Organizations and the Business Environment

To my parents, the Rev. John J. and Mrs Mary Campbell

Organizations and the Business Environment

David J. Campbell
Newcastle Business School
The University of Northumbria at Newcastle

Butterworth-Heinemann
Linacre House, Jordan Hill, Oxford OX2 8DP
225 Wildwood Avenue, Woburn, MA 01801-2041
A division of Reed Educational and Professional Publishing Ltd

A member of the Reed Elsevier plc group

OXFORD AUCKLAND BOSTON
JOHANNESBURG MELBOURNE NEW DELHI

First Published 1997
Reprinted 1998, 1999

British Library Cataloguing in Publication Data
Campbell, David
    Organization and the business environment
    1. Business organizations   2. Industrial management
    338.7

ISBN 0 7506 2760 3

Typeset by Avocet Typeset, Brill, Aylesbury, Bucks
Printed and bound in Great Britain by Scotprint Ltd, Musselburgh

FOR EVERY TITLE THAT WE PUBLISH, BUTTERWORTH-HEINEMANN
WILL PAY FOR BTCV TO PLANT AND CARE FOR A TREE.

CONTENTS

Contents

Contents

ACKNOWLEDGEMENTS

I wish to thank the members of the Business School faculty of the University of Northumbria for their support and counsel during the preparation of this text. Worthy of particular thanks is Paul Lee, who assiduously criticised and corrected each chapter as it was produced. Other colleagues advised on and criticised the specialist chapters, and I am indebted to Geoff Moore (ethics) and Tony Blackwood (accounting) for this input. Also to the staff of the UNN library and to the editorial and production people at Butterworth-Heinemann.

In addition, the following organizations have, in various ways, contributed to the composition of this text. I acknowledge them accordingly.

Asda Group plc
British Telecommunications plc
The Commission of the European Union
Cray Valley Limited
Derwent Valley Foods Limited
Drummond Group plc
Glaxo Wellcome plc
Hanson plc
Kalon Group plc
Nissan
OFTEL
Out of this World
Penguin Books Ltd
Philip Morris Incorporated
Rover Group Motors
RTZ Corporation plc
J. Sainsbury plc
Scottish & Newcastle plc
SmithKline Beecham plc
Toyota
University College Hospitals Trust, London
University of Northumbria at Newcastle

INTRODUCTION

A simple metaphor

Consider yourself. You exist in an environmental context. There are two environments that are important to you. Your internal environment concerns the workings of your body, your health, energy and the way you look and feel. Secondly, your external environment concerns all those things from outside your body that can have an effect on you.

Both your internal and external environments are vital to your ongoing health and prosperity. Both good and harm can spring from either. You may develop a nasty disease – a change in your internal environment for the worse. Conversely, you can improve the performance of the body by exercising, stopping smoking and drinking less.

In your external environment, there are two types of influence. Firstly, there are those influences which impact upon you from your immediate environment. These include the things you need to continue to exist and enjoy a minimal quality of life; things like air, water, food, friendship, shelter and your sense of immediate security. Secondly, there are things that have an influence upon your prosperity; your broader quality of life, but changes in which are unlikely to impact on your survival as such. This may include your occupation, your income, the intensity of your relationships, and all of the plethora of factors that have a bearing on these things.

The business environment

In the same way that an individual person has different spheres of environmental influence, the same is true for a business. It too has an internal environment that can profoundly affect its health and prosperity. This comprises the people within an organization, the systems the business operates, its culture and its structure. These components can be either strong or weak, in much the same way that your intelligence or your respiratory system can be strong or weak. For the purposes of this textbook, we will consider the internal environment under the heading *business organizations* (Part One).

In the world of business, again using our metaphor of the environment of the person, we also see two 'types' of external environment. A business primarily exists in an industry which is made up of other companies who are in the same business as the organization in question. Hence, for a brewing company, its industry is composed of its competitors, its suppliers of materials and the pubs and other outlets it supplies to. Changes in the industry environment can have a serious influence on an individual organization, leading to increased prosperity or insolvency. In this text, we will consider this area of the environment under the heading *the external business micro-environment* (Part Two).

Outside the industry, there is an 'outer layer' of influence. Factors arising from this sphere influence the whole industry. Individual organizations can rarely influence these macro-factors and must therefore learn to cope with changes in this part of the environment. Such factors include changes in the national economy, in political policy, in the sociological realm and in technology. Like changes in the micro-environment, changes in *the external business macro-environment* can be either beneficial or damaging to an organization. Indeed it usually the case than any changes are good for some businesses and bad for others. This part of the environment makes up Part Three of this book.

Internal environment

Internal strengths

Internal weaknesses

External micro-environment

Customers

Suppliers

Competitors

Human and other resources

External micro-environment

Political influences

Economic influences

Sociological influences

Technological influences

Table 1 gives examples of how the environments of individuals (organisms) can be compared with businesses (organizations).

Table 1

	Organism	*Organization*
Internal environment	Body systems, health, strength, fitness, energy, etc.	Employees, systems (e.g. reporting systems), quality and type of management, culture, company structure, etc.
External micro-environment	That which supplies air, water, warmth, shelter, food, friendship, etc.	Competitors, suppliers, customers, etc.
External macro-environment	Acquaintances, occupation, society, etc.	Political, economic, sociological and technological changes

Part One
Business Organizations

1

Organizations and organizational theories

Learning objectives

After studying this chapter, students should be able to describe:

- What an organization is.
- The ways in which organizational theories differ.
- The organizational and management ideas of the *classical* thinkers.
- The development and principles of *scientific management*.
- The concept of *bureaucracy*.
- The *human relations* theories and the work of Elton Mayo.
- The essentials of *systems* thinking as it pertains to organizations.
- What is meant by *contingency theory* and how it relates to organizations.

1.1 What is an organization?

This book is divided into three parts. The first part (Chapters 1 to 15) is all about business organizations – the building blocks of the business world. Before we go on in later chapters to examine business organizations in more detail, this chapter will examine some basics. It would seem appropriate to begin with defining just what an organization is.

Buchanan and Huczynski (1991) suggested the following definition of an organization:

Organizations are social arrangements for the controlled performance of collective goals.[1]

This definition, concise though it is, shows us the two most important features of organizations: they are *social arrangements* and they exist to *perform*. We can say the following general things about organizations:

- they all contain *people* (although it may be argued that some natural groupings of animals in the wild may also be organizations);
- the people in the organization *perform* a role and their continued membership of the organization is dependent upon such performance;
- the organization has a *collective goal* to which all members subscribe;
- all of the roles, taken together, help the organization achieve its collective goal;
- the *roles are divided* so that members of the organization perform different tasks according to their expertise, interest or specialism;
- there is a clearly defined *hierarchy of authority* so that each member of the organi-

zation is aware of where he or she 'fits in';
- the limits or *borders of an organization are usually clearly defined*, and thus there is usually no doubt whether a particular person is 'inside' or 'outside' of the organization.

Question 1.1

According to the definition discussed above, decide whether the following collectives are organizations or not.

- Newcastle United football team.
- The typical nuclear family (Mum, Dad, John, Mary and Ben the dog).
- The Church of England.
- British Telecommunications plc (BT).
- The Black Bull darts team.
- The British Army.
- A trainspotters club.
- The local branch of the Elvis appreciation society.
- A pack of dogs in the wild.

1.2 Why do organizations exist?

Why is it that people form themselves into organizations in order to carry out business activities? Why do they not simply act alone to fulfil their individual objectives? The answer is that the format of an organization offers many advantages over the other option which is many people acting alone.

Firstly, organizations facilitate *synergy*. Synergy refers to the benefits that can be gained when people work together rather than apart. Something can be said to be synergistic when the *whole is greater than the sum of the parts*. More popularly, synergy can be expressed as '2 + 2 = 5.' On a simple level, two people *together* lifting heavy logs onto a lorry can achieve far more work than two people lifting logs separately. A rally team of two enables the team to win a race if they work together with one driving and one navigating. If the two were to work separately, then each person would have to drive and navigate at the same time.

Secondly, organizations facilitate the *division of labour*. Our two workers lifting logs are both performing the same task, but the rally team is divided into two separate but complementary jobs – a division of labour. It is quite possible, and maybe even preferable, for the navigator not to even hold a driving licence, but if he or she is a good map reader, the rally team is greatly strengthened. Similarly, the driver does not need to know how to read maps, provided he or she can take instructions from the navigator and drive well. The two specialists working together do not only produce synergy, they also enable a task to be accomplished that neither member could accomplish alone.

Thirdly, adopting the format of an organization enables increased performance owing to the establishment of *formal systems of responsibility and authority*. When such systems are implemented, they enable all members to fully understand how roles are divided and to accept and respect both responsibility and authority. They facilitate synergy and an effective division of labour by co-ordinating activities so that individuals act in concert to the overall benefit of the organization.

1.3 An overview of organizational theories

Now that we have come to broad understanding of what an organization is, we turn to a discussion of the various theories that have been put forward to analyse organizations and explain how and why organizations 'work'.

We can all readily appreciate that organizations differ. Some are big and 'bureaucratic' whilst others are small, 'lean and mean'. Furthermore, the way that organizations are managed also varies widely. Some management styles are highly regimented within formal structures whilst others are *laissez faire* and 'laid back'.

These differences have led to a diversity of individuals' experience at work. Academics have sought to help explain the reasons for these differences in management style and how organizations work, through the use of organizational theories. It is impossible to say that 'good management is …' or that 'an organization should be managed in this way'. It all depends upon the context of the organization, its purpose and the type of people that work in it. Over the course of the past century, academics have evolved theories which aid our understanding of, and hence our ability to explain how, organizations 'work'.

The theories can be grouped under four broad convenient headings. They are presented in chronological order:

- classical theories;
- human relations theories;
- systems theories;
- contingency theories.

We will examine each in turn.

1.4 Classical theories

Definition

We use the word *classical* in various ways during normal conversation. It tends to imply two things. Firstly, it is something that is of some *quality*, and secondly it implies that it has *lasted*. We might describe Mozart's work as *classical music* because (in the opinion of the majority) his works are of a *high quality* and they have *lasted* since the eighteenth century. Conversely, 'pop' music such as the Bay City Rollers in the 1970s can probably not be said to be classical. As well as being of debatable artistic quality (i.e. not everybody recognized their artistic abilities), the Bay City Rollers are long forgotten in most music lovers' collections. A point of some discussion might be whether the Beatles songs of the 1960s are classical – they are still played regularly in the 1990s, 30 years on.

Classical theories of management in organizations are so called because they were the earliest and their influence has lasted throughout the course of this century. The classical thinkers believed that good management could be distilled down into rules, guidelines or principles, which, within limits, would be transferable to all managerial contexts. Broadly speaking, classical theorists focused on an organization's output and productivity rather than the individuals in the organization. Thus, many were concerned with the managing of people so as to extract the most work in the most efficient way.

An underlying assumption of classical theories is that the human being, as a social and working being, is relatively predictable in his or her responses to given situations. This assumption of predictability underlies the work of all the classical theorists. Put simply, it states that *if* a certain managerial style or set of conditions is applied to the working environment, *then* individuals will respond in a predictable way. The theories we consider later in this Chapter make the assumption that man is a somewhat more complex being than the classical thinkers realized.

'Classical' as a title, conceals a broad range of theories. Within this category, there are many important thinkers who have advanced different techniques and philosophies for managing organizations. We will examine the contributions of the most important thinkers, dividing our discussion into three categories: the work of Henri Fayol, the scientific management thinkers and the concept of the bureaucratic organization.

Henri Fayol

Fayol (1841–1925) was a French industrialist who spent his entire working life with a coal mining company. His main contribution to organizational theory was his attempt to break down the management job into its component parts. He defined management as follows:

> *To manage is to forecast and plan, to organise, to command, to co-ordinate and to control.*

His work is best remembered for his 'six activities' and his 'fourteen principles'. He developed these from his own experiences as a manager and he worked them out in his own working life, with beneficial effects.

Fayol's 'six activities' are those he considered to be the principal areas of concern to an organization:

- technical activities;
- commercial activities;
- financial activities;
- security activities;
- accounting activities;
- managerial and administrative activities.

The tribute to the influence of Fayol's work is that his *activities* roughly describe the duties of the modern board of directors. We would use different names today, but the tasks are essentially as Fayol described.

Question 1.2

Find out the composition of a typical board of executive directors in a modern manufacturing company. You will probably arrive at five or six 'job titles'. To start you off, one of them will probably be the marketing director.

The 'fourteen principles' were, in Fayol's opinion the elements of good organizational management. He himself applied them and found them to work. Again, when we consider the list, we will see that many of them are still considered today to form the basis of good management practice.

Table 1.1 Fayol's fourteen principles of management

Principle	Meaning
Division of work	One man, one job. Specialize work.
Authority	Manager must be able to give orders and be sure they will be carried out
Discipline	Respect and order throughout the workplace
Unity of command	Remove confusion by having any employee report to only one boss
Unity of direction	One boss is responsible for the planning and direction
Subordination of individual interests to the general good of the company	Employees should be prepared to put the company first
Fair pay	Pay should be fair to the employee and acceptable to the organization
Centralization	Management authority and responsibility ultimately rests with the centre
Scalar chain	The observance of an orderly hierarchy line of authority from bottom to the top
Order	Housekeeping, tidiness, order in the work environment
Equity	Fairness and a sense of justice
Stability of tenure	As far as possible, provide job security
Initiative	Staff should be encouraged to show initiative
Esprit de corps	Encourage and develop teams and a friendly working environment

'Scientific' Management

Scientific management is so called, not because it is used for managing scientific activities, but rather that it assumes a scientific model of man working in organizations. If quantitative methods are employed to aid management processes, then, it is argued, efficiency gains can be made. For a given work input, more output can be gained when work is organised using measurement, feedback and refinement. There are three major contributors to the scientific management school: Taylor, the Gilbreths and Gantt.

Frederick Taylor (1856–1917) was one of the earliest of all the organizational management theorists. He worked for the Bethlehem Steel Company in the USA, and it was here that he developed his theories of scientific management. In 1911, he published his *Principles of Scientific Management*, a treatise on this subject arising from his own experience as an industrialist and the outcomes of his early research. He was the first to propound the idea of applying quantitative methods to management problems. This evolved into 'work study' – the analysis of work methods and the rate of work. His theories were quite revolutionary in a day when it was believed that increased productivity arose from simply taking on more people and making them work harder.

Taylor introduced the idea of comparing employee performance against a standard. This involved determining the expected 'standard' time for completing a task and then rewarding or punishing workers according to their performance or achievement. His work also involved finding the optimum way for a given job to be done.

In one notable piece of research, Taylor demonstrated his principles by showing the relationship between work output and the size of labourers' shovels. In a study at the Bethlehem steel plant, it is reported that he used a man who was reputed to be a good labourer and who placed a high value on monetary reward. The initial size of shovel was capable of carrying an average of 38 lb and this resulted in the labourer shifting 25 tons of pig iron in a day. When a smaller shovel size was used, the daily load rose to 30 tons. A 25 lb shovel produced even higher daily loads. The worker, in addition to enjoying the praise of his observers, was also promised extra financial reward as an incentive to move more pig iron per shift. The end result was that the work which was formerly done by 500 men could be achieved by just 140 and labourers' wages rose by as much as 60%.

The scientific management idea was further developed by later theorists, most notably the Gilbreths (Frank and Lilian) who concentrated on 'motion study' and Henry Gantt whose principal legacy is his 'chart'.

The Gilbreths contribution of *motion study* was to analyse the way in which a worker performed a task and then to see if there was any way of simplifying it or making it more efficient. The objective of such a study was to increase a worker's actual work output within the limited amount of time in the day that he or she was working. The most quoted example of their success in this was when they worked out how to reduce the number of movements in laying a brick from 18 to 5. The outcome was that more bricks could be laid in any hour or day and the bricklayer put less work expenditure into any given number of bricks laid.

Henry Gantt is best remembered for his development of the *Gantt chart*. He argued that time could be used more effectively if tasks in an operation were carefully planned in sequence and resources were apportioned accordingly. This would have the advantage of management having more control over events and it would prevent time 'leaking' in fruitless or unnecessary jobs. Gantt charts are used today in a wide variety of planning and control processes.

The Gantt chart is a project planning tool which helps plan the use of resources within a limited time period. It is constructed with consecutive activities plotted in a horizontal direction with time along the x axis. It offers the advantage that the project manager can see at any one time what should be going on and which activities will follow on from completed activities. With a simple modification, the chart can be made to highlight which activities, if any, are critical. Critical activities are those which directly influence the finishing time of the overall project.

Bureaucracy

The words *bureaucracy* and *bureaucratic* have, over recent years, become understood as being synonymous with 'red-tape', 'officialdom' and the general impersonality of large and inefficient organizations. Such a conception of bureaucracy, whilst understandable, is a rather cynical description of some of the negative features of this otherwise highly effective method of organizational management.

The concept of bureaucracy was first put forward by the German academic and sociologist, Max Weber (1864–1920). His research, which was translated into English in 1947, sought to establish the reasons why individuals acted in certain ways in organizations and why they obeyed those in authority over them. Put simply, Weber found that people obeyed those in authority over them because of the influence of three types of authority:

- *Traditional authority* is that which subordinates respond to because of their traditions or customs.
- *Charismatic authority* occurs when subordinates respond to the personal qualities of a charismatic ('gifted') leader.
- *Rational–legal authority* is authority brought about solely by a manager's position in an organization. Implicit in rational–legal authority is that subordinates obey a superior because the superior is in seniority over them in the organizational hierarchy.

Weber, whilst recognizing the importance of the first two types in some areas of life, was primarily concerned with rational–legal authority in his study of organizations. This form of obedience is the prominent form in modern organizations – Weber termed this *bureaucracy*. He continued to argue that the authority structures in bureaucracies could be a highly efficient organizational form, and that a proliferation of bureaucracies could result in gains in efficiency for organizations and in the country as a whole.

Question 1.3

In which contexts might we encounter traditional and charismatic authority?

According to Weber, bureaucracies could be described by certain characteristics. Underlying these characteristics were the dual themes of administration based on expertise ('rules of experts') and administration based on discipline ('rules of officials'). Mullins[2] explains these characteristics as follows:

- Tasks of the organization are allocated as *official duties* among the various positions.
- There is an implied clear-cut *division of labour* and a high level of *specialization*.
- A *hierarchical authority* applies to the organization of offices and positions.
- Uniformity of decisions and actions is achieved through formally established systems of *rules and regulations*. Together with a structure of authority this enables the co-ordination of various activities within the organization.
- An *impersonal* orientation is expected from officials in their dealings with clients and other officials. This is designed to result in rational judgements by officials in the performance of their duties.
- Employment by the organization is based on *technical qualifications* and constitutes a lifelong career for the officials.

Stewart[3] summarizes the four main features of bureaucracy.

- *Specialization* applies primarily to the job rather than the job-holder. The specialization of roles 'belongs to' the organization so that the specialization can continue if any given specialists leave the employment of the organization.
- *Hierarchy of authority* stresses a strict demarcation between management and workers. Within each stratum of the organization, there should be clearly defined levels of authority and seniority.
- *System of rules* is intended to engender an efficient and impersonal operation in the organization. The system of rules should normally be stable and continuous and changes in the rules should be in exceptional circumstances only.
- *Impersonality* means that the exercise of authority and the extension of privileges should be carried out strictly in accordance with the laid down system of rules. No partiality should be given to any individual on personal grounds.

Question 1.4

In what ways might bureaucracy be advantageous to an organization and in what ways might it be disadvantageous?

1.5 Human relations theory

Definition

The objectives of the classical and human relations theorists are essentially the same – to achieve the maximum organizational efficiency. The difference can be seen in the *modus operandi* by which they propose to bring this about. We saw previously that the classical theorists proposed a rational model of *if ... then* that assumes a high degree of human predictability. The human relations theories proposed that, because organizations are composed of humans, focusing on human needs and motivations is the way to bring about optimal organizational output.

Central to human relations theory is the belief that people are the key resources of an organization. Harnessing and cultivating their potential and eliciting their willing contribution is therefore the most effective way of increasing organizational efficiency.

Elton Mayo

The work of Elton Mayo (1880–1949) and his experiments at the Hawthorne plant of the Western Electric Company in Chicago are generally thought of as the principal foundations for human relations theories of management in organizations. Mayo, a Harvard University professor, was primarily concerned with people's experience at work and accordingly, his researches at the Hawthorne plant between 1927 and 1932 focused on the worker rather than on the work itself (which is in contrast to the work of Taylor).

The Hawthorne studies centred around the study of individuals and their social relationships at work. Divided into several stages, Mayo and his colleagues varied the conditions under which workers operated, and then studied output to analyse the correlation between the two. Social arrangements in the workplace – the numbers of people who worked together, their seating arrangements, etc. – were varied, and the work output was measured as each variable in working condition was changed.

The findings suggested that individuals at work produced a higher output when management took into account their social relationships. They found that a feature of people at work is that they form groups. It seemed that people felt more comfortable in groups and this could be used by the organization to produce greater productivity.

Hawthorne findings

In summary, the findings of the Hawthorne experiments were as follows:

- An individual's identity is strongly associated with his or her group. They should be considered less as individuals and more as members of the group.
- An individual's affiliation and sense of belonging to the group can be more important to him or her than monetary rewards and other working conditions.
- Groups can be formal (set up by the organization) or informal (chance social groupings). Both can exercise a strong influence over the behaviour of individuals at work.
- Managers and supervisors would do well to take this group behaviour into account when seeking to extract the maximum amount of work from their subordinates.

The lasting influence of Mayo can readily be seen in most of today's organizations. Most employees are organized into teams, groups, task-forces, etc. More modern developments have included briefing groups, quality circles and 'buzz' groups. Management have, over the intervening years, made attempts to influence the norms of groups in order to make them act in accordance with the general objectives of the organization. When this can be achieved, groups can become 'self-policing', and when a high degree of cohesion is achieved a lower level of supervision is needed.

Question 1.5

Do you know what briefing groups and quality circles are? If not, find out. You should find them in any good quality management or operations management textbook.

One way in which group thinking has been found to enhance output over recent years is to reconfigure production lines specifically to increase an individual's opportunity for social interaction. Figures 1.1 and 1.2 show one such example of this. In Figure 1.1, the person sitting at station C on the production line has the opportunity to interact meaningfully with only two people – the people at stations B and D. However, when the line is 'bent round' (Figure 1.2), the same person has his or her potential interactions increased from two people (B and D) to five (B, D, H, G and F).

Workstations

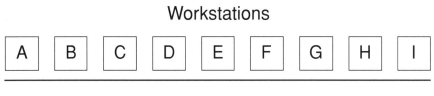

→ Flow of work →

Figure 1.1 Straight production line

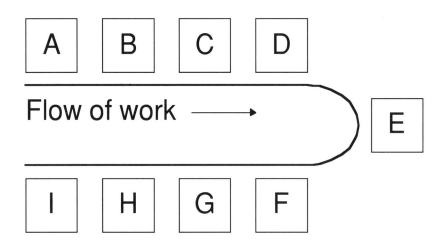

Figure 1.2 'Bent' production line to facilitate more social interaction

1.6 Systems theories

Definition

The distinguishing feature of systems theories is that, whereas classical theories see organizations in essentially scientific terms, and human relations theorists view them in terms of the individuals working in them, systems theorists contend that the most realistic view is to see an organization as a total system. This view, they contend, transcends both of the former theories and takes into account the more holistic context both inside and outside an organization.

An organization is an example of what has been termed an *open system*. An open system is one which must necessarily have a high degree of interaction with its environment. This is in contrast to a *closed system* – one in which there is no interaction with the external environment (a diver's underwater breathing apparatus, for example, approximates to a closed system). An open system of any sort has three stages: inputs, conversion and outputs. All three are essential for the normal workings of the system.

Figure 1.3 An open system

Organizations and organisms

The organization as a body
It may aid our understanding of this concept to consider a simple example. The human body is an example of an open system. It requires several essential inputs such as air, food, heat, shelter and water. The body converts these in its normal functioning and then produces its outputs such as energy, work, exhaled air products and excretions. The body is utterly dependent upon its environment – it would not take long for a lack of air to have a profound effect on the body. A further category of system quickly becomes apparent in this example – that of subsystems in the body. The reasons why the total system of the body can perform the conversions in question is because it contains a nervous system, a renal system, a biochemical respiratory system and many others. Each of these subsystems has its own inputs, conversions and outputs. They are equally interactive with their own respective environments.

It was the analogy between the biological body and the *body corporate* which first gave rise to a systems understanding of organizations. The concept that both types of body contained a number of interrelated and interdependent subsystems was noticed in 1951 by the biologist Ludwig von Bertalanffy[4]. His *general systems theory* was further explored and developed by Miller and Rice, also both biologists, who likened corporate bodies to biological organisms[5]. The complexity of both biological and corporate bodies and their interrelationships with their environments suggested that management of such systems required an understanding that all parts of the body were essential to normal and productive functioning.

A socio-technical system

The systems theorists, in the light of their comparison of organizations to organisms, rejected the simplistic views of the classical and human relations theorists. Classical theories, they argued, emphasized the technical requirements of the organization and its productivity needs – 'organizations without people'. In contrast, human relations theories focused too much on the psychology and interaction of people – 'people without organizations'.

In reality, organizations comprise both the technical features of such things as work study (classical theories) and the human input emphasized by Mayo. Systems theory thus holds that organizations are *socio-technical systems*. In a socio-technical system, it cannot be said that people are more important than an organization's technology, structure, work methods or any other visible or tangible feature. Both are equally necessary and, importantly, both are subject to influence from the organization's external environment (in the context of an open system). A failure of any subsystem in the organization, be it a human or a technical failure, will harm the normal working of the organization.

The pursuit of thought in this area led later writers in systems theory (adopting a holistic view of organizations) to devise a list of four key variables which, it was suggested, were the major determinants of output:

- people and social groups;
- technology;
- organizational structure;
- external environment.

Readers should note that this list includes both social and 'technical' determinants of organizational performance.

Social groups and technology

The relationships between social groups and their employment of technology was also studied by the systems theorists. The implicit suggestion of classical theories is that technology, if properly applied, is the source of increased productivity; conversely, the human relations theorists would have said that output is essentially a function of social groupings.

The Tavistock Institute of Human Relations in London, working in the 1940s and later, conducted research which showed the difficulties of linking output to just technology or just social arrangements. One of the most important studies in this regard was the 'longwall' study.

Prior to the introduction of mechanization in British coal mines in the 1940s, miners worked in small teams in a localized area of the seam. The teams developed a high degree of interpersonal cohesion over the years. They worked together on shifts – possibly going for hours without encountering other teams. Members shared out jobs and this resulted in individuals becoming multi-skilled but non-specialized ('jack of all trades, master of none'). Because the teams worked on only a small part of the coal face at any one time, this method of working was termed the 'shortwall' approach.

When mechanization was introduced, a change in working practices was necessitated wherein:

- a much longer area of the coal seam could be worked on at any one time (the *longwall* method of working);
- the earlier small teams were disbanded and replaced in a shift with a much larger group, all working together on the longwall;
- shifts became specialized in that, on a three-shift system, one shift would work the face, another would clear up the debris and move the coal away from the face and the third would move the wall along the seam to an unworked area;
- shifts, because they involved many more workers together, were supervised.

To the surprise of the pit management, it was found that the introduction of mechanization and the longwall methods actually caused a reduction in output. Furthermore, conflicts arose within and between shifts. Absenteeism increased, morale noticeably decreased and shifts frequently blamed others for poor work.

These findings led Trist and Bamforth[6] of the Tavistock Institute to conclude that effective work arose from an interdependence of social conditions and technology. It involved taking into account the technology used, its layout, ease of use, etc., and the fact that individuals seemed to produce more work in groups in which they felt comfortable.

The problems at the coal face were eventually overcome when the *composite longwall method* was introduced. This was an arrangement which allowed small groups to work together and still make efficient use of the new technologies of the time. The longwall study is seen as a vindication of the socio-technical systems approach taken by systems theorists.

1.7 Contingency theories

Definition

The contingency approach to organizational management had its roots firmly in the systems theory, and in most respects the two are arguably indistinguishable. The essence of the contingency approach is that the manner in which an organization should be managed *depends* upon the wide range of variables which may apply to that organization at any point in time. We can readily appreciate that the environmental conditions, the types of technology employed and the level of human motivation varies over time and according to organizational context. This approach suggests that it is impossible to prescribe any one type of management in all internal and external conditions. It rejects an absolutist approach to behaviour and management and puts forward, in its place, a relativist proposal (we may describe Taylor, Fayol and Mayo as essentially absolutist). The contingency theorists did not reject earlier ideas, in fact they recognized the utility of the philosophies, but only in certain circumstances. Scientific management and the human relations theories each have their place when the environmental conditions were conducive to their use.

Burns and Stalker

The study by Burns and Stalker[7] centred around twenty British companies in what they considered to be five broad environmental conditions, ranging from 'stable' to 'least predictable'. Among this sample of organizations, they also identified two extremes of management practice in the organizations – *mechanistic* and *organic* practice. It was suggested that both of these approaches are equally correct and rational in their appropriate environmental and organizational circumstances.

Mechanistic management systems are rigid in nature. The study showed that these work best in organizations that experience stable environmental conditions. Mullins[8] contends that the characteristics of mechanistic management are similar to those of bureaucracy:

- tasks are specialized;
- clearly-defined duties and procedures;
- clear hierarchical structure;
- knowledge and expertise centred at the top of the organization;
- clear instructions and decisions from superiors as methods of control over organizational activity;
- insistence on loyalty of employees to the organization and to their superiors.

Conversely, it was suggested that *organic* organizations were most appropriate in changeable environmental conditions. The 'surprises' inherent in a changeable business environment necessitated a more flexible and less rigid organizational philosophy than that provided by the inflexibility of a mechanistic organization. Organic organizations have the following characteristics:

- the importance of special knowledge, skills and experience to the success of the organization;
- a continual redefinition of tasks as the environment changes;
- a network, rather than a hierarchical structure of control and authority (characterized by an increased importance of cross-functional rather than hierarchical relationships);
- superior knowledge is not necessarily related to a person's authority in the organization;
- communication is more lateral than up-and-down, reflecting an emphasis on information rather than instructions and commands;
- a widespread commitment of employees to the overall tasks and goals of the organization;
- an emphasis on the contribution of individuals within the organization.

Burns and Stalker contended that organic organizations were best suited to a changeable business environment, which is of course in contrast to the roles of the mechanistic organization. It is important to appreciate that there are shades of grey between the two experiences of mechanistic and organic, and that which is best depends, or is *contingent upon*, the environmental conditions.

Lawrence and Lorsch

Lawrence and Lorsch[9], worked from Harvard University in the 1960s. They were concerned with two key variables in organizations: structure (of the organization) and environment. Their study involved examining organizations in relatively unstable, or changeable environments and others in stable ones. Within these organizations, they sought to see which managerial practices were different and which were the same in the two types of environment. They borrowed terms from mathematics to describe differences in management practice. These are described below.

Differentiation
'Differentiation' refers to the degree to which management practices, attitudes and behaviour vary (or differ) from manager to manager within the organization. In particular, the differences refer to:

- the varying orientation to certain organizational goals (e.g. cost reduction is felt more keenly by accountants and production managers than sales people and engineers);
- the varying time perspectives and time orientations (e.g. research and development (R&D) people tend to work on much longer time-scales than sales and administrative people);
- the varying degrees of interpersonal orientation (e.g. sales people may tend to be more relationship oriented than production people);
- the varying formality of functional department structures across the organization (e.g. production departments tend to have 'taller' and more complex structures compared to the relative informality of R&D departments).

Integration
'Integration' refers to the degree to which management attitudes and practices are common among managers in an organization and the extent of collaboration that exists between managers. It is the opposite of differentiation.

Conclusions
The Lawrence and Lorsch study analysed the sample of organizations for the degree of integration and differentiation that makes for successful business performance in the different business environments. They arrived at a number of conclusions.

- Companies in highly changeable business environments perform better when there is a high degree of both integration and differentiation in the organization.
- Companies in relatively stable business environments perform better when there is a lower degree of differentiation but a high degree of integration.
- One drawback of differentiation is that it is harder to resolve conflict in a highly differentiated organization.
- Conflict resolution is done better in well-performing companies than in their poorly performing competitors.
- In unstable and uncertain environments, integration is more common among middle and lower management levels. In more stable environments, the senior levels exhibit more integration.

Again, we see that the most appropriate management practices for an organization *depend* upon its environment. Both differentiation and integration 'work' in their respective contexts.

Assignment

- Good management is about whipping subordinates into submission.
- If you want people to work harder, you have to be nice to them.
- Strict rules, lavish rewards and swift punishments are the key to organizational success.

Choose one of the above statements and discuss its merits with reference to management and organizational theory.

References

1. Buchanan, D. A. and Huczynski, A. A. (1991). *Organisational Behaviour. An Introductory Text*. Englewood Cliffs, N.J.: Prentice Hall.
2. Mullins, L. J. (1996) *Management and Organisational Behaviour*, 4th edn, pp. 46–47. London: Pitman.
3. Stewart, R. (1986) *The Reality of Management*, 2nd edn. Pan Books.
4. von Bertalanffy, L. (1951). Problems of general systems theory: a new approach to the unity of science. *Human Biology*, **23**(4), pp. 302–312
5. Miller, E. J. and Rice A. K. (1967). *Systems of Organisation*. London: Tavistock.
6. Trist, E. L. *et. al.* (1963) *Organisational Choice*. London: Tavistock.
7. Burns, T. and Stalker, G. M. (1966) *The Management of Innovation*. London: Tavistock.
8. Mullins, L. J. (1996) *Management and Organisational Behaviour*, 4th edn, pp. 378–379. London: Pitman.
9. Lawrence, P. R. and Lorsch J. W. (1969) *Organisation and Environment*. Irwin.

Further reading

Adam-Smith, D. and Peacock, A. (1994) *Cases in Organisational Behaviour. London:* Pitman.

Buchanan, D. A. and Huczynski, A. A. (1991) *Organisational Behaviour. An Introductory Text*. Englewood Cliffs, NJ: Prentice Hall.

Cole, G. A. (1996) *Management Theory and Practice*, 5th edn. London: DP Publications.

Dawson, S. (1996) *Analysing Organisations*. London: Macmillan.

Dixon, R. (1991) *Management Theory and Practice*. Oxford: Butterworth-Heinemann.

Johns, G. (1996) *Organisational Behaviour. Understanding and Managing Life at Work*. Harper Collins.

Mullins, L. J. (1996). *Management and Organisational Behaviour*, 4th edn. London: Pitman.

Pettinger, R. (1996) *An Introduction to Organisational Behaviour*. London: Macmillan.

2

Organizational and business objectives

Learning objectives

After studying this chapter, students should be able to describe:

- The complex nature of defining business objectives.
- The most important business objective.
- What a stakeholder is.
- The view that stakeholder coalitions determine business objectives.
- The view that an organization's principals essentially determine business objectives.
- What a mission statement is and how it can be useful as a means of communicating business objectives.

2.1 Objectives – implicit and explicit

Introduction

The question, 'Why does a particular organization exist?' or 'what are the objectives of this organization?' may, at first glance, seem rather straightforward. We may assume, for example that a private business such as a brewery primarily seeks to make a profit, while a hospital exists to provide healthcare. We will see in the course of this chapter that such simplistic definitions sit uncomfortably alongside the complexity of influences that are brought to bear upon an organization, and that organizations may have many objectives at the same time.

To simplify our discussion, we can seek to divide objectives into two broad categories: those which are expressly stated by an organization, and those which are not, but which we can safely presume to be the case. We can readily imagine that a large company such as the car manufacturer Nissan, as a private company, exists to make a profit. The company states this publicly: '… we aim to build profitably the highest quality car sold in Europe'. Similarly, a hospital trust, such as the University College Hospitals group in London, exists primarily to provide a service – that is healthcare. Again, the trust states this publicly: to '… maintain and develop a local, national and international role as a provider of comprehensive, safe, accessible and high quality care for patients'. We can consider these objectives to be *explicit*, because they are perhaps obvious and (often) stated publicly by the organization.

The activities of such organizations suggest to us that their primary objectives, important though they are, are not the only objectives they pursue. Many organizations, for example, seek to be fair and to act responsibly towards their employees and customers in the belief, perhaps, that such sub-objectives support their explicit goals. Such objectives are said to be *implicit* because they are implied by the organization's policies and activities. Implicit objectives do not oppose the primary objective, they usually complement it and help towards its accomplishment.

Question 2.1

Suggest what you consider to be the primary (most important) objectives of the following organizations:

- Tottenham Hotspur Football Club.
- The Church of England.
- The University of Northumbria.
- BAT Industries plc (a very large company whose main activity is the manufacture of tobacco products).

Out of this World

A new concept in retailing was launched in late 1995. Out of this World (a registered industrial and provident society – a type of co-operative owned by its members – see Chapter 5) is a growing chain of retail outlets – mainly small 'supermarkets'. The shops sell the usual wide range of consumer products that you might find in your regular 'conventional' supermarket. What is unique about Out of this World is that it only sells a product when it is satisfied that both the products sold and the producers meet certain ethical or environmental criteria. Based in Newcastle upon Tyne, Out of this World currently has shops in Bristol, Nottingham and Newcastle upon Tyne itself.

Aimed at people who care about the way that products are produced and the behaviour of the producer companies, Out of this World sells a wide range of organic products which sometimes cost a little more than foods prepared from conventional sources. This is due to the extra costs involved in producing some organic products.

The shops themselves are said by the company to be an 'experience' rather than a conventional shopping environment. Each shop has a database which gives shoppers information on suppliers (e.g. in the Third World) and products to assist them in their choices. Shops are designed not only to provide an enjoyable shopping experience, but also an educational one.

All types of products sold in the shops are carefully chosen for their contribution to:

- the promotion of personal health;
- human welfare;
- environmental sustainability;
- fair trade (the name given to trading relationships which do not exploit or take economic advantage over the producer, often in the Third World);

- community and local development;
- animal welfare.

So what are the objectives of Out of this World? In its share prospectus, the company gives the following explanation:

Is profit a dirty word? Profit is important to Out of this World. It is not a primary objective but it is an essential condition of success. It is a word that we will use ... not as an incentive to personal gain or greed but as the test of the organization's efficiency and sustainability. Profit, for Out of this World, is a significant aspect of business terminology, not a raison d'être.

It follows from the above explanation that profit is not the primary motive of the company but a necessary prerequisite that enables it to fulfil its primary objective.

Question 2.2

Suggest as clearly as possible what the primary objective of Out of this World might be.

Different types of business objective

There are a huge number of objectives which businesses may pursue in addition to their primary objectives (which may be said to be their *raison d'être*). Some of these will be *quantitative* in nature and some *qualitative*.

Quantitative objectives are those whose achievement can be measured using numerical or financial criteria. They can be specific and accurately measured. It follows that the successful achievement of quantitative objectives can be easily seen and it is equally visible when they are not achieved. Examples of quantitative objectives might include:

- targets for market share;
- target accounting or financial performance, e.g. profit margins;
- target levels of year-on-year growth;
- target levels of productivity or efficiency;
- number of new product launches (i.e. two new products this year);
- buy a subsidiary in France to exploit European markets;
- to gain a quality accreditation certificate.

Quantitative objectives – United Biscuits plc (UB)

In his statement in the 1992 accounts, the Chairman of UB gave the following as the company's objectives for the forthcoming year:

- to make a profit before interest and tax not less than 20% of capital employed;
- at least to maintain the increase in profits in line with the increase in sales;
- that the return to shareholders should grow in line with the growth in net profit;
- to maintain the quality of existing assets by investing not less than 5% of sales annually.

(Source: United Biscuits plc) – *Annual Report and Accounts, 1992*

All of the above are quantitative in nature and success or failure to meet the objectives can be easily assessed by examining the company's accounts at the end of the financial year in question. In one respect, such clarity of objective setting is good because it focuses employees' minds towards clear goals, whilst, conversely, it is equally clear if the Chairman has failed to accomplish his stated objective.

Qualitative objectives are more difficult to measure because they are not based on a numerical indicator. This does not mean they are any less important than quantitative objectives – types of objectives will vary from business to business. Examples include:

- a public perception of being a 'good employer';
- to be seen as a responsible 'environmental' or 'green' organization;
- to improve the quality of management;
- to improve customer satisfaction;
- to improve staff training.

Such objectives are essentially intangible in nature and, as such, it is hard to know the exact point at which the objective is satisfactorily realized. If, for example an organization wishes to improve its employees' skills, we can see that this is a broad qualitative objective. We cannot tell from this by how much it wants to improve them or at what point we will be able to say that the objective will have been accomplished.

2.2 The prime objective

There is one objective which applies to all businesses without exception. It is the highest and the clearest objective and it is so obvious that it is rarely articulated. It is universally presumed to apply in all cases. The prime objective in business is to survive – to stay in business.

The individuals in organizations may differ on some other business objectives. It may be the case, for example, that management wish to increase profitability and that the trade union representing the workers wants a pay increase – potentially conflicting objectives. On this and many other examples, there will be debate over business objectives. Over the issue of survival however, there is no debate.

If the company does not survive, then the many possible negative outcomes include:

- employees and management lose their jobs;
- shareholders lose their investment;

- suppliers do not get paid for the goods they have supplied;
- customers must look elsewhere for their supplies;
- the government does not benefit from tax revenues from employees and from tax on profits.

2.3 Who sets business objectives? Two viewpoints

The question 'Who sets the objectives of a business?' is a more complex one than it might at first appear. This question raises the issue of *power* – power enables individuals or groups to impose their will upon the organization. The party with the greatest exertable power will tend to impose more of their purposes upon the company's objectives.

Power – an everyday example

The author of this book has some degree of power over his students. He can ruin their weekends, make them happy, make them despair, make them stay up all night writing essays they don't want to write and reading books they don't want to read. He can, for a short period of time, determine the objectives of his students.

Why is this the case and what is the nature of the power that the author has over his students? The answer is that the author has something that the students want, and they want it so badly that they are willing to subordinate their own social objectives to gain it. The author, as an academic employee of the University of Northumbria, has the power to influence the award of a degree (or at least part of one). Degrees are very valuable as they enable graduates to enjoy a higher income and standard of living over those who are not graduates. Of course, it is also the case that the author has no power over his students when they no longer want what he has to offer; when they drop out of the course or when they graduate from it.

There are two broad approaches to the issue of who sets organizational objectives. They are partly in conflict and partly complementary. The first approach, *stakeholder analysis*, contends that objectives are arrived at by many interested parties in coalition, whilst the simpler model of *principal-agent analysis* argues that the objectives of a business are to be determined by the company's owners and directors alone. In other texts, this dual approach is described as the *stakeholder–stockholder dichotomy*.

2.4 Stakeholder analysis

What is a stakeholder?

A stakeholder can be defined as:

any person or party that has an interest in the activities of an organization, however strong or weak that interest may be. The interests of stakeholders may or may not be primarily financial in nature.

It immediately becomes apparent that many parties fit into this broad definition. Some stakeholders have an urgent and vital interest in the organization whilst others have only a slight concern, and that from a considerable distance. A broad and general list of possible stakeholders would include the following parties:

- shareholders/owners;
- management;
- employees;
- competitors;
- employees' families and dependants;
- suppliers;
- customers;
- workers' (trade) unions;
- bankers;
- money-lenders other than banks (e.g. some individuals lend cash to businesses);
- communities served by the organization;
- near geographical neighbours (i.e. next-door neighbours);
- pressure groups and opinion formers;
- financial auditors (in the case of limited companies);
- regulatory authorities (e.g. Health and Safety Executive and regulatory QuANGOs);
- other businesses in the locality (e.g. the local newsagent, pub);

In addition to the above list, there are many parts of the state which may have an interest in an organization, including:

- the Inland Revenue collects direct taxes from a private sector business;
- Her Majesty's Customs and Excise collects indirect taxes;
- local government collects local taxes from businesses within its area;
- the Department of Social Security collects employers' National Insurance contributions and must pay unemployment benefit to individuals if the company becomes insolvent;
- the Department of Trade and Industry;
- the Department for Education and Employment benefits from businesses as both sources of students and employers of its school-leavers and graduates.

Hence we see a complex picture of interests emerging. We can also see that not all stakeholders want the same things for any given business organization. Whilst some stakeholders will be in concurrence, others may profoundly disagree over the objectives of the organization in question.

Question 2.3

Attempt to generate a list of the specific stakeholders in the following organizations:

- The university or college at which you are studying.
- Your local authority.
- A local sole-trader such as your local window cleaner.
- The local parish church.

Stakeholder coalitions

According to the theory of stakeholder analysis, the objectives of a business depend upon the relative strengths of the various stakeholders. The stakeholders who can exert the most powerful influence over the organization will have most input into the objective-setting of the business. Similarly, stakeholders with little influence, strong though their interest may be, will have little influence over the company's objectives (e.g. the pub which benefits from lunchtime business from a nearby large employer has an intense interest in the large employer, but clearly has little or no influence over it).

According to this theory of objective-setting, the predominant objectives of the business will be those of the most powerful stakeholders, or the objectives of the most powerful coalition (purposeful grouping) of stakeholders. It is clear that some stakeholders on their own could not bring any meaningful influence upon an organization, but when they act in concert with other stakeholders, their aggregate influence naturally increases in power.

Whilst it is uncommon for any given stakeholder to want exactly the same as any other, they often have sufficient in common to mount a common assault on one small area of objective-setting within an organization.

A conflict in stakeholder interests – Sellafield nuclear complex

The Sellafield nuclear fuels complex was opened by British Nuclear Fuels in 1957. Situated just north of Whitehaven in West Cumbria, the Sellafield site includes a number of nuclear reprocessing plants, the Calder Hall nuclear power station and the recently opened ThORP (Thermal Oxide Reprocessing Plant). The collective plants in the Sellafield complex employ, between them, around 7000 people with another 1000 contractors being continually used on site. Sellafield is Cumbria's largest employer and it is estimated that 30% of all jobs in West Cumbria are dependent, either directly or indirectly, on the complex. These jobs are seen as being particularly important, as West Cumbria is an area of high unemployment with a relatively depressed economy.

A stakeholder analysis of the Sellafield situation reveals some interesting conflicts and two opposing stakeholder coalitions.

The 'for' coalition
Some stakeholders feel the plants are of enormous importance and must be protected and, if possible, expanded. The Government considers nuclear energy to be a vital part of its overall energy strategy. Electricity can be produced from coal, gas, oil and other sources, but it is considered wise to spread production across as many fuels as possible. This should mean that a drop in the supply of one input would not have too bad an effect on the overall production of electricity in the country. The employees and their unions support the plants as they are a vital source of employment for the communities. The same attitude is taken by the local authorities in the area for similar reasons. Sellafield's customers are spread across the world. Power generators send their used nuclear materials to Sellafield or ThORP and it is returned to them in a form which enables it to be re-used at a cheaper price than sourcing 'virgin' materials. A plant the size of the

Sellafield complex necessarily has many suppliers – local engineering companies, catering businesses, laundries, etc., and it follows that they, too, have a vested interest in seeing the plant prosper.

The 'against' coalition

Just when you think that the Sellafield complex is an unmitigated blessing, it should be remembered that there are some particularly vocal stakeholders who have misgivings about the plants, some of whom would rather see it closed down completely. Environmental pressure groups argue strongly that nuclear power should not form a part of the UK's energy policy owing to the risks of radiation leaks during use and the problems with disposing of spent nuclear fuel once it has come to the end of its useful life (some nuclear fuels can remain radioactive for 10 000 years). In addition, some health professionals and researchers have suggested that the plants are a source of harmful radiation, both to the workers and to the surrounding population. Evidence has been put forward which may suggest that there is a higher incidence of leukaemia and other serious diseases in the locality of the plants. Concern has also been expressed that radiation from the plant may have teratogenic effects (causing problems in pregnancy and birth defects). The Government of the Republic of Ireland is also concerned about the complex. Ireland is separated from Sellafield by the Irish Sea and some citizens of the Republic believe that harmful effects from the plants may affect parts of their country.

Whilst the controversy over Sellafield has been notable and well-publicized, the collective weight of the 'for' coalition has outweighed the 'againsts'. It seems that the 'againsts', however convincing their arguments may be to some people, will have to remain as a vocal but somewhat impotent coalition whilst the economic forces for keeping Sellafield remain as convincing as they are.

Stakeholder 'mapping'

The extent to which any stakeholder is able to influence the objectives of an organization depends upon two variables: the stakeholders' interest and power[1].

- Stakeholder power refers to the *ability* to influence the organization.
- Stakeholder interest refers to the *willingness* to influence the organization. In other words, interest concerns the extent to which the stakeholder cares about what the organization does.

It follows from this that the actual influence that a stakeholder has will depend upon where the stakeholder is positioned with respect to ability to influence and willingness to influence. A stakeholder with both high power and high interest will be more influential than one with low power and low interest. We can map stakeholders by showing the two variables on a grid comprising two intersecting continua (Figure 2.1).

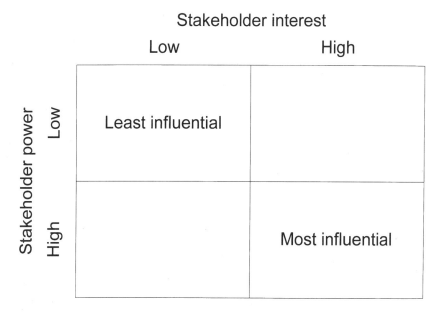

Figure 2.1 The stakeholder map

By examining the stakeholders or stakeholder coalitions of any organization, we can visibly see which stakeholders are the most powerful. We could also use the map, for example, to assess which stakeholder is likely to exert the most influence upon the organization's objectives. It would enable us to see any potential conflicts which may arise if, for example, we see two conflicting stakeholders in the same area of the map, i.e. two conflicting stakeholders with the same degree of power and interest.

The managing director and the board of directors are examples of stakeholders with both high power and high interest. This is because they not only manage the business but also depend upon it for their jobs. The bar to which employees retire after or during the day's work is an example of a stakeholder with high interest but low power.

Question 2.4

Suggest examples of stakeholders who may fit into each section of the grid in Figure 2.1. Concentrate on the categories of low interest, low power and low interest, high power.

Two views of stakeholder theory

We might ask the question 'why' should organizations be influenced in their objectives by their various stakeholder groups. We have seen that the stakeholders may vary in their aspirations for the organization, and so managing the various views may be a bit tricky to say the least. There are two approaches that organizations can take in respect of managing stakeholder aspirations (although academic authors have identified a more complex picture[2]).

The *instrumental* view of stakeholder theory says that organizations take stakeholder opinions into account only inasmuch as they are consistent with the objective of profit maximization (or other conventional indicators of success). Accordingly, it may be that a business modifies its objectives in the light of environmental concerns but only because this is the best way of optimizing profit or achieving success. If the loyalty or commitment of an important stakeholder group (e.g. customers) is threatened, it is likely that the organization will modify its objectives because not to do so would threaten to reduce its profits. It follows from the instrumental stakeholder approach that an organization's values are guided by its stakeholders' opinions – it may not have any inherent moral values of its own except for the over-riding profit motive.

The *normative* view of stakeholder theory takes a 'Kantian' view of business ethics (derived from the German philosopher Immanual Kant, 1724–1804). Kant emphasized the notion of duty and good-will in civil matters and in relationships. Underpinning his ethical philosophy is the notion of respect for the moral duty that one party or person should have towards another. Extending this argument to stakeholder theory, the normative view states that organizations should accommodate stakeholder aspirations not because of what the organization can 'get out of it' for its own profit, but because it observes its duty to each stakeholder. The normative view sees stakeholders as ends in themselves and not as merely instrumental to the achievement of other ends.

2.5 Stockholder (agent – principal) analysis

The argument that the principals of an organization are the only significant influences on objective-setting is one of the foundational and fundamental principles of capitalism. The principals of an organization are those parties that own it – either directly (stockholders) or indirectly (the government in public-sector organizations).

This concept is perhaps a simplification of the notion of stakeholder analysis. It suggests that, as the owners of a business, the shareholders are the only party who have a legitimate right to determine its objectives and policies. The agents of an organization are the directors or those individuals whom the principals have placed in charge of the affairs of the organization. Objectives are conveyed to the agents and, once received, the agents do not need to take cognizance of any other concerns in the execution of their duties. Put simply, according to this concept, the principals say to the agents 'I appoint you and pay your remuneration, therefore you will carry out my agenda for the organization'. The agents, according to this viewpoint, would be acting irresponsibly if they were not to obey their principals.

What are the objectives of agents and principals?

If this theory is to be given credence, then we ought to see in practice the objectives of shareholders taking pre-eminence in commercial organizational objective-setting. The supreme objective of ordinary shareholders is two-fold: to receive the *maximum dividend per share* and to enjoy *capital growth* on the market value of the share. Both of these can only be maximized when the business is enjoying a period of high profitability. Hence, the primary objectives of the shareholder is for the agents to *maximize profit* above all other objectives. As most shareholders are not in regular contact with the agents, they will usually be indifferent to the concerns of other stakeholders and will directly oppose any stakeholders who wish the company to increase its costs for any reason whatsoever.

The basis of market economics is that individuals will place their money where they believe they will receive the maximum return on it. Most shareholders would consequently be displeased if they heard that the agents of their investment (the directors) were paying too much attention to the desires of other stakeholders in a way that would reduce the return on shareholders' investment. In such circumstances, they may have the right to say 'What do you think you are doing with *my* money?'

Agents must manage a much more complex set of variables than their principals. It is the agents' job to balance the many calls upon the business and to take a longer term view than the shareholders. The shareholder will certainly not enjoy the same level of knowledge of the market conditions of the business and must therefore, to a large extent, trust the agents in the vast majority of their decisions and actions. It must be remembered though, that the maximization of profitability is very much in the agents' interests as well as the shareholders'. A failure to maintain high levels of profitability will usually precipitate a fall in the share price and a lower level of dividends to shareholders. Not only will such actions of directors make them vulnerable to being voted off the board by the shareholders (thus losing their job), but an unattractive share falls in value and makes the company vulnerable to takeover (which may also mean the agents being replaced). In addition, directors often have a profit-linked element in their reward packages, meaning that higher profits enables a higher level of remuneration to be achieved.

2.6 Mission statements

Some organizations find it helpful to provide a concise and clear written statement of their broad objectives. Whilst such statements are called by different names, most find the term *mission statement* to be the most suitable. These have increased in popularity over recent years and more and more organizations have come to appreciate their advantages.

Why have a mission statement?

There are a number of advantages to having a clearly set-out and written-down statement of wider objectives.

- It *clearly communicates the objectives* and values of the organization to the various stakeholders groups. This theoretically prevents people from misunderstanding the purposes of the business.
- In the normal operation of an organization, it is important that *all members work towards the same ends*. Clearly stated objectives facilitate this, especially if the organization is decentralized or where the employees tend to work independently of each other. There is great value in all parts of the organization working together, and

coherence is encouraged when overall objectives are clearly understood.

- It can serve to *influence the actions and attitudes of employees* in the company. This is important when the company has clearly defined objectives and the co-operation of employees is necessary to ensure that strategies and plans are implemented.

Question 2.5

Find out if the college or university you are studying at has a mission statement. If it has, try to obtain a copy and identify the key phrases that inform the reader about its objectives.

What does a mission statement contain?

The style and content of mission statements, as we might expect, varies enormously. Some are long and detailed whereas others are short and to the point. There are no 'rights' or 'wrongs' of how it should be presented or what it should contain – it all depends upon the organization and its culture. In practise, mission statements usually contain the following:

- Some *indication of the industry* or business the organization is mainly concerned with. In many cases this will be obvious from the company name (e.g. Imperial *Chemical* Industries plc (ICI)) but in others some elucidation may be of value (e.g. the name *SmithKline Beecham* conceals the fact that the company makes pharmaceuticals and health care products).
- An indication of the *realistic market share* or market position the organization should aim towards. This may be stated as 'we aim to become the leading supplier' or 'we aim to become a major company in the textiles industry'. Most statements of this type in mission statements are reasonably realistic as management realize that an unreachable objective may demotivate the workforce or bring ridicule from outside observers.
- A brief summary of the *values and beliefs* of the organization. Such a statement may be actual (as it is) or aspirational (as management want it to become). Phrases like 'caring company', 'friendly staff', 'valued employees' and 'working as a team' are examples of the company putting across its values in a mission statement.
- Specific and *highly context-dependent objectives* are sometimes expressed in the mission statement. This type of statement will obviously vary greatly from organization to organization and some mission statements contain no expressions of this type. It may refer to a particular competitive environment or uniquely to the industry in which the organization competes.

A detailed mission statement –
Nissan Motor Manufacturing (UK) Limited

In the early 1980s, the motor company Nissan made an investment of almost £1 billion in a 'greenfield' plant in Sunderland, Tyne and Wear. The building of a new installation meant that almost all employees were new to the company. There was therefore an implicit need for a clear statement of cultural norms in the business, coupled with an overview of business and commercial objectives. This need was satisfied with the publication of a document called *Our Company's Philosophy*, distributed to all employees and signed by Ian Gibson CBE, Managing Director and Chief Executive of Nissan's Sunderland plants.

Nissan's *Our Company's Philosophy* reads as follows:

As a Company, we aim to build profitably the highest quality car sold in Europe. We want to achieve the maximum possible customer satisfaction and ensure the prosperity of the Company and its staff.

To assist in this, we aim to achieve mutual trust and co-operation between all people within the Company and make NMUK a place where long term job satisfaction can be achieved. We recognise that people are our most valued resource and in line with this spirit believe that the following principles will be of value to all.

People
- *We will develop and expand the contributions of all staff by strongly emphasizing training and by the expansion of everyone's capabilities.*
- *We seek to delegate and involve staff in discussion and decision making particularly in those areas in which each of us can effectively contribute so that all may participate in the efficient running of NMUK.*
- *We firmly believe in common terms and conditions of employment.*

Teamworking
- *We recognise that all staff have a valued contribution to make as individuals but in addition believe that this contribution can be most effective within a teamworking environment.*
- *Our aim is to build a Company with which people can identify and to which we all feel commitment.*

Communication
- *Within the bounds of commercial confidentiality we will encourage open channels of communication. We would like everyone to know what is happening in our company, how we are performing and what we plan.*
- *We want information and views to flow freely upward, downward and across our Company.*

Objectives
- *We will agree clear and achievable objectives and provide meaningful feedback and performance.*

31

Flexibility
- *We will not be restricted by the existing way of doing things. We will continuously seek improvements in all our actions.*

These are tough targets and we aim high. With hard work and goodwill we can get there.
(Reproduced with kind permission of Nissan.)

Not all mission statements are as long and detailed as Nissan's. Others are shorter and perhaps more 'to the point'.

Mission statement – British Telecommunications plc (BT)

BT, as a very large company, expresses its objectives in a relatively brief document which is designed to communicate its objectives to its wide ranging and disparate types of employee and stakeholder. The document is divided into two parts. The first part is its Vision and the second, its Mission.

Vision
- *To become the most successful worldwide telecommunications group.*

Mission
- *To provide world class telecommunications and information products and services,*
- *to develop and exploit our networks at home and overseas, so that we can ...*
- *meet the requirements of our customers,*
- *sustain growth in the earnings of the group on behalf of our shareholders,*
- *make a fitting contribution to the community in which we conduct our business.*
(Reproduced with the permission of British Telecommunications plc)

Mission statements in smaller companies – Derwent Valley Foods Group Limited

Derwent Valley Foods, now part of the large United Biscuits plc group, was previously an independent food manufacturer of 'adult' snack foods. It is based in the former 'steel town' of Consett, County Durham, from which it distributes its own Philias Fogg brands and a range of products made for supermarket 'own-brand' distribution. As a small to medium sized business, its directors have believed since its foundation in 1982 that all employees should share the same objectives and enjoy a teamworking environment which, it is believed, has contributed to the company's above-industry-average growth and profitability.

Its simple mission statement reads thus:

We will become the best UK adult snack company through dedication to quality, the bold use of new ideas, and the determination to succeed.

As we strive to achieve this goal, it is important that we maintain an environment of friendship, co-operation and respect.

(Source: Derwent Valley Foods Limited)

Recent years have seen an increased realization that public as well as private sector organizations should establish clearly defined objectives. It has thus become increasingly common for institutions such as universities, hospitals and schools to construct mission statements.

A public sector organization's mission statement – The University College Hospitals NHS Trust, London

The University College Hospitals NHS Trust is an 'opted-out' grouping of healthcare facilities in and around the Euston Road and Upper Woburn Place area of North London. The grouping comprises general and specialist hospitals which together offer a wide range of services to the community in its locality and beyond. The University College Hospital is complemented by the National Hospital for Neurology and Neurosurgery, the Eastman Dental Hospital and the Medical, Postgraduate and Dental Schools of the University College, London.

Since the Government enabled hospitals to assume trust status, healthcare institutions have had greater autonomy to develop their own strategies and objectives rather then merely 'following the line' set out by the Department of Health. University College Hospitals is one of the many hospital groups to 'opt-out' in this manner.

The Trust describes its objectives in its published 'vision', as follows:

The new Trust is seeking to:
- *Enhance and develop the reputations of each of the hospitals for providing the highest quality service and ensure that the combined Trust's aims become a reality on 1 April 1996;*
- *Pool our collective talent, expertise and commitment to clinical excellence by forming one organization with shared aims and objectives;*
- *Maintain and develop a local, national and international role as a provider of comprehensive, safe, accessible and high quality care for patients;*
- *Capitalise on our leading national and international role in research, education and training through close alliances with a combined Medical School and associated Postgraduate Institutes to translate research and development into direct benefits to patients;*
- *Provide scope for collaboration, innovation and advances in the continuing education of healthcare professionals;*
- *Ensure that we continue to be open and honest in our dealings with staff*

and are flexible and innovative to enable us to recruit and retain the best people;

- *Employ strong leadership and effective decentralized management to determine the strategic direction and foster a sense of corporate responsibility to achieve the Trust's aims.*

(Source: University College Hospitals Trust.)

Assignment question: Brighton and Hove Albion Football Club

By Saturday 27 April 1996, Brighton and Hove Albion football club had already been confirmed as relegated from the Endsleigh League division two – it had not been a good season. The fans' misery was further compounded by the plans of the club's Board, headed by chief executive, David Bellotti, to sell the club's ground (Goldstone Ground) to a property developer and to relocate to a ground-sharing arrangement in nearby Portsmouth. The fans' affection for Goldstone Ground was not only due to its locality in the town but also because of its age and the fans' association of it with 'happier days'. The financial situation of the club, nevertheless, required some improvement and the sale of the ground was seen by the Board as a suitable way to bring the improvement about.

Having already been relegated, Brighton were due to play York City at the Goldstone Ground on 27 April. The previous week, some fans had broken into the ground at night and daubed graffiti on walls and on the pitch itself calling for the resignation of Mr Bellotti and a reversal of the decision to sell the ground. After sixteen minutes of the match on 27 April with the game still goal-less, a large number of Brighton fans invaded the pitch to make a further public protest. After some of the more militant fans dismantled the goal-posts, the referee was forced to abandon the match. Police restored order shortly afterwards.

Questions

- Generate a list of the most significant stakeholders in Brighton and Hove Albion football club.
- Comment of the legitimacy of the supporters' protests on 27 April.
- To what extent do the supporters 'own' the football club?
- Are the supporters a powerful group of stakeholders?
- What other mechanisms might the supporters use to attempt to influence the board's decision to sell the ground.

References

1. Johnson, G. and Scholes, K. (1993) *Exploring Corporate Strategy, Text and Cases*. 3rd edn. Englewood Cliffs, NJ: Prentice Hall. (Adapted from Mendelow, A. (1991) *Proceedings of 2nd International Conference on Information Systems*, Cambridge, MA.
2. Donaldson, T. and Preston, L. E. (1995) The stakeholder theory of the corporation: concepts, evidence and implications. *Academy of Management Review* **20**(1): pp. 65–91.

3

Non-incorporated organizations

Learning objectives

After studying this chapter, students should be able to describe:

- What is meant by a legal entity or *juristic personality*.
- What is meant by a *sole proprietor*.
- The advantages and disadvantages of holding sole proprietor status.
- What is meant by a *partnership*.
- The advantages and disadvantages of holding partnership status.

3.1 What is a non-incorporated organization?

There are two broad categories of privately owned business organizations, i.e. those not owned by the state. The distinction rests upon the status of the organization in the eyes of the law (the legal status). In this chapter we will discuss one of these categories, *non-incorporated organizations*, whilst in Chapter 4, we will examine the second category, limited companies or *incorporated* organizations.

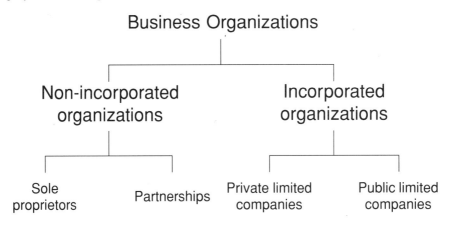

Figure 3.1 A taxonomy of private sector business organizations

The distinction between these categories revolves around the rather odd question: 'What is a person?' This question does not refer to the biologist's definition of a person, but the legal definition. In business, a person (or a *legal entity*) may be a biological person, like you or me, but it might not be. It can be a collection of people.

We shall see in Chapter 4 that incorporated organizations are unique in that the law primarily recognizes the organization as a legal entity in its own right, and not the employees of it. This is not the case in unincorporated organizations.

What is a 'legal entity'?

In legal and business studies, the concepts of human and legal personality can be different. That which legal people call a *juristic personality* is any party that the law recognizes as a single entity ('person'), in that the state will enforce contracts made by that 'person'. A legal entity has certain rights:

- to make contracts;
- to carry out business transactions;
- to own property;
- to employ people;
- to sue and be sued for breach of contract.

It is immediately obvious that these things all apply to you and me. Take the author of this book as an example. He can make contracts (say to buy a car or write a book), he owns a house, he employs tradespeople to repair property, and so on. In all respects, the law recognizes the author as a person.

In the case of the simplest form of business, the sole proprietor, the law does not recognize the business entity of 'the sole proprietor', but it does recognize the human person who is the sole proprietor.

The issue becomes a little more complex when we consider limited companies (see Chapter 4). The law recognizes the company as the legal personality in its own right. Hence, it is the entity of the company which makes contracts. The employees of the company who are empowered to make contracts *on the company's behalf* are called its agents. These are usually senior or specialized employees of the company.

The two major types of business enterprise we shall consider in this chapter are essentially individual 'human' legal entities, and, as we shall see, this has some important implications for the individuals concerned.

3.2 Sole proprietors

What is a sole proprietor?

The sole proprietor or sole trader is the simplest form of business arrangement. Such a person is usually, but not necessarily, a sole person carrying out some sort of business. Because there is no legal requirement to declare oneself as a sole trader, nobody knows exactly how many there are, but it is thought that there are well over one million such businesses in the UK. There is no formal setting-up procedure for sole traders – they simply begin in business. Furthermore, apart from keeping records for tax purposes, there is no requirement to keep records of any kind.

Most sole proprietors are one-person concerns, but others employ a few staff as helpers. Some, albeit in exceptional circumstances, may employ up to 100 staff. Most 'self-employed' people operate as sole proprietors, common examples of which include:

- tradespeople (e. g. joiners, plasterers, electricians, painters, roofers);
- market-stall holders;
- small independent retailers (e.g. fish and chip shops, newsagents, greengrocers etc);
- 'cottage industry' proprietors (e.g. craft workshops);
- farmers;
- window cleaners.

The nature of the sole proprietor means that setting-up costs are limited to the tools or premises required to carry out normal business activities. Whilst this can be reasonably sizeable (e.g. for a shop or a milk-round), in most cases, it is relatively small. Consider the cost, for example, of setting-up as a window cleaner: the price of a ladder, a mop and a bucket. Many sole proprietors carry out business on an occasional basis (e.g. when they have no income from any other source), whereas others spend all of their working lives in this form of business arrangement.

Question 3.1

In addition to the examples given above, can you think of any other businesses which are usually carried out by sole proprietors?

As we might expect, sole proprietors enjoy some advantages from their status in law, and some disadvantages.

Advantages of holding sole proprietor status

- Because there are no legally required setting-up procedures, it *costs nothing* to begin trading as a sole proprietor, apart from the necessary capital costs. It follows that it is also quick, with no approvals needed or complicated forms to fill in.
- The sole proprietor, as the owner of the business (or more correctly as the business – the sole proprietor *is* the business), has total claim on all the business's earnings. All *profits and earnings belong directly to him or her*.
- The owner is 'his own boss' as the only employee of the business. This has several advantages. Firstly, *decisions can be made quickly* as he has nobody else to consult. Secondly, he has *total autonomy* to organize his work as he sees fit. Thirdly, he is *independent* of any other working partner – he can please himself.
- With the exception of tax returns, there is *no requirement placed upon sole proprietors to submit formal documentation* annually as limited companies must (see Chapter 4). This saves a lot of time and costs that other forms of business entity must spend on book-keeping and auditing. It also means that confidentiality can be preserved – nobody except the tax authorities need ever find out how much the sole proprietor earns or how much he has 'saved for a rainy day'.

Disadvantages of holding sole proprietor status

- The very nature of the business as a small or one-person concern, means that *all of the tasks in the business must be performed by the owner/manager*. Such tasks include the operations (e.g. the window cleaning or the plumbing work), selling and advertising (if appropriate), invoicing and collecting debts, filling in tax documentation, and so on. This necessarily puts pressure on the workload of the sole proprietor.

- The *skills and abilities that the business has access to are limited to those of the owner*. If the owner is particularly poor at any skill, the skill deficiencies are to the detriment of the business. This is usually a key consideration because although he may be proficient in his trade, the owner may be poor at administration, selling or any number of important business functions.
- The work of a sole proprietor is usually *labour intensive*. This means that when the sole proprietor is not working, no money is coming in. This tends to mean that 'luxuries' like holidays, sick days and other reasons for 'time off' may be a rare occurrence, especially if there is pressure to keep working to bring in money.
- The small size of the sole proprietor business means that they usually suffer from *poor economies of scale*. This means that the sole proprietor has little buying power, and will consequently pay a higher price per unit of material (e.g. per nail, piece of wood, tin of paint) than larger businesses, which are more likely to buy in bulk.
- A sole proprietor suffers from what is known as *unlimited liability*. This is a major disadvantage of all forms of non-incorporated business. As the sole proprietor is a human legal entity, he does not benefit from limited liability. In practice, his means that the owner of the business (the sole proprietor) is liable for any or all of the business's losses from his own personal reserves, without limit.

Unlimited liability – a sad story

Johnny Banana is a sole proprietor who specializes in decorating and plumbing. He accepted a contract to work in a large country mansion, with a focus on redecorating and replumbing in and above the art gallery. The art gallery in the mansion was of international renown and housed several rare Renoirs, Picassos and a few valuable Lowrys.

What the owner of the mansion didn't realize was that Johnny was not very good at his job. On arriving at the house, Johnny decided to start with the plumbing. He re-routed several water and sewage pipes above the gallery and re-housed some channels under the expensive tiled floor. After this, on the second day, Johnny started to repaint the walls on which the expensive paintings were hung.

Things started to go wrong when he removed a Picasso from the wall to paint behind it. Laying it on the floor, he kicked over a can of paint and unfortunately most of it landed on the painting. Whilst furiously trying to wipe the paint off with some rags, one of the pipes above the gallery ruptured allowing sewage to dribble onto one of the Renoirs. Leaving the Picasso to rush to the sewage pipe, he nudged the ladders, toppling over another tin of paint, which also landed on the unfortunate Picasso. By now, the dribbling foul water was causing irreparable damage to the Renoir. The copious expletives uttered by Johnny caused the mansion's owner to enter the gallery.

The two paintings were judged to have been ruined. Johnny was advised that he owed a total of £14 million in respect of the two paintings. Because Johnny was a sole proprietor, the entire value of the demand had to be met from his personal reserves. His total worth comprised the value of his house (£30 000) and the

---

value of his van (£500). Johnny was declared bankrupt – a situation which meant that he could not take advantage of mortgages or any other loans; thus he lost his home and his business with little prospect of rebuilding either of them again.

3.3 Partnerships

What is a partnership?

The second major form of unincorporated business is the partnership. *The Partnership Act 1890*, defines a partnership as,

> *... the relationship which subsists between persons carrying on a business with a view to profit.*

This definition is a little unclear and it does leave room for some interpretation. It will therefore come as no surprise to learn that a number of different partnership arrangements have been employed by business people over the years.

A partnership is like a sole proprietor in some respects and unlike it in others. Like a sole proprietor, a partnership is *not incorporated* and therefore suffers from *unlimited liability*. In contrast to the sole proprietor, partnerships are a legally acknowledged and recognized form of business organization.

By definition, there must be at least two partners in a partnership. There is no legal upper limit, but in practice, the number of partners rarely exceeds twenty.

Partnership arrangements are occasionally found in the 'trades' (e.g. electricians, builders), but are more common among professional concerns such as:

- surveyors;
- architects;
- accountants;
- management consultants;
- lawyers and solicitors;
- general practitioners.

Partnership agreements

Partnerships are usually set up by all partners signing a legally binding partnership agreement. This is a simple and cheap procedure which requires the services of a solicitor or a similarly appointed legal professional.

A legally binding agreement is meant to avoid two possible unpleasant situations arising:

- Partners are equal in their positions in the partnership unless the other partners agree to elevate one of their number to the position of senior partner. All profits ensuing from the business of the partnership are equally divisible between all partners (unless it is agreed that senior partners should receive more). Without a legal agreement, there would be nothing to prevent some of the other partners 'ganging-up' on one partner (who they may perceive as having done little work) to not give him his rightful share of the partnership's profits.

- We have already seen that partnerships do not enjoy limited liability. In the event that the partnership has to absorb a loss, the amount must be made good from the personal reserves of the partners. In such a circumstance, some partners may be tempted to say 'I am not a part of this organization, I was just helping out. Therefore I am not liable for any of these losses'. This would leave the other partners 'carrying the can'. A formal declaration of partnership leaves no doubt as to who the partners are, thus preventing this situation from arising.

Advantages of holding partnership status

- The fact that there are more people in a partnership than a sole proprietor means that *more capital can be raised*. This will enable the business to benefit from a higher capacity than a smaller business. It follows that the more partners take part in the venture, the more capital may be invested.
- In common with all non-incorporated business organizations, there is *no need to submit accounts* as limited companies have to. This saves time and costs, particularly the costs of having accounts externally audited (a compulsory requirement of limited companies)
- The partners, as the sole owners of the business, are *entitled to distribute all the profits among themselves*. There is no complicated ownership structure to take account of, which is sometimes the case with incorporated organizations.
- The fact that there are several people in the partnership means that there is likely to be a *breadth of skills and abilities* from which the business can benefit. This is in marked contrast to the predicament of the sole proprietor, who only has his own skills to call upon.
- Organizations which benefit from the labour inputs of more than one person can *divide up tasks between individuals*. This means that there can be a degree of specialization and no single partner need shoulder too much of the workload. One partner may specialize, for example, in the administration of the business, whilst others perform the operational tasks.
- Whilst the business has unlimited liability, the fact that there are more individuals involved means that *any losses can be shared equally* among the partners. This reduces the burden of risk that any single partner must endure.

Disadvantages of holding partnership status

- In common with all non-incorporated organizations, partnerships have *unlimited liability*. Furthermore, the situation of losses can be somewhat more complex than losses for a sole trader, as the losses must be borne by all the partners, even if they are caused by the defective actions of just one (although this may be modified by the terms of the partnership agreement).
- The need to set up a *legal partnership agreement* incurs a nominal charge.

- The nature of a partnership in contrast to a sole proprietor means that *decisions must be arrived at by consultation* and agreement between partners. This usually makes for slower decision-making than in sole trader arrangements, and opens up the possibility of conflict between partners.
- The *individual independence of the sole trader is lost*. An equal partner in a partnership does not of himself have the authority to decide on time off, the types of work carried out, the standards of quality observed, and so on. Such decisions must normally be taken in consultation with the other partners.
- The nature of the partnership agreement is such that if one partner leaves the partnership for any reason (e.g. a 'bust-up' or death), then the *partnership is automatically dissolved*. Most partnerships make a special clause in their agreement to account for this possibility.

Except for the statutory requirements that the business should keep records for tax purposes, a partnership, like the sole proprietor, need not keep or publish any other financial information (unlike limited companies). Because of this, it is possible for partnerships to keep financial details secret (such as the magnitude of their total sales). This feature may be of value in some competitive circumstances.

Whereas most sole proprietors remain as relatively small businesses, some partnerships grow to be of considerable size. The large accountancy auditing firms are partnerships (e.g. Price Waterhouse, Spicer and Oppenheim) as are some multinational surveying and architects' practices.

Assignment

You have a friend who has just received a bequest of £10 000 from the will of his recently departed grandmother. When you ask him what he intends to do with the money he informs you that he intends to open a fish and chip shop and to run it himself. He says that he intends to run it as a sole proprietor, but then suggests that you may be interested in joining him as a partner in the venture.

Questions

- Advise your friend of the pros and cons of running a fish and chip shop in the legal form of a sole proprietor.
- Discuss the merits of joining your friend as a partner in the fish and chip shop business.

Further reading

Worthington, I. and Britton, C. (1994) *The Business Environment*, Ch. 7. London: Pitman.

4

Limited companies

Learning objectives

After studying this chapter, students should be able to describe:

- The nature of a legal entity.
- The meaning of limited liability.
- The nature of shares and shareholding.
- The differences between public and private limited companies.
- The legal requirements for limited companies.
- The advantages and disadvantages of limited company status.
- The nature of holding companies.
- The roles of a company's senior officers.
- The nature of corporate governance and the contents of the Cadbury Report.

4.1 An organization as a legal entity

In the case of a sole proprietor, we saw in Chapter 3 that the law recognizes the human person carrying out business with a view to profit. Similarly, for partnerships, the law recognizes the partners as individuals, albeit working together under a legal agreement.

The type of organizations we shall consider in this chapter is quite different from those we considered in Chapter 3. A *limited company*, or an *incorporated organization*, is one wherein the law primarily recognizes the organization as a person. An organizational 'person' acts just like a human person in law (as we saw in Chapter 3):

- it can make contracts;
- it can carry out business transactions;
- it can own property;
- it can employ people;
- it is capable of suing and of being sued for breach of contract.

Hence, when customers, suppliers or employees deal with a limited company, the contracts they make are with the company and not with the employees they deal with. The juristic personality, in this case, is a limited company.

4.2 Limited liability

The need for a form of business organization other than the ones we have so far considered first arose not long after the beginning of industrialization in the nineteenth century. Clearly, for a business to grow in order to allow it to benefit from economies of scale and meet market demand, more investment would be needed than just a few people could provide. The problem was that investors would be reluctant to invest in a business if they could be personally pursued for losses, especially if the investor did not intend to take an active role in managing the business. To answer these disincentives to invest, the idea of limited liability was developed.

Limited liability allows many people to invest in a business, which is good for the business's growth and development. If the business succeeds, the investors benefit from a share of the business's profits (as a *return* on their investment). If, however, the business fails or incurs large losses, the investors will not be liable for anything other than the value of their initial investment. It is said that their liability is limited to the value of the money invested in the business. Of course, business failure means that shareholders lose this money investment, but they would not be pursued for money from their own personal wealth, as is the case in non-incorporated businesses.

How limited liability works

Limited liability, in its simplest sense, works as follows:

- The founders, on behalf of the entity of the company announce that they intend to carry out business activity and that investors are welcomed. The mechanism by which this happens varies from the informal ('Do you want to invest in my business idea?') to the highly formal, such as the when a public company (see later in this chapter) publishes a 'prospectus'.
- The value of the business (either its actual or its proposed value) is divided up into small 'chunks', typically of between 25 p and £1. Each of these 'chunks' is called a *share*.
- Individuals buy a number of shares in the business and, in doing so, become *shareholders*.
- In exchange for the use of individuals' investment, the *agents* (see below) of the company make certain commitments. Pre-eminent among these is that they will manage the company for the benefit of the shareholders and will, to the best of their ability, provide an acceptable financial return on the shareholding.
- The company's agents use the shareholders' money to buy equipment and stock to use in the normal course of business. If the company succeeds, the value of the shareholders' funds will grow as demand for the shares drives the share price upwards. If the company fails, the shareholders lose the entire value of their investment.
- Under no circumstances can shareholders be pursued for more than the value of their shareholding. Parties owed money at the time of company failure can only make claims against the value of the assets of the company.

Agency

A very important concept in the context of limited companies is that of agency. In simple business organizations such as the sole proprietor, it is obvious who has the power to act on behalf of the business – the person who is the business. When the business itself is the juristic personality, it is more difficult to decide who can act on behalf of the company. The law recognizes an important category of human person who is empowered by the shareholders to act on their behalf in respect of the company – the *agents*. A company's agents are usually its directors and are empowered to make contracts on behalf of the company. The shareholders to whom the agents report and are accountable are called the organization's *principals*. The principals, collectively, oversee the work of the agents and may replace agents if they feel they are incompetent or are not acting in the principals' best economic interest.

Case – Polly Peck plc

Polly Peck plc experienced rapid growth as a limited company during the 1980s. As a large company, its business interests included the Sansui electronics company, the Del Monte fruit business, Russell Hobbs consumer products (e.g. electric toasters) and Tower kitchenware. On 24 October 1990, the group became insolvent when the company's bankers made demands upon company funds after they 'got whiff' of some financial irregularities.

When the company failed, it had outstanding debts of £1.2 billion. The failure was also of great concern to its 35,000 employees and its 20 000 shareholders.

The failure precipitated a great deal of legal and financial activity – the collapse of a company of the size of Polly Peck is of interest to a large number of stakeholders. The creditors of Polly Peck (those who were owed money) made claims against the assets of the company to try to recover their cash, but the magnitude of the company's debts meant that it was unlikely that they would receive their debts in full. The shareholders lost all their investment as there was nothing left once the creditors had been paid, but because of their limited liability, they could not be pursued by the creditors for outstanding debts which couldn't be made good from the company's assets.

4.3 Shares and shareholders

At one time, shareholding was the almost total purview of insurance companies, banks and other institutional investors. Changes in the structure of industry in the 1980s, including the privatization of many former state monopolies (see Chapter 19), made it more likely that many thousands of individual people would hold shares. This meant that as well as buying your gas from British Gas, you could also hold shares in the company, and hence be one of its owners.

The number of shares that a company issues is known as the *share volume*. Larger companies obviously have larger share volumes than smaller ones due to the larger company value that is divided into shares.

Question 4.1

Find out the share volumes for the following companies. You will find this information in the share pages of a broadsheet newspaper, such as the *Financial Times*:

- Asda Stores plc.
- Guinness plc.
- British Aerospace plc.
- Drummond Group plc.
- Barclays plc.

Types of shares

Shares are not all the same. Companies in the UK issue three types of share:

- *Preference shares* give their holders rights that other shareholders do not enjoy. Preference shareholders are usually guaranteed a dividend, whatever the financial results of the company. If the company is unable to pay a dividend, the dividend is carried over to the subsequent year when the shareholder is paid for the two years – a principle known as *cumulative dividend payment*. In many cases, in the event that the company is wound up, preference shareholders are entitled to repayment of their investment in preference to ordinary shareholders. Against the benefits of preference shares is the drawback that dividends are often fixed in advance and do not vary. If the company has a good year, it is possible that the ordinary shareholders will receive more than preference shareholders.
- *Ordinary shares* are by far the most common type. The precise rights of ordinary shareholders depend upon the company's articles of association (see later). In most cases, ordinary shares entitle the holder to attend and vote at the company's annual general meeting. In addition, they may expect a variable dividend, dependent upon the level of profits made in any given financial year. Unlike preference shares, ordinary shares do not carry a right to a dividend. In the event that the company is wound up, ordinary shareholders are usually last in the 'pecking order' and will only receive any cash if there is anything left once all the operational debts have been settled. Ordinary shares carry with them the possibility of high return, but also carry more risk than preference shares. This is not only because of the variable dividend, but also because of the almost certain loss in the event of company failure.
- *Deferred shares* are very rarely used, but are worthy of note. Sometimes issued to the founders or employees of a limited company, holders receive dividends only if there is cash available after preference and ordinary shareholders. However, once the other shareholders have been paid, the deferred shareholders may be the beneficiaries of the rest of the profit, divided between them.
- *Share options* are not shares as such, but represent a right to buy shares at a certain predetermined price. Usually granted to a company's managers and directors, they are designed to act as an incentive to achieve higher productivity and profitability. It may be that an executive director is offered a share option at £1. If the share price is

below £1, the director has no financial incentive to exercise his or her share options. If, however, the share price rises to £2 per share, the director can buy shares at £1 and then sell them immediately at £2 (the current market value). In doing so, he or she makes a profit of £1 per share with no risk and no investment (unless the director decides to hold the shares for some time in anticipation of future rises in share price). Executive share options are described by the number of shares that the executive can buy at the fixed price. Senior directors are usually granted more share options than others.

Shares and control

The way in which shares are distributed can determine the overall control of the company. Ordinary shares, as we have seen, give their holders the right to vote on resolutions at company meetings. It follows that the higher the shareholding, the greater the degree of power over the company's affairs. Any single shareholder who holds 51% or more of the company's ordinary (voting) shares has, by definition, absolute control over the company. It may also be the case that a shareholder with a lesser holding has a high degree of power, depending on the structure of the rest of the shareholding. If one single shareholder has, say, 40%, but no other shareholder has more than 1%, it follows that the larger shareholder has a great deal of influence, even though he or she may not have overall control.

Companies limited by share and by guarantee

When a company is formed by the investment of share capital, it is said that the company is *limited by share*. As we have seen, this means that the share capital is the limit of the investors' liability. In the unfortunate event of company failure, the creditors will seek payment from the company's assets, including, if necessary, the share capital. If the company's assets and its share capital runs out before all of the creditors have been paid in full, then it is unfortunate for the creditors.

There is, however, an alternative, but much less common type of limited company. It relies not on investors buying shares, but on individuals agreeing to underwrite part of the company's debt if it fails. It is said that the individuals guarantee to pay so much money in the event of failure so that the company is *limited by guarantee*. Companies limited by guarantee are uncommon because, unlike those limited by share, they have no way of raising capital from shareholders. The individuals guaranteeing the company do not inject capital, but rather they agree to accept some of the liability.

In consequence, companies limited by guarantee tend to be small. Furthermore, because the guarantors are required to provide money (in the event of failure) for no return, such companies tend to be organizations engaged in non-profit-making, benevolent or charitable pursuits. Examples include social clubs, research associations, community businesses and professional bodies. Any profits that the company makes are ploughed back in – having no shareholders, there is nobody to benefit from dividends. In most cases, the amount of money guaranteed by the guarantors is small, sometimes as little as £1.

4.4 Public and private limited companies

There are two broad types of limited company. The distinction rests upon the access to the company's shares.

The *private limited company* is the most common form of limited company. The shares in this type of business are held by private individuals who, in many cases, also work for the company (e.g. the managing director). Shares in private companies are not generally available to the public. If an individual wishes to buy shares in the company, they must approach a shareholder directly and seek his or her consent to transfer the shares upon payment of an agreed sum. It may be the case that share transfers must be approved by other shareholders in the company as well. Private companies are denoted by the term 'Limited' (e.g. Brown Limited, Campbell Limited).

In a *public limited company*, anybody can buy shares in the company. This is the key distinction – it is one of access. The public at large do not have general access to the shares of a private company, but they do in public companies. The shares in a public limited company are freely bought and sold through a stock exchange – a central point which manages all public share dealings. In Britain, we have the London Stock Exchange, located near the Bank of England in the City of London. The London Stock Exchange is one of the world's most important financial institutions and handles more transactions in shares than any other exchange in the world. Public companies are denoted by the term 'plc' (e.g. British Gas plc, British Aerospace plc).

It is usually, but not necessarily, the case that larger companies tend to be public limited companies. During the growth of a company, which almost always starts off as a private limited company, successful trading brings the need to make larger investment in the business. By making the privately held shares publicly available – by turning it into a public limited company – cash can be generated for such purposes. This change in share structure is called a *floatation*, because its shares are 'floated' on the stock exchange.

4.5 Qualifications for limited liability

The state considers the extension of limited liability to a business something of a privilege. After all, in the worst circumstances, it is possible for a company to cease trading leaving debts unpaid and shareholders out-of-pocket. In exchange for the granting of limited liability status, the law makes certain demands on a company, contravention of which would result in the privilege being withdrawn.

A limited company must:

- upon its inception, file its articles of association at Companies House;
- upon its inception, file its memorandum of association at Companies House;
- annually, without exception, file audited accounts of the business at Companies House.

Companies House is an executive agency of the state which is charged with the job of maintaining records on all limited companies. It must retain all records and ensure that all audited accounts are received from each company annually. All information in Companies House is publicly available, so anybody can inspect the articles, memoranda or accounts of any company at their leisure. For companies in England and Wales, Companies House is based in Cardiff, and for Scottish companies it is based in Edinburgh.

The articles of association

These documents are concerned with the internal affairs and the rules of the company. In particular they include:

- the identities of the shareholders (if a private limited company);
- whether the company is private or public;
- the names and home addresses of the directors of the company;
- the identity of the company secretary;
- the name of the accountant or accountancy practice who will be the auditors of the company's annual accounts;
- the powers and responsibilities of the above-mentioned directors;
- the rules regarding the calling of meetings of shareholders (which will include the annual general meeting).

Throughout the life of the company, many of these statements will change. The company can modify its articles of association at any time subject to shareholder approval.

The memorandum of association

These documents include:

- The name that the company intends to adopt or has adopted. This must not be a direct copy of any other company name (e.g. if an existing company is called *J. Smith Ltd*, a new company would not be allowed to adopt that name. It could, however, call itself *J. D. Smith Ltd*).
- The address of the company's head office (called the 'registered office').
- The broad purpose of the company. Most companies intentionally make this reasonably broad to allow them to diversify into other activities if appropriate.
- A statement that the 'members' (shareholders) are claiming limited liability in accordance with the relevant companies legislation.
- The value of the company's share capital.
- The types of shares issued and the numbers of each.
- The distribution of the shares (e.g. 'Mr J. Smith, director, has 30 000 ordinary shares').
- A 'declaration of association' in which the shareholders and agents state their intention to form a company and to take up shares in it.

Again, the memorandum of association can, with shareholder consent, be amended from time to time as becomes necessary.

Annual audited accounts

The accounts of a limited company are a record of its financial state at a particular date (the 'year-end') and a summary of its financial performance over the previous year. There are strict financial rules which dictate how they should be constructed to prevent misrepresentation and so that comparisons can be fairly made between companies (the *financial reporting standards* (FRSs) and the *statements of standard accounting practice* (SSAPs)). We will examine these statements in some detail in Chapter 11.

The accounts must contain three separate documents:

- The *profit and loss account* (or income statement) provides a summary of the performance of the business over the year. It gives the company's total sales, a breakdown of its costs, and hence its profit figure. This statement also discloses how much of the profit must be paid in tax and how much is being retained or repaid to the shareholders as dividends.
- The *balance sheet* is a summary of the company's financial state on the last day of the accounting year (the same day that the profit and loss statement is produced). The statement is called a 'balance' sheet because it contains two 'sides' which, by definition, equal each other. In simple terms, the first side describes where the company has obtained its assets (the amounts from shareholders, loans, retained profits, etc.) and the second side describes how the company has used its assets (how much it has invested in plant, buildings and stocks, external investments, cash at the bank, etc.). Hence, it is not 'magic' when the balance sheet balances – unless something has been forgotten, it simply has to.
- The *cash-flow statement* describes the net cash movements in and out of the company over the course of the financial year. The important feature of the cash-flow statement is that, as its name suggests, it records the inward and outward net movements of cash.

After each of the statements has been prepared, the accounts must be *audited*. This involves an independent firm of accountants coming into the company and checking that all of the information in the accounts is correct. They will look at the company's records behind the accounts to make sure that the accounts represent a true and fair view of the company's financial position on the year-end date.

Once the accounts have been prepared and audited, they must be submitted to Companies House.

4.6 Limited companies – pros and cons

We have seen that the organization known as a limited company is significantly more complex than those of the sole proprietor and the partnership. There are several conditions that limited companies must meet. Yet it is the case that the vast majority of medium to large business are limited companies. In this section, we will identify the major pros and cons of opting for this legal form of business.

Advantages

- By taking on limited company status, the owners of the company can benefit from *limited liability*. No matter what the company's agents do, and regardless of the size of the losses made, a shareholder's liability (or risk) is limited to the value of his or her shares.
- The fact that most limited companies, even small ones, have several shareholders, means that *more capital is likely to be available* for the business than would be the case for a sole trader or a partnership. If necessary, the company can create new shares for sale to the market as a means of raising extra finance.

Disadvantages

- The setting-up and running of a limited company is decidedly more cumbersome than that of an unincorporated business. There are several *legal constraints and procedures* which must be observed, and these invariably involve both cost and expensive management commitment.
- The fact that the business benefits from limited liability may make some organizations *reluctant to lend money* under some circumstances. If a bank knows that any outstanding debts can only be paid from company assets, then a weak asset base may make some lenders wary. This is a particular problem for smaller companies or those that are already in heavy debt.
- In the cases of both sole traders and partnerships, the managers of the business are also its owners. Hence, their investors have total say as to the distribution of profits, and can, if they wish, pay all profits out to themselves. The fact that limited companies are run by shareholders' agents means that *investors are not automatically entitled to all the profits* of the business and may have little say in how the operation is run (unless you are a majority shareholder). Agents rarely pay out all the profits as dividends because it is the shareholders' longer term interests to retain some profit for future investment.

4.7 Holding companies

What is a holding company?

A holding company is a special example of a limited company. We have seen that, by definition, any party which owns 51% or more of a company's shares has control over the owned company. This is because, assuming the shares owned are voting shares, the shareholder can impose his or her will and policies upon the owned company. If more than 51% of the shares were owned by a shareholder, say 100%, this would not give the shareholder any more power, but he or she would obviously be entitled to more payment in terms of dividends.

Company shares can be owned by either individual people or by other organizations. Some companies, however, exist solely to own other companies – by buying a controlling shareholding in the business. These are holding companies.

Holding companies, in one respect, do not do anything directly. Usually based around a single head office, all holding company activity occurs in its *subsidiaries*. The term 'holding' derives from the fact that the head office 'holds' the shares of other companies. The head office may buy and sell entire companies or they may build the companies which they own by investing in them and enjoying the dividends from their activities. By virtue of the nature of their business activity, holding companies tend to be larger organizations and many of the UK's most important companies have opted for this form of organization. Most are also public limited companies.

Understandably, the name of the holding company tends to be less well known than the companies owned. You may not have heard of Grand Metropolitan plc, but you will know of Burger King, Smirnoff vodka, Cointreau and Metaxa brandy – all of which are owned by the holding company head office of Grand Metropolitan.

Shareholders who invest in a holding company are actually investing, indirectly in several companies rather than just one. Some investors take the view that this is a lower risk investment than putting money into a single company which does not have the breadth of interests of a holding company.

In all legal respects, holding companies are the very same as any other limited company. They must file their articles and memorandum of association and must produce an annually audited set of accounts, although we might expect their corporate purposes – set out in the memorandum of association – to differ from those of an 'ordinary' company.

Owned and owning companies – some terminology

Accountants attach different names to companies owned by holding companies, depending upon the percentage of the shares owned. Generally speaking, we refer to the holding as the *parent company* – referring to its role as guardian and senior. For the owned company, accountants use three terms.

- If the parent owns in excess of 50% of (and therefore has control over) the owned company, the owned company is called a *subsidiary* of the parent.
- If the parent owns between around 20% and 50% of the owned company, the owned company is called an *associate* of the parent.
- If the parent owns less than around 20% of the smaller company, the smaller company is called a *related* interest of the parent.

Holding companies and the creation of wealth

The mechanism by which a normal business creates wealth is easily understandable. It produces an output which is of value to the market, and in selling products the company reinvests profits and grows. Because holding companies do not themselves produce anything, they must increase in value through the activities of their subsidiaries.

There are two essential ways in which a holding company can increase its wealth:

- It can extract profits, in the form of dividends, from its subsidiaries. By having majority voting rights, the parent can determine the dividend, which on some occasions may involve overturning the recommendations of the subsidiary's board.

- It can buy a company for one price, increase its value and sell it off at an increased price. This can sometimes take the form of buying an existing group of companies and gaining a cash surplus by splitting the group up and selling the member companies individually.

A holding company making (a lot of) money – Hanson plc

Hanson plc is a British based company which, prior to a recent restructuring, owned companies all over the world. As one of the UK's biggest companies, Hanson's group turnover in the year to 1994 was over £11 billion. In January 1986, Hanson bought 100% of the shares in the US based SCM Group. At the time of the purchase, SCM was a group of 17 companies in a wide variety of industries including paint, chemicals, food, paper and typewriters. Hanson made its money on the SCM purchase by splitting it up and selling off its constituent companies separately. The chronology of events was as follows:

1986   Hanson bought SCM for $930 million.
1986   Hanson sold off former SCM companies for $935 million.
1987   Hanson sold off former SCM companies for $28 million.
1988   Hanson sold off former SCM companies for $266 million.
1989   Hanson sold off 52% of the shares in one former SCM company for $309 million.
1990   Hanson sold off former SCM companies for $41 million.

The total receipts from the sales of former SCM companies to 1990 was thus $1579 million ($1.579 billion). Compared to the purchase price of $930 million, Hanson made a cash surplus on the deal of $649 million. This in itself would have been a shrewd piece of business, but it didn't sell all of the SCM companies. The one company retained, SCM Chemicals, based in Baltimore, is the world's third largest supplier of an industrial chemical called titanium dioxide. This company alone is capable of generating over $300 million a year in profits.

(Source: Hanson plc.)

Holding company structures

The head office of a holding company is usually relatively small compared to the size of the rest of the company. It will be staffed by the group's senior directors, accountants, strategists and, often, legal people.

The way in which subsidiaries fit into the group and the fact that they are kept quite separate from other group companies (Figure 4.1) means that they can be excised and sold with no effects on any other company in the group. Similarly, new acquisitions can be 'tagged on' to the structure.

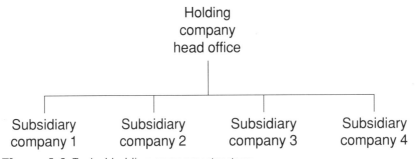

Figure 4.1 Typical holding company structure

Scottish & Newcastle plc (S&N) – a typical holding company structure

S&N plc is a large company divided into three operating divisions. Each division contains a number of companies engaged in similar activities. The company adds to its company portfolio from time to time by means of acquisition and has sold off businesses to concentrate on its three core areas of activity. Figure 4.2 shows a simplified representation of the company's structure and some of S&N's major subsidiaries.

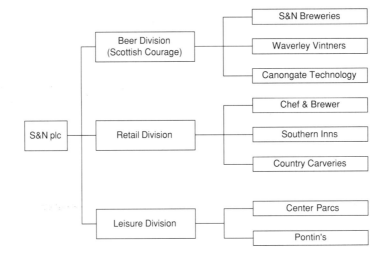

Figure 4.2 Structure of S&N plc

S&N plc is probably best known for its beer division. Scottish Courage is the UK's biggest brewer and became much more significant following the acquisition of Courage plc in 1995. Its brands in this sector include many premium and best-selling products, including McEwan's Lager, Newcastle Brown Ale and Theakston's Best Bitter. Much of its growth over recent years has been by acquisition and 'bolting on' the new companies to the company's existing structure. In addition to the purchase of Courage Limited, S&N has also acquired Chef & Brewer (1993), Center Parcs (1989), Pontin's (1989) and Matthew Brown plc (1987). S&N sold its chain of Thistle Hotels in 1989.

Why adopt a holding company structure?

There are several reasons for adopting a holding company structure:

- By having a business that has interests in more than one product and market sector, the holding company is said to have a *broader portfolio* of business interests. A business that only operates in one sector, say a paint company, is vulnerable if there is a drop in the paint market. For a company which owns businesses in many sectors, a drop off in one sector will offer a lesser threat to the group as a whole. Spreading opportunity and risk is this way is one of the strategic objectives of a holding company.
- Because subsidiaries are kept as separate businesses by the parent (i.e. they aren't all brought together under one 'roof'), *the parent can easily dispose of or acquire companies*. The emphasis of the group can be quickly adjusted by buying or selling companies, as market conditions dictate.
- The control of many companies from a single head office provides the parent with a *ready-made decentralized structure*. By giving the management of each subsidiary a certain degree of autonomy, the parent can benefit from the company without committing parent management time to the company.
- The value to shareholders of the subsidiary company can be increased by the investment of parent company management skills to its operation. This is not only beneficial to the parent's shareholders but also the employees of the subsidiary.

4.8 Corporate governance

The control and management of limited companies

The internal controls of a limited company are the responsibility of the senior management group (as is the case in all other forms of organization). The form that this grouping takes varies according to the type of organization. In small businesses, overall control may be exercised by a single person, but in most organizations this task is entrusted to a group. In limited companies, this grouping takes the form of a board of directors. The way in which limited companies are managed has been the subject of some discussion in recent years. This area of management though has been labelled *corporate governance*.

The governance of a limited company is guided by a number of influences, some of which are statutory (i.e. required by law) and some of which are advisory. A generalized 'hierarchy' is shown in Figure 4.3. It is clear that there a number of people and groups involved in controlling the activity in a limited company. We will examine each one in turn.

Shareholders

Shareholders are the people and organizations who ultimately own the company. By owning a part of the 'stock' of the company, they necessarily have an important say in the affairs of the company. The objectives of shareholders, in most cases, can be described as follows:

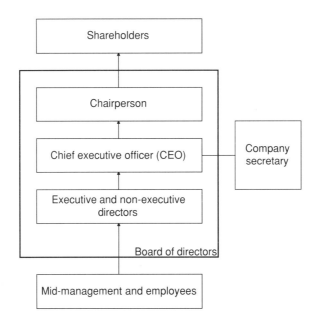

Figure 4.3 *The general structure of a limited company*

- They want to see a return on their investment in the form of a *dividend*. Dividends are paid as a percentage of the profits that the company makes. It follows that the higher the profits the higher the dividend per share.
- They want the value of their shares to rise. A shareholder will buy the shares at a certain price and it would be advantageous if a profit could be made when the shares are sold. Growth in the market value of shares is called *capital growth*.

Shareholders, as a group, have control over the company by their voting rights. Each single share endows the owner with a single vote on company affairs, so the weight of a shareholder's influence is directly proportional to the number of shares held. Votes can be cast at the *annual general meeting* of the company and at any *extraordinary general meetings* that the company may call from time to time.

Both of the central shareholder objectives mentioned above are served by profit-making. It follows that shareholders are principally concerned with the company, not as an employer or a producer of goods, but as a source of profits. This attitude has a knock-on effect on the other controlling influences upon the organization.

Directors and managers – what is the difference?

The role of a director in a limited company is quite unique. Directors have responsibilities unique to their office that other managers do not have.

- A manager is responsible only to his or her immediate superior, whilst a director, in addition to being responsible to a superior, is also responsible, *en masse* with the other directors, to the shareholders (in their role as agents).

- A manager's contract is usually 'permanent'. Most directors must offer themselves for re-election every three years (depending upon the internal rules of the company). This means that, if their performance has not been to the liking of the shareholders, his or her contract is not renewed resulting in the loss of the job.
- A manager is only responsible for the area of work under his or her direct command. Any member of the board, in addition to his or her own functional responsibility, is usually made collectively responsible for the total organization also.

The chairperson

The chairperson of a company is technically its most senior employee, but in many cases, his or her role will be primarily presidential (i.e. he or she *presides*) rather than operational. In the USA, this role is reflected in the job title where a chairperson is referred to as the 'company president'. This means that the chairperson, especially in the case of larger companies, will not be involved in the day-to-day decision-making of the organization. The chairperson has two primary roles:

- To *chair the meetings* of the board of the directors, the annual general meeting and any extraordinary meetings that are held. Because the chairperson is answerable and accountable to the shareholders *only*, he or she must ensure that, at all times, the shareholders' interests are pre-eminent in all company decisions.
- To report to and, if necessary, *liaise with the shareholders* of the company. The chairperson is the 'go-between' who is ultimately answerable to the shareholders on behalf of the company.

The chairperson's statutory requirements include the important task of reporting in a formal document to the shareholders. The *chairman's statement* will appear in the front of the company's annual audited accounts and, if the company produces such, also in the six-monthly interim accounts.

The chief executive officer

The chief executive officer (CEO) is sometimes called the *managing director* or *general manager* and is responsible for actually managing the business. This is in contrast to the job of the chairperson who may assume an overseeing or advisory role but would be unlikely to 'get involved' in the operations of the company. Reporting to the chairperson, the CEO is the *chief steward* of the shareholders' assets and must act in such a way as to achieve maximum return on shareholders' funds.

Among the CEO's most important duties will be the following:

- to manage the company with the objective of achieving the maximum *financial benefit to the shareholders*;
- to ensure that all aspects of company activity are *within the law*;

- to *sign the annual accounts* of the company as being a 'true and fair view' of the company's finances at the time;
- to *formulate strategies* suitable for the company and to implement them in conjunction with the other members of the board;
- to be *responsible for the resources* of the organization and to see that all resource allocations are equitable and in the interest of the shareholders;
- to *approve all major investments* made by the company.

Executive and non-executive directors

In addition to the chairperson and the CEO, the board will also have a number of executive and non-executive directors.

Executive directors
Executive directors are full-time employees of the company and report to the CEO, who also falls into this category. In most companies, each executive director will be charged with oversight of a specific part of the company's activities. In some cases, each director will be responsible for a *function*, such as the marketing function (a marketing director), or the financial function (a finance director). In other cases, for example in the case a company which controls a chain of hotels, each director will be responsible for a hotel. It all depends upon the type and structure of the company in question.

Non-executive directors (NEDs)
Non-executive directors are directors who are not full-time employees of the company. Their involvement will vary from attendance only at board meetings to some degree of involvement as consultants, carrying out special projects for the company. Such people are invited to join the board for a number of reasons:

- they may have a unique *knowledge or expertise* of the industry or products produced;
- they may have a large number of *business or political contacts* that the company can benefit from;
- they may, by their very presence on the board, bring a *credibility to the company* which would be beneficial in their particular industry;
- it may be that an important *stakeholder insists upon the appointment* (a good example of this might be an appointment as NED of a senior employee of the company's bankers);
- companies may appoint NEDs *to comply with the Cadbury code* of best practice (see later – the appointment of NEDs is specifically recommended by the Cadbury Report).

The presence of NEDs on a board is designed to bring objectivity and expertise to discussions. It is sometimes the case that executive directors become so concerned with the day-to-day affairs of the company that a fresh and objective viewpoint from a NED helps to guide and inform board discussions to advantage. Although NEDs receive a salary for their troubles, it is usually less than their executive colleagues.

It has become increasingly common for the chairpersonship to be held by a non-executive person. It is assumed by companies who adopt this approach that objectivity and a certain detachment are particularly useful in the most senior position in the company.

Non-executive directors – Glaxo Wellcome plc

Glaxo Wellcome is one of Britain's biggest companies and the largest manufacturer of pharmaceuticals in the world. Its board is composed of a number of executive directors who are experts in their respective fields of the pharmaceuticals business. In addition, it employs a number of well-qualified and illustrious non-executive directors who together bring a great deal of expertise, experience and balance to the company's governance. The board of Glaxo Wellcome includes former senior politicians, noted academics and a former ambassador. Included in the NED contingent of Glaxo Wellcome plc are (at 1996):

- The Right Honourable Lord Howe of Aberavon (Geoffrey Howe PC, QC), formerly Chancellor of the Exchequer and Secretary of State for Foreign and Commonwealth Affairs. Also a non-executive director of BICC plc.
- Anne Armstrong, formerly US Ambassador to the UK. Also a director of American Express, Boise Cascade, General Motors (the world's biggest motor manufacturer), and Halliburton.
- Lord Kingsdown (Robin Leigh-Pemberton KG, PC), formerly Governor of the Bank of England. Also a director of Redland plc, Hambros plc and Foreign & Colonial Investment Trust plc.
- Professor Sir Richard Southwood FRS, Hon FRCP. Formerly vice-chancellor of the University of Oxford and Chairman of the National Radiological Protection Board.

Company secretary

The company secretary is the most senior administrative officer in the company. Whilst the occupant of this office is not usually a director (although it is possible to combine the offices), he or she will usually be privy to all board business. British company law requires that there are at least two officers in a limited company – one director and one company secretary – such is the importance that the law attaches to the job.

The company secretary should not be confused with the traditional view of a secretary as a personal assistant. It is considered to be an important senior management position and is rewarded with a senior management salary.

The statutory responsibilities of the company secretary include the following:

- He or she is the one who is primarily responsible for the submission of audited accounts – even although it is the directors who sign them.
- He or she is charged with ensuring that the company complies with the law in all respects. This includes company law, contract law and other areas such as health and safety laws. For this reason, many company secretaries have some legal training.

The Cadbury 'code of best practice'

In the late 1980s and early 1990s, there were a number of well-publicized corporate 'scandals' where, it was alleged, some senior managers abused their power to further their own ends or to conduct illegal accounting activities. The most notable cases involved Robert Maxwell and his alleged use of pension money to fund the business, the demise of Polly Peck plc (followed by the arrest and subsequent escape of its chairman, Asil Nadir) and the Guinness 'scandal' where a number of senior directors were convicted of false accounting. The Cadbury Committee, chaired by Sir Adrian Cadbury was commissioned in 1991 to look into the 'best practices' in corporate governance. The central concern of the Committee was the degree of power, which was considered as essentially unaccountable, vested in the board of directors. The committee reported in May 1992 with the following recommendations to redress the main concerns:

- There should be a greater usage of *non-executive directors*. These appointments should be independent of the company and have no financial or business stake in it.
- There should be *regular board meetings* to retain full and effective control over the activities of the company and to monitor its management.
- Responsibilities and duties at board level should be *divided* to ensure that no single person has an overconcentration of power. The independent element of the NEDs should help to accomplish this.
- There should be a *restriction of three years* on the contracts of executive directors which would not be renewed without shareholders' approval.
- There should be a *full disclosure of the emoluments* (total earnings) of each director.
- The company should establish three *subcommittees* of the board which would be staffed or overseen mainly by non-executive directors:
  - an *audit committee* to examine the internal affairs of the company;
  - a *remunerations committee* to recommend the levels of directors' pay;
  - a *nominations committee* to recommend appointments to the board.
- There should be a formal statement in the audited annual accounts that the *business is a going concern*, with financial figures and evidence to back up this claim, as appropriate.
- There should be a *separation of the roles of chairperson and chief executive*, i.e. these two pivotal positions should not be held by the same person (as is the case in some smaller companies).

The Cadbury Committee did not propose that these recommendations be made statutory (i.e. enshrined in company law), but rather that they should be followed voluntarily. They have become almost mandatory, however, for listed public companies, as the London Stock Exchange has recommended that all listed companies comply with the recommendations and formally state the extent to which they do not comply in their annual report. The Cadbury Report has been very influential in reshaping corporate governance over the past few years.

Compliance with the Cadbury Code – compliance and partial compliance

J Sainsbury plc

Like most large plcs, J Sainsbury, the well-known multiple grocery retailer is, concerned to comply, and to be seen to comply, with all matters of 'good practice' in corporate behaviour. The company holds the leading market share in food and non-food grocery supplies selling to over 11 million customers a week through its 355 stores (1995). In its 1995 accounts, the company states that:

...the Group has complied throughout the period under review with all the provisions of the Code of Best Practice contained in the Cadbury Committee's Report which were applicable during that period.

Drummond Group plc

The Drummond Group is a listed company based in Bradford, West Yorkshire. Comprising four divisions under a 'holding' head office and employing just under 700 people, the Group had a turnover in the year to March 1995 of just under £47 million. The four divisions are each involved in a separate sector of the textiles industry, designing and manufacturing fabrics which are sold on to be made into clothes for major high street shops.

In common with all public limited companies on the London Stock Exchange, Drummond is required to comply with the Cadbury Committee's recommendations and to state in its accounts any parts of its governance with which they are not in full compliance.

In its accounts of 31 March 1995, the company made the following statement under the title 'Statement on corporate governance':

The Company is now in full compliance with the code of best practice published by the committee on the financial aspects of corporate governance, generally known as the Cadbury Committee, apart from the following provisions:

- *That relating to the reporting by directors on internal controls, which applies for accounting periods beginning on or after 1st January 1995. Accordingly, the directors do not yet report on that provision.*
- *That relating to the independence of non-executive directors since one non-executive director is nominated by Chargeurs Textiles [one of the divisions of the Drummond Group]. That director does not participate in or vote on any matter which relates to Chargeurs Textiles.*

The first point refers to a technicality of good accounting practice. The second, referring to the independence of NEDs (that they should not own shares in the company), is 'got round' by not allowing the director in question any input into any matter that may compromise his independence.

Assignment

A friend asks your advice about investing in (buying shares in) a company called ABC plc. In its last corporate report, the following statement was included:

ABC plc has complied with the Cadbury Code except for the following provisions:

- *the company's CEO and chair reside in the same person;*
- *the company has no audit, nominations or remunerations committee;*
- *the directors do not retire by rotation and all directors are on permanent contracts;*
- *directors emoluments are not disclosed.*

Advise your friend about the wisdom of such an investment, considering the implications of each of the areas in which the company has failed to comply with the Cadbury Code.

Further reading

Bain, N. and Band, D. (1996) *Winning Ways through Corporate Governance*. London: Macmillan.

Worthington, I. and Britton, C. (1994) *The Business Environment*, Ch. 7. London: Pitman.

5

Other business organizations

Learning objectives

After studying this chapter, students should be able to describe:

- Why some business organizations do not readily fit into the *'incorporated/non-incorporated'* distinction.
- What is meant by a *not-for-profit* organization.
- The features of *charities*, *QuANGOs* and *public sector organizations* which make them good examples of not-for-profit organizations.
- The idea of a *co-operative* and explain how co-operatives work.
- What is meant by *franchising* and describe the features of such a business relationship.

5.1 Introduction

In Chapters 3 and 4 we saw that most business organizations can be divided into two categories: *incorporated* businesses (i.e. limited companies) and *unincorporated* businesses. We shall see in this Chapter that some organizations do not readily fit into either of these categories.

The profit motive

An underlying assumption of the two types of organization we have considered so far is that they exist primarily to make profits. This is not to say that they do not have other important objectives, but that without the prospects of making profit they could not exist. Profits are used to reinvest in the business to enable it to grow, prosper and to repay the investors. We can easily understand that a motor car manufacturer does not exist primarily to make cars *per se*, important though that is, but to make cars in order to make money and profits.

Other organizations exist which do not have profit as a primary motive. This is not because they do not need money, but because profits are necessary only to enable them to pursue other, more important (to them) objectives. We shall examine three examples of such organization. For obvious reasons, this category of organization is said to be in the not-for-profit sector.

What do for-profit and not-for-profit organizations have in common?

These two categories of enterprise share certain common features:

- they all *require revenues* with which to carry out their operations;

- they all *incur expenditure* in the execution of their operations;
- they all *need people* to perform the many and varied duties involved;
- they all *produce a product or service* of some description in that it has an output which its customers or beneficiaries value;
- they all have *consumers* of the organizational output, i.e. they have customers, clients, or individuals (or plants and animals) for whom they aim to provide the product or service;
- they must all be *managed* to enable organizational objectives to be achieved.

In many ways, the management and administration of for-profit and not-for-profit organizations will be similar. Hence management skills and techniques may be largely transferable between the two sectors. In this chapter, we will examine three types of not-for-profit organization and two 'other' types of business.

The not-for profit organizations we will look at are:

- charities;
- government organizations;
- QuANGOs.

The 'other' forms of business organization are:

- co-operatives;
- business franchises.

5.2 Charities

Charities are characterized by their primary objective of providing a product or service to a specific target group rather than to extract money in exchange for goods and services. Such a product or service is usually, but not always, *charitable* in nature, a term which implies that it is provided from a benevolent motive (the word *charity* is an old English word meaning 'love').

The beneficiaries of charities are many and varied. We are all familiar with those which seek to provide relief from human suffering, such as Oxfam, Christian Aid and World Vision, but many others exist. Medical charities aim to support sufferers of certain illnesses, and include support groups and charities that carry out research into diseases, such as the Multiple Sclerosis Society and the Cancer Research Campaign. Other charities include animal protection societies, environmental groups and religious organizations (e.g. churches).

Charities and tax

The state recognizes the works that charities do and allow them exemption from the taxation that would apply to normal *for-profit* businesses. Tax benefits apply to charities on both donations and in regard to surpluses. Taxpayers who make a commitment to pay regularly to a certain charity may fill in a *covenant* form. The covenant enables the charity to claim back the tax (up to the standard rate) that has already been paid on the money earned by the donor. Secondly, whereas for-profit organizations must pay tax on their profits, this requirement is not made of charities. It is assumed that charity surpluses are not used to benefit the owners, but to be re-used by the charity in the pursuance or its benevolent objectives.

Not-for-profit terminology

Not-for-profit organizations use different terms to describe 'profits' and 'losses'. If a for-profit organization has excess money left over at the end of an accounting period, it is called a profit because it is assumed to profit (bring benefit to) the owners. Similarly, a shortfall of money is termed a loss, because the owners must endure the loss if reserves are not available to cover it.

Not-for-profit organizations, because they have different ownership arrangements, refer to excess money as *surpluses* and shortfalls as *deficits*. Surpluses are carried over to the subsequent accounting period to be used by the organization, and deficits are expected to be made up from subsequent donations or other cash injections.

The UK's biggest charities (1996)

Name of charity	Total income/year (£ thousands)
National Trust	144 408
Royal National Lifeboat Institute	64 666
Cancer Research Campaign	59 142
Oxfam	86 798
Imperial Cancer Research Fund	53 640
Save the Children Fund	91 983
Salvation Army	72 321
British Red Cross Society	84 768
NSPCC	43 111
Help the Aged	38 707
Barnardo's	84 567
Cancer Relief Macmillan Fund	37 642
RSPCA	37 604

(Source: *The Times*, 23 August 1996.)

Charities and people

Like their for-profit counterparts, charities can vary in size from the very small to the reasonably large. Because such organizations exist primarily for a charitable purpose, they are understandably reluctant to spend large sums on staff remuneration. Whilst some staff in charities enjoy salaries and terms comparable to those of employees in the for-profit sector, many of the more important people fall into two unique categories:

- Some charities make extensive use of *volunteers*. A volunteer, by definition, gives his or her time and energies free of charge, and they would only do this if they were in broad agreement with the objectives of the charity. Such volunteers may be those who assist in 'doing the books' for a charity, people who help in the local Oxfam shop or the organist at the local parish church.
- Professionals sometimes supply their labour and expertise to charities at a rate of pay below the market rate they would enjoy in the for-profit sector. These may be individuals who use the later part of their careers to invest their efforts in charitable work, or skilled people who believe so firmly in the charity's objectives that they are willing to forego monetary reward.

Both of these employee types enable charities to operate on a much lower cost base than for-profit enterprises. Lower operating costs mean that the majority of income can be used to provide the charity for which the organization exists.

5.3 Government organizations

Government organizations in the form of central departments and local authorities comprise the administrative part of the state (see Chapter 21 for a detailed discussion of these organizations). As such, they are funded mainly through taxation revenues which are channelled to the organizations by Her Majesty's Treasury. Because they are funded by the taxpayer, it is assumed that they exist primarily for the collective taxpayers' benefit. The goods and services provided by such departments are those which, it is argued, cannot or would not be reliably or adequately supplied by the private sector.

Local government is located in town halls, civic centres and county halls, and is intended to manage some government functions at the local level. By having this part of government 'closer to the people', it is assumed that local responsibility and accountability will be greater.

What do government departments and local authorities provide?

The goods and services provided by these organizations fall into two broad categories.

Public goods are goods and services that are provided for the population in general. They tend to be things that are needed by everybody, regardless of an individual's specific need. Among them are:

- defence;
- police;
- transport infrastructure (in the most part).

Merit goods are provided by the state to be taken advantage of as and when the population has need of them. Whilst we all benefit from the protection offered by the police and defence services, we only use merit goods in certain circumstances. Common examples are:

- health service (used when we are sick);
- social security and unemployment benefits (when, for example, we are unemployed);
- education (when we are young or wish to extend our learning).

Question 5.1

There are over twenty central government departments. Find out the names of each of these departments. You could try the governmental publications section of your university or local library.

Governments as not-for-profit organizations

Neither central nor local government is designed to make a profit in the same way that a private sector company is. The emphasis is therefore not on profits, but rather on achieving value for money and on reducing costs. Each part of government (each department or local authority) is apportioned a budget which is more-or-less fixed for any given financial year. Hence, government ministers and local councillors must provide all the necessary services required of them within the strict cash limit set (although some services will be charged for). Increases in efficiency and productivity are generally encouraged by senior politicians, and the effect of such efficiency drives is often felt by individual public sector employees, such as nurses and teachers.

5.4 QuANGOs

What are QuANGOs?

The word QuANGO stands for *Quasi-Autonomous Non-Governmental Organization*. As the name suggests, they have a unique role.

Quasi-autonomous means that the organizations act largely autonomously (under their own supervision). The term *quasi* refers to the fact that, whilst on a day-to-day basis they are autonomous, their objectives and operational briefs are set by the government or individuals acting on its behalf. They are entrusted with carrying out certain tasks on behalf of the government, but are given a high degree of autonomy in how they actually carry out their duties.

Non-governmental refers to the feature of these organizations that they are not part of the government itself. They do, however, implement many parts of government policy and spend a lot of government money.

What do QuANGOs do?

The government sets up a QuANGO when it needs to carry out part of the government's policy but does not feel that it should be carried out directly by a government department. It is assumed that appointees to the QuANGO will bring an objective, independent and informed viewpoint to an area. This, it is thought, is preferential to having the area overseen by a government minister who may be seen as carrying out policy for political advantage.

The range and remit of QuANGOs are many and varied. The best-known examples include the BBC and the regulatory bodies that control the prices of utilities such as gas, electricity and water. Others include the Business and Technical Education Council (BTEC) and many regional development bodies, which are charged with spending government money in a politically impartial way to encourage industrial investment in the regions. If you are studying in England, the university at which you are studying will be funded in large part by a QuANGO called the HEFCE (Higher Education Funding Council for England) which is charged with spending the higher education budget (a figure of several billion pounds) independently of government for the benefit of the university sector. QuANGOs are staffed by specialists in the respective fields, thus bringing expertise and an independent view to their administration and spending.

Criticisms of QuANGOs

Some criticism has been levelled against QuANGOs on the grounds that they spend billions of pounds of taxpayers' money and that they are electorally unaccountable. This means that, whereas government ministers remain accountable to Parliament with regard to their actions and policies, those that work in QuANGOs do not. The increased use of QuANGOs in the implementation of government policy over recent years has given rise to the somewhat critical term *quangocracy* (rule by QuANGOs). It should be born in mind that such criticisms are prevalent amongst those groups who feel that they have had a 'raw deal' from a QuANGO or who feel that government money should be spent by those who are directly electorally accountable. QuANGOs do, however, have a number of distinct advantages.

- Because QuANGOs are quasi-autonomous, they act largely as they see fit, regardless of which government is in power. If their roles were taken by government ministers, the politicians may be more open to the charge that actions were influenced for party political advantage (e.g. by inordinately increasing the funding to a university in a marginal constituency).
- QuANGOs are generally staffed by individuals who have expertise in the field over which the QuANGO has control. This theoretically means that their performance will be optimal, which may not be the case if the tasks undertaken were carried out by 'generalist' politicians, who may not have expertise in the field (imagine if the BBC was directly controlled by the government).

Question 5.2

Suggest reasons why a large sum of money in the Higher Education budget is allocated by a QuANGO and not directly by the Department for Education and Employment.

Evidence to the fact that QuANGOs do not favour an incumbent government can be found when it is remembered that QuANGOs are often critical of government policy. The former head of one QuANGO, the Chief Inspector of Prisons, Judge Stephen Tumim, was at times highly critical of government policy with regard to his area of responsibility. Such criticism could not have conceivably been made if such a task was not delegated to an independent person, in that you wouldn't expect a government minister to criticise his own government's prisons policy.

5.5 Co-operatives

What is a co-operative?

After the industrial revolution of the late 1700s, the ownership of business became largely concentrated in the hands of a relatively few industrialists and entrepreneurs. The 'ordinary' people of the day had a number of criticisms of the shops from which they bought their goods and services, and it was thought that by collectively owning a shop they could achieve certain objectives:

- members could enjoy a share of the surpluses made by the shop;
- members could control the quality of goods sold in the shop;
- ownership of the shop would be devolved to those who actually used it.

In response to these concerns, the idea of shared ownership of a business by its customers was introduced in the 1840s in Rochdale, England. The traditional co-operative is both a for-profit and a not-for-profit organization at the same time. It is for-profit in that goods and services are sold to its members at a price that includes a 'mark-up' against cost, but not-for-profit in that all profits are allocated according to the wishes of the co-operative's members and not used to benefit already wealthy shareholders.

In addition to *consumer co-operatives* such as shop co-operatives, producers also found it helpful to join together in the same way. Such *producer co-operatives* were intended to provide farmers and other small producers of goods and services by pooling their output into a jointly owned business. This gave each small producer the ability to sell produce with the pricing and distribution power of a larger business. Producer co-operatives were and are used to enable members to compete more effectively with larger competitors. Some farming communities adopt this business format to distribute their products. One such co-op, Milk Marque, is a major UK producer of milk.

How do co-operatives work?

We have seen that co-operatives are founded upon the basis that profits should be shared out, not to distant shareholders, but to the members – the customers or producers, depending on the type of co-operative. The principle of the co-operative is that at the financial year-end, the amount of money that would be paid out in dividends to shareholders if it were a conventional limited company is paid out instead to the co-operative members in proportion to the amount they have spent in the shop or the amount they have produced (and hence the co-operative dividend is proportional to the amount they have contributed to the profits).

Those wishing to form or join a co-operative are asked to buy a share. The value of the share is usually nominal and members rarely buy more than one (this is because multiple shares do not entitle members to an increased share of the surplus or greater voting power). Each member of the co-operative is entitled to use one vote when voting on matters concerning the management of the business. This control structure ensures that no single member becomes so powerful that they influence or control the business, which may act to the detriment of the majority of members. The cash raised from the share issue is used as the initial capital to obtain premises and stock. Surpluses are then paid to the members as dividends in proportion to their total purchase values or production volumes.

In the earliest days of co-operatives, every purchase by members was logged by an ingenious mechanical device involving a ball, troughs and pulleys. Latterly, this mechanism was updated to the use of trading 'stamps' which were issued in proportion to the value of the purchase. Trading stamps could then be exchanged for goods in the co-operative shop or, in some cases, claimed as monetary dividend. Co-operatives of the traditional type are rare today, but the principle has been carried on by some companies whose shares are owned by its employees ('employee-owned' or 'workers co-operative' companies). Some coal mines and bus companies, for example, have been bought from the former owners by their employees and have been subsequently run as employee-owned businesses.

Both consumer and producer co-operatives can be registered as limited companies, but they can also opt for registration as *industrial and provident societies* under the Industrial and Provident Societies Acts of 1965 and 1978.

5.6 Franchises

What is a franchise?

Suppose you have good idea for a business. You may well gain some start-up capital and, after some time and a good deal of effort, the business becomes a success. The most obvious thing for you then to do is to increase the size of your business by expansion, which will typically involve opening new premises from which to operate a second outlet. Because your initial business worked, there is a high probability that the second outlet will be similarly successful. At this point in your business's expansion, you have a choice:

- obtain the necessary capital yourself, open the second outlet and manage it yourself; or
- offer the opening of the second and subsequent outlets as franchises.

To franchise a business means to allow somebody else to operate your business idea as their own business. In exchange for his or her use of your successful idea, the franchisee will pay you some money, while he or she manages the outlet and takes on the full financial risk of the outlet. The franchisee will gain the use of your company name, logo, products, etc., and you, the franchisor, enjoy the financial rewards of the enterprise without doing any of the work or taking any of the risk. The franchisor will usually impose strict conditions upon a franchisee in exchange for the franchise. If the parent business observes a certain way of doing things (a certain code of dress or similar), this will apply to the franchised outlet in order to protect the image of the enterprise as a whole.

As a mechanism of business growth, franchising seems to work best in the area of retailing. This is because 'high street' presence rests greatly upon brand images and immediately identifiable shop facias. In addition, retail consumers have traditionally placed a premium on buying from a trusted and proven shop or chain of shops.

Many of the shops that we frequently use operate as franchises. Some of the larger chains, such as Burger King (owned by British multinational Grand Metropolitan plc), operate thousands of franchises all over the world. Smaller, but just as well-known operations include Body Shop, Tie Rack and Avis Rent-a-Car.

Pros and cons of franchising

For the franchisor
The advantages of this form of business arrangement are that financial returns can be made from the business idea with little drain on the head office management resource. In addition, whilst the business is seen to expand, no financial responsibility is assumed by the head office.

Whilst the franchisor will benefit from a number of payments from the franchisee (typically a signing-on fee, an annual fixed payment and an agreed percentage of sales or profits), these will not amount to the total that would be realized if the new outlet were operated centrally. In exchange for the benefits, the franchisor thus foregoes some financial income and must endure a loss of direct control over the business.

For the franchisee
The franchisee, who is usually a small business person, benefits from a ready-made business proposal. This has a number of advantages, not least being that the risk of failure is significantly lower than if he were to launch his own 'cold' idea. In addition, he will probably find that loan capital is more forthcoming from banks and other lending institutions. The franchisor is usually available to give advice and consultancy as an experienced operator in the field. This may be helpful when deciding where to locate and how to arrange the interior of the outlet.

The disadvantages for the franchisee include the fact that the costs of taking and maintaining the franchise are likely to make a sizeable dent in the profits. The franchisor will usually lay down strict rules of conduct, dress and behaviour which, as well as incurring cost for the franchisee, reduces his or her independence as a business manager. Failure to observe the franchisor's rules may well result in the loss of the franchise.

Assignment

In the year to 1996, the UK's largest charities spent the following percentages of their incomes on administration (i.e. not directly on charitable pursuits).

Name of charity	Spend on administration (%)
National Trust	14
Royal National Lifeboat Institute	14
Cancer Research Campaign	10
Oxfam	8
Imperial Cancer Research Fund	9
Save the Children Fund	12
Salvation Army	3
British Red Cross Society	16
NSPCC	16
Help the Aged	20
Barnardo's	11
Cancer Relief Macmillan Fund	18
RSPCA	26

(Source: *The Times*, 23 August 1996.)

Questions

- Suggest reasons for the wide disparities between, for example, the administrative costs of the Salvation Army and the RSPCA or Help the Aged.
- If you were a director of RSPCA or Help the Aged, how would you respond to a regular financial benefactor (donor) who is concerned how much of his donation does not go on the cause he is giving money to support?
- How do these figures for administrative costs compare with those for other organizations such as for-profit businesses?

6

The location of a business

Learning objectives

After studying this chapter, students should be able to describe:

- What is meant by the various dimensions of business location (micro and macro-decisions).
- The principal factors that determine where a business is located.
- The relative significance of these factors for some types of industry.

6.1 What is business location?

This may seem a very straightforward question. The location of a business refers, in this context, to its physical location, literally referring to the ground upon which the organization mainly operates. We can examine this matter on a macro- or a micro-scale, the relevance of which will be different for different types of business.

Macro-decisions are those concerning the location and physical organization of a business in 'big' terms. For some companies, this will mean determining the countries, or even the continents, in which the business will operate. For others, it may refer to which parts of the UK the business should operate in. Such matters are generally considered to be *strategic* as they can have a significant effect on the success or failure of the business.

Micro-decisions, as the name suggests, refer to location decisions taken once the macro-decisions have been made. It might be that a company decides to build a factory in Europe (the macro-decision), but it then needs to be decided which European country and which city in the chosen country is most suitable. For smaller companies, micro-decisions would concern the street on which to locate, or even which part of a given street.

Macro-decisions in business location – Glaxo Wellcome plc

Glaxo Wellcome is the biggest pharmaceuticals (drugs) company in the world. It is a British company which was formed in 1995 by the takeover by Glaxo of one of its major rivals (Wellcome). Prior to this acquisition, Glaxo had undergone a programme of significant geographic expansion. Whilst its activities had previously been centred around Western Europe and North America due to the buying power of health services and individuals in those regions, several moves were made towards other regions of the world. Some parts of the world were showing signs of growth, both in economic and population terms, and it was seen fit to make investments in such countries to take advantage of these favourable conditions. In consequence, Glaxo established centres in parts of South America, Eastern Europe and China. The micro-decisions, important though they would become, were less important at the outset than just 'being there'.

Micro-decisions in business location: the retail outlet (shop)

It has been said that there are three important aspects of retailing: location, location and location. Whilst this is an obvious simplification, it underlines the importance of the location decision. A retail outlet must be located where it is most convenient for its customers to reach it, whilst also catering for the customers' sensibilities and wants. Such is the importance of the micro-decision in retailing that, whilst one part of a street in a city may be ideal for the business, another part of the same street may be useless. This is for two reasons.

Shops cater for a certain type of person (the *demographic profile* of the customer) and must be located at a point of easy access for the target customer group. One need look no further than the main high street stores to see that they are located where the target profile group is in high concentration. Shops like Marks and Spencer would usually seek a location where a high concentration of quality conscious people have easy access to the shop. In contrast, the 'budget' chains like Aldi, Kwik Save and Netto are usually located out of town centres in suburbs predominantly populated by individuals and families who are principally concerned with value for money and price.

The second aspect of retail location is the *volume of traffic* that will regularly pass the shop. Traffic, in this context, does not mean cars and buses, but the number of individuals in the target market segment who will pass the shop frequently or who will find the shop convenient to get to.

6.2 Factors in business location

With the foregoing in mind, we must now turn our attention to the factors that a business takes into account when deciding where to locate. These factors will be equally applicable for both macro- and micro-location decisions, depending upon the individual business.

There are a number of factors that can help to determine business location. The contribution that each factor has will naturally vary from case to case. The most significant factors are shown in Figure 6.1.

Proximity to customers

It is obvious that the success of a business relies heavily on customers having straightforward access to the business's output. This factor is more important when the nature of the supplier–customer relationship is one which involves frequent personal contact and where customers buy little and often from the business. It becomes less significant as a deciding factor when business is conducted largely on a mail-order or telecommunications basis. Hence, this factor is one of the pre-eminent factors when deciding upon the location of a retail business (shop), but less important when locating a catalogue mail-order business.

It is also a major factor in cases where transportation represents a significant cost to a business when, for example, the products are bulky or perishable in nature. It is common to locate near to the largest concentration of customers in this case, or to operate a distribution outlet for the business in close proximity to the customers.

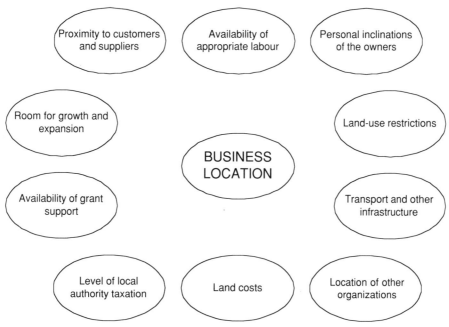

Figure 6.1 Factors that determine business location

The importance of proximity to customers and suppliers – JIT supply

The JIT (Just-In-Time) manufacturing philosophy is one which, among other things, stresses the sourcing of incoming materials being little and often rather than in bulk (we examine JIT in some detail in Chapter 15). The advantage of this for the JIT customer is that low stocks are held and this helps cash-flow significantly. In consequence, materials must be supplied to the customer at very short notice and often in relatively small quantities. For this reason, suppliers, particularly those who supply the majority of their output to one big customer, often set up close to the customer. When the large Nissan development began in Tyne and Wear in the early 1980s, the JIT operation at Nissan demanded frequent supply of car components. Many suppliers located new plants close to the Nissan plant and one supplier even installed an internal rail linkage to the Nissan plant over the short distance to the car production line.

Proximity to suppliers (and other inputs)

Proximity to suppliers is the other side of the same coin to proximity to customers. We would consequently expect this factor to assume greater importance when goods are expensive or inconvenient to transport. We usually, for example, find large installations such as oil refineries on the coast at a point near to the oilfield. This is because the transport cost of oil via pipeline is relatively expensive. Similarly, we typically find fish processors near to the quays at which fish are landed. In this case, the location is decided by the perishability of the product.

Proximity to customers and suppliers – a summary

Proximity to *customers* will be an important factor when:

- customers buy little and often;
- a single customer (or small group of customers) buys a large proportion of a business's output;
- the business operates on a personal contact basis with its customers;
- the business's goods are perishable or expensive to transport;
- the business's major customers operate a low-stock manufacturing policy (e.g. JIT).

Proximity to *suppliers* will be an important factor when:

- the business has a large requirement for material (tangible) inputs;
- the business buys little and often;
- material inputs to the business are bulky or expensive to transport;
- there are few choices of suppliers (i.e. supply is highly concentrated);
- goods inputs to the business are perishable;
- the business employs a low-stock manufacturing policy (e.g. JIT).

The location of other parts of the organization or similar organizations

Some types of organization benefit or suffer from close proximity to partner divisions of the same organization or organizations of similar type ('suffer' in the case of some organizations' proximity to their competitors). We can sometimes observe the various departments or subsidiaries of the same organization concentrating in one region or town or a 'cluster' of businesses in the same industry. In some decisions, the location of a department will be an obvious decision if there is unused land or buildings on the main company site. For other location decisions, there may be more operational reasons for the choice.

We can observe, for example, a concentration of government departments around Whitehall, whilst Teesside has a high concentration of chemical companies. 'Silicon glen' around Livingston, Scotland, is so named due to the high concentration of electronic circuitry manufacturers.

This factor may assume some importance when:

- there is the likelihood of a high degree of personal contact between the different sites;

- there is special 'earmarked' land for a particular type of business or where one part of the organization has spare capacity (e.g. land) on its site that it would be cheaper for another part of the same business to occupy than to build a new plant elsewhere;
- it would be of commercial advantage to be located in close proximity to each other (e.g. so that customers can visit more than one shop in one trip to a retail park);
- when transport costs could be reduced by the location (e.g. distribution points may be located near to the manufacturing plant to avoid transport costs).

Availability of appropriate labour

Labour, as one of an organization's key inputs, is necessarily an important factor in location. The key consideration here is the availability of appropriate labour rather than the availability of labour *per se*.

Some businesses in, for example, heavy industries (e.g. ship-builders, steelworks) require relatively large numbers of skilled and semi-skilled workers. Furthermore, in practice, much of this labour is male. It follows that businesses of this type would be located in regions where the key labour input is plentiful. Of course, one could plausibly argue that the employer attracts the key labour input to its vicinity. Other types of business require staff with key intellectual skills such as science, computing or accountancy. This is one reason for the concentration of banking and finance in the City of London.

In addition to the availability of labour inputs, business location is sometimes influenced by government regulation. Some organizations are guided in their choice of country of location by the degree of regulation of the workforce in the country. In some countries, employers must, by law, make more provisions for employees than in others. Countries with less regulation of the workplace may attract more relocation than those with more. This is one of the reasons why the UK government refused to subscribe to the terms of the Social Chapter of the Treaty on European Union 1992 (Maastricht Agreement), a charter increasing employee rights in the workplace.

Access to transport links and infrastructure

For some organizations, the need for transport links assumes great importance in location decisions. In this context, transport infrastructure includes suitable road networks in the vicinity, rail connection, sea ports and airports.

This factor is especially important for businesses that rely heavily on the transport of goods to and from their plants. For this reason, most manufacturing industry is centred around areas of the country which are well supplied by motorways and rail-freight termini. Local authorities are aware of the importance of this factor for manufacturers when they seek to encourage companies to invest in their locality. The first step in setting up a local business park is often to upgrade the roads linking the park to the nearest motorway or trunk road.

For some industries, this may be the single most important factor. It is obvious, for example, that ship-builders must locate on a major waterway, as ships cannot be transported overland once completed. Similarly, nuclear-power generators are usually located on the coast as the power generation process requires a large amount of circulating water.

Access to energy and utilities

All organizations have some requirement for utilities such as gas, electricity and water. It follows that this is a factor to businesses in the same way as it would be for an individual looking to buy a house. Whilst all main centres of population are well served by the utilities, some outlying areas are not. This is particularly true of gas supplies which are somewhat more expensive to carry to remote areas than electricity.

In addition to utilities, some businesses have a high dependency on a modern telecommunications network (some may include telecommunications as a utility). Countries differ in the modernity of their telecommunications systems. Countries in the First World (Western Europe, North America and the Pacific Rim) all have highly advanced telecommunications, but anybody who has tried getting through to India on the telephone will know that not all countries are equal in this respect. Even within a country, services vary. The increasing use of mobile telephones has shown users that, until recently, not all parts of the UK have been 'covered' equally for mobile phone usage. This may be an important factor for some types of business.

Costs of land

The cost of land varies significantly across the UK according to the differences between the supply (of land) and demand. It has historically been the case, for example, that land is more expensive in the south east of England than in, say, the far north of Scotland. The reasons for the disparity are not difficult to understand. The higher population density in the London area (see Chapter 25) means that there will be a higher demand for land which is subject to finite supply (i.e. there is so much and no more). The highland region of Scotland has much lower land prices resulting from supply being plentiful and demand being relatively (compared to London) low.

Some businesses, particularly those involved in manufacturing, have the need for a lot of land. Whereas many service businesses can operate from a small suite of offices, a manufacturer may require land space for warehousing and production in addition to offices. High land costs are thus bound to affect such businesses more than others. For this reason, manufacturers do not tend to locate in areas of very high land cost unless there is some other very compelling reason for doing so.

Local authority taxation

In order to support local authority services, local government charges residents and businesses in their area with local taxation. The amount charged to each business will depend upon both the level of expenditure of the local authority and the amount of grant money from central government (see Chapter 21). It follows that not all local authorities charge the same level of local council tax.

Areas with lower local authority taxation will obviously be more attractive to businesses than will areas with higher local tax.

Availability of grants

Funding is available from a number of sources to stimulate business activity in certain areas of the country. Assisted areas are selected for their need for industrial investment to offset higher than average unemployment. Grants are offered to encourage new business investment and to encourage existing companies to grow and expand within the same locality. The regions which qualify for grant support are chosen according the levels of unemployment that the areas suffer.

The Department of Trade and Industry (DTI) identifies three categories of assisted area (Figure 6.2):

- development areas (DAs);
- intermediate areas (IAs) which offer different types of assistance to DAs);
- Northern Ireland (seen as a special case due to its singular problems in attracting businesses to locate into the region).

Development areas are mainly those which have suffered from decline in traditional industries such as mining, ship-building, steel and other heavy engineering businesses. Accordingly, DAs are centred around Clydeside, Tyneside, Teesside, South Wales, Merseyside, South Yorkshire and parts of the West Midlands. Intermediate areas, which attract a lower level of grant support, include some outlying areas of the country which have been unable to attract as high a level of investment as more central regions. The DTI offers two types of grant assistance: regional selective assistance and regional enterprise grants.

Regional selective assistance (RSA) is designed to stimulate manufacturing investment in assisted areas. Grants range from 5% to 15% of the fixed capital costs. The average DTI RSA support per new job in DAs over recent years has been £4600 whilst in IAs it has been £2900. For exceptional projects such as those providing a very large number of jobs, grant packages can be specially negotiated to a higher level of support.

RSA is available for three types of investment:

- plant and machinery;
- some associated one-off costs such as patent rights, professional fees, re-installation and removal costs;
- associated land, site preparation and buildings.

To qualify for RSA, a business must provide evidence that:

- without the grant, the project would not otherwise go ahead;
- jobs would be created or safeguarded;
- the resulting business would be viable and self-sustaining (i.e. it would not need ongoing grant support);
- the business will contribute positive benefits to both the regional and national economy;
- other finance will be provided for the business by the private sector (e.g. from shareholders or loans).

Regional enterprise grants (REGs) are specifically designed for small businesses.

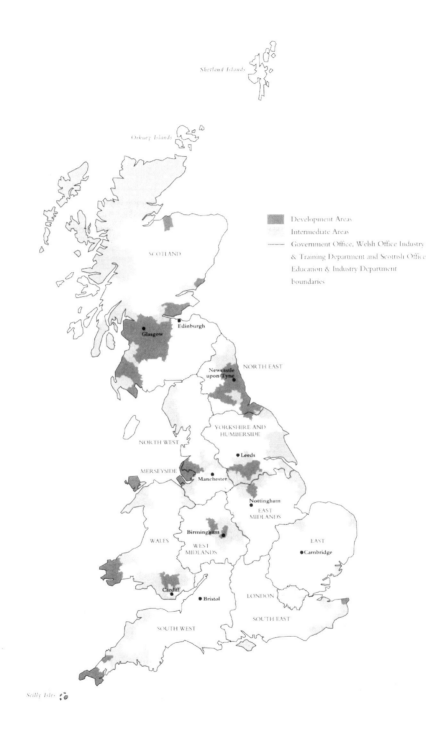

Figure 6.2 Assisted areas from August 1993. (Source: Department of Trade and Industry – HMSO, Crown copyright)

They may be given in the form of investment grants or innovation grants.

- *Investment grants* are available to businesses with no more than 25 employees for investment projects being undertaken in DAs and only in areas affected by colliery closure. They are available for businesses in both the manufacturing and service sectors at a rate of 15% of eligible fixed costs up to a maximum of £15 000.
- *Innovation grants* are available to businesses with no more than 50 employees for innovative R&D (research and development) projects which lead to the introduction of new products or processes. Such projects must take place in DAs or IAs. Innovation grants are available of up to 50% of the agreed project costs up to a maximum of £25 000.

Investment in assisted areas is available from sources other than the DTI. Regional QuANGOs such as development agencies are often instrumental in attracting new business to the areas in which they operate. In addition to non-repayable grants, loans at preferential rates are available from European institutions such as the European Investment Bank and the European Coal and Steel Community.

Restrictions on land use

Restrictions on land use can be imposed by both central and local government. An example of land-use restriction includes the imposition of a 'greenbelt' around a major conurbation. In this case, special planning permission is required for any development in the greenbelt – a measure designed to ensure that cities do not simply continue to expand into surrounding countryside.

Local authorities may also impose restrictions. Some left-leaning local authorities have made their areas 'nuclear-free zones', which include a ban on, among other things, businesses based on the use of nuclear technologies. In some cases, the quality of the land itself (i.e. the soil) may be important, as might the quality of drainage, the risks of subsidence, etc.

Personal inclinations of the owners

The personal preferences of business owners regarding location comprise a particularly important factor when the business is run by an owner-manager. Businesses run in this way are usually relatively small. In most cases, it is common for small businesses to be set up in the region in which the owners and their families are already established. It may be traumatic, for example, to uproot a family, away from friends, schools, etc., for reasons of locating a business in a region which may be in closer proximity to suppliers, customers, or whatever.

There may be business as well as personal reasons for 'staying' in a locality with which the owner is familiar. Owners of small businesses tend to build up business contacts over the years which may be used to advantage when carrying out business activities.

Room for expansion

As part of their strategic planning, some businesses locate in a specific place because the site in question has land around it which offers the opportunity for future expansion. Such businesses tend to be ambitious and may be relocating as part of a market development strategy (see Chapter 8 for a discussion of market development).

This is one reason why manufacturing businesses tend to be located on the peripheries of towns and cities. By constructing a plant adjacent to 'spare' land, the opportunity remains for new building work to take place if needed without having to demolish other buildings first. Local authorities vary in their willingness to grant permission for business expansion into adjacent land and this is another important factor in some business location decisions (although central government can overrule a local authority).

6.3 Examples

Perhaps the best way to understand how the various factors vary in importance from business to business is to consider some examples.

Siemens Electronics – new microchip plant

The Guardian of 25 July 1995 carried an article entitled 'Microchips deal may net 2000 jobs'. Following an announcement from the German Siemens group that it intended to consider a number of locations for its new plant, Prime Minister Major and Deputy Prime Minister Heseltine met with the Siemens President, Dr Heinrich von Pierer. This 'highest level' approach was evidence of the importance that the Prime Minister attached to ensuring that the new investment came to Britain. It was reported that 'He [Dr von Pierer] had been left in no doubt … that the Prime Minister and his deputy attached the utmost importance to Britain's securing what would be one of the biggest European investments in the country'.

Siemens was faced with a difficult decision. In addition to the UK, there were also good reasons to build the plant in several other countries, including, it was thought, Ireland, Austria and Germany itself. At a press conference in Vienna on 24 July 1995, Dr von Pierer outlined the criteria he would be using to decide on the new location. It was reported that 'these include the availability of skilled workers and engineers, the right infrastructure, suitability of the plant's main markets and availability of state or regional aid'.

On 4 August 1995, Siemens called a press conference in London and, together with Mr Heseltine, it was announced that a site had been chosen in Wallsend, Tyne and Wear. The Hadrian Industrial Estate is just two miles from the Swan Hunter shipyard in Wallsend which had suffered severe contractions in its demand for labour. The residents of the North Tyneside area, suffering one of the highest unemployment levels in the country, welcomed the decision and the 2000 jobs that would be created.

A report by Christine Buckley in *The Times* newspaper reported on 5 August 1995 that the financial incentives offered to Siemens to set up on Tyneside may have been as much as £200 million. This represented just under 20% of Siemens estimated £1.1 billion investment in the plant. Ms Buckley reported that:

Jürgen Gehrels, chief executive of Siemens UK ... was reluctant to say what had swung the decision ... He said: 'The commitment of Michael Heseltine [Deputy Prime Minister] *and the Prime Minister has played an important role.' Herr Gehrels said that much had happened over the past month to influence Siemens: the flexibility of the UK workforce, after the UK opted out of the Social Chapter* [of the Maastricht Treaty], *which Germany signed, proved attractive.*

Derwent Valley Foods Limited – snack foods factory

Derwent Valley Foods Limited (DVF) is the manufacturer of the Phileas Fogg range of 'adult' snack food products. It also makes a range of 'own brand' products for a number of supermarket chains. The company was founded in 1982 in Consett – a former 'steel town' not far from Durham city in the north east of England. When the steelworks was closed down in 1979, unemployment became a problem in the region and grants became available from a number of sources for new business developments in the area.

DVF was the idea of four entrepreneurial individuals who became the company's founding directors, each of whom had significant prior experience in the crisps and snack foods industry. The initial growth of DVF was impressive, with sales growth outpacing the industry average in the snack foods sector. In the late 1980s, increased demand for its products led DVF to expand into a new-build factory near to its existing plant.

One of the founding directors, John Pike, outlined the reasons for the choice of Consett for the establishment of DVF as follows:

You asked why we chose Consett. There were a number of reasons. Given that we were unprepared (nor in truth would any great advantage have been gained) to move house, we reviewed a number of locations within the North East which carried maximum grant support. Consett offered a suitable rent-free factory as well as space to expand. The support from D.I.D.A. (Derwentside Industrial Development Agency) – then run at British Steel Corporation's cost, was a significant factor. There was a council and a town happy to welcome us who could provide the labour we required.

(Source: Derwent Valley Foods Limited, with kind permission)

Cray Valley Limited – relocating a laboratory and resin plant

Cray Valley Ltd is one of Europe's biggest manufacturers of synthetic resins – products used in the manufacture of paints and structural plastics (e.g. in glass-fibre products). In 1991, Cray valley was bought by the French petrochemicals company Total. Prior to this acquisition, Cray Valley operated from three sites in the UK (in addition to its sites on mainland Europe), but Total put plans in train to reduce this number to two. It was thought that by concentrating activities on two sites, Total's objectives for Cray Valley could be furthered.

The three sites were previously as follows:

- a polyester resin plant located at Stallingborough near Grimsby, South Humberside;
- a surface coatings resin plant at Machen, South Wales;
- an administration, research and development centre at Farnborough, Kent.

Total's study of its new acquisition indicated that the best course of action was to close down the Farnborough site. In 1991, the decision was taken to relocate the administrative, research and development functions to the Machen (pronounced 'Macken') site. Realizing the importance of its key staff at Farnborough, Cray Valley offered transfers to Machen and a significant proportion of the affected staff accepted. Those who chose not to move to Wales were offered redundancy payments.

The Machen site needed to be expanded to accommodate the new parts of the business. Space was available for this because, unlike at Farnborough, the plant was located in a semi-rural setting.

The reasons for the relocation to Machen included the following:

- South Wales, as an assisted area, offered the possibility of grant support to help with the new capital investment;
- wage costs have traditionally been lower in semi-rural Wales than in Kent;
- the Machen plant offered plentiful room for current and future expansion;
- there were some advantages to be gained by having technical personnel (e.g. chemists) near to the manufacturing facility (for sorting out problems in the factory, etc.);
- communications between the different parts of the company are made quicker and cheaper if they are located on the same site.

The move to Machen was finally completed in 1992 and the Machen site was expanded to meet the demands of the new personnel, the Farnborough site was subsequently sold. (Source: Cray Valley Limited)

Assignment

Choose a business from the following list.

- A firm of management consultants.
- A chemicals manufacturer.
- A nuclear power station.
- The head office of a major multinational company.
- A grocery hypermarket.

Assume the business is considering relocating or establishing a part of the business to the town or city in which your college or university is located. Prepare a report for the senior managers of the business, discussing the advantages and disadvantages of the area for a business of the type in question. This will involve you examining the factors that would be most important to a business of the type you have chosen and then finding out the 'state of play' of these factors in your area.

Once you have researched the issues and written the report, make a final recommendation to the senior management (i.e. should it or shouldn't it relocate into the area). You should be able to complete the report in under 2000 words.

Further reading

Salvaneschi, L. (1996). In: B. Howell (ed.), *Location, Location, Location: How to Select the Best Site for Your Business*, 2nd edn. Grants Pass, OR: Oasis Press.

7

Power, leadership, culture and control

Learning objectives

After studying this chapter, students should be able to describe:

- The things that influence activity inside an organization.
- The nature of power, authority and responsibility.
- The nature and types of leadership in organizations.
- The principle of control and the nature of control in organizations.
- The nature and meaning of corporate culture.
- How culture is determined and its importance in organizations.
- The essentials of Handy's types of culture.

7.1 The influences on activity inside an organization

Why do people in an organization act and think in the way that they do? Activity in organizations varies enormously. In some organizations, people rush around under continual stress, whilst in others, the pace of life is much more relaxed. Compare, for example, the nature of work in your local fast-food hamburger retailer (e.g. McDonald's or Burger King) with the academic staff of a university. In the fast-food outlet, staff are trained in a few essential skills, they tend to engage in mainly repetitive tasks and they work within strictly defined limits. In the university, staff have a broader range of skills, their job involves a great diversity of experiences and their work is interpreted, with equal legitimacy, in a wide range of different ways.

Such a contrast in peoples' experience of work depends in large part on four features of the organization:

- the nature of power and authority;
- the nature of leadership employed;
- the types of control;
- the forms of corporate culture prevalent within it.

These features of an organization are inextricably linked to each other in that they partly determine each other.

7.2 Power and authority in organizations

Power and authority

In attempting to define the term 'power', it may be helpful to look at what it is not. Power is not the same as authority.

- *Power* is a person's *ability* to influence others, to allocate resources or to control situations.
- *Authority* is a person's *legitimate right* to influence others, to allocate resources or to control situations.

We can see that there may well be a difference between a person having the ability to influence and their having a right to do so. Ability to influence can occur in any moral or organizational context, whereas a legitimate right tends to be within the context of a moral or legal framework. Authority, therefore, is invested in a person by a superior body, be that the state, an organization or God. We accept the authority of a judge in a court of law because he or she has the authority of the state – a judge has the right, on behalf of the state to cast judgement upon you. Conversely, you would probably accept the power of a maniacal criminal wielding a gun in a dark back alley, not because of his legitimate right to control you (he has no such right), but because of his there-and-then ability (i.e. power derived from the possession of a gun).

Of course, in one respect, our agreement to obey a person may result from either power or authority (or both) and it is here that the demarcation lines between the two can become blurred. We might readily appreciate, for example, that a policemen has authority and a terrorist exercises power, but what is the source of the influence of a trade-union leader over an employer or a religious-cult leader over some gullible followers? It is here that we must introduce the concept of responsibility.

Authority and responsibility

We have seen that authority is a person's right, from a legitimate source, to influence others. In practice, authority can be distinguished from power as the former is matched with an equal degree of responsibility. If authority is a person's legitimate right to influence or command others, responsibility is the person's degree of accountability or answerability for that over which they have authority.

It is possible for authority and responsibility to be either matched or mismatched.

- Responsibility matches authority when the person is accountable for precisely the area over which he or she has authority.
- Responsibility and authority are mis-matched when one of two situations exist:
  - a person has a greater responsibility than he or she has authority over – this is unfair to the manager who will be held accountable for things outside the area over which he or she has control;
  - a person has a greater authority than he or she has responsibility for – this is unfair to the subordinates and may result in unrestrained power and overbearing authoritarianism.

The principle of matching authority and responsibility has a number of important implications. Personnel professionals use the principle when designing jobs and allocating people to positions of responsibility. It is used as a basis for personnel appraisal, as people are assessed according to their degree of authority and responsibility. If both are matched, then an individual charged with an area of responsibility *and* given the appropriate authority may be either:

- praised for the favourable accomplishments of the charge;
  or
- penalized for the unfavourable performance of the charge.

Either way, when authority and responsibility are balanced or matched, the manager cannot say 'Don't blame me, I didn't have the authority to manage the area of responsibility you allocated to me'. This principle of accountability is carried across to many other areas of life, including politics. A senior politician, such as the Prime Minister, is invested with a great deal of authority, and, accordingly, a great deal of responsibility. In consequence, if the Prime Minister's Government fails to perform well, he or she is voted out of office and replaced.

Types of power

Both power and authority have in common the ability to influence the behaviour of others. In this section, we leave behind our discussion of the legitimacy of such ability and turn to the generic sources of a person's ability to influence another. This ability hinges on the question: 'What makes one person obey another?' Different authors have used different names to describe the types of power and authority. We shall consider two complementary classifications.

J. K. Galbraith
Professor John Kenneth Galbraith[1], the noted American economist and political thinker, has suggested that power can arise from three sources and has proposed names to describe each one.

- *Condign power* is influence exerted over another by offering an unpleasant alternative to obedience. This might take the form of 'Perform this task or else ...', or 'If you do not do this, you will be punished'. Of course, the alternative to obedience need not necessarily be punishment; it might be withdrawal of privileges, social ostracism, dismissal or banishment. The qualification for exercising power is access to the means of punishment.
- *Compensatory power*, as its name suggests, is the opposite of condign power. This type of power works by offering a reward for obedience. If condign power is the stick, then this is the carrot. It might take the form of 'If you perform this task, I will give you ...'. In order to wield compensatory power, one must have access to the means of reward, such as money, privileges or social status.
- *Conditioned power* is influence exerted upon people who have been previously conditioned to obey. This type of obedience (e.g. to conform to norms of societal behaviour) occurs because people have, by their previous experiences and taught values, come to accept certain authorities without question. A leader who employs

this means of power must appeal to people's sense of conditioning and need not use condign or compensatory methods of control.

Examples of power – Why does the author 'go to work'?

The author of this book is a senior lecturer at the University of Northumbria. During term time, he goes into the university to deliver lectures, receive students and conduct seminars. He has a 'boss' to whom he reports and, on an annual basis, negotiates his workload. What types of power are operating to make the author turn up to work and accept the authority of his academic superiors?

Firstly, the author is subject to condign power. If he repeatedly failed to turn up for lectures or acted in another unacceptable way, it is likely he would be disciplined and eventually dismissed. In this event, he would lose his salary and all the benefits that come with it, such as his house, car and standard of living.

Secondly, the author is subject to compensatory power, in that conforming to expectations at work entails monetary compensation (i.e. salary). One might also argue that further compensation is gained by the status enjoyed by the author as a result of his position and other benefits such as working with nice people, etc.

Conditioned power also has a significant bearing in that, like most others, the author was brought up and was educated with the implicit understanding that he was being prepared to enter the world of work. Furthermore, when the author is due in for a lecture, he 'automatically' prepares and leaves for work. There is no 'Should I or shouldn't I go in to work?' – it is a matter of conditioning.

Such a complex set of compelling factors is not at all uncommon in organizational life – very few managers or leaders lean on just one type of power.

A. Etzioni

A similar and complementary view of types of power is given by Etzioni[2] in a model which, it may be argued, is simpler in its approach than Galbraith's. It is a model which does not recognize influence arising from a person's preconditioning.

- *Coercive power* is power that relies upon the use of threats, of unpleasant sanctions or force. In this respect, it is similar to what Galbraith calls condign power.
- *Remunerative power* involves gaining influence through the manipulation of rewards and other material resources. This is approximately equivalent to Galbraith's compensatory power.
- *Normative power* is compensatory in nature, but relies upon intangible rewards rather than material benefits. Examples of such rewards include the conferment of esteem, status and prestige. Galbraith would include this as a type of compensatory power.

7.3 Leadership in organizations

What is leadership?

At its simplest, leadership is the quality evident in a leader. A leader can be defined as *an individual who knows where he or she is going and is able to persuade others to go along as well*. There are consequently two dimensions to leadership; the *conceptual* and the *interpersonal*. It follows of course, from this definition that a person with just clear objectives but no abilities to take others is not a leader. The same can be said for someone with powers of persuasion but no objectives for the followers.

The *conceptual* qualities in a leader are those which enable him or her to identify and resolve clear objectives and a route to accomplish the objectives. Of course the objective in mind may be in any sphere of life – in politics, in business, in matters of religion or in one of many other areas. Furthermore, the objective may vary from a great long-term cause to a trifling short-term ploy. Winston Churchill identified clear objectives during the Second World War whilst the biggest boy in a gang of thugs may generate clear objectives regarding aggression towards rival football fans.

The *interpersonal* aspect of leadership is that quality that persuades others to adopt the same objectives as the leader and to follow him or her towards them. We have already identified the types of power that can be used to facilitate this compliance. Some leaders bring about compliance by promising reward once the objective has been accomplished, others promise punishment for failure to follow and yet others rely on followers' preconditioning to follow. The effects are more or less the same – people following a leader.

Leadership styles

We find leaders in several contexts in and around organizations. We would obviously expect the senior management to lead the staff in the strategic directions identified for the organization, but leaders are found at lower levels as well. Managers who oversee the work of a shift in the factory or the research in a laboratory are leaders, as are shop stewards and other trade union officials. However, the way in which each of these leaders actually leads will differ – and for good reasons. Clearly, the style of leadership depends in large part on the personality of the leader but, in addition, leadership style will be influenced by the nature of the followers and the context of the leader–follower relationship. As in most things in business, we cannot say that any particular style is right or wrong (or good or bad), it is more a case of appropriate or inappropriate in its specific context.

Leadership styles are often shown in the simplified form of a complex continuum (Figure 7.1). The two extremes of the continuum are as follows:

- Fully autocratic leadership is the style in which the leader makes a decision with no consultation at all with those affected by the decision and announces it as a *fait accompli* to the followers.
- Fully participative or democratic leadership is the style demonstrated by a leader fully involving the followers in the making of a decision. The team is encouraged to 'chip-in' to the debate and the leader acts entirely upon the consensus of the group.

Between the two extremes are any number of variations. Leaders tend to the autocratic end of the continuum when there is a high *power distance* between leader and follower when, typically, the followers' opinions are likely to be unfavourable to the decision (such as the leadership of prison wardens over prisoners). More democratic and participative leadership occurs in situations with a lower power distance when, typically, the followers' views are seen as being intrinsically valuable or when their willing agreement is essential once the decision is taken.

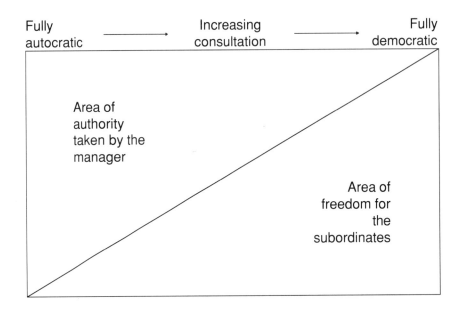

Figure 7.1 *Management and leadership styles*

Definition – power distance

This is a term attributed to Hickson and Pugh[3], both British writers on organizations. They use the term to describe 'how removed subordinates feel from superiors in a social meaning of the word "distance". In a high power distance culture, inequality is accepted … in a low power distance culture, inequalities and overt status symbols are minimized and subordinates expect to be consulted and to share decisions with approachable managers'.

Types of leader

Leaders, as we have seen, are in evidence in many areas of life. A working distinction between the various types rests upon the context of the leadership and the nature of the leader. There are five general types.

The *charismatic* leader's influence arises principally from the leader's personal charisma or personality. This is typically an unusual combination of attractive personal qualities or traits. Such charisma may include outstanding oratorical or literary skills, high intellect, a powerful 'presence', a pleasing appearance and many others. Leaders that fit into this category may include Winston Churchill, Napoleon, Margaret Thatcher and religious leaders like the Rev. Sun Myung Moon (leader of the 'Moonies' sect).

The *traditional* leader assumes a leadership position due to birth. This category thus includes monarchs, tribal chiefs and, in some cases, managers in long-standing family businesses.

The *situational* leader assumes leadership when a certain situation arises, that is, a unique set of circumstances that thrust him or her to the fore. It follows that situational leaders may only lead for a relatively short period of time, whilst the specific circumstances persist. Situational leaders tend to take command when, for some reason, a vacuum is left in the usual leadership structure, perhaps in times of crisis. Examples might include an otherwise ordinary person who takes command in the chaos following a road accident or a fire.

The *appointed* leader gains his or her influence as the result of an appointment. Appointed leaders are found in bureaucratic or hierarchical organizations and their power rests upon their appointed position within the organization. Hence, managers and supervisors in organizations are good examples of this leadership type.

The *functional* leader gains influence by intentionally adopting a form of behaviour that has subsequently made him or her a leader. It might be that an individual has observed the traits of other leaders and has reached a position of influence by emulating the same traits. A functional leader is thus in the position of leadership because of what they do rather than what they are (compare this with, for example, the charismatic leader). Functional leaders, or those that aspire to functional leadership, are sometimes found in politics. There may be a general acceptance that political leaders dress in a certain way, speak in a certain way and 'carry themselves' in a certain way. Politicians seeking high office thus act accordingly to gain such office.

Question 7.1

Which of the above leadership types best describes the following:

- Adolf Hitler.
- Neil Kinnock, the former Labour Party leader who changed his image (e.g. by wearing smart double-breasted suits) during his time as Leader of the Opposition.
- Henry VIII.
- Sir Iain Vallance, chairman of BT plc.
- A university lecturer as he or she exercises leadership over a class of students.
- A class representative.

7.4 Control in organizations

The principle of control

The notion of control pervades most parts of life – it is a far wider concept than just control in organizations. In all cases, a *control system* has three essential components (Figure 7.2).

- A stage wherein *performance standards are set*. The units by which the standard is measured will depend entirely upon the context of the control system.

- A mechanism which allows the *actual performance to be compared with the standard* previously set.
- A *feedback mechanism* to allow the actual performance to move closer to the standard and eventually match it precisely.

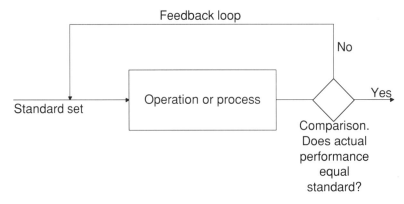

Figure 7.2 A simple control system

A common control mechanism – the thermostat

Imagine the scene. You go into your house and it is cold. The most obvious thing to do is to switch on your central heating system. When you switch it on, the system takes information from the thermostat. This is a device which senses the temperature of the air in the house and is usually mounted on a conspicuous wall. You set the pre-set temperature to a comfortable 20°C (the *performance standard*). The thermostat senses the air and *makes a comparison* with the temperature you have just pre-set (the comparison). The system then goes round the cycle continuously (Figure 7.3).

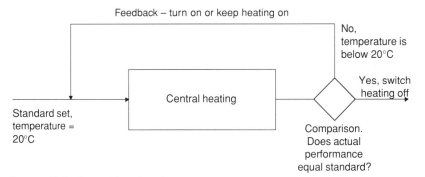

Figure 7.3 Control in a heating system

- If the actual temperature is below the standard, the thermostat engages the heating system, which sends hot water to the radiators to increase the room temperature.
- If (or when) the actual temperature equals the pre-set standard, the heating system is turned off until the temperature falls below standard (when it will switch it on again).

The nature of management control

In Chapter 1 we examined the major theories of management in organizations. All of these should be viewed essentially as attempts to gain the most effective system of control over the various activities of the organization. In the case of Taylor, for example, the outputs of a man's day's work can, Taylor propounds, be controlled according to the conditions under which the work takes place and the reward structures put in place. This is an attempt to impose management objectives upon workers. The work of Mayo and his human relations theories were centred around the use of the work environment and groups to control operational outputs and to increase human efficiency. The work of Henry Gantt was centred around the control of sequential activities to ensure that organizational objectives could be satisfactorily met on time and within resource constraints.

The nature of control measures in an organization will depend greatly upon the organization's environmental situation and its culture (see later in this chapter). Some will adopt a 'tight' regime where activities are controlled by frequent checks and low deviation tolerances, whereas others will favour a 'loose' control regime. 'Loose' or 'flexible' control allows more freedom of action within set limits where work is allowed to assume a certain fluidity. It is, of course, possible for both of these regimes to be present in the same organization as different work conditions dictate.

Question 7.2

Suggest work situations where it would be most appropriate to adopt a tight control regime and some where a loose approach would be most beneficial.

The mechanisms of management control

In attempting to identify the ways in which organizational control is actually exerted, Stewart[4] proposes that there are three different ways. Again, we can readily see that each mechanism is highly context dependent – the method adopted will depend upon the work being undertaken and the type of people involved.

- The first control mechanism is direct control by the use of *direct orders, direct supervision, strict rules and regulations*. This method is more acceptable where the employees are poorly skilled, during training and during times of crisis. It would not be acceptable to situations wherein the employees are expected to take a part in decision-making or where a 'loose' or 'flexible' culture is most appropriate.
- Secondly, according to Stewart, control can be exercised through the use of *standardization and specialization*. Particularly relevant to a bureaucratic culture, this type of control rests upon the prerequisite that the work undertaken is of a standard nature and that employees act within predetermined standard guidelines. It can be used to effect in organizations using repetitive procedures (such as workers on a production line) or where managers have so much authority and no more. An example of this may be the limited autonomy given to a franchisee – ability to act provided

he or she doesn't change the appearance of the shop, the nature of the product, etc.

- The third control mechanism is control through *influencing the way that individuals think about what they should do*. Such an 'intrinsic' method of control is probably the hardest to achieve but, equally, it is probably the most effective. Unkindly labelled 'thought control', this method is widely used in organizations as individuals gradually acclimatize to behavioural and cultural norms wherein it is instinctively understood that certain forms of behaviour would be unacceptable. According to Mullins[5], it can be cultivated in organizations by such things as (for example):
  - selective recruitment (only recruiting those who will think and act in the desired fashion);
  - specific training and socialization;
  - through the use of peer pressure (peers' and colleagues' combined pressure to conform).

7.5 Corporate culture

What is corporate culture?

Culture, along with the nature of control, is a key determinant of activity in business. Furthermore, the culture of an organization is very closely linked to the control mechanisms set in place by the board of directors – they influence each other.

The culture of an organization is easy to experience but harder to define. Consider the following definition:

> *The culture of any group of people is that set of beliefs, customs, practices and ways of thinking that they have come to share with each other through being and working together. It is a set of assumptions people simply accept without question as they interact with each other. At the visible level the culture of a group of people takes the form of ritual behaviour, symbols, myths, stories, sounds and artefacts.* Ralph Stacey (1996)[6]

It follows that culture concerns the organization's norms, and forms of acceptable thought and behaviour. A number of adverbs have been used to describe culture, where each one tells only part of the story. It is the shared beliefs, the 'smell', the 'feel', the 'morale', the personality and the character of the organization.

Culture varies greatly between organizations. Some organizations are 'warm' and 'genial', whereas others are competitive, 'hard' and unfriendly. It is important that we do not become judgmental over certain types of culture – each type may be appropriate in its own organizational and environmental context.

What are the determinants of corporate culture?

The parallel between the personality of an organization and the personality of a person is one which is of some value. The personality of an adult human is the product of a plethora of influences, including his or her genetic make-up and the influences of his or her parents, teachers and peers. The desire to emulate role models and the ethical or religious framework with which the person has been imbued also has a powerful effect.

Similarly, over time, the net effect of the various influences on an organization forges its culture. Any list is bound to be incomplete, but the following are some of the most important influences.

- The *philosophy of the organization's founders* can be influential, even although the organization may be relatively old. The lasting influence of Joseph Rowntree upon the confectionery manufacturer or a religious leader upon a sect is testimony to this.
- The *nature of the activities in the business*. The culture of a university will differ tangibly from that of a coal mine or the shop floor of a heavy engineering company.
- The *nature of the interpersonal relationships* and the degree of camaraderie in the organization. In some organizations, the staff find a natural rapport, whereas in others this is not the case. This is, of course, largely a function of the nature of the personalities in the organization.
- The *management style adopted* and the types of control mechanism. We saw earlier in this Chapter that some organizations adopt a 'tight' control regime and others a looser arrangement. Similarly, management style varies from a dictatorial and autocratic approach to one which is more consensual and democratic.
- Any *influences from the external environment* which can affect the employees' perceptions of their job security or personal economic and social outlook. In times of recession, for example, the 'feel' in an organization will be different from that in more buoyant economic conditions.

British Telecommunications plc – an attempt to influence culture

BT is one of a growing number of companies who attempt proactively to influence their internal culture rather than allow it to develop of its own accord. The company's five 'values' are posted throughout BT premises in the prominent view of all employees. People can nominate their colleagues for small non-monetary prizes for notable achievement of the 'values' in the course of their work. The five values are:

- we put our customers first;
- we are professional;
- we respect each other;
- we work as one team;
- we are committed to continuous improvement.

(With the permission of British Telecommunications plc)

Why is culture important?

The diversity of peoples' experience at work suggests that culture does have some significant influences on a number of facets of organizational life. Some people love their work and find that 'work is more fun than fun'. Others dread the thought of work and find every day stressful and almost intolerable. A good deal of such differences are down to culture. Culture is important because:

- It can affect the degree of employee *motivation*.
- It can affect the *staff turnover* (the rate at which individuals join and leave the organization).
- It can affect the *morale and goodwill* of employees, which may determine the willingness of employees to 'go the extra mile' from time to time as required.
- The fact that culture affects motivation and morale means that it can also have an effect on *productivity and efficiency*.
- It can affect the *quality* of work produced.
- It can have an effect on *industrial relations* (the relationship between workers' unions and management).
- It can affect *absenteeism and punctuality*.

The 'artefacts' of culture

Artefacts are things that 'give away' certain features of an organization. In archaeology, artefacts such as pots, toys and tools give us information about what it was like living in a former age. A human person similarly has certain manifestations which inform observers about their personality, e.g. the clothes they wear, their manner of speech and the way in which they interact with others. In the same way, cultural artefacts give an indication to outsiders or newcomers of the nature of the climate inside an organization.

The first artefact, and one which is amongst the most telling, are the *symbols* that the organization uses. Whilst symbols may refer to company logos and the physical appearance of the offices, it may also be the layout of the plant. If, for example, the reception is small and grubby with the receptionist sitting behind an ancient hatch, this gives a very different signal to observers than a reception which is nicely decorated, well lit and altogether more welcoming. Similarly, if the research and development (R&D) department is located in a series of badly maintained Portakabins apart from the main plant, this gives an indication of how the organization views research.

Secondly, *slogans and sayings* can tell us about the culture. These may be ones which the organization's management seek to spread (such as BT's values, e.g. 'we are professional'), or it may be slogans which have grown from the ranks. In some cases, slogans can assist management, whereas in other cases they can be cynical or even subversive.

The third artefact is the form or *forms of language* that are prevalent within the organization. Just as you can tell a great deal about a person by listening to them talk, so the ways in which members of the organization speak to each other and speak to outsiders tells us something about the organizational culture. Compare, for example, the formality of a military situation, where individuals are addressed according to their rank, to an open-plan office of 'equals', where a great deal more informality will be in evidence. The latter situation may contain people known by affectionate nicknames and it will usually be the case that everybody is on 'first-name' terms with everybody else.

Fourthly, we can analyse an organization's culture by its *rituals and routines*. Some companies observe ritualized procedures such as sending all managers of a certain level to a conference, to an outward bound weekend or similar. It may be that people below the level in question will aspire to the particular management level and associate their presence at the ritualized occasion with 'having arrived'. Rituals also concern honouring the past and honouring longevity of service. The presentation of a gold watch after 25 years service to the organization is one example. Staff may refer to there being so many years until they receive their gold watch – not for the value of the watch, but for what the watch says about their service to the company. Routines, as their name suggests, are more mundane and frequent than the organization's more elaborate rituals. Nevertheless, the routines observed within an organization can tell us a great deal about its culture.

Fifthly, an important artefact of culture is *how the culture treats newcomers* to the organization. This parallels, on the human person level, to the impression you get of a person when you first meet. Some people are visibly warm and generous, whereas others appear to be more austere and 'businesslike.' A new employee, in seeking to 'find his feet' in a new job, may find the new colleagues to be open, generous and helpful. Conversely, the new employee may find them resentful at his presence and decidedly unwilling to help him or her to adjust, particularly if the new employee was appointed in preference to internal candidates.

The final major artefact of culture are the various *stories* which circulate as part of the culture of the organization. Stories speak of 'heroes and villains' as they have affected the company over the years, of past battles and famous victories, and of the recent political manoeuvres within the company. The culture of the organization will determine which stories are propagated and which are remembered long after the events in question.

Types of culture

We have already seen that each organization has its own unique culture, but is it possible to sort types of culture into separate categories? Charles Handy,[7] a noted writer in the field of culture, has proposed that corporate cultures can be divided into four broad categories.

A *power culture* is one that is centred around a single powerful individual. The individual in question will engender his or her own personality to the organization and, by the dictation of systems and control mechanisms, will forge the organization's culture. Whilst power cultures are common among small companies which may have a dominant owner-manager, there are also some notable examples among large organizations. Examples of this latter category include Amstrad (Alan Sugar) and Virgin (Richard Branson). A power culture (which has a lot of influence vested in the one powerful person) is usually characterized by quick decision-making, but this same feature can render the organization unstable if the person in question is unable to continue in service. The investment of a lot of power in one individual can also have the negative effect of poor delegation and inadequate management development.

A *role culture* is characterized by a regime in which functional specialists carry out functions according to predetermined roles. Role cultures work best in organizations which operate in relatively stable environments. Examples can be found in larger bureaucracies such as the civil service. The organization comprises many people performing specific roles which are broadly inflexible. Management's purpose in a role culture is concerned with ensuring the roles are carried out efficiently and within defined parameters which is in contrast to the often continually changing management briefs in a power culture.

A *task culture* is based upon a number of people with similar skills being drawn together. The focus of the organization or grouping is upon a specific task or tasks, and the nature of the task can change over time. Companies with a strong emphasis on R&D and professional accountancy practices often have evidence of a task culture. In R&D, many similarly skilled minds may come together to 'crack a certain nut' or overcome a specific problem. Task cultures occur across multidisciplinary teams in matrix organizations where a team is charged with a project, or in a refugee camp where medics, engineers and others work together in a missionary capacity.

A *person culture* is one which exists for the benefit of its members, and this has a strong bearing on the 'feel' of the organization. It is in strong evidence in professional and learned societies, in co-operatives and in communes of various sorts.

Assignment

Upon the retirement of his predecessor, Jim Bean took over as the Governor of HM Prison Parkbench, a high security establishment of prisoners considered to be 'criminally insane' and of high risk to the public. Jim's background was as a senior academic at a well-known university, and consequently he was accustomed to the culture and management styles used in higher education establishments. On his first day in the governor's chair, Jim announced that he intended to manage the prisoners in the same way that he used to manage his lecturers. This meant that he would give them autonomy, freedom, trust and discretion in how they spent their time and with whom they associated.

Within a month, the prisoners had taken advantage of their new freedom by dismantling their cells and by digging up the recreation field. Prison warders found the period difficult owing to their increased sense of vulnerability with the new management regime. Jim Bean was fired by the Director of the Prison Service owing to his 'highly inappropriate management style'.

Questions

- Contrast some of the features of the cultures of a prison and a university.
- Compare the leadership styles that are best suited to managing in the two types of institution.
- Describe the types of power that a prison governor might be able to exert over the prisoners.
- Explain where Jim went wrong in his management of the prison.

References

1. Galbraith, J. K. (1985) *The Anatomy of Power*. London: Corgi Books.
2. Etzioni, A. (1975) *A Comparative Analysis of Complex Organisations*, 2nd edn. New York: Free Press.

3. Hickson D. J. and Pugh D. S. (1995) *Management Worldwide*, p. 21. London: Penguin.
4. Stewart, R. (1991) *Managing Today and Tomorrow.* London: Macmillan.
5. Mullins, L. J. (1993) *Management and Organisational Behaviour*, 3rd edn, p. 550. London: Pitman.
6. Stacey, R. (1996) *Strategic Management and Organisational Dynamics*, 2nd edn. London: Pitman.
7 Handy, C. B. (1989). *The Age of Unreason.* Boston, MA: Harvard Business School Press.

Further reading

Anthony, P. (1994) *Managing Culture*. Milton Keynes: Open University Press.

Brown, A. (1995) *Organisational Culture*. London: Pitman.

Deal, T. E. and Kennedy, A. A. (1982) *Corporate Cultures*. New York: Addison Wesley.

Lukes, S. (1974). *Power: A Radical View*. London: Macmillan.

Moss Kanter, R. (1984) *The Change Masters*. London: Unwin.

Taffinder, P. (1995) *The New Leaders. Styles and Strategies for Success*. London: Kogan Page.

8

Growth in organizations

Learning objectives

After studying this chapter, students should be able to describe:

- Ansoff's generic product/market expansion grid and its contents.
- What is meant by internal growth and why it is adopted as a growth strategy.
- The meaning of external growth and why it is adopted as a growth strategy.
- The types of external growth.

8.1 Trends in business growth

A potted history

Prior to the industrial revolution in the late eighteenth century, businesses were locally based and usually very small. Often located around agricultural communities, such businesses were typically engaged in crafts and simple service industries. The dawn of automation and increased urban demographic concentration brought about a completely new climate in the external business environment. For the first time, businesses were able to make much greater quantities of their products, and increased demand provided the economic incentive for businesses to gear up for higher production levels. In consequence, the first large businesses appeared, employing hundreds or thousands of people rather than just a few. The nineteenth century witnessed the birth of a large number of businesses that eventually grew into large companies, many of which are still operating today.

The extent of business growth was limited by problems with communications and transport between the businesses and their suppliers and customers. Developments in the twentieth century, however, reduced these limitations. The invention and refinements in both the internal combustion engine and in air-flight made the transportation of goods and people significantly easier. Running parallel with these developments was the development of modern telecommunications systems. The result was the removal of many of the factors that limited business growth. Consequently, the twentieth century witnessed the emergence of many very large businesses, the economic interests of which encompassed the world. Today, the business world comprises all sizes of organization and businesses in all stages of growth and development.

Big is beautiful

It is usually assumed in business that growth is good and that bigger is better than smaller. This view is held for a number of reasons:

- Bigger companies, by increasing their sales, have the opportunity to earn more profits (although not necessarily a higher percentage of profit against sales).
- Bigger companies enjoy a higher market share than smaller companies. Higher market shares allow the larger business to have more of an influence over the market price of a product – an opportunity to increase profit.
- Bigger companies are usually more robust than smaller ones. This means that size renders a business more able to cope with economic trauma such as a sudden decline in sales or a sudden change in government policy.
- Bigger companies have the opportunity to benefit from increased economies of scale – the reduction of unit costs resulting from increases in size and buying power.

This chapter is concerned with the ways in which businesses seek to gain the advantages of larger size.

8.2 Ansoff's growth and expansion matrix

The American academic H Igor Ansoff[1], in seeking to distil the complex patterns of business growth into simplified directions, arrived at his product–market expansion matrix. He found that, although businesses take many and varied routes to growth, all of these can be simplified to one of four simple generic growth strategies. It is usually shown in the form of a simple two-by-two matrix (Figure 8.1).

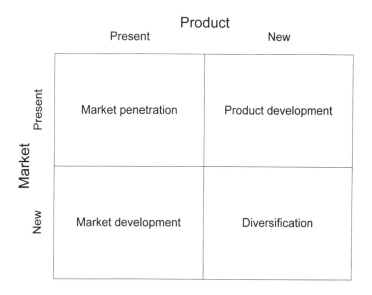

Figure 8.1 The Ansoff product–market expansion matrix

According to the Ansoff matrix, businesses have essentially only four generic mechanisms of growth (Table 8.1, but the ways in which organizations actually follow the four directions will vary.

Table 8.1 A summary of Ansoff's product–matrix expansion grid

Growth mechanism	Characteristics
Market penetration	same markets, same products
Market development	new markets, same products
Product development	same markets, new products
Diversification	new markets, new products

Market penetration

Business expansion which involves the organization growing by the use of existing products in existing markets is known as market penetration. It is said that the organization further penetrates the market which it already serves. It thus involves the organization increasing its market share, i.e. attracting more customers in the market to use the existing products.

Market penetration is an appropriate strategy when:

- the existing market has growth potential and is currently profitable;
- other competitors are leaving the market, thus reducing the competition in supplying the market;
- the company has a great deal of experience in the market which it can take advantage of in understanding what the market wants;
- the company is unable to pursue a strategy involving entering new markets, due to such things as insufficient resources or inadequate knowledge.

There are several ways in which a business can attract more market share. The essence of market penetration is to make the business's products more attractive than its competitors' products.

- The business can *reduce the price* of its products. Depending on the price elasticity of demand (see Chapter 17), lower price may attract a higher volume of sales. Price reductions can usually only be maintained over a protracted period of time if the organization can also reduce its operating costs accordingly.
- *Quality can be improved.* By making products better match the requirements of the customer, the buyers will tend to have more confidence in the products.
- The products can be *differentiated.* By giving the products a unique or distinctive quality, customers may switch brands to the differentiated product.
- Product *distribution can be widened.* By selling the products through more outlets, more customers will be able to access the business's output.
- *Production can be increased* by means of operational investment. Increased output may increase market share if customers are prepared to purchase the extra volume.
- *Advertising* and other marketing promotions, by making more customers aware of the products, can increase market share.
- A business can increase its market share by *acquisition.* The purchase of a competitor making similar products instantly increases a business's market share.

Market development

Market development is growth by means of placing a business's existing products into new market sectors. It is said that businesses who pursue this option develop new markets for their products. It involves 'transplanting' products into market sectors which are 'new' for the products. By doing this, the business sells more of the product by spreading its output across different market segments.

In this context, new markets can be completely new geographical markets (e.g. a different region or country), or a different segment of the same geographical market (see Chapter 12 for a discussion of market segments). The key to market development is that, although markets are increased, products remain essentially unchanged. It follows that the key to successful market development is the transferability of the product. Some products transfer well to other markets, whilst others are specific for one segment only.

It is said that the product is *repositioned* as a player in a new market. An example of market development on a grand scale is the repositioning of the McDonald's fast-food chain from its domestic 'home' in North America to appear as a symbol of western culture in Eastern Europe and Russia.

Product development

Growth by product development occurs when an organization increases sales in its existing markets by launching new products aimed at the same market segment. In this context, the term 'new products' can mean several things:

- it can mean completely new products such as when a manufacturer of crisps launches a product based on toasted bread;
- it can mean the development of additional models of existing products, such as when car manufacturers launch modified versions of cars;
- it can mean the creation of different quality versions of the same product, thus offering a choice of ways of reaching the market with the product.

The product development approach is common among businesses that feel they understand their customers and can thus supply more of their wants and needs. The principal reasons for pursuing this approach to growth include:

- the company already holds a high share of the market and feels that it could strengthen its position by the launch of new products;
- there is growth potential in the market, thus providing the opportunity of a good economic return on the costs of a new product launch;
- changing customer preferences demand new products if they are not to desert the company for a competitor's products;
- as a means of 'keeping up' with competitors who have already launched new products.

There are several ways that product development can be accomplished. Many companies develop new products through their research and development functions (which in some organizations are called 'design' departments). In some cases, organizations increase their product offering by buying a company which currently offers different products to the same customers.

Diversification

Under some business circumstances, organizations elect to make a complete change. Growth by diversification involves approaching new markets with new products. It follows that in most cases, this strategy represents a higher risk of failure than any other of the three we have considered previously, due to the potential lack of knowledge among management about the new situation. Again, this growth strategy can be achieved by the internal development of new products or by the acquisition of a business already in the new market.

Diversification is appropriate when:

- current products and markets no longer provide a financial return that satisfies the shareholders or principals of the organization;
- the organization has 'spare resources' after it has pursued its requisite expansion exploiting existing products and markets;
- the organization wishes to broaden its portfolio of business interests across more than one product/market segment;
- the organization wishes to make greater use of any existing distribution systems in place, thus diluting fixed costs and increasing returns;
- the organization wishes to take advantage of any 'downstream opportunities' such as the use of by-products from its core business activities.

Ansoff's general strategies can be achieved in two different ways. We now need to turn to these two mechanisms: internal growth and external growth.

8.3 Internal growth

Internal growth occurs when a business grows by reinvesting its profits back into the same business entity. By buying new plant and equipment, and by taking on more people to operate them, the business increases its capacity (the volume of output it can produce). With an increased capacity, the business can meet higher demand and accept a higher market share, thus increasing its financial income. The business usually continues to invest its profits over many years, thus consolidating its position. This method of growth is sometimes referred to as *organic* growth due to its effects on the numbers of people that the business employs.

Internal growth has been the prominent method of growth since modern business began during the industrial revolution. Many of the 'big names' in business today began as relatively humble small businesses, but which wisely invested profits over the years to arrive at their current size.

To rely wholly on internal growth as a means of business expansion has both advantages and disadvantages. The advantages include the possibilities of the building of long-term working relationships which lead to a strong team culture and a sense of security and even pride in the organization. Disadvantages include the potential limitations on skills and expertise that may come to light if the organization continually rejects growth by external means.

8.4 External growth

The second mechanism by which organizations can grow is by external growth. Whereas internal growth occurs by investing profits in the same business, external growth involves using the business's money to invest in other businesses. This is achieved by one of two mechanisms: mergers and acquisitions.

Mergers and acquisitions – what are they?

From time to time, a major merger or acquisition is reported on the national news. You may remember the publicity surrounding the acquisition of Rover Group by BMW in 1994, or the 1995 acquisition of Wellcome plc by its bigger pharmaceuticals competitor, Glaxo. Whilst such 'big money' acquisitions may be less frequent, less grand (mergers and acquisitions) (M&A) activity is a very common occurrence in most sectors of business.

Mergers
A merger occurs when two separate companies agree, usually by mutual consent, to come together, not unlike in a marriage of two people. Such an arrangement can obviously only come about by the consent of the two companies' respective shareholders. In most cases, the shareholding in one of the companies is simply commuted to shares in the new business entity, albeit possibly at a slightly different share price.

The issues raised by business mergers are similar to those experienced when two people 'merge'. They frequently involve:

- the surrendering of independence previously enjoyed by the two individual businesses;
- the possibility of a clash of cultures as the two businesses realize they have different ways of doing things and of thinking about things (culture is discussed in Chapter 7);
- the shedding of labour as the two participants seek to save money by avoiding previous duplication (i.e. the merged company will only require one accounts department, one board of directors, etc.);
- taking on a new identity as a result of the merger, which sometimes involves upsetting people who have an understandable affection for their former business identity.

The potential benefits of a successful merger are, however, quite compelling. The synergies that can result from two parties working together rather than against each other, can be marked. In addition, the larger size of the organization means that greater economies of scale can be enjoyed with the resulting reduction in unit costs.

Mergers are usually entered into with a great deal of negotiation and careful thought because, once merged, it soon becomes difficult to demerge. Notwithstanding the undoubted intensity of discussion and negotiation prior to most mergers, the research seems to indicate that the majority are unsuccessful. The management consulting firm McKinsey & Co. made a study in 1986 of mergers involving 200 large businesses. The findings showed that only 23% of the mergers were successful as measured by an improvement in business performance and an increased value to shareholders.

Recent years have, if anything, seen increased merger activity in some business sectors. In banking, for example, 'big is beautiful' as more branches, cash machines and lending power facilitates a better service to customers. The intensification of competition for mortgages and lending to customers together with a need to reduce costs has been the main motivation behind the merger activity in the banking sector.

Acquisitions

If a merger is a marriage, an acquisition is a takeover. By purchasing a shareholding (of voting shares) of over 50%, a company can control another and impose its will upon it. There are two broad types of acquisition.

- A *friendly takeover* occurs when the board of the acquired company recommends that the shareholders sell their shares to the acquirer. A company's directors, as agents of the shareholders, are legally required to act in the shareholder's best economic interests. By examining the proposals put forward by the acquirer, the board have come to the conclusion that the acquisition would benefit the shareholders.
- A *hostile takeover* is when the directors of the acquired company do not wish to become part of the acquirer. They believe that the acquisition is not in the best interests of the company or the shareholders and they thus resist the offer and advise shareholders to reject the price offered. However, the directors' legal obligation to act in the best interests of the shareholders sometimes means that if the acquirer offers a price for the shares in excess of the market's expectations for the share price, the directors recommend that shareholders accept the price. This obligation remains the case, even though they may personally oppose the takeover.

The arguments in favour of acquisition are similar to those for mergers. The increase in size gives the acquirer synergies and increased economies of scale. In addition, acquisitions can be selectively made to pursue any of Ansoff's generic growth strategies.

The track record of acquisitions is not particularly impressive as many end in divestment after a failure on the part of the acquirer to successfully manage the strategy of the acquired business. Professor Michael Porter of Harvard Business School conducted a study of merger behaviour among 33 large US based businesses between 1950 and 1980. He found that 53% of related acquisitions and 74% of unrelated acquisitions were subsequently divested (the terms *related* and *unrelated* are defined later).

Types of mergers and acquisitions

Both mergers and acquisitions ('integrations', meaning 'becoming one') can be divided into subcategories depending upon the relationship of the two companies involved. These distinctions aid our understanding and are shown in Figure 8.2.

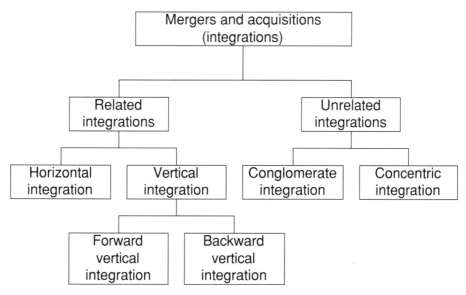

Figure 8.2 Types of merger and integration

Related integration

Mergers and acquisitions are said to be related when the two companies involved in the integration are in the same industry. It is important, however, to define what we mean by 'industry' in this context. In its broadest sense, an industry comprises all parts of the supply chain for a good or service. In the brewing industry, for example, the 'industry' includes the brewers, their suppliers (of malt, hops, etc.), their customers (bars, off licences, etc.) and their competitors. This is shown schematically in Figure 8.3.

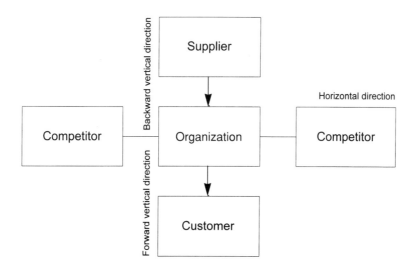

Figure 8.3 Horizontal and vertical integrations

The form of figure 8.3 shows us that related integration can occur in one of two directions:

- *Horizontal integration* is growth by acquisition of, or merger with a competitor.
- *Vertical integration* is acquisition of, or merger with, a business backwards or forwards of the organization in the supply chain. There are thus two vertical directions:
  - backward vertical integration, i.e. integration with a supplier,
  - forward vertical integration, i.e. integration with a customer.

Horizontal integration

This approach, as we have established, involves two competitors joining forces which have previously supplied the same goods and/or services to the same market. The result of horizontal integration (by merger or acquisition) is thus to increase the concentration of supply. The acquirer immediately gains the market share of the acquired business and thus avoids the arduous task of winning it in open competition which would be the task facing the business if it adopted an internal growth strategy. Ansoff would identify this strategy as an example of market penetration.

Horizontal integration offers a relatively low-risk expansion strategy to an organization. This is mainly due to the transferability of management expertise. The main advantages of pursuing this approach rest upon the increased market presence:

- Economies of scale can be gained as the larger (combined) business can exercise greater buying power over its suppliers. The fact that the business now buys higher quantities of common inputs means that it will be able to negotiate lower units prices. This will obviously contribute to a lower unit cost for the organization, enabling higher profits to be made.
- The greater market share may enable the organization to have a greater control over prices in the market. The closer supply comes to a monopoly, the greater the control of prices results. If, by enhancing market presence, a business can increase or maintain prices, an opportunity clearly exists to increase profit.

Vertical integration

The logic behind vertical integration lies in 'locking in' the forward or backward links in the supply chain.

Backward vertical integration enables an organization to gain control over one of its suppliers. This offers the following advantages:

- guaranteeing supply which may be important for some inputs that are subject to shortages;
- prices to competitors (if competitors are existing customers) can be maintained whilst the integrated organization gains goods at a preferable transfer price.

Forward vertical integration enables an organization to gain control over one of its customers. This mechanism of growth offers the following advantages:

- It guarantees an outlet for the company's output, which means the production and sales can be forecast with greater certainty.
- In controlling the customer, the organization can ensure that the customer gives pri-

ority to intergroup sales. This means that the customer's buying power can be used to favour its group partner at the expense of competitors.

Both strategies, in addition to the advantages above, obviously also serve to increase group sales and hence total profits. They also have the beneficial effect of broadening an organization's portfolio as new products and markets are brought under the organization's umbrella.

Unrelated integration

Mergers and acquisitions are said to be unrelated when the two companies involved in the process are in different industries. According to Professor Ansoff, this type of business growth can be described as diversification (i.e. new products and new markets).

It follows from our discussion of related integration that the two parties do not compete with each other in any part of their business and that they do not supply or buy from each other. However, this does not mean that the two companies have nothing in common. There are two types of unrelated integration, depending upon how much the two parties have in common.

Concentric diversification

Some diversifications occur between organizations which are not in the same industry but nevertheless do have something in common in that some skills are transferable between the two companies. Such integrations are said to be concentric.

Companies who pursue concentric diversification see the advantage that they can expand their product and market portfolios without completely 'jumping ship'. This can mean that the integration is less of a risk than a complete move into new products and new markets. Examples of this growth strategy include mergers or acquisitions between businesses which share common technologies, common marketing approaches or manufacturing plants which can be merged together. It might be, for example, that a television manufacturer acquires a manufacturer of hi-fi equipment. Although the two businesses serve different markets, their common core competencies of the design and manufacture of electronic equipment and marketing consumer goods to the retail markets should mean that the acquisition has a higher probability of success.

Conglomerate diversification

In contrast to concentric diversification, conglomerate diversification is characterized by merger or acquisition into a business sector which has no obvious links with existing products or markets. It follows that no organizational competencies or operational expertise are directly transferable between the two businesses. This necessarily introduces a more pronounced element of risk into the integration, but, conversely, it represents the most effective mechanism of widening the total product and market portfolio.

Many of the world's largest and most important holding companies are highly conglomerately diversified (hence they are sometimes called *conglomerates*). Whilst some large companies like ICI are essentially concentrically diversified companies (i.e. entirely in the chemicals sector), others like the UK based Hanson plc and BAT Industries are conglomerates.

An Anglo-American conglomerate – Hanson plc

Prior to a restructuring in the financial year 1996–97, Hanson was a UK based company which successfully pursued a strategy of external conglomerate growth since the 1960s. Its world-wide sales in the year to 1994 were £11.2 billion, making it one of Britain's biggest industrial companies. Hanson's strategy was one of investing in businesses which are spread both by geographical region and by market/product segment. This gave the company a wide portfolio of business interests, spread as they were across ten broad product/market sectors (each of which contained several disparate companies) and across different countries of the world (including the USA, the UK and South Africa).

Hanson's diversity could be seen by examining its portfolio by business sector. Its total workforce of 74 000 people comprised of 16 000 in the UK, 52 000 in the USA and 6000 in the rest of the world. The business sectors of Hanson were as follows (financial year to 1995):

- coal mining;
- chemicals;
- materials handling;
- tobacco;
- propane;
- other consumer products;
- aggregates (e.g. building materials);
- forest products;
- other building products;
- other industrial products.

Assignment

You have just joined the board of directors of a company involved in the manufacture and distribution of beer. It is a smaller regional brewer which does not own any outlets such as pubs and is a one-site business.

At your first board meeting, the financial director puts forward some proposals on the expansion of the business. 'As a result of our recent successful rights issue,' he began, 'We have sufficient funds to pursue a number of possible options.' He went on to explain that he has analysed the possibilities of both an acquisition and a joint venture. 'There are a number of possible acquisition targets', he continued. 'I have had contact with a number of companies. One makes beer in another part of the country to our present location, one makes scrumpy, another is a farming complex in Kent which produces hops and barley malt whilst yet another is a chain of off-licences. The one "outsider" chance we have is to buy up a paint company in Hull. On the joint venture front, there is scope for a joint licensing agreement with a German lager producer. This would involve us brewing and marketing their lagers over here whilst they would do the same for our range of English real ales over there in Germany.' The financial director concluded that the final option was to put the money on deposit at the bank and let it accumulate interest. 'At least we know the money is safe in the bank', he mused, 'even although we might make a lower return on it.'

Questions

- Identify each of the financial director's options according to the growth strategies described in this chapter.
- What factors should the board consider in evaluating each of the options?
- Given that the company is relatively small with a limited management resource, which course of action would seem to be the most appropriate?
- Which options should definitely not be pursued?

Reference

1 Ansoff, H I. (1987) *Corporate Strategy*. London: Penguin.

Further Reading

Cartwright, S. and Cooper, C. L. (1996) *Managing Mergers, Acquisitions and Strategic Alliances*. Oxford: Butterworth-Heinemann.
von Krogh, G., Sinatra, A. and Singh, H. (1993) *The Management of Corporate Acquisitions. International Perspectives*. London: Macmillan.

9

Change in organizations

Learning objectives:

After studying this chapter, students should be able to describe:

- The motivations for change within organizations.
- The types of change that take place in organizations.
- The various attitudes to change that are evident among employees.
- A range of models that explain how to manage change.

9.1 Motivations to change

If one issue gives an organization's management more headaches than any other, it is this one – the management of change. Change is necessary in almost all organizational contexts to a greater or lesser degree. It has been a feature of organizational life for as long as organizations have existed, but recent years have witnessed increasing change in organizations due to more complexities in the external environment. A changing external environment has brought about the need for organizations to change internally in order to match more closely the new external conditions. Hence, the study of internal change has increased both in academic circles and in organizations themselves.

Reactive and proactive change

The first distinction we need to understand in this area is that of the two principal sources of impetus to change.

Reactive change is change forced upon an organization arising from a need to react to a change in the organization's environment. This can apply to an individual as well as an organization – for example, you must change your lifestyle if your student grant is suddenly reduced or discontinued. There are a number of environmental changes that can precipitate reactive change, but they usually have in common an element of necessity, of being unexpected or an element of surprise.

Proactive change, in diametric opposition to reactive change, is planned in advance, usually with a particular objective in mind. Whilst proactive change may be as an indirect consequence of changes in the environment, it is essentially change because the organization wants, or internally feels the need to change. To relate this to the individual, you might proactively improve your presentation skills in order to increase your job prospects, or learn German in order to allow you to work in Germany.

Analysing environmental factors

There are any number of changes in the business environment that can necessitate internal change. The complexity of environmental influences upon an organization will vary significantly from case to case. Some organizations pass from decade to decade with little change in their environments, whilst others must cope with daily or hourly changes which must be addressed.

The stability/complexity grid (Figure 9.1) provides a useful tool for managers to assess the nature of the organization's environment.

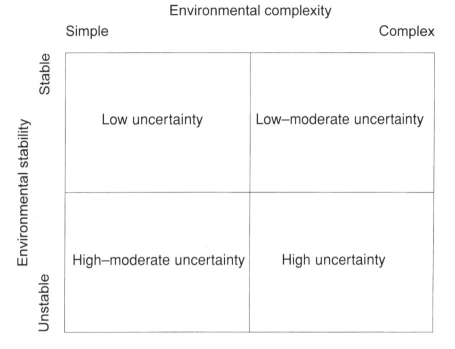

Figure 9.1 *The stability/complexity grid*

Stability, in the context of this grid, refers to *how often* and *by how much* the external environment changes. In a stable environment, there is little external change from year to year, whereas in an unstable situation the environment may change significantly and often. Needless to say, an unstable environment requires more frequent internal change than a stable one.

Complexity refers to the number of potential external influences upon an organization. In a simple environment, the organization will have few material influences upon it. In a complex environment, it will have many possible influences which must be monitored.

Question 9.1

Generate a list of organizations which exist in the four broad types of environment identified in the grid in Figure 9.1. To start you off with some examples, a monastery exists in a simple and stable environment whilst a university's environment is largely complex but relatively stable.

Impetus from the external environment

As with all external environmental analyses, we can identify the sources of environmental influence using an analysis of an organization's micro- and macro- (PEST) environments (PEST refers to an organization's political, economic, sociological and technological environments).

The *industry* will offer impetus to change. The activities of competitors, suppliers and customers will often mean that an organization will have to implement changes. Customers who change their requirements, competitors who merge or acquire within the industry may mean that an organization has to modify its structure, culture or other internal features.

The *political* environment, with its power to legislate and implement government policy, can be highly influential. New laws must be accommodated (e.g. health and safety legislation), whilst such policies as encouraging inward overseas investment can affect domestic companies. Some elements of the political environment will act against a company whilst others will work in its favour.

In the *economic* environment, changes in fiscal and monetary pressures (see Chapter 23) can bring about the need to change. The same can be said for commodity prices (e.g. oil) and currency movements.

A politico-economic impetus for internal change – BT plc

Since the privatization of British Telecommunications plc (formerly British Telecom), the activities and pricing of BT have, by statute, been strongly influenced by the Office of Telecommunications Regulation (OFTEL). OFTEL is a QuANGO, acting independently to ensure that fair competition takes place in the telecommunications industry and that powerful players (particularly BT) do not use their size and near-monopoly status to charge unfair prices to their customers.

After BT was privatized in 1984, OFTEL established a price formula for BT based on the prevailing rate of retail price inflation (the RPI) minus a fixed amount – the 'RPI minus X' formula. The formula was to apply to BT's call charge prices. Between BT's privatization in 1984 and 1989, X was 3%. X was increased to 4.5% between 1989 and 1991 and further increased to 6.25% between 1991 and 1993.

On 1 August 1993, Don Cruikshank, the Director General of Telecommunications Regulation (the Head of OFTEL) announced, after consultation, that the value of X was to be increased to 7.5%. This figure was seen by some as being a difficult target to meet as RPI was then falling and was in the region of 3–4%. This meant that if RPI was 3%, then BT would have to cut its call charges in money terms by 4.5%.

BT's subsequent call charge reductions were all well publicized – usually through national media advertising. They included the abolition of the peak rate morning tariff and a reduction in the price of weekend calls – local call weekend rates were reduced to 1 p a minute. It is important to appreciate that BT did not offer these reductions to remain competitive, but because they were instructed to make such cuts by the regulator.

The effects of such price constraints meant that the company had to make significant cost reductions. This required a significant programme of change. By shedding the last vestiges of its former bureaucratized public sector culture, some layers of management were made redundant. Voluntary redundancies were also offered to staff in an attempt to reduce the company's labour costs as cost-saving technology was introduced to replace many human tasks. Services that were once all handled at a local level (e.g. directory enquiries and computer services) were all centralized. A culture of both cost-cutting and increased quality awareness emerged as remaining staff found themselves working harder to cover for departed colleagues whilst still maintaining a high adherence to quality.

One of BT's mid-managers described the change as:

...a difficult time for all concerned. We often work longer hours and must assume greater responsibilities as a result of lower manning levels. Many things were changed, including an emphasis on PRP [performance related pay] as a mechanism of increasing earnings above indexation. There has been a massive shift towards mechanization coupled with the centralization of many central services such as directory enquiries.

Sociological influences, particularly demographic changes and variations in tastes, fashions and trends will always demand change from organizations. Retailers, for example, will take account of demographic factors to relocate whilst some shops 'make their living' from catering for the latest fashions.

An increasing influence on organizations in recent years has been the changes in *technology*. The continual need to adopt the latest technology in order to remain competitive has meant that an almost continual programme of technological change has become the norm in many organizations.

Impetus from the internal environment

An organization's internal environment, the subject of Part One of this book, can also offer reasons to change. It is frequently the case, however, that a need to change stimulated by an internal weakness or imbalance is precipitated by a change in the external environment. Hence, internal stimuli are usually an indirect consequence of an external environmental influence.

An internal analysis of an organization usually takes the form of a survey of its strengths and weaknesses. In seeking to correct or address its weaknesses, the organization must undergo some change.

The areas which would usually be the subject of review in an internal analysis are as follows:

- *Personnel* – a need to improve skills, to cultivate expertise, to increase or reduce numbers or to modify inappropriate reward systems.
- *Structures* – appropriateness of existing structure, overall 'shape' of structure, degree of decentralization, etc.
- *Systems* – reporting, financial, quality, administrative systems, etc.
- *Culture* – appropriateness of culture for the industry and an organization's customers.

- *Technology* – is the technology adequate for current and projected needs? Can existing employees 'cope' with technological change?
- *Financial* – cash-flow position, profit and loss position, debt and credit position, etc.
- *Marketing* – strength of brands, product quality, effectiveness of promotions etc.
- *Intellectual* – effectiveness of patents, licences, brands, key intellectual personnel, customers' perceptions, etc.

The key consideration in analysing the internal environment is the strength or weakness of each component as it relates to the organization's objectives. The quality of an organization's personnel, for example, may be a critical weakness in one organization, whereas the same quality of personnel in another business may be perfectly adequate.

9.2 Types of change

When we consider organizational change, we must ask the question 'Which aspects of the organization are we seeking to change?' We have seen the complexity of the stimuli to change, but managers of a business must ask themselves *how* and *what* to change to enable the organization to cope with such internal and external influences.

Structural changes

In response to changes in the environment, it is sometimes necessary to modify the structure of the organization. This may simply be a case of changing reporting systems (e.g. moving one department to be under the authority of a different manager), or it may be more sweeping. The degree of structural change depends upon the extent of change in the organization's environment. Over recent years, structural change has typically taken the form of 'flattening' the organization – reducing the number of layers of management (Figure 9.2). Other reasons to bring about structural changes include re-organizations following acquisitions and mergers.

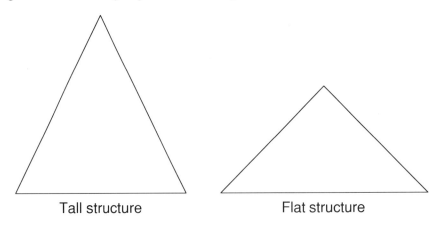

Tall structure   Flat structure

Figure 9.2 Tall and flat structures

The fact that structural change is sometimes accompanied by staff redeployments and redundancies means that it can be source of stress to employees. Employees being asked to move to different parts of the organization, possibly to relocate to another part of the country or to learn new skills, tends to mean that managing the change is problematic, even though changing the structure is, on paper, relatively straightforward.

Technological change

There are few more precipitous changes that have occurred in organizations than the introduction and continual updating of technology. As a force, technology has revolutionized many workplaces as well as dispensing with many thousands of jobs, where technology has taken the place of a human. Furthermore, it seems that technology reaches almost all parts of the organization. In operations, the automation of manufacturing has reduced workforces and increased quality and output. In the office, computer and telecommunications systems have changed and replaced manual systems and made work faster and more reliable. Communications have been improved beyond recognition by improved telecommunications, fax and Email. Designers and research and development (R&D) people make extensive use of many technologies, whether it is to design new garments on a microcomputer or to test new materials on a piece of scientific equipment. The effects of such changes have presented many problems to managers as they seek to manage effectively.

Systems change

Changes in internal systems will often follow naturally from changes in structure and technology. In this context, systems refer to procedures and 'ways of doing things' in the organization.

As the environment changes, changes may be necessitated in many internal systems, for example:

- reporting procedures and lines of authority;
- control systems, for example budgetary control systems;
- financial reporting systems;
- quality systems, for example quality assurance measures or inspection procedures;
- information systems, such as access to information from computers and telecommunications links;
- paperwork systems, for example paper-form design and changes to circulation lists.

The fact that system changes usually mean a change of 'doing' rather than 'thinking' normally means that such changes are brought about relatively painlessly.

Cultural change

A change in the culture of an organization is often necessary if the organization is to cope successfully with changes in the external environment. Changes in the competitive environment sometimes mean that businesses must progress from being and 'old-fashioned bureaucracy' to a modern 'lean and mean' organization. The difference between cultural change and all of the others is that this type of change involves changing people – not just systems, technology, etc. It follows that cultural change is the hardest to bring about.

Whereas other changes can be forced upon an organization in a relatively short time, changing a 'personality' will invariably take much longer. If an organization can change its structure in a few months, it may well take several years for the culture to catch up. For some employees, a cultural readjustment may be painful as, after many years, they have to change the way they think and act within the organization.

9.3 Attitudes to change

Burns and Stalker – the context of attitudes to change

We can intuitively understand that some organizations will change more readily than others. Some appear to accept changes as a matter of course whilst others demonstrate stubbornness and inertia. These variations have been partly explained by two of the theorists we encountered in Chapter 1, Burns and Stalker.

Burns and Stalker contributed to the body of organizational theory which became known as contingency theory. They identified two generic forms of organization depending upon their cultures, structures and systems. Mechanistic organizations are characterized by high levels of formality, hierarchical structures and an insistence upon regimented procedures. In contrast, organic organizational types tend to demonstrate a higher level of informality with a higher likelihood of a network structure and lateral rather than vertical communication links. The authors saw mechanistic and organic type organizations as two extremities of a continuum along which differing degrees of the two could be observable. Furthermore, within larger organizations, both types could be present.

These distinctions have a bearing upon attitudes to change owing to their particular characteristics. Mechanistic type organizations tend to be, by design, 'machine-like' in their *modus operandi*. The increased use of bureaucracy and formality tends to mean, in most cases, that change is relatively difficult to implement. Organic-type organizations tend to encourage a more entrepreneurial and risk-taking approach, and such organizations may well attract individuals who are more inclined to accept change both in the nature of their jobs and in the organization itself.

Organizations have acknowledged this theory by seeking to adopt a more organic culture as part of the change process. Organizations which were previously bureaucratic and mechanistic have attempted to 'free-up' the organization by reducing the formality and delineation in the workplace. In this respect, they are adopting a more organic culture.

Inertial attitudes

In examining an organization's resistance to change, organizational theorists borrow a term from physics – *inertia*. Physicists use the word to describe the force needed to be applied to a body to overcome its resistance to a change in state. It obviously takes a greater force to produce movement in a broken-down car than it does to a football. However, once the initial inertia has been overcome, maintaining its movement is easier. The same is true of organizations. The hard part is beginning the process, but once the process has begun, 'steering' the change, difficult though that may be, is usually relatively easier than overcoming the inertia.

In order to begin the change process, management must overcome the attitudes among people within the organization that would possibly represent a resistance to the onset of change. We can examine such attitudes as follows:

- *lack of understanding* about the nature and objectives of the change;
- *lack of trust* of management's motives and competence;
- *self-interest* and fear of personal loss – a belief that the change process will result in a deterioration of one's personal conditions (e.g. by redundancy);
- *uncertainty* and fear of the unknown – an understandable apprehension where employees fear the unknowability of the outcome of the change (e.g. the change may necessitate moving house, moving from a job in which they feel competent, etc.);
- *social loss* – a fear that the change will result in the break-up of informal groups in the workplace and that they may lose contact with friends or trusted colleagues.

Question 9.2

For each of the inertial attitudes listed above, suggest how management, if possible, may effectively address and overcome each attitude.

Force-field analysis

A noted thinker in the area of change management was Kurt Lewin. In 1951, Lewin proposed the model of a force field where the state of change in an organization can be understood in terms of an equilibrium position. The equilibrium is held in place by one set of forces applying pressure for change and opposing and restraining forces which apply pressure to remain with the status quo (Figure 9.3).

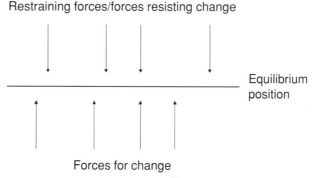

Restraining forces/forces resisting change

Equilibrium position

Forces for change

Figure 9.3 Lewin's force-field model

According to Lewin's force-field model, the pressure for organizational change must be brought about by the pressures for change exceeding the restraining pressures. There are patently two ways in which this can be accomplished:

- by a build-up in the strength of the for-change forces up to the point that they exceed the restraining forces;
- by a reduction in the strength of the restraining forces such that the for-change forces gain supremacy without increasing in strength.

According to Lewin, an attempt to implement change by enabling the for-change forces to 'push harder' will, as the diagram suggests, simply result in the restraining forces digging in to retain the status quo – a conflict resulting in no change. Hence, the proclivity to see the process as a war (where the for-change forces must 'win') should be resisted. A preferable stratagem to overcome inertia is for the for-change proponents to work on reducing the strength of the restraining forces rather than to attempt to overcome them. This is accomplished not by attempting to persuade restraining forces of the arguments for change, but by for-change proponents gaining an appreciation of the reasons behind the restraining forces. By a process of addressing misgivings and respecting fears and uncertainties, change, argues Lewin, can be implemented more successfully.

9.4 Managing change

The matter of how to manage change has been one of the most well-researched and most discussed issues in management circles over recent years. There is consequently much that we could examine in this section. We will discuss some of the most appropriate ideas at this level, but students seeking a more detailed study should access one of the texts listed at the end of this chapter.

There are some principles in relation to change management that are considered as organizational 'best practice', and these are discussed below.

A simple prescription

One of the simplest models for managing change is to assume a hierarchical 'if not, then …' approach. This approach assumes that certain managerial practices are preferable to others. In this respect it is an oversimplification inasmuch as it is self-evident that the most appropriate management approach will be highly context dependent. The process begins with consultation (with those affected by the change) which, ideally, will be sufficient to carry through the proposals. Other stages become necessary if inertia cannot be overcome by previous attempts. The process ends with coercion when all other attempts have failed – the process of forcing through a change by coercing those affected whether they like it or not (Figure 9.4).

Useful models

As in many other aspects of management, the use of well-conceived models can help us to understand otherwise complex things. Although others exist, a review of two models which help to explain the management of change process will be of value.

Figure 9.4 *A simple management of change process*

Kurt Lewin's three-step model

Lewin contended that change involved three distinct stages. Each stage required managing in a different way and each was essential to the overall management of a change process. His model is as follows:

Unfreezing the current level involves abandoning old practices and beliefs before new practices are introduced in order to prevent confusion. It also involves creating a cultural climate of change to the point that individuals expect and will accept the imminent changes.

Moving to the new level involves implementing the change once the old attitudes have been unfrozen. This is the change process itself and involves the management procedures we have previously identified. The third stage, refreezing, involves cementing the new culture and practices into the organization's culture to prevent employees from falling back into old practices. It follows that refreezing may involve some resolve on the part of management. The new point of equilibrium (as described by the force-field model) must be supported by putting support mechanisms in place which enable employees to feel happy with the new position.

The 'champion of change' model

This model suggests that change can be implemented effectively when led by an individual or group who leads and 'champions' the entire change process. To have a champion not only ensures the process is led (as opposed to being allowed to drift), but also provides a focal point to the process in the form of a visible person. The presence of the champion also provides a visible leadership symbol and a constant reminder of the ongoing momentum of the change process. Figure 9.5 shows the varying degrees of involvement over time of the key groups of people in an organization if a champion approach is used.

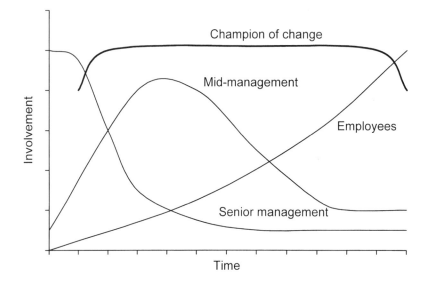

Figure 9.5 The champion of change model

Any change clearly starts with the impetus and unequivocal support of senior management, hence their high initial involvement. Early in the process, the champion is appointed by the senior management who 'pass on the baton' to him or her. The champion cannot implement any changes without the support of the organization's mid-managers, so this group is involved in order to carry the changes through. It then falls to the mid-managers to communicate the message of change to the workforce who are the people who will be the group most affected by the change. As the mid-managers and workforce become increasingly involved in the change, the senior management role declines, and the same is true of mid-managers as the workforce begin to change in their attitudes and actions. Throughout the entire process, the champion is involved in all of the groups to ensure they are properly informed and guided. The champion's role finally declines once the workforce has fully implemented the change.

Assignment

- How would you respond to a manager who says the best way to implement change in an organization is to punish employees who fail to change quickly enough to a new regime.
- Discuss the possible barriers to change in a retail company attempting to implement a new system of electronic stock control and a computerized checkout system in its shops.

Further reading

Bridges, W. (1991) *Managing Transitions. Making the Most of Change*. New York: Addison Wesley.

Carr, C. (1995) *Choice, Chance & Organizational Change: Practical Insights from Evolution for Business Leaders & Thinkers*. Maidenhead: AMACOM.

Grundy, T. (1993) *Implementing Strategic Change. A Practical Guide*. London: Kogan Page.

Handy, C. (1996) *Beyond Certainty: The Changing Worlds of Organisations*. Boston, MA: Harvard Business School Press.

Jarrett, M. and Bowman, C. (1996) *Management in Practice. A Framework for Managing Organisational Change*. Oxford: Butterworth-Heinemann.

Morgan, G. and Sturdy, A. (1996) *The Dynamics of Organisational Change*. London: Macmillan.

Sadler, P. (1996) *Managing Change*. London: Kogan Page/Sunday Times Business Skills Series.

Storey, J. (ed) (1996) *Blackwell Cases in Human Resource & Change Management*. Oxford: Blackwell.

Weiss, J. W. (1996) *Organisational Behavior & Change: Managing Diversity, Cross-Cultural Dynamics & Ethics*. St Paul, MN: West.

10

Structures, divisions and departments

Learning objectives

After studying this chapter, students should be able to describe:

- A range of managerial issues relating to organizational structure – span of control, delegation, unity of command and decentralization.
- The difference between line and staff employees.
- The various types of hierarchical and non-hierarchical organizational structures.

10.1 Specialism and departmentalization

It is a self-evident fact that we all have different skills, aptitudes, levels of intelligence and ability. Some people are academic, perhaps with a scientific 'bent' whilst others are better with their hands but weaker in academic pursuits. The quintessential 'mad professor' may understand the grand concepts of physics, maths or economics but may be completely unable to cook a simple meal or wire a plug. Conversely, people with manual skills may have little ability to understand academic concepts but may be able to produce magnificent food and sort any kind of electrical problem in a house.

Organizations have a need for all types of skills and abilities. The total burden of labour in an organization is divided up so that people with different levels of intelligence and skills can each find their own productive place.

This chapter deals with the ways in which different employees are organized within organizations. Before examining the various types of organizational structures, we will firstly look at the key management issues that must be considered in any discussion of structures. These issues, in part, determine the shape, 'depth' and 'width' of the structure.

10.2 Management issues in organizational structure

Line and staff employees

The first management consideration is to examine how employees are distinguished from each other in terms of how they 'fit in' to a typical organizational structure – the issue of line and staff employees. Different specialist divisions and departments within an organization contain a predominance of either line or staff employees.

Line employees are those that are directly responsible for achieving the organization's objectives. Line employees are therefore found in departments that are responsible for producing, selling or servicing the organization's products (e.g. in operations, marketing and after-sales servicing).

Staff employees are responsible for supporting the line employees in their tasks. Staff are therefore found in departments that advise, support or provide expertise, such as personnel, research and development and finance.

The line and staff distinction can be best understood by the use of an example. A business producing cars is known for its car-making activities. Its primary objective is to produce and market cars in order to make profit. The company needs its staff functions *because of* its line functions. The personnel and finance functions would have no purpose at all unless they were in support of the company's primary (car-making) activities – performed by the line employees. Nissan is not known primarily for the quality of its finance function (important though this is), but for the output of its line employees – its cars.

Span of control

The span of control, sometimes called the span of management, is a simple concept which describes the number of subordinates that directly report to a manager. Some managers oversee large teams of subordinates (a wide span of control) whereas others manage just one or two subordinates – a narrow span. It follows that the span of control will have a large influence upon the structure of an organization.

There is no span of control which is right or wrong. It is not possible to say that a manager must have x subordinates and no more or less – it obviously depends upon the managerial context. It is, however, important that the span is appropriate to the manager's skills and brief, and the nature of the subordinates. If the span is too broad, the manager will have too many subordinates and his or her ability to oversee their activities will be reduced. If the span is too narrow, the organization is paying a manager who is effectively underemployed – a waste of money and human resources.

The optimum span of control in any given context will depend upon a number of factors:

- the skills of the manager in question;
- the ability of the subordinates to work without regular oversight;
- the complexity of the work undertaken;
- the variety of the work undertaken;
- the extent of any automation and the type of technology involved;
- the stability (susceptibility to change) of the organization;
- the health and safety situation of tasks undertaken by the subordinates;
- how much the organization can afford to pay for management.

Hence, a highly skilled manager overseeing a team of competent 'self-policing' subordinates may have a very broad span, whereas (to take the extreme) an inept manager overseeing a team of poorly motivated subordinates in a dangerous environment will require a very short span.

Delegation

A second management issue in structure is the extent to which work is delegated downwards through the organizational structure. Delegation is the mechanism by which managers pass on work to subordinates. This enables the burden of work to be shared and it also relieves a manager of tasks, thus freeing him or her up to carry out jobs more suited to his or her skills.

The implicit rules or guidelines of delegation are not as straightforward as they might at first appear. In Chapter 7, we encountered the notion of matching authority and responsibility. In this context, we can see that, when a manager delegates work to a subordinate (over which, by definition, the manager has authority), then it is the manager and not the subordinate who is ultimately held responsible for the outcome of the delegated act. The manager may in turn, of course, hold the subordinate responsible for that area of authority delegated, but it is in the manager's interest to ensure that sufficient instruction is given to enable the subordinate to carry out the delegated task correctly.

A subordinate to which a task is delegated is formally referred to as a *delegate,* although this term is rarely used in business. The principle of matching authority and responsibility means that the delegate is empowered to act only in accordance to his or her specific brief. If the delegate acts outside of the brief (or set of instructions), the process breaks down, as the subordinate is assuming authority which he or she has not been granted by the manager.

There are a number of pros and cons of delegation, from the point of view of the organization.

Advantages:
- It relieves the manager of some of his or her workload.
- It helps to develop the skills of the subordinate, thus making him or her more useful to the organization.
- It may serve to motivate the subordinate as a greater degree of responsibility is taken on.

Disadvantages:
- A risk is taken that the subordinate may not be 'up to the job' and may consequently make errors.
- Successful completion of a delegated task relies upon the communication of the instructions to the subordinate. It thus relies upon appropriate skills in this area on the part of the manager.
- The manager may be reluctant to delegate owing to the risks associated with it – some managers adopt the attitude that 'if you want a job done, you've got to do it yourself'. This clearly depends upon the personality of the manager.

Centralization and decentralization

Definitions
A key structural consideration is the extent to which the organization is decentralized. Like all aspects of organizational structure, the degree of decentralization will depend upon the nature, purpose and size of the organization.

- *Centralized* organizations are characterized by power and decision making being concentrated in a single powerful 'centre'. The centre may be a single individual or a head office. No major decision-making power is devolved to any other part of the organization.
- *Decentralized* organizations are characterized by, to varying degrees, a devolution of power from the centre to its peripheral parts. The 'parts' of an organization to which power is devolved may be distinct divisions, departments, subsidiary companies (for holding companies), or profit and cost centres.

Like many things in business, the varying degrees of decentralization can be shown as a continuum. At one extreme, fully centralized structures are those which have no evidence of any delegated power to any other part of the organization. At the other extremity, fully decentralized organizations are characterized by power entirely devolved to its peripheral parts. Between the two extremes lie the various possible 'real-life' cases. Many organizations are partly decentralized, and these could be shown as lying at various points along the continuum.

What determines the extent of decentralization?
The fact that organizations exist in many states of decentralization means that no single approach is the best in all cases – the ideal degree of decentralization for an organization has a number of determining factors:

- The mission or objectives of the organization. Businesses which are relatively unambitious in terms of growth may remain centralized. Companies seeking to serve many markets or wishing to grow in other ways will tend to become increasingly decentralized.
- The size of the organization. Larger organizations will tend to be more decentralized than smaller ones as a matter of necessity – control from a centre becomes increasingly difficult as size increases.
- The nature and type of the organization. Sole proprietors will tend to be highly centralized but public limited companies, governments and holding companies will tend to be more decentralized.
- The output that the organization provides and its markets. Clearly, a business which distributes products nationally or internationally will be more decentralized than a corner shop. Similarly, products like petrochemicals will tend to be produced by companies which are more decentralized, and producers of local products (e.g. Grasmere gingerbread or Edinburgh rock) will be more centralized.
- The management style used in the organization. Some managers like to keep their eye on all activities in an organization, whereas others are happy to delegate to decentralized divisions or departments. This, of course, will be highly dependent on other factors such as size.

Advantages of the two approaches

Centralization has a number of advantages.

- It enables managers in the centre to maintain a tight level of control. The risks of problems occurring in the parts of the organization are thus potentially reduced.

- It avoids the potential problems of introducing complex and expensive organizational structures.
- Communications are quicker and cheaper when the entire organization is located close together.
- The risks associated with delegation are avoided.

Decentralization also offers advantages.

- It means the organization can engage in a wider range of activities and can operate in many locations at once.
- It enables increased specialization in the decentralized parts (e.g. those who 'know best' about a certain market, a specific product line or a specific range of activities).
- It can reduce the time taken to make key decisions. If power is devolved, decisions can be made by managers in the decentralized parts without the need to refer to the centre every time a decision needs to be made.
- The devolution of power serves to develop and improve the skills of managers – a feature which may also serve to motivate them.

Examples of decentralized organizations
Most organizations are decentralized to some extent. Some, however, exhibit a high degree of decentralization:

- multinational companies (where the parts are located in different locations of the world);
- holding companies (the parts are subsidiary companies);
- Her Majesty's Government (the parts are Government departments);
- some large private limited companies.

10.3 Organizational structures – hierarchical and non-hierarchical

When we examine the manner in which organizations arrange themselves internally, we are necessarily doing so in fairly general terms. This is because each organization will assume a structure unique to itself in order for it to operate optimally within its environment. The way in which it organizes its line and staff employees, its usual span of control and the extent to which it is decentralized, will all have an important influence on the actual structure.

Whilst it is true that there are as many different organizational structures as there are organizations, our task in studying this area is to look for groupings and general types which are most common, and that will help us to understand the principles involved.

One of the commonest ways of dividing structures is as follows:

- those based on hierarchical relationships;
- those which are not.

The key distinction between the two is the extent to which the organization observes the principle of the *unity of command*.

> **The unity of command**
>
> This is a very simple principle which states simply that any given person in an organization should report upwards to only one superior or, 'one person, one boss.' To some people, this may appear a rather obvious and common-sense approach to management but, as we shall see, it is not universally observed.
>
> Unity of command offers some key advantages. The most obvious of these is that it avoids any confusion on the part of the subordinate as to who to take orders from. Its disadvantages include the possibility that 'taking orders' from one boss may extinguish the subordinate's flair and creativity. The lack of observance of the principle of unity of command is the basis of non-hierarchical organizational structures.

Hierarchical structures

The basis of the different forms of hierarchical structure is the strict observance of the principle of the unity of command. A line of command can consequently be traced from all members up (or down) through the ranks of the organization to or from the chief executive or chairman. Members are usually divided into divisions or departments which are charged with a certain area of responsibility.

The various forms of hierarchical structure are distinguished from each other according to how the parts of the organization are separated. The most common forms are:

- organization by specialism (functional structure);
- organization by geographical concentration (geographic structure);
- organization by customer focus (customer structure);
- organization by product type (product structure).

Each type of structure shares the same generalized 'shape' – see Figure 10.1. The general form is sometimes referred to as an 'M-form' structure, owing to its supposed similarity to the shape of the letter.

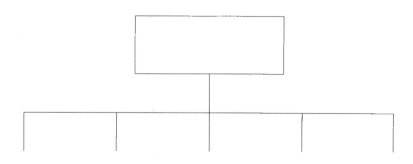

Figure 10.1 *'M-form' structure*

Functional structures
Functional structures are used as a means of concentrating specialists in separate departments, which enables them to work together for the benefit of the whole busi-

ness. Specialists are typically divided into five key functional areas:

* finance and accountancy;
* marketing and sales;
* personnel (or human resources) department;
* technical (e.g. research and development, engineering);
* operations (e.g. manufacturing).

Functional structures tend to be employed by organizations based on a single site, such as a small to medium sized companies or single-site subsidiaries of larger organizations. It is a structure well suited to businesses engaged in manufacturing.

Geographic structures

Geographic structure is appropriate when an organization needs primarily to provide a local coverage of all its functions to a specific region of the country or the world. Large multinationals frequently structure themselves in this way to facilitate a faster and more regionally appropriate response to customer needs. It may be, for example, that a large multinational has a division which concentrates on North America, another on Europe, another on east Asia, and so on.

Smaller companies may use the idea of geographic structure on a less grand scale. It may be the case, for example, that a UK based company operates regional offices as a basis for sales activity and product distribution. On this scale, the company may have an office to cover Scotland, another for the South East, another for the Midlands, and so on.

Geographic structure offers the advantage of keeping the organization near to its customers and, in doing so, providing the 'feel' of a local company, even though it may be based far away. It also means that managers based in the geographic regions will be nearer to the customers to hear what they want to buy and to design and distribute products accordingly. Geographic markets clearly differ in their tastes and preferences and this structure provides for a local response to such variations.

Customer-based structures

A customer-based structure is similar in philosophy to a geographic structure in that it recognizes that the organization must structure itself to meet the needs of specific customer groups. Again, this type of approach tends to be more appropriate for larger concerns, although smaller companies often operate it in part.

When the customer base serviced by a company is broad and comprises several different customer types, this structure offers some advantages. It is self-evident that retail customers (i.e. the public) require a different approach to industrial customers. Accordingly, some organizations operate separate divisions to service each customer segment, e.g. retail, industrial, local government, etc. Larger personal computer companies may find such a structure to be useful, where one division may service business customers, another universities and educational establishments, another retailers, another mail-order customers, and so on. The advantage of such a structure is that each type of customer is catered for on his or her particular terms.

Product-based structures

Product-based structures are suitable for companies that operate within several different product areas (i.e. different product types) where each area requires some degree of specialization in its management. It is usually the case that expertise is not very transferable from one product type to another, so managers remain as specialists in their area, within their own product based division.

This type of structure is in evidence in some larger chemical companies. Many large chemical companies are involved in several types of chemical, each of which requires a high degree of specialist skill in research, selling and strategy. Companies like the German company Hoechst or the UK's ICI are primarily structured in this way. Within their broad chemical expertise are the various specialities (separate divisions), such as plastics, pharmaceuticals, agro-chemicals and intermediates. It is quite possible for a research chemist or a salesperson to be a very good at plastics but to know nothing about pharmaceuticals – hence the wisdom of the product based structure.

Non-hierarchical structures

We have already learned that some organizations do not observe the principle of the unity of command in such a strict way as hierarchically structured organizations. The thinking behind non-hierarchical structures is to 'free' employees from the rigidity of reporting to one boss in order to facilitate a more creative and flexible approach to work. The most common form of non-hierarchical structure is the *matrix structure*.

A matrix structure is actually something of a hybrid in that it contains both an approximate hierarchy and a strong non-hierarchical element. Employees will usually have a nominal 'boss', but the bulk of their time at work will be spent in cross-functional teams. In team-working, employees work closely with a team leader who is not their line manager and, in this respect, they can be said to have two people to whom they 'report.' Some more complex matrix structures involve employees working in several teams at once, thus 'confusing' reporting lines even more.

This potential confusion is the reason why some businesses have elected not to adopt a matrix structure. James Ross, chief executive of the multinational telecommunications company, Cable and Wireless, has said:

> We have rejected matrix management, if by [that] you mean that every person has two bosses ... I have operated within that sort of a system and it is theoretically perfect. Practically, it is expensive ... It leads to slow decision making and confusion of accountability.

Matrix structures are, however, useful in organizations that must carry out a range of relatively diverse tasks and which require staff to be especially flexible. It would rarely be employed in small or simple businesses in which tasks are mainly repetitive and predictable. The cross-functional teams in a matrix structure are typically short to medium term in their constitution, often being formed and then reformed according to the project needs of the organization. Accordingly, staff will often end up working alongside a larger number of colleagues than in purely hierarchical structures.

When shown diagrammatically, matrix structures are usually shown as a 'net' of interconnecting lines of reporting (Figure 10.2). Such a representation is necessarily oversimplified as it implies that any given employee only has two reporting lines – one to his nominally hierarchical line manager and one to a team leader. In practice, an employee may report to more than one team leader, a state that cannot be shown on a net diagram.

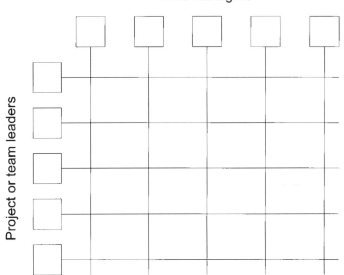

Figure 10.2 The matrix structure

Matrix structures are found in many organizational contexts. An example close to home for many readers is the structure of some university business schools. Academic staff are based in specialized divisions such as management, marketing, accountancy, human resources, and so on. Within the division, lecturers have a line manager called a division leader. From the division, lecturers are appointed to work in course teams alongside specialists from other divisions and, in doing so, have an additional reporting line to the course leader. This means that, in practice, staff often see more of the course leader and other lecturers on the course than they do of their own line manager (the division leader). Because lecturers teach on several courses, the cross-functional team (actually a cross-divisional team) becomes a 'second home' to the lecturers involved. The composition of each course team changes at the beginning of each academic year as staff are shuffled as division leaders see fit. A typical business school matrix structure is (imperfectly) represented in Figure 10.3.

Matrix-type structures can also feature in otherwise hierarchically structured organizations. On occasion, and to meet a specific project objective, staff are seconded to project teams which involve staff from a range of specialisms. A major chemical company recently set up a team of specialists to look into the possibility of setting up a particular set of operational philosophies called 'world-class manufacturing'. The team comprised staff seconded from their respective departments – a scientist, an accountant, an operations manager and a human resources manager – for a period of one year, each of whom possessed knowledge important to the team.

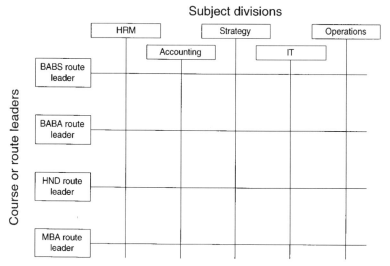

Figure 10.3 A matrix structure in a university business school

Hybrid structures

When we consider the distinctions we have discussed above, we should be aware that it is quite possible for more than one to be evident in an organization. We have already seen that an otherwise hierarchical organization can use elements of matrix management in their structures. Similarly, hierarchical structures can use more than one of the 'types' (product, functional, etc.) within the total corporate structure. Figure 10.4 shows how this may be the case for a typical large business operating in several geographical regions and selling more than one product type.

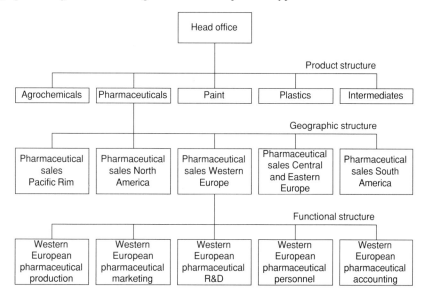

Figure 10.4 A hybrid organizational structure

133

Assignment

Michael Knight is the chief executive of a medium-sized company that has traditionally been organized hierarchically according to function. After attending a management seminar, he decides to encourage interfunctional co-operation by implementing a partial matrix structure in the organization. Michael argues that a matrix organization and cross-functional team working would provide flexibility and enhanced performance to the organization. The company secretary drew Michael's attention to some possible drawbacks. These, the company secretary proposed, included the potential problems that 'people won't know who they are meant to be reporting to, people might skive off when their line boss thinks they are working in their teams and team leaders will have no real authority over the team members.' After speaking to the company secretary, Michael began to have second thoughts about a matrix structure.

Michael decides to ask for a more considered view of restructuring the company. He asks you to prepare a report for him to address the following issues:

- the advantages of the existing hierarchical structure;
- the advantages of a matrix structure;
- how, as management, Michael and his team can address the company secretary's concerns;
- how Michael might gain some of the benefits of a matrix structure without fully restructuring the organization.

Further reading

Chandler, A. D. (1962) *Strategy and Structure*. Boston, MA: MIT Press.

11

Accounting and corporate finance

Learning objectives

After studying this chapter, students should be able to describe:

- Why a business needs money.
- The sources of money.
- The types of accountant and their roles.
- The structure and content of the legally required financial statements.
- The principal methods of analysing financial accounts.

11.1 Money and business

Why does a business need money?

Essentially, business can be said to be all about money – acquiring it, managing it, investing it and spending it. It follows that the management of money in an organization is a job of great importance. In most organizations, this responsibility rests with the accounting function (sometimes called the finance function).

At the beginning of a chapter on accounting and finance, it seems appropriate to ask the question: 'Why does a business need money?'

Firstly, a business needs money to *meet its operating costs*. In the course of normal business activities, a business incurs costs through having to pay for such things as:

- wages and salaries;
- rent and local authority taxation;
- raw materials and purchased items;
- insurance;
- energy (e.g. fuels).

Secondly, money is needed to *purchase new capital items* to enable the business to grow and develop. Included in this category are such things as:

- new land and buildings;
- new plant and equipment;
- new technologies.

Thirdly, money is sometimes needed to *make good short-term cash deficits* that arise from overspends on operating or capital costs. From time to time, a business runs out of money for a short period of time, in much the same way that you or I might in the week before pay-day or at the end of term. Money must be found to enable the business to continue through such periods.

Where does money come from?

Having discussed why a business needs money, we now turn to the sources of money open to a business.

The first and most important source of money is from *sales of goods and services*. Businesses in the 'for-profit' sector produce outputs which they exchange for money. This type of money is called *revenue* or *income*.

Secondly, a business can obtain money from *loans*. Loans take many forms depending upon the size of the loan and the body that lends it. Money can be obtained from banks, building societies and other financial institutions, but also from private individuals.

Thirdly, a business can obtain money from *its retained profits* or *reserves*. This is money earned in previous years from the sales of goods and services which can be accessed to use as and when appropriate (in the same way that you and I might use our savings).

Fourthly, money can be obtained from *donations, gifts or non-repayable grants*. Charities and political organizations make use of gifts, whilst public sector organizations make use of funding from central government, such as the funding a university receives indirectly from central government to operate its courses, research, etc. Grants are sometimes paid by government agencies to attract businesses to set up in areas of high unemployment.

Fifthly, money can be raised by *selling shares*. When a limited company begins in business, it raises its money through selling shares. However, the same method of money raising can be used later in the company's life in a *rights issue*. This approach is not often used as it can exert a downward pressure on the market price of existing shares.

11.2 People and roles in the accounting function

The importance of the management of financial resources means that in most organizations the responsibility is entrusted to a professionally qualified individual called an accountant.

Accountants and accounting technicians

An accountant is a person who has gained a professional qualification from one of the main accountancy bodies. Entry to such bodies is by examination, and passing all of the papers for a given body can take several years (the ACCA, for example, currently requires that each candidate passes fourteen papers to gain admission as a professional member). The bodies recognized in the various parts of the UK are as follows (brackets indicate designatory letters of professional members):

- Institute of Chartered Accountants in England and Wales (ACA);
- Institute of Chartered Accountants in Ireland (ACA);
- Institute of Chartered Accountants in Scotland (CA);
- Chartered Association of Certified Accountants (ACCA);
- Chartered Institute of Management Accountants (ACMA);
- Chartered Institute of Public Finance and Accountancy (IPFA).

A second important type of employee in the accounting department is the accounting technician. These are people who have qualified as members of the Association of Accounting Technicians (AAT), a body which qualifies people to work closely with accountants and to assist them in managing the accounting function. Accounting technicians form an important part of the administration in many accounting departments.

The diversity of the jobs that are performed in the accounting function means that both accountants and accounting technicians are usually assisted by other administrative and clerical staff.

Types of accountant

Accountants are found in all sectors of business and governmental activity. Any organization that uses money (i.e. all but a tiny minority) have a potential need for accounting professionals. Generally speaking, accountants do one or more of four things:

- they *report* on the financial performance or financial state of an organization;
- they *manage* finance and financial information and they advise non-financial managers based on their knowledge;
- they *audit* (check and approve) financial information by carrying out procedures to ensure the veracity of financial statements;
- they *advise* on business and money-related matters such as investments, taxation and forecasting.

Accordingly, there are four broad types of accounting:

- financial accounting – producing financial reports;
- management accounting – assisting with the management of the organization;
- auditing – checking the financial statements and accounting systems of an organization;
- consultancy and specialist accounting.

The majority of accountants work in the first three areas. These are the 'bread and butter' accountancy areas. A minority act as advisers or consultants in specialized areas. In addition to specialism in such things as tax, some accountants work in accounting law or in mergers and acquisitions whilst others work in areas such as international finance, banking and insurance. This chapter cannot possibly be exhaustive in its discussion, but it hoped the discussion acts as an overview of the subject. Readers should bear in mind that, although the accounting areas are considered separately, the tasks may be performed by the same person in smaller companies.

Financial accountants

Financial accountants produce accounting reports and may also assist in the organization's financial management. In practice, this means three things.

Firstly, financial accountants oversee the process of *financial recording*. This involves logging all transactions onto documents called ledgers. Whereas at one time the accounting office in a business was lined with ledger books, all but a minority have now installed computerized systems. Although the financial accountant is unlikely to enter the transactions himself, he will oversee the administrators and clerks as they enter the details of each sale, purchase, expense claim, bank deposit and withdrawal, etc.

Secondly, financial accountants ensure the business has sufficient finance available at any one time to operate normally and to invest when necessary. In consequence, they are often skilled at raising finance in the various ways we considered at the beginning of this chapter. They work out the most cost-effective way of *'financing'* the business and ensuring that cash is available when required. It is thus the financial accountant that organizes such things as bank loans and rights issues. He or she oversees the recording of all the financial transactions of the business such as sales and purchases.

The third area in which the financial accountant is involved is in the *reporting* of the financial position of the business in accordance with the law and agreed accounting standards. This means preparing accounts for publication at timely intervals (typically at the financial year end and at half year intervals). The law requires that each limited company submits three statements annually to Companies' House:

- the profit and loss account;
- the balance sheet;
- the cash-flow statement.

Each statement is compiled by drawing together the year's financial activity in the business. This in itself is a sizeable task, but the accountant's task has been made easier in this by specialized computer packages that are designed to prepare each statement automatically.

Management accountants

As their title suggests, management accountants are engaged in accounting as it relates to helping to manage the business. Their task extends to the preparation of information that helps other (non-accountant) managers perform their jobs with the maximum possible information 'at their fingertips'. In consequence, it will be the management accountant that managers approach to receive advice on such things as investment (e.g. in new machinery), staffing levels, marketing spending and the funding of research and development programmes. In most companies, all senior managers will consult with, or be consulted by, the management accountant on a regular basis.

As a professional who understands the company's financial affairs and who is also in possession of a wide range of planning and forecasting skills, a management accountant can carry out several management tasks for or on behalf of other managers. The most common are described below.

- *Management accounts* – the issuing of financial information on (usually) a monthly basis to inform managers on the financial state of the business to facilitate understanding and to promote intelligent decision-making.
- *Costing* – the process of determining the costs associated with the organization's products and services. There are a number of approaches to costing; the approach adopted depends upon the type of information wanted by the management. It may be that a manager wants to know the cost of materials in a product or it may be that the full cost is required including the share of fixed costs attributable to the product's production.
- *Cash-flow forecasting* – the setting of revenue and payments estimates on a monthly basis for a forthcoming period of time (typically a year). By doing this, a business can see how cash balances vary from month to month and also highlight any months where there is a net cash outflow, in which case a way must be found for making good the shortfall.
- *Budgeting* – the practice of setting income and expenditure expectations for a forthcoming period of time. A spending or *expenditure budget* represents an expectation or a limit at which spending departments, such as operations, should aim towards. An *income budget* applies to those departments that raise money for the organization. Hence, there may be a sales budget or a fund-raising budget (for charities). Budgets are set internally as a means of control where the value of a budget is set (usually) in negotiation with the departmental manager to whom it applies.
- *Variance analysis* – provides a means of comparison of actual performance against budget. Variances against budget are typically calculated monthly and can be good or bad news to the management accountant:
  - *adverse variance*s are those which are unfavourable to the business, i.e. expenditure above budget or income below budget;
  - *favourable variances* are those which are good news, i.e. expenditure below budget or income above budget.
- *Investment appraisal* – involves evaluating the financial viability of investments proposed by departmental managers. It may be, for example, that the manufacturing director wishes to purchase some extra factory space or a new machine. The management accountant will calculate the returns from the investment (in increased sales or reduced costs as a result of the purchase) and compare this against the price of the investment. If the price of the investment can be repaid within an acceptable time period, the accountant will probably approve the investment and release the cash. If, however, it looks like the investment will not give significant benefits to the business, it is likely that the accountant will recommend that it is not approved.
- *Competitor analysis* – involves gaining intelligence on a company's competitors by analysing financial information in competitors' published accounts. Whilst this task could theoretically be done by anybody, the management accountant is often best suited for the task. He or she will usually 'pick through' competitors' accounts to see how the competitor looks against his own business. In a management technique called *benchmarking*, accountants analyse the performance of the leading competitor in an industry (e.g. the most profitable) and seek to learn how the superior performance has been brought about. This can help to inform the practice of departmental managers in the business as they seek to improve the efficiency of their particular specialist areas.

11.3 Financial statements

When accountants (usually financial accountants) report on a company's performance, they must do so using strictly defined formats. The three mandatory reporting statements are, as we have seen, the profit and loss statement, the balance sheet and the cash-flow statement. The law requires that each statement be constructed using specific rules so that observers know that they are making a meaningful comparison when they study the accounts of more than one business. The old Statements of Standard Accounting Practice (SSAPs) are being replaced with instruments called Financial Reporting Standards (FRSs). Companies are thus bound to work within the provisions of these standards when reporting on financial matters.

Profit and loss statement

What is the profit and loss statement?
The profit and loss (P&L) account (sometimes called the *income statement*) provides a summary of the trading activities over the period of a financial year. A financial year can end at any point in the year; some companies operate on a December 31 year-end, but the majority do not. The account gives the total income for the year and shows how the company has spent money in order to generate its income. After costs have been subtracted from income, the account shows a profit on the year or a loss. Its general, simplified form is thus:

Income (sales)	£*xxxx*
Minus costs	(£*xxxx*)
Profit/loss	£*XXXX*

The general principle of the P&L account is very straightforward and can be applied to an individual as easily as it does to a business. If you earn (income) £20 000 in a year and you only spend £15 000 (costs), then you will have a 'profit' over the year of £5000. You can use the surplus to invest in the bank, to buy a car, to take a holiday or any number of other nice things. If, however, you make a loss on the year, you must find a way of financing the shortfall. You might ask your friendly bank manager for an overdraft or you might prefer to dig into some money that a late relative left you in a will. Either way, the loss must be financed.

Items in the P & L statement
The various items in the P&L account:

- *Sales* is the total income in the financial year from trading activities. Income from non-trading activities such as investments are shown elsewhere. For J. Sainsbury, this figure represents the total sales from its superstores across the country and those overseas.
- *Operating costs* are the total costs of running the business. This can be divided into the various types of cost, e.g. purchases of stocks for resale, labour, administration and distribution.

Profit and loss statement (P&L) – Asda Group plc

In practice, of course, company accounts are not as simple as the above general form. The complexities of a real company P&L account are shown below in the accounts of Asda Group plc, the grocery multiple (accounts as at 29 April, 1995 for the financial year 1994–95, simplified for the purposes of demonstration).

	£ millions
Total sales excluding VAT	5285.3
Less operating costs*	(5020.5)
Operating profit (PBIT)	264.8
Less net interest payable	(7.6)
Profit/(loss) on ordinary activities before taxation	257.2
Less taxation	(78.6)
Net profit (PAIT or earnings)	**178.6**

* Includes the release of small sums from other sources.

- *Profit before interest and tax* (operating profit or PBIT) is the sales minus the operating costs. Because the PBIT represents the surplus made on normal operating and trading activities, this figure is sometimes referred to as *operating profit*. Before the business can consider the profit its own, it must pay the appropriate proportion to the Inland Revenue in taxation and interest on any loans it has.
- *Profit after interest and tax* (PAIT), or *earnings*, is the money left over when everything has been paid for. It is this money that is available to the management and shareholders of a company to use at their discretion. There are three possible uses for the PAIT:
  - part of it can be paid to shareholders as dividends, thus providing the shareholders with a 'return' on their investment;
  - it can be retained by the business in the bank for future investment and expansion;
  - it can offset losses made in previous years by paying off long-term debts.

Balance sheet

What is the balance sheet?

We have seen that the P&L statement is a summary of the financial performance of a limited company over the duration of a financial year. The balance sheet is different in that it describes the financial state of a company on the last day of the financial year (the same day on which the P&L statement is reported). It is sometimes described as a 'snap-shot' of the business's finances on the day in question.

The purpose of the balance sheet is to detail two things about the company's total financial resources:

- where the company has obtained its financial resources;
- how the company has used its financial resources.

The statement thus has two sides: the 'assets' side describes the way the company has used its money whilst the 'funded by' side describes the sources of the company's money. These two sides must obviously balance, hence the statement's name.

Balance sheet – Asda Group plc

A look at a real-life example will show us how this looks. The example is that of Asda Group plc for the financial year 1994-95 (as at 29 April 1995 – simplified for the purposes of this demonstration).

	£ millions
Fixed assets	**2020.1**
Current assets	
Stocks	275.2
Debtors	103.0
Investments	428.6
Cash at bank and in hand	14.7
Total current assets	**821.5**
Creditors: amounts falling due within one year (current liabilities)	
Borrowings	(110.7)
Other creditors	(757.7)
Total current liabilities	**(868.4)**
Total assets (fixed and current) less current liabilities	**1973.2**
Creditors: amounts falling due after more than one year	
Borrowings	(328.4)
Other creditors	(0.3)
Provisions for liabilities and charges	(151.3)
Total net assets	**1493.2**
Capital and reserves ('funded by')	
Called up share capital	726.2
Share premium account	302.6
Revaluation reserve	83.9
Profit and loss account (transfer from P&L)	380.5
Equity shareholders' funds	**1493.2**

Items in the balance sheet – assets side
- *Fixed assets* include 'tangible assets', i.e. the value of money invested in plant, machinery, buildings, fittings, vehicles and land. They also include the value of longer term investments.
- *Current assets* are the value of money tied up in things which enable the business to operate in the relatively short term. There are three categories of current asset:
  - *stocks* are items stored by the business to be used in its processes or to sell on;
  - *debtors* is the amount of money owed to the company by its customers;
  - *investments* is the value of short-term investments;
  - *cash* is simply money which is immediately available either in a bank account or in literal notes and coins.

- *Current liabilities* are the value of money that the business owes to its suppliers for goods supplied or for services rendered. These are sometimes called *creditors* and fit into two categories:
  - *due within one year* are loans or debts due for repayment with a year;
  - *due after one year* are loans and debts due for repayment over the longer term.

Items in the balance sheet – funded-by side
- *Share capital* is the money that the company has made use of from its shareholders.
- *Reserves* is money 'put away' from various sources. Reserves can come from the sale of assets (e.g. subsidiary businesses) or from retained profits (money put aside from previous successful years' trading).
- *Profit and loss account* is earnings from the P&L account transferred across to the balance sheet. This is a form of 'reserves' in itself.

Cash-flow statement (CFS)

The CFS is the third compulsory financial statement. The CFS is unique in that examines only movements of cash in and out of the company over the course of the financial year. In this respect, it is different from the balance sheet in that the balance sheet refers to just the last day of the financial year and that it records the value of assets as well as cash on the day in question.

It follows from the statement's *raison d'être*, that it should be structured in such a way as to show each area of inward and outward cash movement. This is indeed the case. The general form of the CFS is as follows:

	£
Cash generated from operating activities	*xxx*
Returns on investments and servicing of finance	*xxx*
Taxation paid	*xxx*
Cash generated from investing activities	*xxx*
Net cash inflow/outflow before financing	*xxx*
Payments to the sources of finance	*xxx*
Net cash flow for the year	***XXX***

Cash-flow statement – Asda Group plc

The following statement is simplified from the Asda Group accounts for the year to 29 April, 1995.

	£ millions
Net cash inflow from operating activities	378.0
Returns on investment and servicing of finance (net)	(65.4)
Taxation paid during the year	(34.3)
Net cash inflow/(outflow) from investing activities	(188.6)
Net cash inflow/(outflow) before financing	89.7
Financing (net cash outflow)	(7.5)
Increase/(decrease) in cash and cash equivalent	**82.2**

Items in the CFS
- *Cash from operating activities* shows cash injections from normal trading. This is often simply the cash gained from profits after all outgoing costs (e.g. dividends) have been paid.
- *Returns on investment and servicing of finance* shows the amount of cash gained or lost as a result of investments and debts. The company pays servicing costs on its debts (rather like a mortgage holder pays a monthly instalment on a mortgage), but it receives income from any investments it has made, such as bank deposits.
- *Taxation* is cash paid on all of the company's taxable income. This includes tax on profits and on income from investments.
- *Cash generated from investing activities* shows cash movements resulting from the acquisition or disposal of assets, which is distinct from the returns on investment category (which shows servicing costs and returns on investments when they are owned). Hence, outgoings in this category would include the purchase of new fixed assets, and income would include the sale of subsidiary businesses or shares.
- *Financing* concerns the provision of cash to the business for use over the longer term and can include such things as new long-term loans (cash income), loan repayment (cash outgoing) or proceeds from the sale of new shares in the company (cash income – a process known as a *rights issue*).

The completed CFS shows a net inflow or outflow of cash over the course of the financial year in question. It follows that a positive figure is significantly more favourable than a negative figure.

11.4 Analysing financial statements

Financial information, at its simplest, is essentially a set of numbers. In order to make sense of it and to make it useful, we must analyse it. We do this by employing a few simple techniques:

- by examining trends in financial numbers;
- by calculating ratios comparing one financial figure with another;
- by comparing one company's financial information with another's.

Financial trends

Accounting numbers are made more meaningful when they are compared with the corresponding numbers for previous years. We might say, for example, that the total sales for J Sainsbury plc, a competitor to Asda Group, in the year to 1995 were £12.065 billion. In itself, this figure, large though it is, is only a number. We will be able to say much more about what this tells us about the company's performance if we compare it with the sales in previous years. Figure 11.1 shows us the trend in sales growth and we can see that, whilst the company has witnessed consistent growth, the *rate of growth* has slowed over recent years (although we ought to take the rate of inflation into account to see whether sales growth is in excess of this).

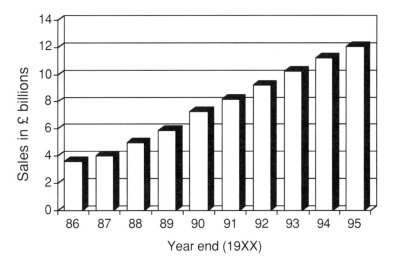

Figure 11.1 *Trend in sales value – J. Sainsbury plc, 1986–95*

There are many other accounting numbers we can examine in addition to trends in sales. We may also construct a graph to show how the company's profitability (see next section on ratios) has grown or shrunk over a number of years. From Figure 11.2, we can see that, whilst the sales trend may look relatively healthy, the growth in profits is not so good. Whilst there is a broad upward trend, there has been an erratic, but generally improving progress in profits.

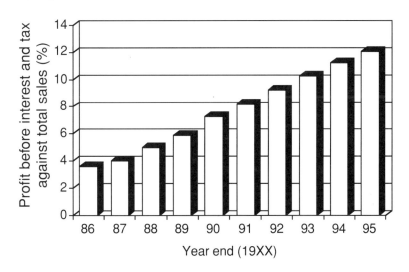

Figure 11.2 *Trend in profitability, J. Sainsbury plc, 1986–95*

The lesson to be drawn from the use of trends is that figures are much more meaningful when they are placed in the context of previous years' results. We can use any of the figures in the P&L account or balance sheet to construct a trend, or use any of the ratios we will consider in the next section.

Financial ratios

The figures that appear in company accounts are not, in themselves, very meaningful. A number in an account is simply that – a number. In order to make the analysis of accounts more meaningful, numbers are compared against each other in the form of ratios.

A ratio is arrived at by dividing one number by another. We can appreciate the value of ratios by looking at a simple example. Suppose you hear of the weight of two people: person A weighs 15 stone and person B weighs 10 stone. You might then conclude that person A is fatter and therefore less healthy than person B. Such a conclusion would be unwise because body weight itself is meaningless unless you also know the person's height. This is because the 'fatness' of a person is defined by the ratio between height and weight. If the two people are the same height then it is clearly obvious the person A is the fatter. If, however, person A at 15 stone is 8 feet tall, it is likely that he or she will actually be thin.

The lesson is clear: figures must be placed within a meaningful context to make them significant. Two companies each with a turnover of £100 million might appear at first glance to be similar, but until we know about their respective profits, capital employed, etc., we cannot make an intelligent comment about the two companies' performance.

In accountancy, financial ratios are used to analyse the financial features of accounts (usually annual accounts). For the purposes of our discussion, we can say that the most useful ratios fall into five broad categories:

- performance ratios;
- efficiency ratios;
- working capital ratios;
- financial structure ratios;
- investors' ratios.

The following discussion focuses on some of the most widely used accounting ratios. Readers should be aware that many more than these can be calculated.

Performance ratios

Performance ratios, as their name suggests, are those which are used to determine how well the company has performed in business terms. The crux of performance is *return*. A return is a financial profit compared with either the company's sales or the company's capital employed. There is, however, as we have seen, more than one definition of profit. We might think of profit in terms of profit before interest and tax, or earnings (after interest and tax). We must consequently specify which one we refer to in any performance ratio.

The commonest performance ratios use profit before interest and tax (operating profit, or Pbit):

$$\text{Return on sales (RoS)} = \frac{\text{Pbit}}{\text{Total sales}}$$

Sometimes called the profit margin, RoS gives an indication of how successfully the company has managed to controlled its costs in relation to sales income generated:

$$\text{Return on capital employed (ROCE)} = \frac{\text{Pbit}}{\text{Capital employed}}$$

(*Note*: capital employed is usually taken to mean shareholders' equity.)

ROCE is a measure of how effectively the company has used the shareholders' investment. For a business to make effective use of this investment, ROCE must at least be greater than the current rate of interest, i.e. the rate or return that the shareholder could get by investing his or her money in the local building society.

Efficiency ratios
Efficiency ratios record how well the company has used its factor inputs. Given that the company pays for inputs such as land, machinery and personnel, efficiency ratios attempt to assess how well the company has used these inputs in its business activities. Examples of efficiency ratios include:

$$\text{Sales per employee} = \frac{\text{Total sales}}{\text{Number of employees}}$$

and

$$\text{Profit per employee} = \frac{\text{Pbit}}{\text{Number of employees}}$$

Both of these ratios measure how efficiently the company has turned its labour inputs into money – either in terms of sales or profits. In some industries, such as retailing, efficiency can be measured by comparing sales or profits with the floor area of a shop:

$$\text{Sales per square metre} = \frac{\text{Total sales}}{\text{Floor area of shop in square metres}}$$

This ratio tells us how well the retail company uses its limited floor space. Efficient retailers will produce higher sales per square metre that inefficient ones. We can apply efficiency ratios to any of the factors of production.

Working capital ratios
Working capital is the amount of money that a company has tied up in the normal operation of its business. Working capital comprises money tied up in stocks, in debtors (money owed to the business), creditors (money the company owes) and in actual cash or current bank deposits. A company's objective is thus either to minimize this figure or at least to make efficient use of it.

To test how well a company uses working capital, a number of ratios can be used.

$$\text{Days-debtors} = \frac{\text{Value of debtors}}{\text{Total sales}} \times 365$$

$$\text{Days-creditors} = \frac{\text{Value of creditors}}{\text{Total sales}} \times 365$$

These two ratios tell us two things. Days-creditors tells us how effective the company is in delaying its payments to creditors. The larger the number, the longer the company takes to pay its creditors and thus the better the company uses its working capital. Conversely, days-debtors tells us how many days the company takes, on average, to collect its money owed. Good working capital management would usually be indicated by a low days debtors.

The effectiveness of a company's stock management can be measured by its stock turn.

$$\text{Stock turn} = \frac{\text{Total sales}}{\text{Value of stock}}$$

We measure stock in the number of times the stock is turned over in the course of the financial year. If, for example, a company's total sales is £2 million and its balance sheet value of stocks is £500 000, then the company turns its stock over four times. A higher stock turn tells us that the company has less working capital tied up in stocks and thus has lower working capital.

An important area of working capital management is to monitor the company's liquidity. The term 'liquidity' refers to a company's cash and other resources than can be turned into cash relatively quickly. It is generally assumed that a company should have sufficient liquidity to meet short-term cash requirements if the need arises. A company may be vulnerable to *insolvency* (running out of money) if its liquidity ratios are unfavourable.

$$\text{Liquidity ratio} = \frac{\text{Current assets} - \text{Value of stock}}{\text{Current liabilities}}$$

The liquidity ratio tests the company's ability to meet its short-term cash needs. We saw above that current liabilities comprise those items in the balance sheet which the company must pay for in the short term. Conversely, current assets represent cash items that the company can 'count on' either because it is money owed or in cash form. To calculate liquidity, stock is subtracted from current assets because they are deemed to be slower to turn into cash than other current assets (because they have to be worked on and/or sold first).

Financial structure ratios

Financial structure refers to the way in which the company finances itself. We learned earlier that a company can use two broad methods of financing capital investment (quite a different thing to working capital, which finances normal operations). Firstly, it can use shareholders' funds which include any retained profits, which obviously also belong to the shareholders. Secondly, it can use debt from a bank or from another lender.

The ratio between these two is called the company's gearing or its debt/equity ratio (*equity* means shareholders funds). There are two common ways of calculating gearing:

$$\text{Debt/equity (gearing)} = \frac{\text{Long-term borrowings}}{\text{Borrowings plus shareholders funds}}$$

This ratio gives borrowings as a percentage of the company's total long-term capital.

$$\text{Debt/equity (gearing)} = \frac{\text{Long-term borrowings}}{\text{Shareholders' funds}}$$

This ratio tells us simply the ratio of the two. A figure of greater than one means the company has more borrowings than equity; less than one, the converse.

Whilst it is common for businesses to make extensive use of debt to fund investment, being in too much debt increases the company's vulnerability to increases in the interest rate (see Chapter 23). A high gearing is also an indication that the company must eventually find the money to repay its debts, this not being a good indicator of future business performance. Debt has the advantage, however, of enabling the company to retain its equity for other purposes.

Investors' ratios

Investors are those people who inject their own money into a company – mainly shareholders, although banks and other lenders can also be considered as investors. Shareholders have three essential interests in a company. Firstly, they want to be sure that their investment is safe and that the company will survive, which they can gauge from ratios such as liquidity. Secondly, they want to receive dividends on their shares of meaningful value against the value of their investment. Thirdly, shareholders want to see the value of the share increase (capital growth) so that they can sell at a personal profit (the value of performance ratios will have an influence on this). Investors' ratios are those which inform shareholders of the state of their investment or which guide potential investors in a company as to the attractiveness of the company as an investment target. It follows that shareholders will potentially be interested in all ratios, although they may be particularly keen to analyse performance ratios.

Some ratios, however, are designed to give information which concerns various aspects of unique interest to shareholders and other investors. The earnings per share (EPS) ratio takes the profit figure from the P&L account and tells us how much of the figure is attributable to each share.

$$\text{Earnings per share (EPS)} = \frac{\text{Profit after interest and tax (PAIT) in most recent annual accounts}}{\text{Number of shares (i.e. share volume)}}$$

The EPS allows a shareholder to know how much profit is attributable to him or her on the basis of how many shares are owned. It should be borne in mind, however, that only a part of the EPS will be payable as dividend.

The price earnings (P/E) ratio is an indication of the confidence that the investment community has in a company's shares:

$$\text{Price/earnings (P/E) ratio} = \frac{\text{Current price of share}}{\text{EPS at last declaration of results}}$$

We might expect the value of a share to rise following an announcement of high earnings (because demand for the share will rise). In this case, the ratio between share price and last earnings will be low. In some cases, however, the shares remain in demand (and hence have a high price) *despite* mediocre earnings. In this case, the ratio will be high, indicating a high confidence in the share and that the future remains bright despite the last earnings announced.

Other investors' ratios inform us about the various issues surrounding dividends on shares. Dividends are paid to shareholders as a return on their investment and are usually paid as a percentage of the earnings (profit after interest and tax). The company's directors recommend that some of the earnings be kept in the company to reinvest as retained profits.

The dividend yield is a ratio informing investors of the current return on the share as a percentage.

$$\text{Dividend yield} = \frac{\text{Gross dividend per share}}{\text{Current price of share}} \times 100$$

The yield is measured in per cent and gives the investor an indication of the attractiveness of the share as a means of providing an economic return on his or her investment. Bearing in mind that the top of the ratio is *gross* dividend (i.e. before tax is paid on it by the recipient of the dividend), an investor would be looking to see that the yield is greater than the current rate of interest – the return that could be gained simply by placing the investment in the local building society or bank.

Comparing financial performance between companies

The final way in which accounts can be analysed is by looking at one company's accounts and then comparing the various accounting figures with those in other companies. We can compare not only the size of two companies (e.g. by looking at total sales or total assets employed) but also their ratios or trends over time of any of their accounting figures (e.g. sales or profit margins).

The two companies that we are comparing may be competitors or in different industries. If we compare the accounts of competitors, we often get a like-for-like comparison, which enables us to draw broad conclusions about which of the companies is in the more favourable position. If we compare the accounts of companies in different sectors of industry, we can discover the ways in which players in the two industries differ.

This will become clearer if we look at some simple comparisons. We could take any base on which to compare the companies, but to keep it relatively simple, we will compare the total sales and operating profit margins of three companies. We have already encountered (earlier in this chapter) two of the UK's biggest retailers, J. Sainsbury plc and Asda Stores plc, and we will also look at a major company in the pharmaceuticals and healthcare sector; SmithKline Beecham plc. All of the data are for the year ending 1995.

Table 11.1 Selected comparisons between three companies (Source: respective annual accounts)

Company	Sales after VAT (£ billions)	Operating profit margin (%)	Sales per Employee (£)
J. Sainsbury plc	11.357	7.9	137 920
Asda Stores plc	5.285	4.65	76 194
SmithKline Beecham plc	7.011	24.7	133 798

Of course, to carry out a fully meaningful analysis, we would need to compare more accounting figures than just those listed above. However, even from our simple analysis, we can draw some conclusions:

- J. Sainsbury is a larger company by sales than Asda;
- J. Sainsbury is more profitable than Asda;
- J. Sainsbury, with its higher sales per employee, makes a more efficient use of its employees than Asda;
- SmithKline Beecham has a lower total sales figure than J. Sainsbury, but a higher one than Asda;
- SmithKline Beecham is much more profitable than either of the two companies in retailing (we cannot conclude from this that all pharmaceuticals companies are more profitable than retailers);
- SmithKline Beecham and J. Sainsbury are similar with respect to sales per employee, and both are superior to Asda in this respect.

Assignment

Obtain the financial accounts of a public limited company of your choice for the past five years (published accounts often contain five- or ten-year trends whilst databases like FAME have five years' results as standard).

Questions

- For the company in question, record or calculate, for the five-year period: the turnover;
  - the return on capital employed;
  - the operating profit margin.
- Comment on the trend in each ratio. Do they show an optimistic or pessimistic outlook for the company? Give reasons for your conclusions.
- By checking the company's current share price (in the financial pages of a broadsheet newspaper), calculate the current price earnings ratio.
- From the P/E ratio, comment on the market's confidence in the company's shares.
- Prepare a short report on the company, its activities and recent performance to a potential investor. Would you recommend purchasing the shares?

Further reading

Atrill, P. Harvey, D. and McLaney, E. (1994) *Accounting for Business*. Oxford: Butterworth-Heinemann.

Bendrey, M., Hussey, R. and West, C. (1996) *Accounting and Finance for Business*, 4th edn. London: DP Publications.

Hussey, J. and Hussey, R. (1994) *Essential Elements of Management Accounting*. London: DP Publications.

Millichamp, A. H. (1995). *Finance for Non-Financial Managers*, 2nd edn. London: DP Publications.

Oldcorn, R. (1996). *Company Accounts*, 3rd edn. London: Macmillan.

12

Marketing and business products

Learning objectives

After studying this chapter, students should be able to describe:

- The nature of marketing.
- The role of marketing in a business organization and the nature of the marketing mix.
- The nature and 'dimensions' of a business product.
- The stages in the product life cycle.
- Pricing strategies in marketing.
- The bases by which markets can be segmented.
- The major methods of marketing communication and product promotion.

12.1 What is marketing?

Marketing has been interpreted in many different ways. In a modern organization, the various facets of marketing are carried out by specialists in a department. In many cases, the marketing department is responsible only for sales and promotions. In other cases, the department has an altogether broader remit.

Consider the following two definitions of marketing.

> *Marketing is the management process which identifies, anticipates and supplies customer requirements efficiently and profitably.*
>
> (The Chartered Institute of Marketing – CIM)

> *Marketing is not only much broader than selling ... It encompasses the entire business. It is the whole business seen from the point of view of its final result, that is, from the customers' point of view.*
>
> (Peter Drucker, *The Practice of Management*, 1954)

These two definitions show us two complementary approaches to marketing. Firstly, the CIM see it as a *management process* – something that management does. A management process involves procedures and systems put in place to implement marketing within the organization. Secondly, Drucker proposes a wider definition than the CIM. In his phrase, 'it encompasses the entire business', we see marketing as a *philosophy of business*. The marketing philosophy is one that is geared to doing everything with the benefit of the customer in mind.

Businesses which adopt marketing as an underlying philosophy of business are said to be *marketing-oriented* organizations. This is in contrast to organizations which are based primarily around a different function of the business. A heavy-engineering facility (e.g. a shipyard or a steel-milling business), for example, will often be oriented towards its operations department. This is because of the nature of the products produced and the imperatives to maintain operational quality and reduce costs. We cannot say that one approach is right or wrong – we can simply say that the orientation should be chosen as is most appropriate for the organization and its products.

12.2 What does the marketing function do?

The role of the marketing department varies according to the needs and situation of the organization. Some are very large and elaborate, whilst others have none at all or perhaps just one marketing person. Furthermore, the responsibilities of the marketing function also vary greatly. Some marketing functions include research and development (R&D) and sales, whilst others merely look after any press releases or promotional activities undertaken. In one respect, therefore, it is impossible to generalize as to the precise activities of a marketing department. This chapter deals with what may be considered to be an idealized marketing department, or one which carries out all the activities assigned to it by noted theorists and academics who specialize in the marketing field.

Marketing manages the marketing mix

What is the marketing mix?
The term 'mix' is used to describe the mix of activities undertaken by a marketing department. We should dispense at once with the notion that marketing is simply about advertising and issuing press statements – it is much more. To enable a simpler understanding of the role of marketing in a business, writers in this field use the '4 Ps' model to describe the marketing mix:

- marketing specifies the design and features of the *product*;
- marketing determines the *price* that will be charged for the product;
- marketing specifies the notional or actual *place* where the product will be sold at the agreed price;
- marketing *promotes* the product to the target market (place) at the agreed price.

Hence, the 4 Ps are:

- *Product*;
- *Price*;
- *Place*;
- *Promotion*.

The congruence of the elements of the marketing mix
An essential feature of good marketing is that each part of the process 'matches' all of the others. When a product is developed, it is usually with a certain place in mind. The price must also make the product attractive to the target market. Promotions must be

geared to effectively communicate the benefits of the product to the target market.

Mismatches can occur when any of the elements of the mix do not match the others. It may be, for example, that an organization develops a good product aimed at a particular segment of the market, but then attaches too high a price to it and promotes it in an inappropriate way.

Marketing directs the R&D function

In an organization which employs the marketing philosophy, it is the marketing people who 'have their finger on the pulse' of what the market wants. It therefore makes sense that is should be the marketing people who ultimately decide on the R&D function's agenda. This may take the form of regular meetings between the marketing manager and the R&D (or design) manager, or it may be the case that a marketing specialist actually oversees the activities of the product development staff.

Marketing sets prices

Part of the marketing process is to attach a price to products sold. Usually working alongside an accountant, the marketing specialists will be aware of the prices that the target market will be willing to pay for the product. Careful marketing research will tell the marketing department the price that will yield the maximum long-term profit for the product, and the price chargeable will almost certainly inform the design function as it produces the product at its inception. It may be, for example, that the price chargeable for a small car, mainly targeted as a 'second' vehicle at women, is around £7000 to £8000. Working backwards, the price will guide the design function as it designs the car.

Marketing decides who to aim the product at

Apart from the necessities of life, no single product can be aimed at everybody. The product and price will usually be designed to appeal to only part of the total market. Marketing specialists have ingenious ways of dividing people up according to their ability or willingness to buy certain products. They can predict who a new product will appeal to and where such customers can be found.

Marketing sells and promotes the product

This part of the marketing department's job is the best known but, as we have seen, is only part of the total workload. After all the other parts of the mix have been carried out, the marketing department will work out how best to communicate the benefits of the product to the target market. The style of communication will be carefully chosen to appeal to the target market. For technical products, such as industrial products, promotions will often be restricted simply to a statement of the product's technical specification – this is all the buyer requires to make a decision. For many consumer products, communications are aimed at a 'mass market' and the promotion reflects this by including a persuasive element in the promotion.

12.3 Business products and prices

What is a product?

The first misconception we must immediately dispense with is the notion that a product is merely something physical. A product can be a physical object, but need not necessarily be. Consider the following definition.

> *A product is any organizational output which satisfies a consumer's wants or needs.*

Output
The output of an organization falls into two broad categories: goods and services. *Goods* are tangible, physical products which can be touched and seen. *Services* are intangible. Goods are things you own, services are things done to you or things done on your behalf. A service may involve the use of goods in the course of imparting the benefit or the product. Similarly, the impartation of the benefits of a good may involve an element of service (such as when a petrol pump attendant dispenses petrol into your car).

Cars, chemicals and the book you are holding are all examples of goods. You take advantage of service products when, for example, you visit the hairdresser, when you employ a mechanic to repair your car or when you enrol at a university.

Wants and needs
Individuals are motivated to take advantage of an organization's output when they believe it will be of some benefit to them. The distinction between needs and wants is rather blurred. A consumer will tend to be prepared to pay a higher price for a product which fulfils a felt or real need.

The economic nature of organizations means that the output must be paid for in some way. It is not, however, always the case that the individual enjoying the benefit of a product is the same person who pays for it. Whilst this is the norm, some organizations operate in such a way as to provide a product which is not necessarily aimed at those who pay. Government organizations provide services which every tax payer pays for even though only those in need benefit from the output. Similarly, charities provide benefits which, in most cases, the beneficiaries do not pay for directly.

Types of product
There are several ways in which products can be subdivided. We have seen that the first way of dividing products is according to whether they are goods or services. We can also divide products according to the general types of customers that consume them. One such mechanism is the industrial – consumer goods distinction.

Industrial products are those used by businesses rather than individual people. They are rarely in their finished form and tend to undergo further processing by the business. A manufacturing business buys in raw materials and parts which it uses in its manufacturing processes. Service industries may purchase products which enable them to carry out the services. A plasterer will use plaster (an industrial product) as an essential input to his service business.

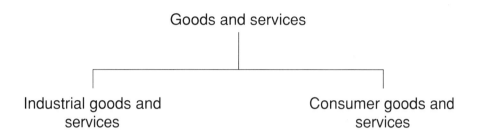

Figure 12.1 Types of product

Consumer products are goods and services which are purchased by the end user. It is usually the case that little or no further transformation is performed on consumer products – they are consumed. Consumption, in this context, does not necessarily mean eaten, but rather used in the product's existing form. A consumer is unlikely to make modifications to his or her washing machine, it is simply used. The two major categories of consumer products are *consumer durables*, such as electrical goods, cars, etc., and *fast-moving consumer goods* (FMCGs) which are products we tend to buy little and often, such as food products.

Features of a product

Marketing specialists, when describing a product, see it as having two 'dimensions'. It is these two dimensions which define the totality of the product.

Generic product
The generic or *core* product comprises the features of the product which meet the basic needs of the customer. It is totally basic and has no embellishments at all.

The generic car would be a totally basic vehicle which meets minimum legal standards but has no 'add-on' features at all. It may, for example, have hard vinyl seats, a floppy plastic steering wheel and a 750cc engine. It meets the basic needs of a car in that:

- it goes;
- it stops when brakes are applied;
- it prevents the ingress of rain.

The generic food product is one which fulfils the essential purpose of volume, sustenance and bulk for the body. It may possess little in the way of flavour, texture or convenience.

Question 12.1

Describe the core features of the following product types:

- Chocolate bars.
- Houses.
- Anti-perspirants.
- Beer.

Whilst most products contain the benefits of the core product, we can readily appreciate that most products we use have 'extra' benefits as well.

Augmented product

The augmented product comprises the totality of features of a product. It includes the core benefits and any number of 'add-on' or *premium* benefits which make the product more acceptable to certain segments of the market.

Premium features are included to appeal to the senses of the consumer and increase sales and profits to the business. The nature of premium features added to a product will obviously vary. For food products, premium features may include taste, texture, convenience, 'healthy image', etc. For our basic car, we could add premium features such as appearance, metallic paint, engine size/design, leather seats, increased reliability, fuel economy, etc.

The presence of augmented features can significantly increase the cost (and hence the price) of a product. It is possible, for example, to pay £5000 or £500 000 for a new car. Both provide the core benefits, but the more expensive models contain much more in the way of augmentation. Not all premium benefits are tangible. Some are perceptual in nature – the image that the consumer associates with the use of certain products. In the case of an expensive car, almost all the price goes towards paying for premium or augmented benefits.

A great deal of emphasis is placed on premium features in the process of marketing communications. Advertisements for cars, for example, are usually concerned with communicating premium benefits such as style, utility, reliability, etc. We can imagine the response to an advertisement which only communicated the core benefits, e.g. 'Here is a car. It goes, it stops and it keeps the rain out! Buy it'.

Question 12.2

For the following products describe some of the premium features which apply to each one:

- Chocolate bars.
- Houses.
- Anti-perspirants.
- Beer.

The product life-cycle

An essential feature of almost all products is that of its life cycle. The position of a product on its life cycle will have a large bearing upon its marketing. It may determine its design and will be relevant to its pricing and promotion. As shown in Figure 12.2, there are four distinct phases in the product life cycle.

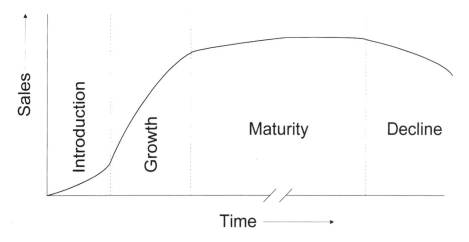

Figure 12.2 The product life cycle

Introduction

The introduction stage of a product follows its design although, as it is introduced to the market, it is not uncommon for further 'tweaking' to be made to render the product more acceptable to customers. If the product is unique (i.e. it is not a 'me too' product), it will benefit from a lack of competitors, although it risks early failure if the market does not take to it quickly. The company usually incurs extra costs at this stage due to promotional expenditure and, as a consequence, failure during introduction, before the company makes any meaningful sales, is especially costly.

The percentage failure rate varies according to the product type and the amount of market research that precedes the launch. New processed food products have a success rate of approximately one in ten. For more capital-intensive products like electronic and defence equipment, the success rate is more favourable. There have been some very expensive and notable 'flops' at the introduction stage. Certain products have become almost infamous due to their well-publicised failure: the video disk, the V2000 video and the Sinclair C5 electric car are good examples.

Growth

Products that successfully emerge from introduction enter the growth stage. Growth is characterized by several features, particularly rising sales and the appearance of profits which can initially be used to offset the development and introduction costs. If the product type is one which is readily 'copyable', then competitor products may come on-stream and threaten the rate of growth.

As demand for a product rises, the business can take advantage of this by increasing the product's price and thus can enjoy higher profits. Much of the promotional activity will be geared to establishing the product as a leader in its product/market sector. However, as the product becomes better known due to increased usage, the business will usually reduce its promotional costs as a percentage of sales to allow higher returns to be made. The company will also pay great attention during growth to the product's distribution in order to ensure optimum exposure of the product to the target market.

Maturity

In the same way that the majority of people are in maturity (aged between about 14 and 65 years), so are the majority of products. Maturity is characterized by:

- static or slowly increasing growth in sales;
- a lot of competitive products;
- manoeuvring by competitors to 'steal' market share;
- lower prices than in the growth stage (and hence lower profits).

The fact that sales have stopped growing by any significant amount means that sales increases can only be achieved by taking a competitor's market share. For this reason, the mature phase is the most competitive. Companies go to great lengths to buy brand loyalty from customers. The product may be adjusted or 'tweaked' to make it more attractive to customers. For consumer products, such adjustments may take the form of new premium features or more attractive packaging. Advertising is widely used by companies seeking to promote mature products (e.g. coffee, washing powder). If the product's demand is price elastic (see Chapter 17), market share can be increased by reducing the price, but this has obvious implications for profitability.

Decline

Decline occurs when customer preferences change away from the product. Whilst decline can be postponed by adroit product redesign, it cannot be avoided. It is characterized by:

- falling sales for all producers of the product;
- price cuts to maintain sales for as long as possible;
- declining profits;
- competitors abandoning the market.

When products begin to decline, the key decision is to when to discontinue production. Most companies producing declining products attempt to 'milk' sales for as long as possible. No investment would be made under such circumstances (i.e. no further development or marketing funds would be committed to the product).

Question 12.3

- Which stage of the life cycle do you think the following products are in?
  - VHS video recorders.
  - Computers containing the 486 processor chip.
  - Personal computers as a whole.

- Corn flakes.
- Video cameras.
- Twelve inch vinyl records.
- Apart from the examples listed above, give three examples of product types that are currently in each stage of the product life cycle.

Life cycle – a metaphor from life

The concept of life cycle does not just apply to products, it applies to you and me. Human beings undergo a life cycle that has a huge bearing, not just on our biological changes, but on behaviour.

We undergo *introduction* when we are conceived and grow inside our mothers. After birth, we begin to *grow* – a process that continues until, after puberty, we reach our full height and weight. Our *maturity* phase is the longest. For most people, it will last from our mid-teens until the time when our faculties begin to fail us – perhaps in our sixties or seventies. When we reach old age, we begin to *decline*. Our eyesight may begin to deteriorate, we slow down and we may lose some of our intellectual sharpness. Finally, when decline has run its course, life is no longer viable, and we *die*.

The duration of the product life cycle

Just like the spans of human life, not all product life cycles are of the same duration. Some products go through the life cycle very quickly, whereas others last for centuries.

Products which are subject to fashion tend to have relatively short life cycles. The life cycle of flared trousers in the 1970s was around four or five years in total, from introduction to the end of decline. The same time-scale applied to shell-suits and T-shirts with the words 'Bros' or 'Take That' printed on the front. For staple food products such as rice and grain, it is difficult to imagine them leaving the mature phase.

Question 12.4

Apart from those products mentioned above, list five products which have had a short life cycle and five others which have enjoyed a very long cycle.

Pricing strategies

The ways in which businesses attach prices are complicated. The price that a product is given by its producer has a number of determining factors:

- the cost of production;
- the price of competitive products;
- the customer's expectations of what the price should be (the *utility* the customer

attaches to the product);

- temporary tactics to influence the volume of sales (e.g. short-term price reductions to shift slow-moving stock);
- the elasticity of demand of the product (i.e. how responsive the quantity demanded is to changes in the product's price – see Chapter 17);

With such a complex set of determinants, the price attached to a product depends in large part on the stage of the product on the product life-cycle and the product's price elasticity of demand (see Chapter 17).

New-product pricing

Pricing decisions at the point of a new-product launch are a little more complicated than pricing existing products. On the one hand, there is good reason to attach a high price to the product to start recovering the new product's development costs. On the other hand, a high price may deter consumers from trying the product and so a lower price may help the product to become established.

The approach taken will depend in large part on the number of consumers that are expected to buy the product, its distinctiveness or uniqueness and its price elasticity of demand (i.e. how responsive demand is to price). There are two broad introduction pricing strategies: price skimming and price penetration.

Price skimming involves attaching a relatively high price to the product at its launch. It is an appropriate strategy when the early buyers of the product comprise a small part of the total market and who are prepared to pay the high price to enjoy the product's benefits (i.e. it has a price inelastic demand). It also relies on the presupposition that there are few competitors to match the product's benefits. Price skimming is used in sectors such as pharmaceuticals and military equipment. If appropriate, new consumers are encouraged to buy the product with phased price reductions as time passes.

Price penetration involves the attachment of a relatively low price to the new product with a view to attracting a broad customer base early in the product's life. Price increases may then be applied as a loyal customer base is established. Penetration is appropriate when the product's demand is responsive to price (price elasticity) or when the product is entering a competitive market and market share is consequently a major consideration.

12.4 Placing the product

What does placing mean?

The matter of product placement concerns two aspects of marketing. The two aspects are:

- identifying the customer group at which the product is to be aimed;
- the best method by which to make the product available to the target market.

Accordingly, the placing process begins with an attempt to describe the type of customers who may be most interested in buying the product. This is done by the use of 'dividing tools' that can separate people from each other. These are distinguishing features that circumscribe a *market segment*. Following this, the next marketing decision is to establish the distribution channel to most effectively reach the market segment for the product.

Market segmentation

No single product can possibly be aimed at everybody. Marketing specialists have ways of dividing up the total market into smaller 'chunks'. These are called market segments. Such segments are used as the basis upon which to 'target' products. For industrial products, market segments are almost self-suggesting, in that if a product is a part for an aircraft, the producer will target aircraft manufacturers in its marketing. For consumer products, the picture is a little more complicated.

Because consumer products are aimed at the end user (the consumer), marketing people must find ways of dividing up the total population. A common way of doing this is by taking advantage of *demographic variables*. It is obvious that people are very different, and it is these differences which make some products appeal to some people but not to others.

Demographic segmentation bases

This part of marketing examines the ways in which people differ. The reasonable assumption underlying market segmentation is that different people will have different demands for products. It is self-evident, for example, that older people will buy fewer toys than the parents of young children, women will buy less after-shave than men. and wealthy professional people will eat in exclusive restaurants more than manual workers.

The most frequently used segmentation bases ('people dividers') are:

- age;
- gender;
- stage in the family life cycle;
- occupation and income;
- type and place of residence;
- level of education.

Demographic variables

The most widely used demographic variables are described below.

Age

The period of life that a person is at will have a large influence upon both their spending power and their preferences. Obvious examples of age-related products include children's toys and zimmer-frames for the elderly. Others are not so obvious. It is typical for magazines to have an age-related target market. The editorial styles employed and the contents of magazines are designed to appeal to differing levels of maturity – compare the readership of *Viz* with that of *Inspirations for your Home* or *Tatler*.

Gender

Like segmentation by age, gender differences allow for an obvious type of market segmentation (e.g. in the cases of clothes, razors, fragrances, hygiene products) and some less obvious examples. It is believed that one's gender creates certain product preferences as a result or male and female psychology rather than physical differences. Some alcoholic beverages are predominantly aimed at just one sex, as are some food products and cars.

Question 12.5
How many products or types of product can you think of that are generally aimed at one sex or the other?

Stage in the family life cycle

As people pass through the various stages of their family life, their preferences and spending power will change. Whereas a young married couple with no progeny may take holidays skiing in Austria, when they have two children, say five years later, it is more likely that they will opt for something less ambitious, such as a cottage in Cornwall. A family with young children will tend to purchase less expensive furniture, not only because of their restricted spending power, but because of the higher probability that it will have to endure a higher level of wear and tear. At the other end of the life cycle, the older couple, whose children have 'flown the nest' are likely to have more spending power (mortgage paid off, higher income, etc.). Such people will tend to be more discerning in their preferences, opting for higher quality furniture and holidays, as well as engaging in activities such as hobbies which they previously may have had less time for.

Family life cycle – Wells and Gubar's classification

A commonly used classification of family types is as follows:

- Bachelor stage – young singles, not living with parents.
- Newly married couples – young with no children.
- Full nest I – youngest child under six years.
- Full nest II – youngest child aged six years or more.
- Full nest III – older married couples with dependent children.
- Empty nest I – older married couples, with no children at home and with the head of the family still working.
- Empty nest II – older married couples, with no children at home and the head of the family retired.
- Solitary survivor – employed.
- Solitary survivor – retired.

Occupation and income

Segmenting people according to their jobs is one of the most powerful and most widely used 'dividers' of people. The underlying assumption of this approach is that a person's job will not only say something about their income, and hence spending power, but also indicate certain preferences in taste.

Marketing specialists band people together into socio-economic groups according to the occupation of the major wage earner in a household. They use letters to describe each group.

Group	Percentage of population (approx)	Status	Occupation of head of household
A	3%	Upper middle class	Senior managerial, senior administrative, 'true' professionals (accountants, lawyers, doctors), inheritors of wealth.
B	13%	Middle class	Intermediate (mid) management and administrative, other professionals.
C1	23%	Lower middle class	Supervisory, junior managerial, clerical, some professionals. (including most nurses, teachers, policemen, etc.).
C2	32%	Skilled working class	Skilled manual workers (electricians, plumbers and other tradespeople).
D	19%	Working class	Unskilled and semi-skilled manual workers (factory operatives, labourers).
E	10%	Subsistence class	Unemployed, state pensioners, low-grade workers, casual workers.

Type of residence and neighbourhood

Some products can be targeted at people according to the type of house they live in and the area in which the house is located. It would be appropriate, for example, to target lawn-mowers at those who live in houses with gardens, but not those who live in tower blocks. Security systems (for properties) may well be most efficiently targeted at residents in inner city areas, as the demand for such systems may be less in sleepy rural villages.

The ACORN classification (a classification of residential neighbourhoods) is used to separate one type of neighbourhood from another. Marketing people, when targeting products according to neighbourhood, select the most appropriate ACORN categories where they may promote their products with a greater chance of success.

The most commonly used ACORN classification groups are listed below:

A   Agricultural areas.
B   Modern family housing, higher income.
C   Older housing of intermediate status.
D   Poor quality older terraced housing.
E   Better-off council estates.
F   Less well-off council estates.
G   Poorest council estates.
H   Multi racial areas.
I   High status non family areas.
J   Affluent suburban housing.
K   Better-off retirement areas.

Level of education

The population as a whole has a very wide range of educational standards. The assumption underlying the use of education level as a basis of market segmentation is the belief that the level of education a person has enjoyed will influence buyer behaviour and determine certain preferences. It is probable that most graduates and professionals have a more enhanced 'intellectual appetite' than less well educated people. This preference determines many things, including the newspaper they read and their choice of television programmes and radio stations. Among newspaper readerships, more highly educated people tend to prefer 'broadsheets' such as *The Times* and *The Daily Telegraph* due to their more thorough coverage and discussion. The 'tabloids' such as *The Sun* and *The Daily Star* tend to be read by those with a lesser appetite for detail – often those with lower educational accomplishments.

Special interests

In addition to the demographic variables hitherto discussed, an important 'divider' of people is the fact that some people are distinguished by their uniqueness or special interests. Some products are clearly targeted at highly specialized segments, whether it be railway modelling enthusiasts, motorcyclists, evangelical Christians or sufferers of a disease such as diabetes. Such people will have specialized product requirements by virtue of their special interest – diabetic chocolate is of little interest to anybody except diabetics.

Distribution channels

The second aspect of placing a product is the establishment of a suitable distribution channel for the product. Some products benefit from a very short distribution channel in that they pass directly from the producer to the consumer. You may, for example, buy a dozen eggs direct from a farmer near your house. In this case the producer is in direct communication with the consumer. In other cases, the product may pass through several stages from the producer (e.g. a factory or a farm) to the end user. If you buy an imported motor car, it is likely that the vehicle will have passed through a relatively lengthy channel before you take delivery.

Some of the more commonly observed channels are shown in Figure 12.3. Note that the length and complexity of the channel becomes successively longer.

The method of distribution chosen for a product will depend on two important considerations:

- the required level of market exposure;
- the costs associated with each stage of the channel.

Market exposure concerns the percentage of the target market that will have ready access to the product. It is usually the case that the longer the channel length, the higher the market exposure. It will typically be the case, for example, that a FMCG manufacturer will use the major national retailers (e.g. Tesco, Asda, etc.) to provide a high level of market exposure. This naturally necessitates a lengthening of the distribution channel.

The *costs* associated with channel length are said to be *proportional*. A longer channel means that more businesses are involved, each of whom will wish to make a profit on its handling of the goods. All of these costs will eventually be paid for by the consumer in the final price. This feature explains why it is usually the case that the nearer the producer a good is purchased, the cheaper it will be. You may, for example, save money by buying from a factory shop, from a wholesaler (e.g. a 'cash and carry') or even direct from an importer.

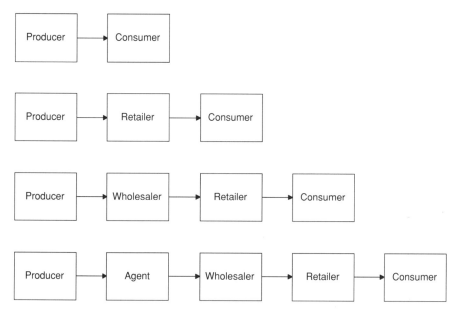

Figure 12.3 Basic models of distribution channel

It follows that any distribution decision involves a trade-off or compromise. A producer will obviously want to increase its market exposure, but in doing so, it must accept that its products will eventually be sold at prices that reflect the profit margins of each stage in the channel.

Question 12.6

Some manufacturers of personal computers (PCs) sell their goods through the major national electrical retailers (e.g. in Dixon's). Others advertise in the national press and invite customers to order equipment directly from the manufacturer via a mail order arrangement.

Suggest a rationale for both of these two approaches.

12.5 Promoting the product

Once the product has been designed, priced and the target market segment identified, marketing turns its attention to promoting the product to the market segment.

Promotions are more correctly called *marketing communications*, because it is concerned with communicating the benefits of the product to the segment in question.

There are four commonly used techniques or vehicles for marketing communications:

- above-the-line promotions;
- below-the-line promotions;
- direct selling;
- public relations, press and community involvement.

Above-the-line promotions

The term 'above-the-line' is a marketing jargon term for promotions using various types of media advertising. A business takes advantage of several media upon which to communicate its marketing messages. The one chosen will depend upon the nature of the product, target segment, budget available, etc. The most commonly used formats are as follows:

- commercial television;
- commercial radio;
- magazines and newspapers;
- buses and other transport;
- posters;
- leaflets and handouts.

The need to gain optimum exposure to a target segment means that advertising campaigns tend to be carefully planned within budget constraints. The different media available also each have distinctive pros and cons. Whilst TV exposure offers the opportunity to convey a complex message owing to the ability to combine images and speech, it is the most expensive. Other media, such as posters and press are much cheaper, but only allow for a simple message, possibly only a single picture and a slogan.

The choice of media will partly depend upon the type of product. It would be inappropriate, for example, for industrial products to be promoted on TV, but it would make sense to promote such products in the specialist industrial press, where a highly targeted readership could be addressed. Advertising specialists work upon the assumption that certain TV programmes, radio stations, papers and magazines attract different demographic profiles.

Question 12.7

Try to describe the demographic profile that would be most likely to watch, listen or read the following. Use the market segmentation demographic variables to describe each one (e.g. the readership of *Mother and Baby* might be: sex, female; socio-economic group, ABC1; age, 20–40 years; stage of family life cycle, married with young children). Some productions may have a highly specific audience (e.g. the profile for *Church Times* would include the description Christian' or 'Church-goer').

- Blind Date.
- Channel 4 News.
- Children's ITV programmes.
- Classic FM (radio station).
- Virgin 1215 (radio station).
- *The Sunday Sport.*
- *The Financial Times.*
- *Motor Cycle News.*

For each one, suggest a product that might be successfully advertised in it (i.e. one which is aimed at the profile in question).

The message conveyed will also vary according to product and target segment. Consumer product promotions may contain an element of emotional appeal whilst industrial products such as chemicals will tend simply to communicate their technical specification (because this is what the buyer cares about). Promotional communication messages are designed to convey the product's benefits to the target segment. This task is made easier if the product is in some way differentiated from its competitors. If it has a *unique selling proposition* (USP) and can be readily distinguished from others, then it makes sense to centre the marketing message around the unique features.

There is an interesting recent history of the use of innovative messages and ideas in advertising. Cigarette manufacturers, who must abide by strict guidelines in their advertising have used the restrictions to their advantage. Readers may remember the 'Reg' campaign for Embassy Regal, or the ongoing images used in Silk Cut press and poster adverts. A successful and memorable symbol or slogan can embed the brand image into consumers' consciousness – a very valuable asset in maintaining and increasing market share.

Question 12.8

How successful is television advertising? Test your recall.
Which companies or brands are associated with the following slogans:

- The listening bank.
- The bank that likes to say 'yes'.
- The appliance of science.
- Helps you work, rest and play.
- The car in front.
- It's good to talk.
- Drives the imagination.
- The power to hit pain where it hurts.

Below-the-line promotions

Below-the-line promotions are marketing communications which do not use the media. The fact that they can be very highly targeted means that they have grown in importance over recent years, such that in some sectors below-the-line expenditure exceeds above-the-line spending. The nature of this type of promotion means that it is especially suited to activity in the consumer goods retail sector, although it can also be used for industrial products.

As a category, below-the-line promotions can be conveniently divided into two types.

- *push promotions* are incentives for salespeople to increase their sales of products;
- *pull promotions* are those which encourage customers to increase their weight of purchase.

Unlike above-the-line promotions, which tend by their nature to be relatively unfocused, below-the-line communications can be very closely targeted to gain a high exposure to the target market segment. Efforts can be focused on a single product or market at relatively modest cost.

Push promotions can be centred upon one product which a business particularly wishes to promote or they can apply generally. Examples include:

- commission on sales for sales staff;
- increases in dealer margins (i.e. price reductions to distributors);
- trade or shop demonstrations or exhibitions;
- 'best salesperson of the year' award.

Pull promotions include:

- short-term price decreases (e.g. a *loss leader* – a price reduction on a selected item designed to get customers 'through the door' in the belief that additional sales will recoup the profit reduction in the loss leader);
- more favourable credit terms (e.g. lower interest rates, longer credit periods or both);
- 'buy one get one free' offers;
- coupons and trading stamps;
- improved guarantees (e.g. extended guarantees – some car companies offer up to three years 'free' servicing);
- point-of-sale displays (features in a shop designed to attract customers' attention);
- checkout savers (where the 'ringing through' of one item through a supermarket till will automatically trigger a money-off voucher for a direct competitor brand – paid for by the competitor).

Pull promotions assume great importance in some sectors. A notable example is petrol retailing, where competitors are expected by customers to offer a range of vouchers, etc. Customers may remain brand loyal to a particular brand purely because of a below-the-line promotion.

Direct selling

Direct selling, in most instances, is the most closely targeted marketing promotion. Sales representatives and salespeople in shops generally do not find themselves discussing the benefits of a product unless the potential customer has at least a reasonable interest in buying it.

The way in which a company carries out direct selling again depends upon the nature of the product and the characteristics of the customer. Typical formats used include:

- retail outlets employing salespeople as opposed to checkouts (e.g. for electrical goods, motor cars);
- trade counters and factory shops;
- showrooms and warehouses;
- travelling sales representatives (reps) – usually involved in the sale of industrial goods;
- telephone sales (the practice of telephoning potential customers of a certain product, often by the use of an ACORN-based segmentation).

The thing which all direct-selling approaches have in common is that they involve person-to-person communication. This affords the business the opportunity to understand closely the needs and motivations of the customer and to fashion the sales presentation accordingly.

Public relations and community involvement (PR)

Public relations is marketing communication which is usually geared primarily to cultivate a favourable impression of the organization, rather than a product, in the eyes of its various stakeholders (see Chapter 2). In consequence, PR tends to be less focused than other forms of marketing communication. An organization may have many reasons to enhance its public perception. Common motivations include:

- to stimulate investors' interest in the company's shares;
- to enhance the organization's reputation for quality, service, etc.;
- to answer criticism or scepticism about certain commercial activities;
- to enhance the organization's reputation as a good employer in order to encourage good people to apply for jobs;
- to make the organization appear to be caring, environmentally responsible, etc.

Organizations use several vehicles for PR:

- 'open days', where stakeholders are invited to visit and see the organization in action;
- press and PR departments, where staff are happy to answer queries from any interested stakeholders;
- press statements – items written by the company for publication in newspapers, etc.;
- 'roadshows' such as visits to local schools, exhibitions at conferences, etc.;
- videos issued to stakeholder groups;

- sponsorship of sports events, football teams, etc.;
- charitable donations and sponsorship of community projects;
- visitor centres, where interested people can come and learn about company activities (such as the elaborate visitor centre at the Sellafield nuclear reprocessing centre in Cumbria).

Public and community relations: Scottish & Newcastle plc (S&N)

Scottish and Newcastle plc is Britain's biggest brewer. Based in Edinburgh, it has a broadly based business portfolio including brewing, retailing and leisure interests. It follows from the breadth of markets served that maintaining a high profile of both the company and its products will be beneficial in supporting its advertising and in cultivating a favourable image of the company and its products.

Accordingly, S&N has developed a range of ways of contributing to the broader community, some of which are ostensibly benevolent, while others are more likely aimed at enhancing product exposure while at the same time helping to develop the organizations who have received S&N PR funding. Community involvement at S&N is centred around three areas.

Firstly, the company, through its beer division (Scottish Courage) is involved in the *sponsorship* of sport and the arts. It has sponsorship deals with five soccer teams: Blackburn Rovers, Newcastle United, Chelsea, Glasgow Rangers and Northern Ireland, each of which wears shirts depicting an S&N brand on the front. The brand shown may vary from season to season. The 1994–95 football season was a particularly good one for S&N, with both Glasgow Rangers and Blackburn Rovers winning their respective championships – and both showing the words 'McEwan's lager' on their shirts. Other sporting activities sponsored include golf, cricket, rugby union and league, horse racing and formula one motor racing. Arts sponsorship has traditionally been broadly based, including such events as The Beck's Art Programme, The Edinburgh International Festival, ABSA Scotland and the Tyne Theatre and Opera Trust.

Secondly, the company often sets aside some funds for *charitable donation*. In the year to 1995, S&N donated £375 000 to over 500 organizations, whilst many individual pubs organized their own fund-raising events for local charitable concerns.

Thirdly, the group attempts to take a positive role in the area of *environmental issues* – matters of concern to many of the company's stakeholders. Internally, S&N has a group-wide environmental advisory council that meets to address the environmental impact of the company's activities, while externally, S&N has funded a Chair (professorship) of the Environment at the Glasgow Caledonian University.

Assignment

Connelly's rest homes is a company engaged in the long-term care of elderly citizens. The chief executive, Jimmy Connelly is a qualified nurse with a business degree who opened his first home in a converted large house in 1970. Since then, Connelly's has opened 23 'nursing homes' in towns along the south coast of England. Jimmy argues that his services are used by 'senior professionals who have worked hard all their lives and who want to relax and be well cared for in their late retirement. We tend not to attract people of more modest means because the service we provide is of an exceptionally high standard with a very high nurse to resident ratio. We provide a comprehensive service to guests who are no longer able to cope on their own at home by offering them comfort and privacy whilst at the same time providing round the clock medical and domestic assistance. There are no "rules" like some other homes impose. Guests can come and go as they please, have visitors whenever they like and partake in a wide range of interesting activities. We recently, for example, started a monthly malt whisky appreciation meeting in each of our homes and we run day-trips to local race courses and other venues.'

After inspecting the HMSO's projections for the numbers of elderly people over the next thirty years, Jimmy has decided to expand his business with the purchase and conversion of another ten homes over the next few years with the first of the new homes to open in five years time. His early thoughts on the locations of the new developments include ideas about opening homes in more attractive towns outside the south east such as Bath, Harrogate and, possibly semi-rural Derbyshire.

Questions

- Explain the core and premium features of the product that a senior citizens' care business like Connelly's provides.
- Explain the purpose of the premium price that Connelly's charges for its services.
- Given that Connelly's will welcome the first guests into its new homes in five years' time, define the market segment limits that should form the basis of any proposed marketing promotions.
- Discuss the range of options that Jimmy could consider in seeking to promote his new homes to prospective guests. What might be the content of such promotions?

Further reading

Adcock, D., Bradfield, R., Halborg, A. and Ross, C. (1995) *Marketing. Principles and Practice*. 2nd edn. London: Pitman.

Baker, M. J. (1995) Marketing: Theory and Practice, 3rd edn. London: Macmillan.

Baker, M. J. (1996) *Marketing: An Introductory Text*, 6th edn. London: Macmillan.

Christopher, M. and McDonald, M. (1995) *Marketing – An Introductory Text*. London: Macmillan.

Dodge, R. and Hanna, N. (1995) *Pricing. Policies and Procedures*. London: Macmillan.

Fletcher, A. C. and Jones, N. (1996) *Value Pricing. How to Price Products and Services*. London: Kogan Page.

Hart, N. (ed.) (1995) *Strategic Public Relations*. London: Macmillan.

Hutchings, A. (1995) *Marketing. A Resource Book*. London: Pitman.

Kinnear, T. C., Bernhardt, K. I. and Krentler, K. A. (1995) *Principles of Marketing*, 4th edn. London: Harper Collins.

Lancaster, G. A. and Reynolds, P. (1995) *Marketing*. Oxford: Butterworth-Heinemann.

Lancaster, G. and Massingham, L. (1993). *Essentials of Marketing*. 2nd edn. New York: McGraw Hill.

McDonald, M. (1995) *Market Segmentation*. London: Macmillan.

Morden, A. R. (1993) *Elements of Marketing*, 3rd edn. London: DP Publications.

O'Brien, E., Cooper, M. J. and Madden, C. (1995) *Introduction to Marketing. International Edition*. Harper Collins.

Smith, R. (1995) *Essential Elements of Marketing*. London: DP Publications.

Stokes, D. (1994) *Discovering Marketing*. London: DP Publications.

Stone, N. (1995) *The Management and Practice of Public Relations*. London: Macmillan.

13

People, personnel and employee issues

Learning objectives

After studying this chapter, students should be able to describe:

- Why human resources are important to organizations.
- The differences between personnel management, personnel policies and the personnel department.
- What the personnel (or human resources) department typically does in an organization.
- The essentials of 'good practice' in key personnel tasks, especially appointments, training and development and rewarding employees.
- The differences between the 'personnel' and the 'human resources' schools of thought.
- The features of the two 'sides' of the employee – employer relationship with a focus on trade unions.
- The major theories of human motivation.

13.1 The importance of human resources in organizations

People are one of the key inputs into organizations. The input provided by people to organizations constitutes one of the *factors of production*, along with capital, land and the physical inputs of stock and equipment. Factors of production are those inputs that are needed to make an organization productive, i.e. to enable it to maintain a normal level of performance.

There is, however, a uniqueness about the human factor of production – unlike the other inputs, people think and have a mind of their own. They are able to make their own decisions, to withhold their input, to argue and disagree and to make costly mistakes. Of course, it is equally true that this factor of production is also able to make a unique contribution to an organization's success by generating ideas, by working productively, by managing others and by contributing intellectual and creative power for the benefit of the organization.

It is a simple fact that all organizations need people. It is an organization's human resources that are the key to added value (the adding of value to goods and services as they are produced). People design the processes and attend work environments in which stocks are increased in value by a process of transformation. Without this resource, or with an insufficient level of it, an organization could not make the most productive use of its other factors of production.

As with the other organizational inputs, human resources cost money. It follows from this that an organization has a need to make a return on its outlay. This need is the nub of personnel management – to extract the optimum productivity from its investment in human resources. Apart from those organizations which exist primarily for the benefit of their members (such as Handy's person cultures – see Chapter 7), all organizations use their human resources for productive purposes. All the areas we will consider in this chapter are designed to maximize human productivity for the organization. It is a happy coincidence if this also entails satisfaction and fulfilment for the human resources themselves.

13.2 The 'personnel' function

Unlike some other functions, 'personnel' work takes place throughout an organization, not just within a specific department. In one sense, every manager who has subordinate staff has a personnel role to his or her job, inasmuch as managing people is a part of it. In addition, though, many organizations have a separate personnel department which contains people who are specialists in this function.

We have therefore encountered two key concepts:

- *Personnel management* is the management of people in their jobs and is carried out by line managers throughout the organization.
- The *personnel department* or personnel function is a function in an organization which contains specialists in all matters of personnel management. It performs a supporting role to line managers in their jobs, advising them and helping to administer matters like appointments, training and reward systems.

Both personnel management and the personnel function are concerned with *personnel policies*. These are statements of the manner in which personnel affairs in the organization will be conducted. Designed to ensure that employees are treated and dealt with equally and fairly, personnel policies apply uniformly throughout all parts of the organization. Typically, organizations will have a personnel policy to cover each part of the job of personnel management.

Personnel policies – the University of Northumbria at Newcastle (UNN)

The University of Northumbria is not unlike any other large organization. It has a personnel policy to cover each area of the personnel process. They are strictly applied to ensure fairness and equality. Examples include policies on:

- recruitment and selection of new staff;
- equal opportunities;
- health and safety;
- staff training and development;
- staff disciplinary procedures;
- trade union recognition;
- disputes and grievance procedures;
- redundancy and redeployment.

The actual work that is undertaken by the personnel department falls into two categories. Some work is concerned with *administering* the day-to-day functioning of the business, that is, the maintenance of 'good order' in relation to 'people' activities. This category includes issues such as salaries, routine problems, advising managers and negotiating with trade unions. Other work in the personnel department is more *strategic* in nature. Included in this category are any activities involved in preparing for the future such as recruitment, selection, training and development.

13.3 What does the personnel department do?

Given that we now know what personnel management is, we now ask what the personnel department itself actually does. It goes without saying that personnel departments vary from organization to organization. Some organizations have large and elaborate personnel functions, whilst others have no such function at all (where personnel management jobs are entirely carried out by line managers). We can consider the work carried out by the department by looking at the 'passage' of an employee through the organization – from when the vacancy is identified to when the employee finally leaves. The personnel department is therefore involved, to a greater or lesser degree (depending upon the organization in question), with the following activities:

- identification of a vacancy;
- job analysis;
- job description;
- person specification;
- recruitment;
- selection;
- induction;
- training and development;
- relocation and redeployment;
- termination of employment (by means of resignation, retirement, redundancy, dismissal or death).

The range of tasks required of the personnel function means that the senior staff in the department are specially qualified for the job. The Institute of Personnel and Development (IPD) is a qualifying body to which many personnel professionals are associated. The personnel director or personnel manager who heads the department will typically either be qualified by the IPD or will be qualified 'by experience'. Either way, the range of manpower activities into which he or she will have an input makes the jobholder a highly influential person in the success or failure of the organization.

13.4 'Best practice' in the appointments process

The importance of appointments

Appointing new people to work in an organization is perhaps the most important part of the personnel function's role. This is for four reasons:

- because the right person can make a strong positive effect on the organization;
- because appointing the wrong person can be potentially devastating for the organization;
- because it can be very difficult to 'get rid' of a less than perfect employee once he or she has been engaged;
- because a new employee may stay with the organization for as long as fifty years.

The case of Baring's Bank is an example of an unfortunate appointment. A single employee (Nick Leeson), whom presumably the management would regret appointing, caused the entire organization to fail. Conversely, the transfer of a key football player from one club to another can be an example of a particularly favourable appointment, especially if he is of the standard of Alan Shearer, Les Ferdinand or Robbie Fowler. Similarly, the scientists who devised the formulations for the best-selling prescription pharmaceuticals were clearly particularly important and favourable appointments.

The stages in the appointments process

The general procedure followed in an appointment is as follows:

Identification of vacancy
↓
Job analysis
↓
Job description
↓
Person specification
↓
Recruitment
↓
Selection

Identification of a vacancy
The process of appointing a new employee to an organization begins with the identification of a vacancy that must be filled. There are a number of ways in which vacancies are identified.

- *Replacement* of staff that have left the organization.

- *Organic growth* that requires extra employees to cope with expansion.
- Particular staff or *skill shortages* in a department or function (e.g. a company may decide to appoint an advertising specialist, a gardener, a specialist in a particular computer package).
- Some appointments are made on the basis on *ratios*. Academic staff in a university faculty are typically appointed on an approximately ratio-based approach. Most staff members are required to teach a specific number of hours, so the number of staff is arrived at by dividing the total number of lecture hours in the faculty by the required lecturing load of each staff member.

Job analysis and job description

Once it has been established that a vacancy exists, the personnel department is responsible for carrying out a job analysis. When the job is analysed, the personnel specialist is concerned with examining the tasks involved in performing the job. This sometimes involves a procedure called *work study* – the examination of a job to establish the tasks involved, the hours required and the best place (in the structure) to perform the job within the organization.

Once the job has been analysed, the next step is to generate a job description. This is the outcome of the job analysis. The job description is a document which (obviously) describes the various facets of and tasks involved in the job in question. It may begin with the words, 'this job involves …'

Typical areas covered by the job description include:

- a summary of the duties involved in the job;
- where the job fits in to the organization's structure;
- the responsibilities and authority of the job;
- the expected hours of work.

Person specification

Following the issue of a job description, the personnel specialist will use it as the basis for a *person specification*. The person specification is a document listing the qualities, skills and characteristics of the ideal person to carry out the duties listed in the job description. It is thus important that the person for a job is not under- or overspecified. Underspecification will result in the appointment of a person who may not be competent in all aspects of the job. Overspecification will result in the appointment of a person who is overqualified and who may become bored or disillusioned in a short period of time. It is clear, then, that person specifications vary enormously – compare the different skills that might comprise the person specifications for a factory's cleaner or its operations manager.

The person specification is thus a person *descriptor* which uses factors to distinguish and discriminate between types of people. It may include a description of the ideal person according to:

- age – minimum and maximum (e.g. 'the ideal candidate will be aged between 25 and 32');
- experience – the type and length of experience;
- qualifications – anything from 'no formal education required,' to 'a doctoral degree in organic chemistry is essential';

- personal attributes – intelligence, ambition, interpersonal skills, appearance, etc.;
- special abilities unique to the job – ability to speak foreign languages, aptitudes in special areas such as dexterity, art, computer literacy, etc.

(*Note*: It is illegal, in most cases, to discriminate on the grounds of sex or race – see Chapter 22).

The information contained in a person specification is typically divided into two categories:

- criteria which are *essential* for any appointee to the job;
- criteria which, whilst not being essential, are nevertheless *desirable*.

It follows that the successful candidate will be in possession of all of the essential requirements, but the organization may have to settle for a person who possesses only some of the desirable criteria. If the field of applicants contains nobody with the essential criteria, it is unlikely that the organization will make the appointment at all (it may then be re-advertised).

Job description and person specification – a University of Northumbria lecturer in business

Job description
Appointees to the position of lecturer will be required to undertake any of the duties below.

- All forms of pedagogic [teaching] work including classroom teaching, tutorial work, together with associated administrative work.
- Student counselling and pastoral care activities.
- Curriculum development, including the planning and development of new courses.
- Staff development, including participation in staff appraisal.
- Research and consultancy.
- Management and administration of courses.

Person specification
- Possession of a degree and preferably postgraduate qualifications.
- Ability to teach effectively on academic and professional courses.
- Ability to contribute to course management.
- Ability to work as a member of a team.
- Potential for successful research.
- Interest in furthering his/her personal development both as a teacher and as a subject specialist.
- Possession of relevant experience in business/commerce, the public sector or professional practice.

Question 13.1

Attempt to generate person specifications for the following jobs. Divide the contents of your specification into essential and desirable criteria.

- Financial director.
- Consultant surgeon.
- Bricklayer.
- Pregnancy counsellor.

Recruitment and selection (R&S)

Once the person specification has been finalized, the personnel function turns its attention to finding and appointing an appropriate person to the post. This involves two further stages: recruitment and selection.

Recruitment is the process by which an organization generates a pool of applicants for a vacancy. At this stage of the process, the organization is seeking to generate the largest possible number of suitable applicants to give itself the widest possible choice. The need to attract applicants is usually reflected in the personnel policies on personnel recruitment. Such policies may, for example, state that:

- all vacancies will be advertised in the appropriate press media;
- all vacancies will be advertised internally;
- the company operates an equal opportunities policy;
- the company encourages applications from all sectors of the community.

The means by which organizations attract applicants are many and varied. The channel chosen will depend upon the nature of the vacancy, and the media can be segmented for jobs in the same way as it can for marketing promotions. For senior positions, it is likely that the organization will decide to advertise in the national newspapers, whereas specialists tend to be attracted through their own specialist press (e.g. *Accountancy Age, Chemistry in Britain, The Engineer*). Jobs requiring a less specific level of skill or expertise are more likely to be advertised through Jobcentres or the local press. For particularly important positions, organizations sometimes employ *recruitment consultants*. These are private businesses with expertise in seeking out and attracting applications from appropriate people, and then interviewing them in accordance with the organization's person specification before sending a short-list to the company for selection.

Because the purpose of recruitment is to attract applicants, job adverts tend to take the form of 'selling' the organization to its potential applicants. For senior positions, job adverts attempt to attract high calibre applicants by using 'attractive' statements. Some examples follow (all quoted verbatim from *The Sunday Times*, 12 May 1996):

- AT&T is the leading telecommunications company in the world. In the UK, our goal is to be a premium telecommunications services provider ….
- As worldwide market leader, Bespak supplies major international pharmaceutical companies with the latest technology in drug delivery systems … You will be

responsible for the current and future business growth ....

- Orange is one of the best known mobile phone networks in the UK. We're also the fastest growing, with our expansion based on dynamic branding, innovative products and an emphasis on value for money.
- Acclaimed for its world-class standards and dynamic approach, this progressive international high technology company, with a solid financial base, is confident of continuing its expansion.

Once the pool of applicants has been generated, applications are filtered according to the criteria of the person specification. This 'whittling down' process results in a *short-list* of the few applicants who best match the essential and desirable criteria in the person specification. Note that the short-list does not contain the best people as such, but the people who best match the person specification. Once the short-list has been generated, the unsuccessful applicants are rejected and the short-list goes forward to the selection stage.

Selection is the process that takes the short-list generated by the recruitment stage and from it selects the single person who most closely matches the person specification. Picking out the best person from the short-list involves the use of a range of selection techniques. The selection techniques chosen will depend upon the nature of the appointment and the nature of the skills and aptitudes stated on the person specification.

Common selection techniques include:

- interviews;
- the examination of application forms and curriculum vitaes (CVs);
- presentations or skill demonstrations by applicants;
- psychometric testing (the testing of personality, intelligence, team-working ability, etc., by means of complex written tests);
- observation of applicants' manner, appearance, demeanour, confidence in social situations, etc.;
- 'assessment centre' activities (the testing of applicants in intensive situations in which candidates can undertake a range of social, skill and psychometric tests relevant to the job).

Because of the diversity of criteria on the person specification, most selections involve more than one of these techniques. For matters of qualifications and experience, an examination of an application form or a CV will usually suffice. For testing aptitudes and competencies, it is common to ask candidates to demonstrate the skills to the selectors. Secretaries, for example, are often required to perform typing demonstrations to show their speed and accuracy of typing or their command of word-processing packages. Applicants to the position of university lecturer are often required to give a brief lecture as part of their selection to demonstrate their competence in coherent 'public' speaking.

Once the selection process has been completed, the selectors will have narrowed the short-list down to the one candidate who most closely matches the person specification. It is then the task of the personnel manager to persuade (in some cases) the most suitable candidate to accept the offer of a job. This is not as straightforward as it might appear. The fact that a candidate has applied and undergone selection for a job does not necessarily mean that he or she will accept the offer. The personnel function must design an appropriate rewards package that will swing the individual in favour of accepting the offer. Failure to persuade the successful candidate to accept may require going to the candidate who is the second closest to the person specification, and this may involve some degree of compromise on such things as the desirable criteria.

The R&S process – the University of Northumbria

The UNN employs around 2200 individuals and is therefore a relatively large employer. Any organization of this size will necessarily have a turnover of staff requiring a more-or-less ongoing need to appoint new staff members. In consequence, the university's personnel department is well practised in all aspects of recruitment and selection. In its recruitment documentation, the university states its aim in recruitment and selection is to 'attract highly qualified and highly motivated teachers, administrators and service staff'.

The procedure followed arises from the personnel policy that is relevant to the task. The stages are as follows:

- identification of vacancy;
- job description is drawn up;
- person specification is generated from job description;
- decision on where to place advertisement for the vacancy;
- advertisement is written/designed;
- advertisement appears in relevant newspaper/magazine;
- applicants respond to advertisement;
- short-list is made up from applicants;
- short-list candidates are called for interview;
- interview using a range of selection techniques, depending upon nature of appointment;
- verbal offer is made and this is accepted or declined;
- health check on successful candidate;
- references are checked;
- formal letter of offer is sent (returned by successful candidate);
- new employee starts work.

13.5 Induction, training and development

Once the successful applicant has been appointed, he or she joins the organization as a new member of staff. Individuals who are thus 'locked in' may then undergo procedures, overseen by the personnel function, to improve performance at work and make the employee better at serving the organization's needs. One of these procedures takes place when the employee joins the organization and the others can take place at any time during the employee's service.

Induction

Induction is the process whereby a new employee is welcomed and acclimatized into the organization. The complexity of the induction process varies greatly from organization to organization. Larger organizations tend to have more elaborate induction procedures than smaller ones who frequently have no formal induction at all. The issues covered in induction include:

- 'welcome' to the organization;
- meeting new colleagues and finding out 'who does what';
- learning about the organization's history and culture;
- learning where things are located such as canteens, different departments, etc.;
- 'any questions' to managers about the organization;
- explanations of company policy on such things as health and safety, fire procedures, grievances, etc.;
- initial training and brief.

Training and development

These two activities are quite different in nature but share the same essential objective, i.e. to improve an employee's performance at work. Both can be undertaken either 'on-the-job' or 'off-the-job.' The requirements for an employee's training and development are arrived at by the training and development 'equation':

> Training and development needs =
> What the employee needs to do the job (including any future needs) minus what the employee can do now.

Training and development needs are often arrived at during an *appraisal*. Some organizations have formalized appraisals in their personnel policies and these typically take place annually. During an appraisal, the employee meets with his or her immediate line manager and the two parties discuss the employee's performance in the job, together with any problems and ideas that either party has for improvement. Appraisals are usually designed to be open and 'stress-free' occasions where the manager can discuss the employee's short-comings as well as giving due credit and praise where appropriate. The terms can be defined as follows.

Training is the instruction of employees in specific techniques that are used in the working environment. For example, employees may be trained:

- to use a piece of equipment such as a new lathe or similar machine tool;
- to operate a new computer application such as a word-processing package;
- how to escape in the event of fire or how to use a fire extinguisher;
- how to chair a meeting;
- how to engage in public speaking;
- how to 'close' a sale (for salespeople);
- in improving telephone technique, etc.

Development is an attempt to improve the person as a whole rather than just the employee's individual skills. It follows that development programmes are intended to broaden and deepen an employee's ability to cope with a wider range of working situations. The approach taken to develop staff is different from the approach taken in training. Examples include:

- educational development by allowing staff to attend day-release classes or by secondment to attend universities or colleges (e.g. to undertake BTECs, HNDs or degrees);
- management development by sending staff on postgraduate degrees such as MBAs;
- mentoring – the practice of a junior employee being 'taken under the wing' of a more senior and experienced colleague;
- job rotation to enable staff to gain from a broader experience of working environments;
- conference attendance for specialist staff to exchange ideas with peers from outside the organization.

Advantages of training and development
Organizations tend to view training and development in a similar way to any other investments. Both training and development cost money, whether it is by giving staff time off work, course fees, or accepting a longer learning curve by such things as staff rotation. It follows that the organization expects a return on its investment. Some of the returns are readily quantifiable in financial terms, but the majority are not. Benefits include:

- a more highly skilled workforce;
- increased competence in the working environment;
- higher productivity;
- greater staff confidence in their work;
- the possibility of higher staff morale if staff appreciate that the organization values them sufficiently to invest in their improvement;
- the possibility of lower staff turnover and greater staff loyalty as a result of the potentially higher staff morale;
- lower waste and higher quality;
- a more flexible workforce that is more able to accept change;
- a workforce that is more culturally homogeneous (i.e. one that thinks and 'does things' in a similar way).

13.6 Human resources and rewards

Since the abolition of slavery, an important consideration of personnel management has been the concept of reward or compensation. A key feature of the labour market is that suppliers of labour (employees) *sell* their labour to buyers of labour (employers). The process of selling necessarily involves an exchange. In exchange for the supply of labour, the buyer (the employer) provides a number of rewards to the employees.

Types of reward

A reward can be defined as *any form of gratification that an employee gains from his or her employment with an employer*. With such a broad definition, we would rightly expect there to be a wide range of rewards that organizations can use. There are two broad categories of reward: intrinsic and extrinsic.

Intrinsic rewards are those that arise from the nature of the job and of actually *doing* the job. Intrinsic rewards include:

- job satisfaction;
- working conditions;
- social relationships at work;
- job security;
- recognition and appreciation at work.

Extrinsic rewards are rewards that are tangible or that can be enjoyed outside of the work environment. Examples include:

- pay or salary;
- fringe benefits (e.g. company car, company pension, health insurance);
- holiday entitlements;
- commission on sales or productivity bonuses;
- status and social standing as a result of holding the job or the specific job title (e.g. 'And what do you do?' 'I'm a doctor', or, 'I work for BT').

The purposes of reward

There are a number of purposes of rewards, Examples include:

- to reward and recognize different levels of performance;
- to recognize seniority and 'wisdom';
- to motivate;
- to reduce dissatisfaction and disquiet in the workplace;
- to retain staff and prevent them from seeking employment elsewhere;
- to maintain and encourage employee loyalty;
- to attract staff into the organization.

13.7 'Personnel' and 'human resources'

There has, over recent years, been something of a debate with some resultant development of thought within the 'people' area of business. At the centre of the debate is the view that the organization takes of its employees. According to proponents of the newer 'human resources' (HR) ideology, traditional personnel management took the view that employees were a cost to the organization. Like all costs, cash spent on the recruitment, reward and development of employees should thus be kept to a minimum. In contrast, human resources theory views employees as key organizational inputs or *resources*. Accordingly, employees, like all other resources (e.g. financial, plant and equipment) should be cultivated, invested in and improved.

Although the above view of 'old' personnel management is something of a caricature (i.e. it isn't as bad as some HR theorists suggest), there have been a number of changes in the way that people are managed in the workplace. The changes are driven by the underlying conviction that employees are a vital resource rather than an inconvenient cost. It is important to understand, therefore, that human resources management (HRM) is a *philosophy* rather than a *style* of management.

The 'infection' of modern organizations with HR ideas has signalled the introduction of a number or practices such as involving employees in decision making, increased staff development and a heightened sense of employees' 'comfort' at work. These changes do not, by themselves, mean that an organization has adopted HRM. Most writers in this area contend that the adoption of HRM involves a change in the culture of the entire organization – rather more than a simple change in practice.

The differences between 'old' personnel and 'new' HRM are, albeit with some inevitable stereotyping, described in Table 13.1.

Table 13.1 Comparison of 'personnel' and HRM

'Old' personnel management	*'New' HRM*
Employees are treated as *collectives*. This means that negotiations take place between management and unions on an adversarial (enemies) basis. In other words, a culture that espouses collective bargaining or *industrial relations*	Employees are treated as *individuals*. Negotiations therefore are carried out on an individual rather than collectivist basis: *employee relations* – a non-adversarial co-operative approach. Trade union membership is not necessarily discouraged, but the emphasis is nevertheless upon individuals
The administration of employees is *marginalized and segregated* into one of the organization's functions (the personnel department). The personnel manager is informed of strategic decisions but has no part in making them	The administration of employees is devolved from the HR department to *empower line managers*. The head of HR is involved in all strategic decision-making and will usually be on the board of directors. HR comes 'from the top'
Personnel work is *largely routine* and does not necessarily tie in with the broader mission or strategy of the organization	HRM is totally dedicated to enabling the organization achieve its overall strategy or mission. All activities are designed to facilitate the *accomplishment of strategic objectives*
Personnel management is a *set of administrative techniques* that can be used in any corporate culture whether they 'fit' the culture or not	HRM is *adaptable* according the culture in which it exists. Furthermore, HRM depends for its success on a 'conducive' and appropriate corporate culture
Reactive in nature in that personnel activity takes place in response to other factors	*Proactive* in nature in that it takes place in the context of an organization's long-term strategy

Many organizations have espoused HRM, but to varying degrees. Some organizations have implemented HRM in full, accompanied by a significant change in corporate culture. Others have, perhaps a little cynically, merely changed the name of their personnel department to the human resource department. To a certain extent, HRM is fashionable, but its full implementation has proved to be problematic in many cases.

13.8 Employer–employee relations

The two 'sides'

The two 'sides' of the employment system (employers and employees) interrelate with each other in the work environment. In most situations, they are in agreement (i.e. they work together), but on occasions the two can be in conflict. Such conflicts arise due to the two sides seeking essentially different objectives in the working environment:

- employers aim to extract the maximum amount of useful labour from the employees at the minimum reasonable cost to the organization (this is not to say that the employer wishes to exploit labour, but rather that it wants to obtain value for money from it);
- employees aim to achieve security of employment together with rewards commensurate with an acceptable standard of living.

Because of the nature of the relationship, it is generally assumed that the employer is the most powerful 'side'. Individual employees have little influence over the terms and conditions under which they work for an employer; so, in order to further their aims with respect to employers, employees sometimes organize themselves into collectives called unions or trade unions.

Types of trade union

A trade union (in the UK) is defined by the Trade Union and Labour Relations Act, 1974 as an organization whose principal purpose is the regulation of relations between union members and their employers (the definition of a trade union was narrowed further by The Trade Union and Labour Relations (Consolidation) Act, 1992). They are financed entirely by the contributions of their members (to ensure that they exist only for the benefit of the membership) and must submit annual accounts in a similar way to limited companies.

There are six broad types of union:

- *Craft unions* are unions whose membership comprises specialists in a particular craft or skill. To join, one must have served an apprenticeship or have other recognized training in the craft. An example of a craft union is the Amalgamated Engineering and Electrical Union (AEEU), which represents engineers and electrical workers across a wide variety of industries.
- *General unions* do not require any qualifications for membership. Members can consequently be skilled, semi-skilled or unskilled. The Transport and General Workers

Union (the TGWU or T&G) is a general union and is the largest of all trade unions in terms of membership.

- *Industrial unions* comprise members from specific industries only. Within the industry, members can be drawn from all levels of employee from unskilled workers through to managers. Examples of industrial unions include the National Union of Mineworkers (NUM), which represents all types of employees in the mining industry, and the Civil and Public Service Association (CPSA), which represents public-sector employees.
- *White-collar unions* represent exclusively staff, clerical and professional workers. Manual workers are consequently excluded from membership. Many university lecturers are members of the National Association of Teachers in Further and Higher Education (NATFHE) – an example of a staff union.
- *Company unions* are rare in the UK but more common in other parts of the world, such as the USA. A company union is formed when the employees of a specific employer organize themselves into a union to increase their bargaining power over the employer.
- *Professional associations* are the final type of workers' collective. In most cases, professional associations would not describe themselves as trade unions, but they are unions in that they occasionally represent their members with employers and provide representation (see later for a discussion of this) as necessary. Examples of professional associations include the British Medical Association, the Royal Society of Chemistry and the Inns of Court, which represent barristers.

Why do employees form and join unions?

The simple fact that union membership requires the payment of a subscription means that members will naturally expect some benefits in return. The benefits of membership arise from two angles.

Firstly, members benefit from the *collective action* of the union. The fact that members are organized into a single collective increases the employees' ability to influence the employer in their favour (in comparison with the weak bargaining power of a single employee). The commonest form of collective action is *collective bargaining*. This is the practice of the union negotiating contract terms (such as pay rises) with the employer on behalf of all members of the union.

Secondly, members benefit from *union representation*. This includes such things as legal representation by the union solicitor in the event of unfortunate occurrences such as an industrial injury or an employer's claim against a member for improper conduct at work.

Forms of union action

Employees, by acting together under their trade union, can increase the power of their case against an employer. They do this by using a number of 'weapons' or forms of *industrial action*. Such measures may be used (usually after a ballot) when the union membership feels it has a legitimate case against the employer, such as when a desired level of wage increase has not been forthcoming or when the employer has imposed adverse changes to the work environment.

The most radical form of action is the *strike*. This involves two things:

- A withdrawal of labour for a period of time, thus causing gross inconvenience to the employer.
- The picketing of the employer's premises with the aim of discouraging other employees from going to work and to prevent supplies from arriving or leaving. Pickets are also designed to draw media attention to the strikers' case against the employer.

Secondly, the union may introduce a *work-to-rule*. This is the practice of employees conforming exactly to their job descriptions and refusing to go beyond the strict 'rule-book.' Whereas employees would normally be relatively flexible in their relationship with the employer, work-to-rules exclude all flexibility in the work-place – a measure designed to inconvenience the employer and increase production costs.

Thirdly, and linked to the work-to-rule, is the *slowdown*. This is when employees deliberately perform work tasks more slowly than they normally would. Such a practice has obvious effects on production costs.

The fourth form of union action is the *overtime ban*. Overtime is frequently offered to and accepted by employees to help the employer meet such things as production deadlines. A refusal on the part of employees to accept it can mean that deadlines are not met. This potentially causes harm to the employer through such things as a loss of customer goodwill.

In practice, trade unions are reluctant to implement measures such as those above and only do so when they feel that their aspirations can not be met through normal negotiations. This is for two reasons:

- Some forms of industrial action *cost union members money* through lost earnings. Strikes are accompanied by the employer withholding pay for the time that the strike is in progress. In some cases, the union itself makes good the loss of earnings from its own financial reserves. Overtime bans also reduce employee earnings.
- All forms of industrial action, by definition, are designed to cause inconvenience and loss to the employer. Union members are usually aware that if they take industrial action 'too far' it may ultimately *threaten their own jobs*.

Mediation and arbitration

When unions and employers are in dispute, the first means of resolving the disagreement is to meet to attempt to reach an acceptable compromise. The management is represented by a suitably briefed member of the senior management team (e.g. the personnel director) whilst the union is represented by a union member appointed by the other members to negotiate on their behalf (e.g. the works convenor). If, however, agreement cannot be reached, the two sides in the dispute may elect to appoint an independent mediator or an arbitrator.

- A *mediator* acts simply as a communicator between two sides when normal communication has become difficult or impossible.

- An *arbitrator* is empowered to determine a settlement between the two parties – an outcome which is binding on both parties and which may be a compromise between the two positions. An arbitrator is only engaged in a dispute at the invitation and with the agreement of both parties.

In 1974, the UK government established the Advisory, Conciliation and Arbitration Service (ACAS). ACAS is managed by a council of nine members:

- three from the Confederation of British Industry (CBI), representing the employers;
- three from the Trades Union Congress (TUC), representing the unions;
- three independent members.

The role which ACAS performs in negotiations depends on the invitation of the two sides. In some cases, ACAS is engaged purely as a mediator, whereas in other cases the two sides agree that ACAS should perform an arbitration role.

Recent trends in the world of trade unions

Declining membership
Figure 13.1 shows the trend in total trade union density (membership compared to total workforce) between 1971 and 1991. We can see from this graph that there has been a marked decline in membership, but particularly in the years since 1979. There are a number of reasons for this phenomenon:

- The change in political power in 1979. When Margaret Thatcher's Conservatives took over from James Callaghan's Labour Party, a number of laws were introduced that increased the regulation of trade unions. This is considered in detail in Chapter 22. The laws that were introduced had the effect of imposing restrictions on both trade union activity and the ways in which they should be operated. The effect of these laws was to reduce union power with respect to employers.
- A marked decline occurred in industries that were hitherto highly unionized. The reduction in size of industries like coal-mining, steel and ship-building has meant that union membership in these key industries has declined.
- A growing belief that union membership does not bring the benefits with it that once it did. A number of key union defeats (e.g. the miners in 1984) and the changing nature of the job market in favour of employers have brought with them a heightened perception that unions have become increasingly impotent.

Mergers between unions
The decline in membership and the problems of lower bargaining power over employers brought about by increased regulation has triggered a spate of interunion mergers. This means that two unions which have suffered from declining membership join forces to create a new, merged union. The larger size of the merged union brings two benefits:

- an increased ability to influence employers in favour of union members;
- increased financial stability of the union itself (resulting from economies of scale), thus providing continued support for its members.

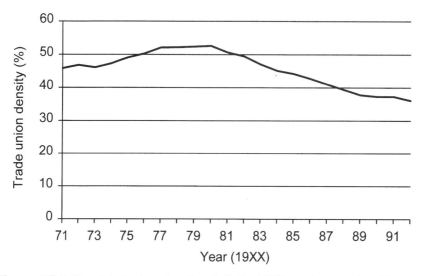

Figure 13.1 Trends in trade union density in the UK (i.e. union membership as a percentage of all workers). (Source: Social Trends, 1995, London: HMSO)

Recent union mergers have brought about a slight blurring in the types of union we learned about above. There have, for example, been mergers between white collar and industrial unions. Such mergers, whilst not necessarily being what the union officials would ideally have wanted, were thought to be necessary as a means of gaining the benefits that a merger engenders.

Some of the more reported recent union mergers include:

• the GPMU (Graphical, Paper and Media Union) in 1991, from the merger of SOGAT (Society of Graphical and Allied Trades) and the NGA (National Graphical Association);
• Unison (1993) from a merger of three public sector unions – NALGO (National Association of Local Government Officers), NUPE (National Union of Public Employees) and COHSE (Confederation of Health Service Employees);
• the AEEU (Amalgamated Engineering and Electrical Union), completed in 1996, from two craft unions – the AUEW (Amalgamated Union of Engineering Workers) and the EETPU (Electrical, Electronic, Telecommunications and Plumbing Union).

13.9 Human resources and human motivation

Given that personnel (or human resources) management is concerned with maximizing the economic return on the organization's investment in its human resources, the matter of how best to motivate the work-force is naturally a matter of concern. The problem is that an understanding of the ways in which humans are motivated is very complicated and this is mainly because people are very complicated.

The fact that there are several major theories on human motivation is testimony to the fact that none of them is sufficient in itself. Each theory adds to the total body of knowledge in this area, but we need to acknowledge each one to gain an overall picture of this issue. A number of writers have added their theories to the debate:

- Abraham Maslow;
- Frederick Herzberg;
- Clayton Aldefer;
- D. C. McClelland;
- Victor Vroom.

Their theories are described below.

Abraham Maslow's hierarchy of human needs

Maslow's theory of motivation was first published in 1943[1] and remained the most influential for many years. His theory rests upon the premise that humans are motivated by the satisfaction of needs. Furthermore, human needs can be categorized into 'layers' or 'levels' – some are very basic and others are more advanced. The various levels can therefore be expressed as a hierarchy (Figure 13.2).

Figure 13.2 *Maslow's hierarchy of human needs*

Once one level of need has been satisfied, the individual is motivated to satisfy needs in the next level. This pattern continues upwards until the individual is motivated to meet the needs of self-actualization. If, however, an individual seeking to satisfy higher needs experiences a threat to lower level needs, his or her attention is drawn back to the fulfilment of the threatened lower level needs. An individual who has his or her needs met up to the point of self-actualization will, if drowning, be more motivated to meet immediate physiological needs, that is, the need for air. In such a circumstance, the unfortunate person will care little for his or her shelter, relational or esteem needs, such is the motivation to simply stay alive. The levels of need in the hierarchy are explained below.

- *Physiological needs* are those which are essential to the simple continuance of life. Such needs include the needs for air, water, food, good health, etc. Some have argued that this category of needs also includes more basic 'quality of life' issues such as sleep, maternal or paternal fulfilment and the satisfaction of sexual appetites.
- *Shelter and protection needs* refer to an individual's need for a sense of personal security, freedom from danger, the need for order and predictability and, in most cases, the need for a shelter or 'nest'.
- *Love and relational needs* are sometimes called social needs. They refer to an individual's need for human interrelationships such as friendship, a sense of belonging, affection, etc.
- *Esteem needs* refer to the individual's need to be held in esteem by oneself and by others. Such needs include the need for some degree of status, prestige, recognition and appreciation from others.
- *Self-actualization* is the final level of needs fulfilment. These needs are consequently addressed only when all others have been satisfied. An individual's need to self-actualize is connected with the desire to 'find yourself', to be creative, to compose, to invent and to do things for their sake alone, and not as a means to other ends.

Maslow's theory is attractive in its simplicity but has a number of flaws. It is clearly an oversimplification of the complexities of the human make-up. Whilst it may hold for some people that they follow the hierarchy upwards as Maslow described, others seem to be a little different. Some individuals, for example, may be motivated to self-actualize (e.g. by painting, writing, etc.) with only the most modest means of shelter and with little or no apparent need for affectionate interaction. So the work of Maslow, albeit a valuable contribution to the debate, cannot be considered to be a watertight and all-encompassing description of human motivation.

Frederick Herzberg's motivation–hygiene theory

Whereas Maslow's work attempted to describe the totality of an individual's motivation in all parts of life, Herzberg's writings focused on human motivation at work. In examining the various features of a person's working environment, he concluded that some features served to motivate an employee to greater performance, whereas other features served to prevent the employee from becoming dissatisfied with his or her work. He attached names to these groups of features:

- *Hygiene factors* are those features of work that prevent employees from becoming dissatisfied with their work. They do not motivate, but serve to maintain the employee's co-operation and loyalty.
- *Motivating factors* are those features which motivate employees in their work.

Both hygiene and motivating factors are important if the employee is to be satisfied *and* motivated in his or her work.

Hygiene factors include:

- salary and remuneration;
- the quality and level of supervision in the working environment;
- the working conditions;
- company policy and administration;
- the interpersonal relationships that the employee enjoys (or does not enjoy) in the working environment.

Motivating factors include:

- the opportunity to achieve worthwhile goals at work;
- recognition of good work;
- the status attached to a job;
- the level of responsibility and authority attached to a job;
- opportunities for growth, development and promotion afforded by the job.

Herzberg's theory has been influential in management thinking and in job design. By using Herzberg's ideas, the features of a given job can be adjusted to meet an employee's particular circumstances, i.e. hygiene or motivating factors can be addressed according the employee's needs. One of the oft criticized parts of Herzberg's theory is the inclusion of pay as a hygiene factor and not a motivating factor. By doing this, Herzberg is arguing that money in itself doesn't motivate, but this is not to say that money as a part of recognition or higher achievement isn't in part motivating. Salary, Herzberg argues, prevents employees from becoming dissatisfied with their work.

Clayton Aldefer's ERG theory

Aldefer published his theory in 1972 which post-dates both Maslow and Herzberg by a number of years. In his ERG theory, Aldefer contends that motivation can be expressed as a continuum containing three interconnecting zones:

- *existence* (E) – motivations relating to simple matters pertaining to the continuance and simple enjoyment of life;
- *relatedness* (R) – motivations relating to the need to be personally connected through meaningful personal relationships, friendships, networks and intimacy;
- *growth* (G) – motivations pertaining to the need to develop oneself, to grow and improve oneself.

There is an apparent link between Aldefer's theory and that of Maslow. The difference arises in the fact that Aldefer does not see levels of need as a strict hierarchy, but as a continuum (Figure 13.3). It is possible to be seeking fulfilment of both existence and relatedness needs simultaneously if an individual is on the part of the continuum between the two zones. Similarly, once existence needs have been satisfied, the individual moves onto the stages of relatedness and growth and may be motivated to fulfil both needs simultaneously. Hence, the ERG theory accounts for a more complex model of human psychology that the simple hierarchy proposed by Maslow.

Existence	Relatedness	Growth

Figure 13.3 The ERG continuum

D. C. McClelland's achievement motivation theory

D. C. McClelland and his colleagues worked at Harvard University in the early 1960s. He suggested that humans are motivated by four main arousal-based motives:

- the *achievement* motive (which McClelland called *n Ach*);
- the *affiliation* motive (*n Aff*);
- the *power* motive (*n Pow*);
- the *avoidance* motive.

According to McClelland, different people show one of these motivations above the others. Some are primarily motivated by the need for achievement, some by the need for affiliation (relational needs) and others by a need for power and influence. Still others are seemingly motivated by indolence and a desire to avoid work altogether.

McClelland's study focused on just one of these motivating forces, the need for achievement (n Ach). This is because this factor is apparently more important than the other factors in the workplace. The *achievement motivation theory* states that individuals with a highly pronounced n Ach factor demonstrate:

- a constant need for achievement;
- an eagerness to accept positions of responsibility;
- a desire to set themselves realistic goals (i.e. they are 'self-starters');
- a willingness to respond positively to feedback on their performance;
- the trait that achievement is more important to them than affiliation needs.

McClelland contended that those with a pronounced n Ach factor would make ideal managers. Such individuals, in seeking achievement above all other goals (e.g. affiliation needs), would be conscientious workers and effective managers. The theory has been influential inasmuch as personnel specialists frequently seek n Ach characteristics when appointing key managers in an organization.

Victor Vroom's valence theory

Vroom's contribution to motivation theory is his valence (or expectancy) theory. Like Herzberg, Vroom's theory concentrates mainly upon motivation in the workplace. The valence theory asserts that the degree of motivation that an individual feels towards a particular course of action depends on the strength of two variables: valence and expectancy.

Motivation = valence × expectancy

The two variables are defined below.

Valence expresses the degree of satisfaction that an individual thinks will be enjoyed as a result of pursuing the course of action in question. It is thus future-oriented and refers to the individual's *anticipated* satisfaction from the course of action. Put crudely, valence refers to the intensity of desire that an individual feels towards an outcome or, 'how badly' it is desired.

Expectancy refers to the strength of belief that the action will lead to the particularly favourable outcome. It follows that expectancy is usually subjective in nature and depends upon the individual's perception of the probability of the successful outcome. It is possible that an individual may have an inaccurate perception of the probability (i.e. an unrealistically high expectancy), but the important thing is the expectancy from the point of view of the individual, not the objective truth.

High motivation results, according to Vroom, when both valence and expectancy are at their highest. If either is weakened, either by uncertain desire (lower valence) or by a lack of certainty (lower expectancy), then overall motivation, which Vroom called *force*, will be reduced.

We can understand this better by constructing a simple example. Suppose a company's marketing director is due to retire in 12 months time and you, as an employee in the marketing department, are one of the people who may be considered to replace the director.

The motivation you have towards your work will depend upon two variables:

* The value you attach to the benefits you believe will accrue as a result of the being appointed as the new marketing director (e.g. high salary, power, status, company car). This is the valence.
* The strength of your belief in the possibility of actually getting the job. If you think there is a high probability of getting the job, you will have a higher expectancy than if there is a front-runner ahead of you.

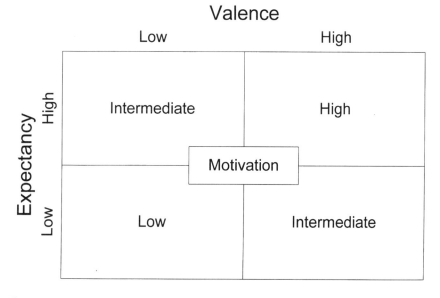

Figure 13.4 A representation of Vroom's valence – expectancy theory

Your motivation at work over the 12 months until the present marketing director retires will depend upon these two factors. If you place a high value on the benefits of holding the marketing director's position (high valence) *and* you believe you have the best chance of being appointed, then your motivation is maximized. If, however you do not value the rewards of a directorship (such as an indifference to increased financial reward, status, etc.) or you do not believe you are in a strong position to get the job, your motivation will be reduced accordingly.

The possible outcomes using Vroom's two variables are shown in Figure 13.4.

Assignment

Sister Jones of Ward 14 (paediatric services) at the Monkcliffe general hospital thinks that her staff are overworked and has rung the personnel department asking for another nurse, preferably two. As the newly appointed assistant personnel manager, the director of personnel has asked you to take charge of the situation, to see if Sister Jones has a case and then to manage the new appointments process from start to finish if the vacancy is approved.

Questions

- What steps might you take to establish whether Sister Jones has a legitimate case for a new member of staff?
- Given that the vacancy is approved, discuss the type of steps you would take to appoint a new qualified nurse to Ward 14.
- Suggest what might comprise the contents for a job description and person specification for the new paediatric nurse.
- Explain how would you carry out the recruitment and selection stages for the new nurse.
- What ongoing training and development might a nurse and the hospital benefit from on Ward 14?

Reference

1. Maslow, A. (1943) A theory of human motivation. *Psychological Review*, **50** (July).

Further reading

Adair, J. (1996) *Effective Motivation*. London: Macmillan.
Attwood, M. and Dimmock, S. (1996) *Personnel Management, 3rd edn*. London: Macmillan.
Beardwell, I. and Holden, L. *et al.* (1994) *Human Resource Management. A Contemporary Perspective*. London: Pitman.
Bratton, J. and Gold, J. (1994) *Human Resource Management, Theory and Practice*. London: Macmillan.

Cole, G. A. (1996) *Personnel and Human Resource Management*, 4th edn. London: DP Publications.

Hendry, C. (1995) *Human Resource Management*. Oxford: Butterworth-Heinemann.

Hollinshead, G. and Leat, M. (1995) *Human Resource Management. An International and Comparative Perspective*. London: Pitman.

Howe, S. (1995). *Essential Elements of Human Resource Management*. London: DP Publications.

Kempton, J. (1995) *Human Resource Management and Development. Current Issues and Themes*. London: Macmillan.

Miner, J. B. and Crane, D. (1995). *Human Resource Management. The Strategic Perspective*. London: Harper Collins.

Smith, M. and Robertson, I. T. (1993) *The Theory and Practice of Systematic Personnel Selection*. London: Macmillan.

Storey, J. (1992) *Developments in the Management of Human Resources*. Oxford: Blackwell.

Torrington, D. and Hall, L. (1991) *Personnel Management – A New Approach*, 2nd Edition. New York: Prentice Hall.

Tyson, S and York, A. (1996) *Human Resource Management,* 3rd edn. Oxford: Butterworth-Heinemann.

Weiner, B. (1992) *Human Motivation. Metaphors, Theories and Research*. Thousand Oaks, CA: Sage.

Werther, W. and Davis, K. (1995) *Human Resource and Personnel Management*. New York: McGraw Hill.

14

Operations and manufacturing

Learning objectives

After studying this chapter, students should be able to describe:

- The nature of operations in business.
- The types and costs of stock.
- The processes involved in purchasing and in the management of inbound logistics.
- The common types of manufacturing system.
- The processes involved in distribution and outbound logistics.

14.1 What is operations?

Introduction

Operations is perhaps the most important part of any organization. This is because of its crucial role in the success or otherwise of the business. Let us first define this function: *operations is the part of the organization that is directly responsible for achieving the organization's objectives.*

We can note immediately that this 'direct responsibility' is what distinguishes operations from other functions. In a car manufacturer, the operations function is that part of the business which makes the cars. Without this part of the business, it makes little sense to have a personnel function, a finance function or any other – important though those functions are. Other functions exist to support operations, without which, they would have no reason to be (see the distinction between line and staff employees in Chapter 10).

It is perhaps appropriate to consider some examples:

Type of organization	*Operations function*
Manufacturing company	Factory
Newcastle United Football Club	Newcastle United football team
Restaurant	Kitchen and waiters
University	Lecturers and researchers

An example close to home to most readers will be the university. A university employs many people apart from lecturers such as administrators, finance managers, clerical staff, site services staff (e.g. car park attendants, gardeners) and technical staff. However, the university exists primarily to educate students and to research – only academic staff (lecturers) can do this. All other parts of a university exist to support academic staff in their important duties.

Manufacturing as an example of operations

We have seem that manufacturing is one example of an operations function. However, owing to its complexity and importance, the majority of thinking in the operations sphere has been focused in the area of manufacturing. It is for this reason that the majority of this chapter is concerned with manufacturing, although it should be borne in mind that many of the principles we will discuss are transferable to non-manufacturing operational contexts (e.g. university, bank, restaurant).

Manufacturing is a process involving the passage of physical goods through an organization from buying materials in, to distribution of the finished goods to the customer – and all that happens in between. A generalized representation of the manufacturing process is shown below.

Purchasing
↓
Goods inward and raw materials storage
↓
Manufacturing
↓
Finished goods storage and distribution

Stock

Types of stock

An important part of manufacturing must be introduced at this point: the actual material involved in the process – referred to as stock or *inventory*. Stock is divided into three types, depending upon where it is in the transformation process:

- *Raw materials* (RMs) or purchased parts are stocks in their 'raw' state. RMs are those goods that are purchased before they undergo any processing within the manufacturing process.
- *Work-in-progress* (WIP) is the name given to stocks that are actually being worked on in the manufacturing process.
- *Finished goods* (FG) stocks are those which have passed through the process and are ready for distribution to the customers.

Costs of stock

Central to all stock purchasing and management is the fact that stock of all kinds costs money. We can appreciate the nub of this issue by relating it to our own personal stocks, such as stocks of food. It is a singularly pleasurable experience to open the fridge door to find it packed with immediately consumable fresh foods – cheeses, patés, cold meats, fresh juices and many others. It is obvious, however, that such luxuriant stocking costs money. Whilst, with a full fridge, you are prepared for any eventuality, such as friends calling unexpectedly, you must accept the variety of costs that accompany such stock levels.

This has been an issue that has much exercised the minds of the business and academic elite over the past two decades – to find the level of stock that will facilitate normal business functioning without incurring excessive costs for the 'luxury' of excess stocks.

The costs of stock to a business (many of which are equally applicable to the stock of food in your fridge) are as follows:

- The *price paid for the stock* is the most obvious cost. Whenever stock is bought in, money must be paid out for it, thus reducing the amount of money left 'in the kitty'. It follows that stock has an 'opportunity cost' – by buying stock, you have less money to spend on other things and you are foregoing interest on the money that you could earn if the money paid for the stock was deposited in the bank or otherwise invested.
- The *cost of stock storage* has several constituents: the purchase or rental cost of space required to store it, the insurance paid on the stock and its storage space, and wages to staff who are paid to manage the stock.
- The *risk associated with stock storage* is the third cost. If you overstock on food, you run the risk that some of it may 'go off', and in the same way, some business stocks can become obsolescent or become subject to theft or damage.

Operations in everyday life

The author decides to cook. Not being very ambitious, he decides to make a shepherd's pie. Opening his fridge, freezer and larder, the author realizes that he has none of the required ingredients. In consequence, he goes to the local supermarket to buy the ingredients in (the purchasing stage). After carefully selecting half a kilo' of mince, an onion and some potatoes, he returns home to unpack the goods. Unpacking the food (raw materials) on the kitchen bench, he checks the mince for gristle, the onion for bad bits and the potatoes for damage or black bits (goods inward and inspection). The ingredients are then put away until dinner time (raw materials storage).

When the time comes to prepare, the author retrieves the ingredients from the storage units (e.g. fridge) and begins the cooking process by chopping up the onion and frying the mince (the manufacturing or production process). There are obviously several stages in this process, such as boiling, frying and finally baking or grilling. The ingredients, whilst undergoing the process are work-in-progress stocks.

Finally, the shepherd's pie is finished. The author takes the masterpiece from the oven and serves it up on to plates and carries them through to the dining room table for consumption (distribution – no finished goods storage in this case).

The example of making a shepherd's pie illustrates the principles. In practice, however, the processes involved in operations are rather more complicated. We will examine each stage in turn.

14.2 Purchasing and inbound logistics

What is purchasing?

Purchasing is sometimes referred to by rather grand-sounding names such as procurement or inbound logistics. Essentially, it is about buying in materials to facilitate the normal working of the subsequent manufacturing process.

The job of the purchasing manager is thus to buy:

- the right material or part;
- of the right quality;
- in the right quantity;
- at the right price;
- from the right supplier;
- with the right delivery arrangements;
- to arrive at the right time;
- with the right payment or credit terms.

The purchasing manager clearly has an important job, as getting any part of the purchasing process wrong can be very damaging to the overall operations process. An inept purchasing manager may, for example, order the wrong materials to arrive too late or possibly forget to order them at all. In either case, the manufacturing process is severely adversely affected. Similarly, a purchasing manager who pays too much for incoming materials will increase operational costs and thus reduce profits.

In a typical UK manufacturing business, the purchasing manager spends around 65% of the company's total income. This means that, if the business achieves sales of £100 million, the purchases needed to generate that level of sales will be around £65 million. It follows that the quickest way to increase profits is to reduce the cost of purchases rather than to sell more products (important though that is). It is consequently something of a mystery why most purchasing managers are 'back-room boys' (or girls) on a mediocre salary. The strategic importance of the purchasing manager's spending is difficult to overstate.

What does the purchasing manager do?

The purchasing manager, as we have seen, is an important person in an organization. The job includes a number of distinct activities:

- administering and organizing all material inputs into the organization;
- acting as a 'window on the world' by monitoring changes in the supply industries such as new products, price changes, etc.;
- visiting suppliers to check on quality and the reliability of suppliers to meet the company's input needs;
- negotiating supply contracts with suppliers;
- 'shopping around' for cheaper prices, better service or more reliable supply;
- meeting with suppliers' representatives to find out about new products and any changes in the terms of supply and cultivating good relationships with suppliers;

- inspecting and examining suppliers' sales information to establish the most appropriate products to buy and the optimum order quantity.

Goods inward and raw materials storage

The goods inward part of operations is important for three reasons:

- it manages the raw materials, thus ensuring they are properly kept so they don't go off, decay, rust or become obsolescent in any way;
- it issues raw materials to production when requested in precisely the right quantities so that the production process has just what it needs, when it is needed;
- it monitors stock levels of raw materials so that there are no excess stocks or that no understocking occurs (although in many cases, this part of the job has been replaced by computerized stock management systems).

The actual level of raw materials stocks held and how they are held will in part be determined by the type of operational philosophy used by the organization (see Chapter 15). Some operational systems, for example just-in-time (JIT), favour no stocks of raw materials, in which case, the goods inward stage will assume a different role to that discussed above.

14.3 Manufacturing processes

The manufacturing part of operations is when raw materials become work-in-progress. The conversion (or processing) of materials results in the output of finished goods from the organization. Of course the actual process of conversion will depend entirely upon the nature of the business; it might be assembly, reaction, transformation, mixing or any number of other mechanisms of conversion. Similarly, the scale of production varies enormously, from the one-person back-shed business making trout flies to the multinational company producing cars in 40 different manufacturing plants in as many countries.

Added value – the aim of manufacturing

The essential purpose of manufacturing is to *add value*. This means that, by working on stocks, a business increases the value of the stocks and thus enables a profit to be made. When raw materials are bought in, they are just that – *raw* materials. A tonne of sheet metal is of little use to a customer who wishes to drive to Norwich. By taking the sheet metal, some plastic and some rubber and transforming it, a motor car manufacturer can turn such unlikely materials costing a few hundred pounds into a magnificent motor car valued at many thousands of pounds.

Each stage of manufacturing through which the materials pass adds more value to the stocks. When a sheet of metal is pressed and cut into the a front wing of a car its value is increased, as a front wing is worth more than a sheet of metal. When it is painted, it is worth even more, and when it is bolted or welded onto an assembled car body its value is maximized.

It follows from this principle that value is only being added to stocks when they are actually being worked on. If, at any time, the stocks are sitting idle or are waiting to be worked on, value is not being added and thus costs are being incurred (we have already identified the costs of stock). One of the aims of manufacturing is thus to keep stocks moving through the process. Stock queueing is thus the enemy of added value (Figure 14.1).

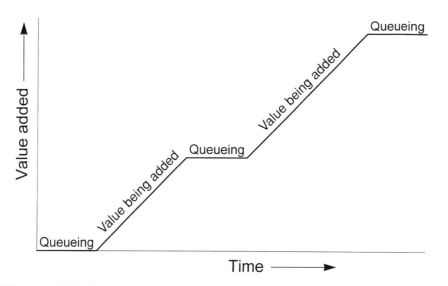

Figure 14.1 Progress of added value in a manufacturing process with stock queueing

As we discuss the various types of production, we will see that some add value more rapidly than others.

Types of production

There are five generalized forms of production in manufacturing business:

- project manufacture;
- job manufacture;
- batch manufacture;
- flow and line manufacture;
- continuous manufacture.

The method chosen will depend in large part on the nature of the product being made. Some products can only be made by one method, whereas other products can be made by more than one method. We will briefly examine each in turn.

Project manufacture

As its name suggests, project manufacture is concerned with making 'one-off' jobs. Projects are characterized by a number of features:

- in most cases, each project undertaken is unique and is made to a design explicitly specified by the customer;
- projects are usually large objects, which means that once they are built they cannot be moved (although there are exceptions);
- orders are won not on the quality of the product produced (although this becomes important), but on the capabilities of the business (its track record at carrying out similar projects);
- value is added continually as the project is being worked on all the time until it is finished – the entire operations function of the business is brought to bear on the project.

Examples of products which are made by project manufacturers include:

- civil engineering projects such as buildings, roads, railways and special projects such as the channel tunnel;
- building refurbishments and modifications, such as the building of extensions;
- shipping;
- off-shore installations such as oil-rigs.

Jobbing manufacture

Job manufacture is like a project in that it involves making one-offs, but jobs tend to be on a much smaller scale – they are jobs rather than grander projects. The two approaches also have other things in common:

- They both add value more-or-less continuously in that the product is being worked on all of the time until it is finished.
- They both produce products which are built according to customers' specifications (i.e. they are not standard 'off-the-shelf' products).
- They both employ relatively skilled workers who are specialized in a specific part of the manufacturing process (e.g. bricklayers, welders).
- They both suffer from relatively low machine utilization. This means that a machine is used for one part of the manufacturing process only. It is thus quite possible for an expensive piece of equipment to sit idle for most of the time. Sometimes, manufacturers 'get round' this drawback by renting machines as needed, but this is not always possible.
- They both rely on the competencies of the business and its track record as the key qualifier in winning an order.
- They both rely on a relatively steady flow of orders. If the business enters a period with no orders, it is not possible for project or job manufacturers to make for stock, as none of their goods are standard stock products.

In this respect, it is difficult to say where projects end and jobbing starts. Whilst we may agree that a large oil tanker taking over a year to make is a project, we may be less sure about a small fishing boat (i.e. we may say the fishing boat is a job). Examples of products which are usually seen as jobs rather than projects include:

- smaller engineering jobs (e.g. one-off prototypes);
- works of art, sculptures, etc.;
- tradespeople's jobs (e.g. plastering a wall, repairing a washing machine);
- car repairs.

Batch manufacture

Some types of product can be made in 'lots' rather than separately or individually. Batch manufacture thus results in the manufacture of 'lots' of identical products – a feature which contrasts sharply with the unique nature of each project or job. Whereas a job or project manufacturer will produce one ship, one motorway, etc., a batch process may produce 10 000 gallons of beer, 5000 bolts or 45 tins of paint.

Features of batch manufacture include:

- An ability to cope with much higher production volumes than project or batch processes.
- Products typically pass through several distinct stages in the batch process, as is also the case in project and job processes. Each stage may be based at a separate location or workstation and so there is the possibility of time being wasted in non-added-value activities such as stock moving from place to place and in waiting to be worked on.
- The equipment and plant used in batch manufacturing is modified each time a new batch goes through the plant. This is because each batch is different and requires different settings or material inputs. After each batch, the workstation must be *tooled down* in order to be *tooled up* to run a different batch (this may of course be a washing or purging process, or similar). Such modifications represent time delays which prevent value being added to stocks.
- The focus of a batch manufacturing business is on its products, and customer's buying decisions are based upon the products rather than on the organization's competence – the opposite of project and job.
- The fact that batch operations are based in factories rather than out 'on-site' means that an increased emphasis is placed on maintaining factory volumes and in keeping machines busy.

Batch manufacture is very widely used in manufacturing industry owing to its flexibility. Products made by this method include:

- beer, often in very large batches of several thousand gallons;
- paints, in batches of anything from 5 to 20 000 litres;
- pharmaceuticals, where batches run to millions of individual pills – products like inhalers and vials are made in batches of up to 200 000 units;
- nuts, bolts and other engineering products such as car parts (e.g. a batch of 'patterned' exhausts for a Vauxhall Cavalier).

The advantages of a batch process include its ability to cope with variations in product and volume demand, its higher utilization of equipment (compared to project and job processes), and the fact that it enables personnel in the factory to become specialized in the operation of their particular process.

Batch manufacturing's disadvantages include the difficulties in organizing and scheduling batches through the factory. The fact that different products take different times to produce and that customers require products on different dates means that decisions on what to make where and on what machine can be a headache. In addition, the flexibility of batch manufacturing usually necessitates the holding of relatively high raw material stocks as well as higher work-in-progress stocks when queues between stages are involved.

Flow and line manufacture

Flow manufacture – balancing production stages
If you can imagine a batch manufacturing facility in which stocks never queue between workstations, then you have an idea of what flow manufacture is about. Imagine that the manufacture of a product involves three separate processes – process A, process B, and process C. Now suppose that, due to the nature of the three processes, they take different times periods:

- process A at work-station A takes 1 hour;
- process B at work-station B takes half an hour;
- process C at work-station C takes 2 hours.

The passage of stocks through this facility thus runs as follows. Stock for batch 1 enters process A and is completed after 1 hour. After it is finished, process B can begin work on the stock immediately as process A receives more raw materials stock to begin another job (batch 2). After another half an hour, process B has finished working on the batch 1 stock and upon passing the work-in-progress (WIP) on to process C, must sit idle for half an hour until the next consignment of WIP (batch 2) arrives from process A. Process C begins work on the batch 1 stock immediately, thus ensuring that batch 1 passes through all stages without queuing.

After sitting idle for half an hour, process B eventually receives the WIP for batch 2, which it then works on for the requisite half an hour. However, once batch 2 has finished at process B, the WIP itself must wait (or queue) for half an hour before it can pass to process C which requires 2 hours to finish working on batch 1. Once several batches have begun in the factory, the result is a frustrating scenario in which process B sits idle for half the time whilst large queues build up waiting to enter process C. Both of these things – machines not being used and stocks sitting idle – cost money.

Both problems can be sorted by 'line balancing'. If we install two machines at process A then there will be a delivery of WIP from process A once every half hour – perfect for process B. Process C must then be modified so that it can accept WIP from process B every half hour. Because process C takes 2 hours, we will need four process C machines. The line is now balanced: there is no queuing and all the machines are fully utilized.

With the bottleneck between processes B and C removed, stock now *flows* through the factory. We have thus turned batch manufacture into flow manufacture.

Line manufacture

Line processes go one step further than flow processes. When a factory is geared up to run higher volumes than most batches through a range of processes, the 'line' of stages can be designed so that they are literally in a line, thus making the passage of stock through the processes as simple as possible. Furthermore, if higher volumes of the same product are being produced, the times between tooling up and tooling down are much longer. Lines can thus be dedicated to making a standard product in high volume. Of course, such 'dedication' of a line to one product means that we lose the flexibility of a batch process – we lose the ability to just tool up to run a different product through the process.

Features of line production are therefore:

- a higher investment in plant than batch production;
- high volume production;
- dedicated lines which are inflexible to changes in the product being made;
- a given line produces just one product;
- very high machine utilization (constant usage in most cases);
- workers on the line become very specialized in just one process along its length – work can be tedious and repetitive.

Products which are usually made on line processes include:

- motor cars;
- electronic consumer goods such as televisions, video recorders and microcomputers;
- consumer kitchen appliances such as washing machines and cookers.

Continuous manufacture

The final type of general manufacturing system we will consider is continuous manufacturing. Just as line is an extension of batch, continuous is an extension of line. As its name suggests, a continuous process is one that never stops – rather like a line process for which demand is ongoing and where the product is never subject to fluctuations in demand due to changing fashions or consumer preferences. Continuous processes often run continually for years or even decades without being switched off.

It follows from this that continuous processes produce far higher volumes of output than any of the other production methods we have discussed. The nature of the products produced by this method also means that usually, the cost of setting up a continuous process is huge – usually dwarfing investments in any of the other methods. The size of the investment alone means that production must run constantly in order to generate sales that will pay for the large investment.

Continuous processes are usually controlled rather than worked on (all the other methods of production need at least some people to work on products as they pass through the plant). This means that while the continuous process is running, staff monitor production from a separate control room rather from the 'factory floor'.

Clearly then, continuous manufacture is a suitable production method for products which have a high and relatively predictable demand, such as:

- energy (e.g. power stations);
- petrochemicals (e.g. oil refineries producing petrol, diesel);
- steel (where iron is produced by smelting iron ore and converted into steel in the same production process);
- gas.

14.4 Distribution and outbound logistics

Finished goods stock

Once the operational stock has passed through all the stages of manufacturing, including any quality control filters that may be in place (see Chapter 15), it becomes finished goods (FG) stock. FG stock attracts the same costs as raw materials or work-in-progress inventory, and so it usually the case that a business wishes to distribute it to customers as soon as possible. In some cases, however, a reasonable FG stock is useful as it enables unexpected customer orders to be met rapidly. The alternative – to make to order – usually incurs a longer lead time than supplying directly from FG stock.

The optimum time of FG stock storage depends upon the value of the stock and the nature of the product. FG stocks in which a large amount of money is invested, such as shipping or defence orders, must be delivered immediately upon completion to gain payment. Other products need to be distributed quickly because they are perishable (e.g. fresh fruit, cooked food, such as chips or bakery products).

Distribution

The process of distribution is the procedure by which finished goods stocks leave their point of manufacture and arrive at the point of consumption (e.g. the next stage in the supply chain or the end consumer). The nature of distribution systems varies from the very complex, such as the distribution of petrochemical products across the world, to the very simple, such as the distribution of fish and chips from the local chippy.

The distribution of goods – the science of logistics – is a complex subject in its own right. Academics study it at length and many companies earn revenues from it by means of road, rail, air and shipping haulage. We have probably all seen the ubiquitous Eddie Stobart lorries on UK roads – just one example of a medium to large business involved in this area of activity.

The method of distribution chosen by a given business will be guided by such things as the nature of the product and the requirements of the customer. Some products are delivered little and often, whilst others are distributed on a batch at a time basis. In both cases, the same criteria for a good distribution system apply. A suitable system will ensure:

- that the product *actually arrives* at the point of consumption, i.e. the distribution company is reliable;
- that deliveries will be *on time*, i.e. within the time-scale as determined by the customer;

- that the product *will not be damaged* in transit;
- that the deliveries will be *cost-effective*, meaning that the cost of distribution does not make the selling of the product uneconomical at normal market prices.

The operational process is completed when the goods finally and successfully arrive at the customer.

Assignment

A local engineering company has decided to make its goods-inward manager redundant because it feels that it can trust its suppliers to always supply goods reliably. According to the operations manager, there hasn't been a 'duff batch' delivered for years. 'By saving on goods inward inspection, we can save on employee costs. We were paying for a man we simply didn't need'. the operations manager said. Discuss the wisdom of the operations manager's decision by identifying the pros and cons of the redundancy and arriving at a conclusion.

Further reading

Anderson, E. (1994) *The Management of Manufacturing. Models and Analysis.* New York: Addison Wesley.

Baily, P., Farmer, D., Jessop, D. and Jones, D. (1994) *Purchasing, Principles and Management.* London: Pitman.

Barnett, H. (1996) *Operations Management*, 2nd edn. London: Macmillan.

Bowersox, D. and Closs, D. (1995) *Logistics Management.* New York: McGraw Hill.

Christopher, M. (1992) *Logistics and Supply Chain Management.* London: Pitman.

Dilworth, J. (1996) *Operations Management*, 2nd edn. New York: McGraw Hill.

Gattorna, J. L. and Walters, D. (1996) *Managing the Supply Chain. A Strategic Perspective.* London: Macmillan.

Hill, T. (1995) *Manufacturing Strategy. Text and Cases.* London: Macmillan.

Mair, G. (1993) *Mastering Manufacturing.* London: Macmillan.

Muhlemann, A. P., Oakland, J. S. and Lockyer, K. G. (1992) *Production and Operations Management*, 6th edn. London: Pitman.

Slack, N. *et al.* (1995) *Operations Management.* London: Pitman.

15

Operational philosophies: quality and JIT

Learning objectives

After studying this chapter, students should be able to describe:

- Why the operations function is important to business performance.
- What makes an operations function successful or otherwise.
- What is meant by quality and why it is important.
- The types of quality regime that businesses employ.
- The features of total quality management (TQM).
- The features and benefits of just-in-time (JIT).

15.1 The strategic significance of operations

We saw in Chapter 14 that operations is that part of the organization which is primarily concerned with 'making' or 'producing' the product or service. It follows that the operations department is the most important function in a business: a car manufacturer does not exist to report on financial performance or to manage its personnel – it exists to make cars and, by doing so, money. All other functions such as personnel and finance must therefore be in support of the operations function.

Furthermore, operations can be said to be the most important function because it provides the output which the customer actually pays for and uses. Poor personnel policies or poor financial reporting would rarely, in themselves, make customers stop buying from a business, but poor products or bad service certainly would. So we can arrive at a generally accepted principle:

Good operations department = Competitive business

and

Bad operations department = Unhealthy and uncompetitive business

What then makes one company's operations department better than others? Or, put another way, in what ways can the operations function add to or take away from the success of the business as a whole? We can answer this by looking at several 'success factors' (which, of course, can also be 'failure factors').

- The *materials used* is the first and perhaps the most obvious success factor. It is clearly essential that the materials taken into and used by an operations process must be correct and of appropriate specification for the process. The appropriateness of materials will have a great bearing on the final product.

- *Quality* is the second success factor. In this context, quality means fitness for the job, which means that materials used must be right at each stage of the process. Materials bought in for the process must be of the right quality; too low quality and the product will be substandard, too high quality and the organization will be paying more than necessary for its inputs. The same principle applies to the quality of the final product output.

- The third success factor is the *lead time*. This refers to the time taken between an order being received and the delivery of the final product to the customer. It follows that companies with shorter lead times have an advantage over those who are slower. The lead time obviously depends upon such things as how the organization manages its orders, its queues in process and the efficiency of its procedures.

- Fourthly, success depends upon an organization's *distribution*. This refers not only to such things as the number and locations of outlets and depots, but also the method and efficiency of transport of finished goods to the customer. Reliable distribution can win orders, whereas unreliability in this area can soon erode customers' confidence in an organization's ability to supply on time.

- The final success factor, but perhaps the most important of all, is the level of *cost* incurred by the operations function. In most organizations, the operations function, is, by necessity, the 'biggest spender' of company money. There are many ways in which the operations department can and does incur costs, and successful businesses have ways of keeping them under tight control:

  - raw materials and other material inputs;
  - wages, salaries and personnel costs;
  - fixed costs such as rent, rates and insurance;
  - energy costs, such as electricity to power processes and machines;
  - investment costs, such as the acquisition of new plant and equipment;
  - packaging and distribution costs;
  - maintenance costs of equipment.

Both of the operational 'philosophies' we shall discuss in this chapter, quality and just-in-time (JIT), seek to gain competitive advantage by addressing the factors we have discussed above. By placing an emphasis on a certain key operational objective, these philosophies aim to achieve a superior operational performance. We should understand that quality and JIT are not mutually exclusive and many successful companies combine an emphasis on quality with a JIT regime. When taken to their extremes, such philosophies involve and affect entire organizations rather than just operations departments.

15.2 Quality

What is quality?

When we discuss quality, we must immediately dispense with the common understanding of the word. When we mention quality in the operations function, we do not refer to any notions of luxury, superiority or premium. If we say, for example, that a Rolls-Royce is a quality car, we usually mean that it is a premium car or a luxury car. It is, however, quite possible for an eastern European car or a budget Chinese moped to be of equal quality to the Rolls-Royce when we use the word in its precise business context.

Some definitions of quality follow. Quality means:

- the product is fit for the purpose for which it is intended;
- the product precisely meets its specification;
- the product meets the customer's expectations of it.

Hence, strictly speaking, it is quite possible for a product which is designed to be 'budget' – and which then meets the customer's low expectations – to actually be a high quality product. An example might be a cheap sausage comprising a high percentage of gristle and fat which perfectly meets the requirements of price-conscious customers for food within a tight budget. The sausage is thus a quality product in that context.

Why is quality important?

The quality of products, i.e. how well they meet customers' expectations, is very important in all types of organization. This is for two broad reasons:

- good quality wins orders, stimulates demand and retains customer confidence and loyalty;
- poor quality loses orders, erodes demand and damages customer confidence in the organization and its products.

Whilst the benefits of high quality are perhaps self-evident, the problems created by poor confidence require some elucidation. One of the reasons why so many organizations have viewed the issue of quality with increased seriousness is a belief that poor quality costs money. What are the sources of these costs of poor quality?

- At worst, poor quality products cannot be sold to the customers (for some products such sales may actually be illegal). In this case, the business incurs the *cost of the stock* plus the costs incurred in producing the product. In cases where 'off-specification' products can be re-worked, costs are incurred in putting stocks back through the factory.
- Costs are incurred in *correcting faults under warranty* or guarantee. If the material or construction is not capable of the performance expected by the customer, the product may fail, thus necessitating repair or compensation from the supplying organization.
- Probably the highest potential cost of poor quality is the *cost of losing customer confidence*. In competitive markets (i.e. those in which there are many suppliers), it doesn't take much to put customers off repeat purchases from poor quality suppliers. We all have stories about bad experiences we've had with a certain make of washing machine, motor car or restaurant. Often, bad reputation spreads by word of mouth,

so a bad experience not only precludes the disgruntled customer from repeat purchases, but also from those informed of the problem. Conversely, of course, good quality brings about repeat purchases, recommendations and hence intensified customer loyalty.

15.3 Quality regimes

Quality in operations is imparted into products using one or more of several possible systems, or quality *regimes*. The choice of an appropriate regime depends upon the nature of the operations function and the attitude of the organization to its particular competitive environment.

The various approaches can be set out in an approximate hierarchy according to the degree of employee involvement in the quality process:

Total quality management (TQM)
↑
Quality assurance backed by international quality standards
↑
Quality assurance (QA)
↑
Final quality control with in-process checks
↑
Final quality control (QC)

We will discuss the various regimes from the bottom up.

Final quality control

As its name suggests, final quality control (QC) is the checking of the quality of products once they have finished the entire operations process. QC is thus tagged onto the end as the final hurdle which must be 'jumped' before products are cleared for delivery to customers. Each product will have a specification set for it, and staff in QC will check the products to ensure that they meet the basic specification.

The amount or number of products tested in QC will vary according to the type of product. Sometimes, QC will check every single product produced, typically when the production output is low (e.g. the output of one shift). For processes producing thousands of nuts and bolts, however, testing every single product simply isn't possible. In this case, a statistically significant *sample* will be taken from each batch for testing.

Final quality control with in-process inspections

This regime, as its name suggests, adds extra safeguards to final QC in that the product is tested for conformance to specification at certain points in the process itself. This may include testing materials at the inbound logistics stage to make sure raw materials conform to requirements in addition to key points in the process.

The thinking behind this regime is to root out any problems at the earliest possible stage, just as you would wish to know if you have a disease as early as you possibly could. There is clearly no point in continuing with a batch which you know will fail final QC when it gets there. Whilst there is necessarily a higher cost associated with more testing (such as employing more testers), organizations that employ this regime argue that more is saved by catching poor quality early than is incurred in extra testing.

What happens after QC?

When work-in-progress stocks reach a QC point, whether it is in-process or at the end of the process, there are clearly two possible outcomes of the tests performed: the product is within specification (pass) or it is not (fail). If the stock passes the tests, then there is no problem; it can proceed to the next stage of production or go into finished goods stock ready to go to the customer. If, however, the test is failed (and is hence 'off specification' or 'off spec.'), there are a number of possible routes the stock can take. The most appropriate will, of course, depend upon the nature of the product.

- Some products that fail at the end of the process can be *sold off cheaply* to customers as 'off-spec.' products – sometimes called *seconds*. Not all products lend themselves to this type of rescue, but typical examples include clothes with mis-stitched seams and mis-shaped chocolates. The products will still offer some benefit to the customer, even though they are not 'perfect' (an odd-shaped chocolate still tastes acceptable even though it couldn't be sold at the normal price).
- Some products can be taken back into production and *reworked* to bring them back within QC specification. A paint that is not precisely the right colour when it reaches QC can usually be re-tinted to meet the precise colour required. Similarly, a computer with one defective circuit can be returned to production to have the one circuit replaced.
- Other products which fail QC must simply be *disposed of*. Disposal is obviously the option of last resort and is only taken when there is no scope for rework or selling on cheaply. Typical candidates for disposal would be products such as beer or food with a fatal contaminant or anything that would be unsafe to sell on or to rework.

Quality assurance

QA systems do not necessarily replace conventional QC regimes, rather they attempt to reduce the need for QC by assuring quality in advance. This means that quality is *designed into* products and processes in order to reduce the chances of things going wrong once they get into production. This is something of a shift in philosophy away from QC. Quality control more or less accepts that a certain failure rate will occur, whereas QA attempts to *create good quality* rather than control poor quality.

Quality is assured in advance by ensuring that all materials and processes involved in the manufacturing procedure conform to key quality criteria. The QA regime must therefore account for the following:

- *Design* – products and services must be designed with quality in mind. This means that research and design professionals design in features which will meet the customers' expectations. Product features will not be over- or underspecified and each part of it will be testable (if appropriate) during the product's production.
- *Materials* – these must be appropriate to the process. Again, they must not be under- or overspecified (i.e. too bad or too good for the product) and must be consistently of the appropriate quality.
- *Suppliers* – these will be chosen for their reliability and consistency to supply in addition to the quality of the materials themselves.
- *Plant and machinery* – these must be procured and maintained to operate within stricter tolerances than might otherwise be the case. By having machines that the organization knows it can rely on, the worry that a defect in plant may be responsible for poor product quality is removed.
- *Human resources* – whilst human error is always a potential source of poor quality, the risk of this happening can be reduced by appropriate training, development, human resource planning and by reducing the impact of human error by technologically based safeguards.
- *Operational procedures* – these must provide a framework which is consistent with good quality. If, for example, production is organized so that there is room for slovenly practice, that will tend to act against good quality. Clearly, the way that operational procedures are planned, managed and carried out will have a significant influence on the quality of the output.

Quality assurance standards

A standard, in this context, means a published document from either the British Standards Institute (BSI) or the International Standards Organization (ISO). These standards are prescriptive in nature and set out technical specifications which apply to a huge range of products and processes from the composition of petrol, to the strength of a motorcycle crash-helmet, to the nature of plastics that are included in ship designs.

In the 1980s and 1990s, both the BSI and ISO introduced a standard that would prescribe quality assurance as a means of giving customers confidence in an organization's output and procedures. The two standards are equivalent to each other.

BSI version	ISO version	Areas covered by standard
BS 5750: Part 1: 1987	ISO 9001: 1994	Quality of all aspects of operations and product design.
BS 5750: Part 2: 1987	ISO 9002: 1994	Quality in all aspects of operations.
BS 5750: Part 3: 1987	ISO 9003: 1994	Quality in final product inspection only.

Compliance with a QA standard must be proven to a body of independent inspectors. These inspectors, either from the BSI itself or from a suitably accredited alternative consultancy, inspect the organization's systems to test whether internal quality procedures are actually and consistently being followed. The organization seeking BS 5750 or ISO 9000 (which are equivalent) accreditation will produce documentation setting out how they will perform each part of the operational process. Once written down in this way, the company will be judged by the assessors according to how consistently it observes the procedures in practice. Once granted, the assessors can call on the organization at any time (without warning) to check that procedures are still being followed.

Accreditation is indicated by the award of the BSI or ISO 'kite mark' which can be shown on company letterheads, vehicles, etc., to indicate the organization's quality assurance. The assurance of quality is of obvious competitive advantage in the organization's attempts to increase its customers' confidence.

Total quality management

According to some, total quality management (TQM) is the 'next step' in quality consciousness after QA. Others see TQM as more than this – an overarching philosophy of business. Whereas other quality regimes are concentrated on the operations function, TQM in its 'purest form' is quality applied to the entire business. It is thus embedded into the culture and structures of the organization and requires everybody to adopt a quality consciousness in all aspects of their work.

A number of management thinkers have been associated with the development of TQM. In the fifty or so years since the Second World War, the changes in management thinking in the USA, and later in Japan, led by 'gurus' like Edward Deming and Philip Crosby, have seen an evolution of quality regimes into modern TQM. We could go to one of several writers to gain a good working definition of TQM. One of the best is given by Philip B. Crosby in his book *Quality is Free*.

Crosby's four absolutes of TQM
Crosby argues that systems in TQM rest upon 'four absolutes of quality':

- *Quality is defined as conformance to specification.* This view of quality concurs with our earlier definition – that it is concerned with matching expectations rather than with any ideas we may have of luxury or premium.
- *The systems for causing (or ensuring) quality are based upon prevention (of poor quality) rather than appraisal or control.* In this respect, TQM is more like QA than QC. The emphasis is thus on bringing the organization's systems to bear upon preventing bad quality by emphasizing good design, staff training and a culture of caring about quality.
- *The performance standard is zero defects* (ZD). This means that the emphasis shifts from trying to get products within QC tolerances to creating products which are perfect every time. Under TQM, every product will be produced correctly every time, thus avoiding all the costs associated with reworking or disposing of off-specification stocks or in losing customer confidence through poor quality. Customers can thus be absolutely certain that every delivery of product will precisely match specification.
- *The measure of quality is the financial cost of non-conformance.* We have already

seen that bad quality costs money and, whilst TQM may have some costs associated with its implementation, it is argued that bad quality costs more than guaranteeing good quality.

Seven principles of TQM

The above four absolutes set out the underlying philosophy of TQM. Its management in organizations obviously rests upon much more 'concrete' ideas than the four absolutes. The so-called 'seven principles' of TQM are designed to guide managers in managing systems under a TQM regime.

- *Get it right first time*, thus eliminating the risk of failure at QC, possibly facilitating the closure of the QC department altogether. It also means that quality must be designed into each part of the business.
- *Make quality easy to see*. This means that product design and the production process should be such that faults can be detected at the earliest possible stage. Visibility and simplicity in all aspects of operation should consequently be encouraged.
- *Insistence upon compliance* with the quality philosophy. All employees should be fully convinced of the value of TQM and must be 'sold' the idea by management or 'coerced' into it if necessary.
- *Line stop authority*. We have seen that one of the most important features of TQM is to prevent poor quality as soon as it occurs. TQM makes this possible by making the prevention of bad quality the responsibility of everybody. Hence, all employees working on the production process are given the authority to stop the production process to correct bad quality if they find it in any part of the process.
- *Correct your own mistakes*. This is in keeping with the TQM idea that quality is everybody's responsibility, so an employee is expected to ensure that any faulty workmanship is made good before the stock is passed on to the next workstation. Faults should be corrected as soon as they occur rather than leaving them to be corrected at some later time.
- *100% checks* means two things. Firstly, that inspection does not just occur at a few points along the production process but takes place all of the time a product is in production. Such an undertaking clearly cannot be carried out by just a few testers and so this responsibility falls to everybody to maintain a high level of vigilance at all times. Secondly, all parts, or all components, of a product should be assured to be within specification, from the most critical parts right down to the 'nuts and bolts' and other ancillary parts that may be considered less important.
- *Continuous improvement* is the final principle of TQM. Behind this principle is the idea that products and processes are never so good that they cannot be improved upon. In some companies, this principle is formalized into groupings like quality circles where employees meet regularly to discuss ways of improving products or processes.

TQM and culture

We have seen that for most organizations, the adoption of TQM will require a shift in the corporate culture. Its introduction may prove to be problematic unless the concept is fully taken on board by all members of the organization. For this reason, in many cases, it takes some time to implement in its 'purest' form.

The culture of TQM requires several key cultural changes in thinking.

From	To
Reactive management (reacting to problems and circumstances)	Proactive management and forward planning
Inspection (QC)	Prevention (QA)
'Acceptable' quality ('that's good enough')	Zero defects ('right first time, on time, every time')
Placing the blame for a problem	Solving the problem, regardless of blame
Low cost *or* quality	Low cost *and* quality
Good quality costs more	Good quality actually costs less

15.4 Just-in-time

We have seen that TQM involves a concentration or focus on quality. The second philosophy we shall consider, just-in-time (JIT), is complementary to TQM rather than contradictory of it, even though its emphasis is different. JIT and TQM have many features in common and it is perfectly possible for a company to operate both simultaneously.

The focus of JIT is waste. JIT thus aims to eliminate waste in all the forms in which it occurs in an operational process. By doing this, JIT cuts the costs involved in operations and thus increases an organization's profitability.

What is waste?

Waste arises from any stock or activity that costs the organization money but does not add value or generate income. Examples include:

- Any stock that is not actually being processed (and to which value is therefore not being added). This includes all raw materials, all finished goods and any work-in-progress that is queuing between production processes.
- Stocks that have failed a quality test, either in-process or at final QC.
- Machine 'down-time,' that is production time lost through machines not being operable for any reason such as breakdown or through tooling up or tooling down between batches.
- The time and stock involved in producing unsold or unsaleable stocks.

The core themes of JIT

The core themes of JIT address the cultural climate necessary for its successful implementation. In the same way that TQM requires a conducive culture, JIT must also have the support and understanding of all employees – especially, of course, in the operations function.

- *Simplicity* – all procedures in operations should be kept as simple as possible. This does not mean that complicated things should be made artificially simple, but that nothing should be more complex than it needs to be. Overcomplicating procedures means that more costs are incurred than needs to be the case.
- *Visibility* – waste can only be eliminated when it can be seen. In practice, this means that all systems and work-places should be functional and tidy. It also implies that waste can conceal potential problems – for example high stock levels can be used as a buffer to hide poor production planning.
- *Continuous* – JIT is not a 'fad', it is part of the ongoing success of the organization, and indeed, the success of the organization may depend upon JIT.
- *Involvement* – even although JIT may be centred around the operations function, everybody in the organization must be committed to it and involved with it.

JIT and operational practices

When we considered TQM, we saw that it, too, had some key underlying 'absolutes' which underpin its implementation in practice. The core themes of JIT and the focus on the issue of waste set out the philosophical underpinnings of JIT. The main features of JIT in practice can be summarized by the segments in the 'JIT cycle', as shown in Figure 15.1.

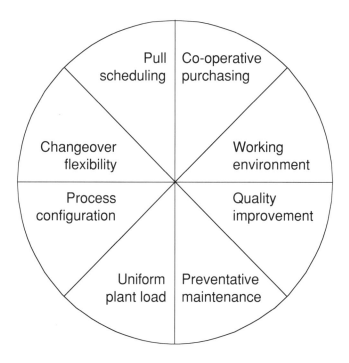

Figure 15.1 The JIT cycle

The key operational features of JIT are discussed below.

Environment
This refers to the management of space and the working areas. Tidiness and order are considered to be important features of a JIT system – 'a place for everything and everything in its place'. Similarly, all information and paperwork systems need to be transparent and orderly.

Quality
JIT takes the same view of quality as TQM. Because poor quality costs money, it is obviously a source of waste. For this reason, many organizations that operate JIT also observe principles of QA or TQM. Prevention is better and cheaper than cure.

Preventative maintenance
Given that one form of waste is machine down-time due to breakdown, JIT emphasizes maintaining plant and equipment proactively rather than waiting for something to go wrong. This parallels with having a car regularly serviced to keep it in good order, as opposed to waiting until the radiator springs a leak on a cold wet night when you are in a hurry to get somewhere. In consequence, JIT observes regular and thorough maintenance schedules on all equipment. Furthermore, all employees are encouraged to immediately report any irregularities in machine operation (such as a 'funny noise').

Uniform plant load
JIT requires skilful planning of the workload through the operations function. A 'lumpy' passage of work can result in periods of underwork or overwork. Underloading of work results in both employees and equipment 'sitting idle' (i.e. not adding value). Overloading results in stocks queuing to get through the various stages in operations and possibly an extension of lead times (possibly leading to an erosion of customer confidence in the business to supply its needs on time). Both of these situations, in their different ways, cost money and introduce waste (i.e. non-value-adding activity).

In consequence, JIT seeks to even out the flow of work through the operations function. Whilst the pattern on customer orders may make this objective difficult to achieve at times, production planners attempt to smooth out workload as far as possible to eliminate 'lumpiness'.

Process configuration
Process configuration refers to the manner in which processes in a production facility are physically laid out. There are two general ways in which factories can be laid out:

- *Process-based configurations*, where plant is arranged according to the type of process. Batches pass from process area to process area depending on the station which is able to receive the batch at the earliest time.
- *Product-based configurations*, where plant is arranged according to the type of product being produced.

Figures 15.2 and 15.3 show typical routes for three batches under the two regimes.

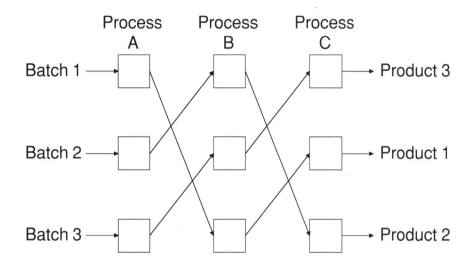

Figure 15.2 Possible route for three batches (1, 2 and 3) through three processes (A, B and C) under a process-based configuration

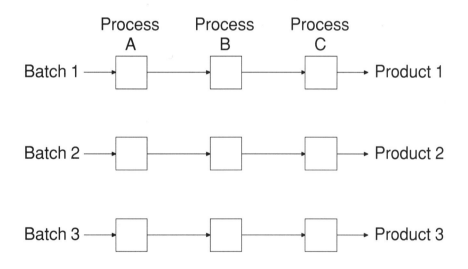

Figure 15.3 Simplified route for the three batches through a product-based configuration

In keeping with the JIT core theme of simplicity, most JIT operations attempt to avoid clutter and confusion. In theory, JIT prescribes that a business uses whichever configuration provides the most visibility and simplicity. In practice, the majority opt for a more or less product-based layout. This offers the possibility of more precise line-balancing (see Chapter 14), thus reducing work-in-progress queuing between stations.

Changeover flexibility
We have seen that one of the sources of waste is the time taken to tool-up and tool-

down between jobs or batches. It follows that a key way of reducing such waste is to make such changes faster and easier. The parallel is sometimes drawn in this area between the time it takes for a motorist to change a wheel by the side of a road to a team changing the wheels on Damon Hill's formula one racing car. One takes twenty minutes; the other less than ten seconds. The point being that when staff are sufficiently trained and motivated, changeover times can be significantly reduced.

This factor is of importance when designing an operational process. By designing-in a facility for rapid and flexible product-to-product changeover, down-time can be reduced and hence waste avoided.

Pull scheduling

We have seen that one of the sources of waste is stock to which value is not being added – raw materials and finished goods stock. Pull scheduling avoids the creation of such stocks. Under this regime, nothing happens in an operations function until a customer 'pulls' stock through it in the form of ordered stock. This represents a significant change of thinking for many businesses which, when orders are light, will 'make for stock' – making finished goods stock for anticipated future orders.

The process of 'pulling' extends backwards through the operations function by a system the Japanese have termed *kanban*. A kanban (the Japanese word for 'card') is a signal from one workstation to another to provide goods for the next stage of working. In a JIT operation, work is forbidden unless a kanban is obtained from a forward station – from the customer, to despatch and backwards through the operation. The final kanban is a signal to the supplier to provide the necessary raw material stocks to fulfil the customer's order.

Kanban works as a trigger to start production activity. A simple kanban system is as follows:

- a customer places an order (a kanban to the despatch department);
- the despatch department kanbans the final stage of production to supply goods to fulfil the customer order;
- the final stage of production kanbans the second-last stage to supply goods so that the final stage can finish the process to provide the goods requested by despatch;
- each work-station kanbans the one before it to supply goods in the appropriate state of assembly until the purchasing department kanbans the supplier.

It follows from the kanban principle that, providing there are no delays in any of the stages, the lead time for an order is the same as the time it takes to produce it. Such a system requires a very well organized operations function and a very special relationship with the suppliers.

Co-operative purchasing

The kanban principle means that JIT operations make special demands upon their suppliers. They require suppliers to deliver stock:

- immediately or within a very short time period;
- to the point on the production line at which it will be used;
- in the precise quantity to meet customer orders;
- to a consistent quality and often to the buyer's design.

Such demands necessitate a special relationship with a supplier. JIT manufacturers achieve this by cultivating long-term and co-operative relationships with suppliers. The conventional supplier–buyer relationship is based on achieving the maximum amount of concession from the other. This means that suppliers seek to supply at quantities that are convenient at as high a price as possible, whereas buyers seek to buy at the lowest possible price.

In a co-operative purchasing environment, a buyer (the JIT manufacturer) recognizes that the ability of the company to operate its JIT system relies upon reliable supply. In consequence, partnerships tend to be built up wherein suppliers are rewarded with long-term supply contracts, agreed pricing structures and regular communication with the JIT customer. In many cases, the supplier's flexibility is also rewarded with a slightly higher price – reflecting the supplier's higher stockholding and transport costs.

The benefits and drawbacks of JIT

JIT offers a number of potential benefits.

Firstly, the reduced stockholding reduces the working capital needed to run the business. Working capital is money tied up in stocks, cash-in-hand or in debtors (money owed to the business). Stock is therefore a way of tying up money which cannot be used for other purposes such as investment. A lower working capital not only provides the opportunity for higher profitability, but also increases liquidity (see Chapter 11).

Secondly, JIT provides an opportunity to reduce the costs of the operations department. JIT's focus on reducing stocks, preventing breakdown and on reducing changeover time all help to reduce costs and thus increase profitability.

Thirdly, under JIT, all products are made to the requirements of the customer. This provides increased flexibility as a customer can order the precise quantity needed and to the required specification (i.e. the customer does not merely have to choose from existing finished goods stock).

Potential drawbacks include the possibility of higher unit costs arising from the requirements made of suppliers. Additionally, the fact that finished goods stocks are not held renders the business vulnerable if for any reason the order cannot be fulfilled (such as through machine breakdown or supplier failure).

Assignments

- Discuss the problems that a company might experience in attempting to implement a JIT system into a 'traditional' corporate culture.
- The director of a company producing ball-bearings says that 'Implementing TQM in my company would be a waste of money. We only make little round metal balls. Our QC is consistently within tolerance. What else do we need?' Discuss the wisdom of the director's comments.

Further reading

Crosby, P. B. (1979) *Quality is Free*. New York: McGraw Hill.

Hoyle, D. (1994). *ISO 9000 Quality Systems Handbook*. Oxford: Butterworth-Heinemann.

Labovitz, G., Chang, Y. S. and Rosansky, V. (1994) *Making Quality Work*. London: Harper Collins.

Munroe-Faure, L. and Munroe-Faure, M. (1992) *Implementing Total Quality Management*. London: Pitman.

Oakland, J. S. and Porter, L. (1995). *Total Quality Management: Text and Cases*. Oxford: Butterworth-Heinemann.

Oakland, J. S. (1993) *Total Quality Management*. Oxford: Butterworth Heinemann.

Omachonu, V. K. and Ross, J. E. (1995) *Principles of Total Quality*. London: Kogan Page.

Wickens, P. (1987) *The Road to Nissan*. London: Macmillan.

Wilson, G., Cairns, N., McBride, P. and Bell, D. (1994). *Managing Quality*. Oxford: Butterworth-Heinemann.

Part Two
The External Business Micro-environment

16

The market system – prices and costs

Learning objectives

After studying this chapter, students should be able to describe:

- The meaning of the terms 'market' and 'market system'.
- The difference between goods and services.
- The difference between prices and costs.
- The various types of cost.
- The purpose and meaning of price.
- The various types of revenue and how they are arrived at.
- How prices, costs and revenues can be used to determine the break-even point.
- How prices, costs and revenues can be used to determine the point at which profit is maximized.

16.1 What is the market system?

The 'market'

If you or I want to buy some food, we naturally head for a food shop. Why is this? Because we know that, at a food shop, there is a business that is willing to part with the goods we need in exchange for our money. Similarly, if I want to sell my car, I may put an advert in the local paper in the hope that I can attract interested buyers who will buy the car from me. People who want to buy second-hand cars may well look in the classified section of the local paper.

We can thus readily arrive at a simple definition of the term 'market'. *A market is a place where buyers and sellers come together.* We use the term market in many contexts in everyday conversation. The job market consists of buyers (of labour) who advertise in papers, Jobcentres, etc., and sellers (suppliers of labour – employees and potential employees) who access those sources knowing that they can 'meet' buyers in those pages. The food market exists in your local supermarket as sellers set up a business and buyers go to the shop for the sole purpose of buying food.

The word 'place' in the above definition may or may not mean a physical location. In some markets, it may do (e.g. the quayside market in Newcastle upon Tyne, the fish market in Billingsgate), but in many cases it means a non-physical 'location', which may be in the media, through word of mouth or, increasingly, through computer communications. We speak, for example, of the chemicals market, which consists of thousands of buyers and sellers all over the world who, through a plethora of interrelationships, make themselves known to one another.

Goods and services

Markets are concerned with buyers and sellers of goods and services. The term 'goods and services' is used frequently in this text and is taken to mean the various types of product that are exchanged in business.

A *product*, in its most general sense, is the output of an organization that is offered for use or consumption by the buyer. We can immediately see that the nature of organizational outputs varies enormously and it is here that we use our 'goods and services' distinction.

- *Goods* is generally taken to mean products that can be touched and seen. They are classified by economists and the Government (for recording purposes) as *visible products*. Examples include foods, cars, chemicals, pharmaceuticals and electronic goods. It follows that goods are things we can *own*.
- *Services* are products that cannot be touched, They are things that are done for our benefit and are classed as *invisible products*. Examples include insurance services, tradespeople like plasterers and mechanics, health provision and legal advice. Services are things that we *use* or *have done* rather than own.

> **Question 16.1**
>
> For each the organizations listed below, state:
>
> - The main product offered to the market.
> - Whether the product is a 'good' or a 'service'.
> - The buyer of the organization's product.
>
> - J. Sainsbury – supermarkets.
> - General Accident – insurance company.
> - The University of Sussex – educational and research establishment.
> - National Power – power generator.
> - The Army – one of Her Majesty's armed forces.

The market price

Every time you make a purchase, say of a food item at your local Asda, you are (probably unconsciously) attesting to the efficiency of the market system. Asda offers its baked beans for sale at a certain price – say 20 p a tin. You go to Asda because you know it sells baked beans. You look at the price of 20 p and you have a choice. You can either say,

- 'No, 20 p is too high a price' (result: no sale takes place), or you can say,
- 'Yes, I am willing to pay 20 p to enjoy the benefit of these beans' (result: sale takes place).

If you decide that 20 p is too high a price, you may look elsewhere for your beans. You may try a cheaper supermarket or you may decide to buy peas instead.

On the other side of the market relationship, Asda will be asking itself some questions. If the sales on baked beans (at a price of 20 p) are high, it will conclude one of the following:

- the price of baked beans is about right, we will leave it as it is; or
- the price for baked beans may be too low, we may be able to increase it slightly and make even more money from the sale of this product.

Conversely, if sales of baked beans are low, it may conclude that the price of baked beans is too high. In such a situation, the most obvious thing to do is to reduce the price and see if the total sales rise.

The market system is thus composed of millions of individuals buying and selling decisions. In this chapter and the one following, we will examine the features of the various parts of the buying and selling decisions that, in their totality, make businesses 'tick' and national economies 'work'.

Prices and costs – what is the difference?

In common language, we tend to use the terms 'price' and 'cost' interchangeably. In strict business and economic terms, there is a clear difference. Put simply: *the seller's price is the buyer's cost.*

In the above example we saw that the *price* of a tin of baked beans was 20 p. When Asda bought the beans from its supplier (e.g. Heinz) , it would incur a *cost* by buying it. The cost to Asda would be some amount less than its asking price so that by selling the beans it could make a profit. To you, the buyer of the beans, the Asda price of 20 p becomes a cost (to you) of the same amount.

Hence, a business will often speak of its costs to mean the total amount of money needed to operate the business. It will use the prices charged for its products to (hopefully) cover the costs it had incurred.

16.2 A closer look at business costs

Types of costs

When examining business costs, a business first identifies the monetary value of the *total costs* that the business has incurred and then attempts to see how the total cost is made up.

The first component of the total cost is the *fixed cost*. Fixed costs are those which do not vary with an organization's output. In other words, they must be paid even if the business does not make or do anything. Examples of fixed costs in most businesses include:

- rent on the factory, land, offices, etc.;
- local authority taxation;

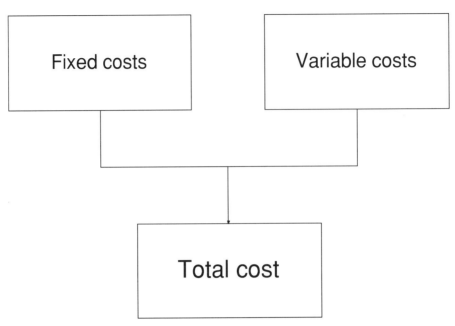

Figure 16.1 Composition of total cost

- some staff/employee costs;
- water rates (if water is not metered);
- repayments on any loans that the business may have.

The second component of total cost is the *variable cost*. Variable costs are those which do vary with organizational output: if the business makes nothing, it incurs no variable costs. Examples include:

- raw material costs;
- some labour costs (persons employed on a piece-rate basis);
- energy costs (needed to operate machines, for example);
- transportation costs.

Hence we arrive at a very simple mathematical definition of total cost.

Total cost (TC) = Fixed cost (FC) + Variable cost (VC)

or

TC = FC + VC

In examining costs, economists tend to distinguish between what are termed *short-run* and *long-run* costs. In the short-run, it is assumed that production inputs like rent on property are fixed in that the company cannot immediately terminate the use of the property and thus reduce its costs of the rent. It is thus considered as a short-run fixed cost. In the long-run, however, the fixed costs can be reduced by giving up use of the property (or selling a machine, building, etc.). What was a short-run fixed cost can thus become a long-run variable cost.

Most calculations in micro-economics are based on the short-run basis. When we enter a discussion of economics in the longer run, it can get very complicated, as all fixed costs can become variable eventually (i.e. in the very long run).

Average and marginal costs

Economists, in analysing the costs of a business use the terms average and marginal costs to get a better understanding of how costs are incurred by a business. Let us first define the terms.

The *average cost* of a business describes the cost, on average, attributable to each unit of output (e.g. each can of beer, washing machine, car). Whilst businesses may know some costs (e.g. the material cost) of each item it makes (but, in practice, even this is often unknown), it can allocate fixed costs to an item by performing a simple calculation. We find the average cost by dividing the total cost by the output in units or quantity.

$$\text{Average cost (AC)} = \frac{\text{Total cost (TC)}}{\text{Quantity(Q)}}$$

or

$$AC = \frac{TC}{Q}$$

The *marginal cost* is the total cost incurred by the business for each extra unit of output it produces. Initially, we would expect the marginal cost to fall as output (quantity) increases. This is because each extra unit produced 'dilutes' the fixed costs by that little bit more and, although the variable cost attributable to each unit may remain relatively constant, the total cost per unit incurred is likely to fall.

When output rises past a certain level, however, the marginal cost usually starts to rise. At the point at which it starts to increase, the business is beginning to increase its total costs faster that it can recover them through simply producing more units. This is due to short-run diseconomies of scale that creep into a business through having to, say, purchase a new machine to make more units. The point at which marginal cost is at its lowest is therefore the point at which production is at its most efficient.
Marginal cost is defined as:

$$\text{Marginal cost (MC)} = \frac{\text{Change in total cost (}\Delta\text{TC)}}{\text{The change in quantity (}\Delta\text{Q)}}$$

or

$$MC = \frac{\Delta TC}{\Delta Q}$$

(the symbol Δ (delta) denotes a change in, so ΔTC means the change in total cost)

The costs schedule

The best way to understand how these costs all fit together is to construct a table. You are given the following information:

Table 16.1 Costs schedule

Quantity	Fixed cost	Variable cost	Total cost	Average cost	Marginal cost
0	20	0			
1		10			
2		16			
3		22			
4		36			
5		60			
6		100			

Using the information and equations we have already learned we can now fill in the rest of this table. Fixed costs, by definition, will stay the same for all quantities produced. Total cost can be obtained by adding together the fixed and variable costs. Average cost can be obtained by dividing the total cost by the quantity. Marginal cost, in this case, can be calculated by subtracting the previous total cost from the current one.

The completed table is thus as shown in Table 16.2.

Table 16.2 Completed costs schedule

Quantity	Fixed cost	Variable cost	Total cost $(=FC+VC)$	Average cost $(=TC/Q)$	Marginal cost $(\Delta TC/\Delta Q)$
0	**20**	**0**	20	0	-
					10
1	20	**10**	30	30	
					6
2	20	**16**	36	18	
					6
3	20	**22**	42	14	
					14
4	20	**36**	56	14	
					24
5	20	**60**	80	16	
					40
6	20	**100**	120	20	

Note that we enter marginal cost in-between the lines of other figures. This is because marginal cost describes the difference between the two sets of values in the line (total cost and quantity). It also reminds us that when we come to plot marginal costs, we plot the values between the other values on the x axis.

If we now plot this data on a graph, we arrive at an important principle. The point 'X' in Figure 16.2 is important. Levels of output to the left of point X mean that average cost is falling with increased output, so it makes business sense to produce at those quantities. To the right of point X, average costs start to rise. Hence, the point at which the marginal cost line intersects the average cost line represents the most efficient short-run output level of the business. In this example it is about 3.5 units.

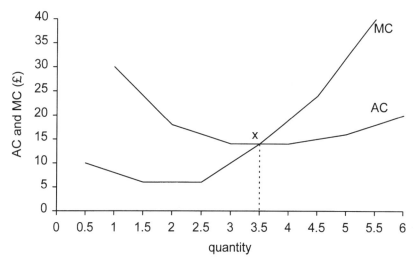

Figure 16.2 *Average cost and marginal cost against quantity (short run). AC, average cost; MC, marginal cost*

Question 16.2

Complete the following table and plot the graph. Establish the most efficient level of output.

Quantity	Fixed cost	Variable cost	Total cost	Average cost	Marginal cost
0	15 000	0			
1000		15 000			
2000		24 000			
3000		33 000			
4000		54 000			
5000		90 000			
6000		150 000			

Hint: When plotting marginal cost, plot the numbers between the points of average cost. This is because MC figures represent the difference between the two total cost figure from which average cost is calculated.

16.3 A closer look at business prices

The purpose of the price

The price that a business charges for its goods and services has a number of purposes.

It is a means of *covering the costs* that the business has incurred in bringing the product to the market. Such costs may typically include the cost of the materials in the product, the costs of labour, rent on premises, transport costs, marketing or advertising costs, packaging costs, etc. In this respect, the price charged ensures that the seller does not make a trading loss.

It is a means of gaining wealth and of *making a profit* if the price charged includes a net surplus over all costs incurred. Profits are used to reinvest in the business (e.g. buying more equipment) and to pay the owners of the business a return, such as the giving of dividends on shares.

Profit

We use the term 'profit' in a number of ways in ordinary conversation. In economic terms, the profit is the surplus a business is left with once a price has been achieved in a business transaction and all the costs have been paid.

It can represent the cash surplus on one business transaction, in which case we express it as:

Profit (π) = Price (P) – Total cost (TC)

It can also represent the total surplus made by a business over a period of time. This would be expressed as:

Profit (π) = Total revenue (TR) – Total cost (TC)

for the time period in question.

The price can sometimes be a *signal to the buyer*. A buyer often makes the assumption that 'you get what you pay for'. In this regard, a low price will communicate certain features of the product to the buyer (e.g. 'cheap and cheerful', functional, basic) whereas a high price will have the opposite effect (e.g. quality, premium, luxurious).

Revenue

The term revenue is sometimes referred to as sales value, turnover, or income. It is the total sales for a business over a period of time and is expressed as:

Total revenue (TR) = Price (P) × Quantity sold (Q)

or

TR = PQ

Hence, if the price of a good is £2 and, over the course of a month, the business sells 1000 units, then its revenue for the month is £2 × 1000 = £2000. If sales are consistent over a year, the quantity for the year would be 12000 and the revenue, £24000.

Average and marginal revenues

In the same way that we calculated average and marginal costs, there is also value in calculating the same for revenues.

Average revenue (AR) is the revenue that a business earns from each unit at any given level of output.

$$\text{Average revenue (AR)} = \frac{\text{Total revenue (TR)}}{\text{Quantity (Q)}}$$

or

$$AR = \frac{TR}{Q}$$

We should note at this point that we have seen the term *TR/Q* before. By rearranging the equation we used to calculate total revenue, we can see that the equation:

TR = PQ

can be rearranged as

$$Q = \frac{TR}{P}$$

or

$$P = \frac{TR}{Q}$$

Because TR/Q = P, it follows that if

$$AR = \frac{TR}{Q}$$

then, because both P and AR = TR/Q, it must be the case that

AR = P

So for our purposes (making some assumptions), we can describe the average revenue as price.

Rearranging simple mathematical equations

There are two types of simple equation. The first type involves a plus or a minus and the second type involves a multiplication or division.

Equations which are of the type

$a = b - c$

can be expressed correctly in three ways

a = b − c, or
b = a + c, or
c = b − a

Equations that are of the type

$a = b \times c$ (sometimes expressed as $a = bc$)

can be expressed correctly in three ways

$a = bc$

$b = \dfrac{a}{c}$

$c = \dfrac{a}{b}$

You can check if your rearrangement is correct by making a, b and c equal 1, 2 and 3, to see if the equation works.

Marginal revenue (MR) is the additional revenue earned by selling one extra unit of output. This figure can be found by calculating as follows:

$$\text{Marginal revenue (MR)} = \frac{\text{Change in revenue } (\Delta TR)}{\text{Change in quantity } (\Delta Q)}$$

or

$$MR = \frac{\Delta TR}{\Delta Q}$$

A feature of prices is that the more of an item there is on the market, the lower the price of that item will be. If there was only one motor car for sale in the whole country, it would attract a hefty price. Similarly, if there were more than a billion for sale in the UK, sellers could hardly give them away – they would certainly go for a very low price. We would thus expect both the price per unit (average revenue) and marginal revenue to fall as quantity rises.

We can see how this works by looking at a schedule as shown in Table 16.3.

Table 16.3

Quantity	Price	Average revenue	Total revenue	Marginal revenue
1	100			
2	90			
3	80			
4	70			
5	60			
6	50			

By using the equations we encountered above, we can fill the table in.

Table 16.4

Quantity	Price	Average revenue (= price)	Total revenue (= PQ)	Marginal revenue (= $\Delta TR/\Delta Q$)
1	100	100	100	-
				80
2	90	90	180	
				60
3	80	80	240	
				40
4	70	70	280	
				20
5	60	60	300	
				0
6	50	50	300	

We can now plot the data as a graph (Figure 16.3).

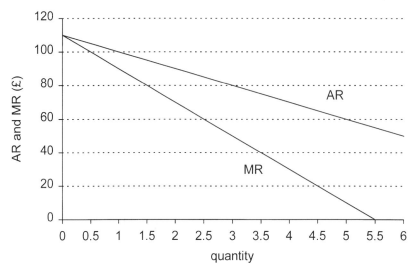

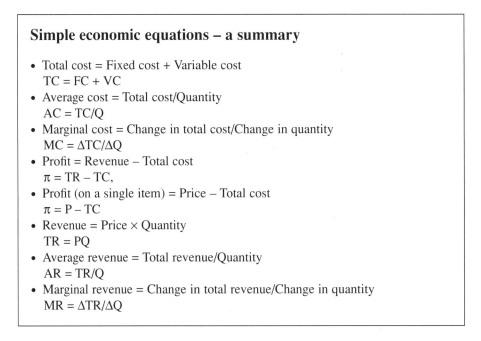

Figure 16.3 *Average revenue (AR) and marginal revenue (MR)*

Simple economic equations – a summary

- Total cost = Fixed cost + Variable cost
  TC = FC + VC
- Average cost = Total cost/Quantity
  AC = TC/Q
- Marginal cost = Change in total cost/Change in quantity
  MC = ΔTC/ΔQ
- Profit = Revenue – Total cost
  π = TR – TC,
- Profit (on a single item) = Price – Total cost
  π = P – TC
- Revenue = Price × Quantity
  TR = PQ
- Average revenue = Total revenue/Quantity
  AR = TR/Q
- Marginal revenue = Change in total revenue/Change in quantity
  MR = ΔTR/ΔQ

16.4 Using prices and costs in business

We may well ask what the purpose is of the foregoing discussion on the various aspects of prices and costs. We will examine two of the most important uses of what we have learned.

Break-even point

By understanding the information we have so far discussed, we can introduce the concept of break-even point – the quantity beyond which the business's revenues exceed its total costs. We can intuitively see that if a business has no output, it is still incurring its fixed costs such as rent and local authority taxation. Using the equation $\pi = TR - TC$ it is clear that if $TR = 0$ (because nothing is being sold) and TC (which is partly fixed cost) is a positive figure, then π would be a negative figure, i.e. a loss.

The break-even graph in Figure 16.4 is explained as follows. At zero output, the business incurs the full burden of fixed cost, but no variable cost. There is, of course, no revenue. The loss on operations is the value of the fixed costs.

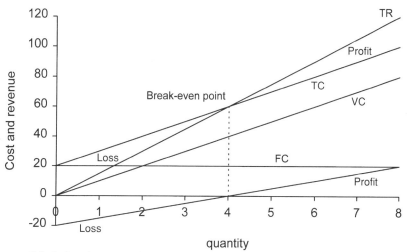

Figure 16.4 Break-even point

As output rises, the business begins to incur variable costs and hence total cost rises parallel to variable costs (because total cost equals variable cost plus fixed cost, which remains constant). Revenue rises at a faster rate than costs due to the price being in excess of costs with a view to more then covering variable costs. For simplification purposes, the TR line makes the assumption in this case that an increase in quantity does not produce a reduction in price. We know this to be something of a simplification, but it enables us to understand the principle of break-even.

At the break-even point, output reaches a level at which the total revenue earned from all units produced overtakes total cost. Production below the quantity at break-even point incurs an overall loss to the business, whereas at levels above it an overall profit is made.

Profit maximization

We can use the theory discussed above to answer the question: 'What is the optimal output of a business at which profit is maximized?' Using the information we have already learned, we can calculate the output of maximum profit in two ways:

- by plotting total cost and total revenue on the same graph;
- by plotting marginal cost and marginal revenue on the same graph.

The *total cost and total revenue* approach is as follows. Let us remind ourselves of the behaviour of these two variables. Total costs will be the fixed cost at zero quantity and will then grow increasingly slowly as the increased quantity dilutes the fixed costs. Eventually, however, total costs will rise with increasing output as the business experiences diseconomies of scale in the short run. It follows that the shape of the total cost curve will assume a sigmoidal (S-shaped) form. For total revenue, we may expect revenues to grow rapidly as a function of quantity at first, but as the market price for the good falls with increased quantity, the total revenue against quantity will level off.

Using some appropriate figures, as given in Table 16.5, should aid our understanding.

Table 16.5

Quantity	Total cost (= FC + VC)	Total revenue (= PQ)	Total profit (= TR − TC)
0	100	0	−100
1	150	100	−50
2	180	180	0
3	210	240	30
4	280	280	0
5	400	300	−100
6	600	300	−300

We can now plot the graph shown in Figure 16.5.

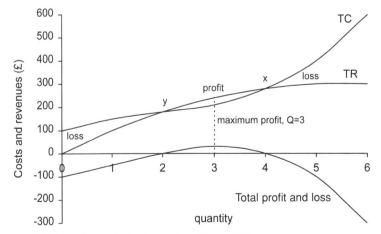

Figure 16.5 Profit maximization using TR and TC

We can see that the total profit curve reaches its highest at a quantity of three units, but by plotting the other two curves as well we can see why it is the case. To the left of point *y*, output levels have not yet provided sufficient revenues to outweigh total costs (which at this stage are mainly fixed costs). Between point *y* and point *z*, revenues exceed costs and this is the area of profit. Output of anything between *y* and *z* (which in this case is between two and four units) would yield a profit, but it is at three units that the gap between the TR and TC is at its widest – hence the point of profit maximization. To the right of point z, the two factors of short-run diseconomies of scale (on costs) and reduced price per unit (on revenues), makes for a nasty combination. The curves grow further apart as costs rise and revenues fall.

The *marginal cost and marginal revenue* approach rests upon the following principles. We know that the marginal cost is the cost incurred by producing one more unit of output and that marginal revenue is the extra revenue gained by selling that one more unit of output. We can intuitively understand that if a business incurs more cost than it makes in extra revenue by making one extra unit, then it is unprofitable to make that unit. Using the same figures as in Table 16.5, we can calculate the average and marginal costs and benefits (Table 16.6).

Table 16.6

Q	TC	AC	MC	TR	AR	MR
0	100	0	–	0		
					100	100
1	150	150	50	100		
					90	80
2	180	90	30	180		
					80	60
3	210	70	30	240		
					70	40
4	280	70	70	280		
					60	20
5	400	80	120	300		
					50	0
6	600	100	200	300		

If we now plot marginal revenue and marginal cost against quantity (Figure 16.6), we can see how this approach works. We note immediately that the two lines (MC and MR) intersect at a quantity of three units – the same quantity as profit was maximized in Figure 16.5. This is not an accident, as it is natural that profit should be maximized at this point.

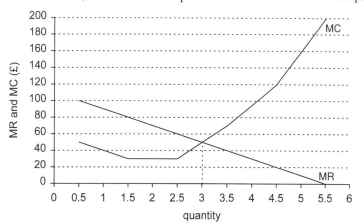

Figure 16.6 Profit maximization from marginal revenue and marginal cost

Assignment

The Turtonian brand of fly-fishing rods is produced by the Turton Company Limited, a small company in Skelmersdale, Lancashire. The company's owner, Nigel Turton, has given you some information about the company's prices and costs and he wants you to calculate the following information for him:

- the most efficient output of production;
- the company's break-even quantity point;
- the output level at which Turton's profit is maximized.

The information you are given is this:

- Company's short-run fixed costs: £2000 per year.

Q	VC at the level of Q	Price per rod at the Q
0	0	–
10	300	130
20	300	126
30	600	122
40	900	118
50	1300	114
60	1800	110
70	2400	106
80	3100	102
90	3900	98
100	4800	94
110	5800	90
120	6900	86

Further reading

For further reading associated with this chapter, see the list at the end of Chapter 17.

17

The market system – supply and demand

Learning objectives

After studying this chapter, students should be able to describe:

- The features and determinants of demand.
- What is meant by the demand schedule and the demand curve.
- The features and determinants of supply.
- What is meant by the supply schedule and the supply curve.
- The mechanisms of price determination and disequilibrium.
- The principles of price elasticity and income elasticity of demand.
- The principles of cross elasticity of demand.
- The features of factor markets, particularly the labour market.

17.1 Demand

Demand and effective demand

Whenever we express an interest in purchasing a good or service, we are indicating a demand. Note though, that it is possible to demand a product without actually buying it. You may demand a new motor car, but for various reasons (e.g. poverty) you are unable to express your demand in the form of a purchase. It is for this reason that economists distinguish desire for a product with its *effective* demand. Producers of goods and services are less concerned with how badly you desire their products, and more with how many you will actually buy and at what price.

Effective demand, as distinct from demand, has three components:

- the actual *quantity demanded* of a good or service;
- the *time period* over which the quantity is demanded;
- the *price* at which the quantity will be demanded over the time period.

Effective demand thus takes into account the customer's ability to buy, not just the desire – however intense that may be. We may say, therefore, that the total demand for product A is 10 000 units a month if the price is 45 p per unit. Thus all three components must be in place before the demand can be said to be effective.

The determinants of demand

In seeking to answer the question *why* the demand for a product is as it is, we must explore the reasons behind consumer choices. We can intuitively appreciate that demand for goods and services varies, both according to the type of product and over time. There are five broad variables which determine the demand for any given product:

- the financial ability to pay;
- changing tastes and fashions (i.e. changing preferences);
- the prices of other, related products;
- the consumer's perceptions of what will happen in the future;
- the type of product it is.

We will examine each in turn.

Ability to pay

The ability to pay for goods and services will obviously have a huge influence on demand. If consumers have a lot of spending power (or disposable income), demand for most products will rise. Conversely, it consumers are 'hard up', demand will tend to fall. The power of consumer spending will depend, among other things upon macro-economic features such as:

- the level of wage or income increases;
- tax rates;
- interest rates;
- employment and unemployment levels in the country.

Consumer preferences

The second determinant of demand is the changing face of consumer preferences. If financial issues determine the consumer's ability to buy, preferences concern the consumer's *willingness* to buy. It is obvious that people change over time in what they want to buy. It may be that one type of product is in demand one year, but not the next. Preference can be influenced in several ways:

- It can be subject to *fashion*, as is the case with clothes, some forms of art, furniture, music and many other things.
- It may be influenced by increasing or decreasing *trends*, such as a decline in the consumption of cigarettes or an increase in the use of condoms.
- It may be influenced by *advertising*, where a producer persuades people to increase consumption of its products.
- Some goods are subject to *seasonal variation* in demand. We might, for example, expect more ice cream to be sold in hot weather whilst we would collectively demand more duffel-coats in the winter.
- Consumption is sometimes informed by *expert opinion*. If an eminent doctor announces that the use of sun-lamps contributes to skin cancer, we might expect a downturn in demand for the purchase and hire of sun-lamps. Conversely, announcements about the cholesterol-reducing properties of bran fibre and red grape juice would tend to stimulate demand for these items.

Prices of other products

The third determinant of demand is the price of other products. This concerns the nature of a product in question and how it relates to other products. A product can be related to other products in one of two ways: it can be a complementary product or it can be a substitute product.

- *Complementary products* are related inasmuch as you will need to buy product A if you buy product B. It follows that an increase in demand for product A will stimulate an increase in the demand for product B. For example, if you buy a petrol-driven car, you will need to buy petrol for it. An increase in the number of cars sold will tend also to increase the volume of petrol sold by oil companies. Cars and petrol are therefore said to be complementary goods. A second example might be video recorders and video tapes.
- *Substitute products* are related inasmuch as you will not need product A if you buy product B. This is because product A performs essentially the same function as product B. Hence, an increase in the demand for product A will cause a decrease in the demand for product B. If, for example, there is an increase in the demand for butter, we would expect a reduction in the demand for margarine. Similarly, if the price of coffee increases due to a bad Brazilian harvest, we might expect more tea to be demanded in place of (as a substitute for) the more expensive coffee.

Question 17.1

How many pairs of products can you think of that are either complements or substitutes? Try to think of at least four pairs for each category.

Consumers' perception of what will happen in the future

The fourth determinant of demand is the consumer's perceptions of the future. If the consumers of a product collectively believe that there will be a future shortage of the product, then demand will increase in the short term. Conversely, if they believe that the price will come down, they will delay purchases, thus reducing short-term demand.

Levels of consumer income and the nature of the product

The fifth determinant of demand is determined by the nature of the product itself. There is a link between the demand for different products and other variables, such as personal income. A comparison between the quantity demanded of goods compared to personal income shows three broad types of product (Figures 17.1 to 17.3).

Figure 17.1 Normal goods

Figure 17.2 Inferior goods

Figure 17.3 Inexpensive necessities

A *normal good* is one wherein demand increases with income – the more you earn, the more you buy. Examples of normal goods are legion; with rising income we will tend to buy more bottles of wine, more holidays, more houses (i.e. we would move more often), etc.

Inferior goods show increased use with rising income, but only up to a point. When a certain level of income is reached, people switch to superior products and hence demand for inferior products declines. Examples of inferior goods would include the cheaper food brands and the use of 'cash-only' supermarkets. In some parts of the country, the use of the bus as a commuter vehicle would be an inferior good as higher income groups switch to private cars to get to and from work.

Inexpensive necessities show an initial increase in demand with income, but there comes a point at a very low level of income where consumption remains constant whatever the income. Examples include salt, sugar and bread. However much you earn, your demand for salt remains the same.

The demand schedule

In seeking to understand the demand for a product during a time period, we must analyse how the quantity demanded is related to the product's price. We do this by means of a simple table called the demand schedule.

The general rule of demand is that there will usually be an inverse relationship between the price and the quantity demanded. In other words:

- the higher the price, the lower the quantity demanded;
- the lower the price, the higher the quantity demanded.

We can illustrate this with a simple example. Product P has the demand schedule shown in Table 17.1. The quantity refers to the number of units that would be bought by the market in a given time period if the price was set at the figure on the left. Hence, if the price per unit was £100, one unit would be demanded by the market. If, however, the price was set at £40, the market in total would buy five units.

Table 17.1 Demand schedule

Price (£)	Quantity demanded
100	1
82	2
66	3
52	4
40	5
30	6
22	7
18	8
16	9

The demand curve

We can now plot the demand schedule to see on a graph how the quantity demanded of a good or service relates to its price. Figure 17.4 shows the demand curve for the data in Table 17.1.

The top left to bottom right slope is typical of the shape of a demand curve. At the top left, the price is high but the quantity demanded is low. At the bottom right, the opposite is the case – low price, high quantity.

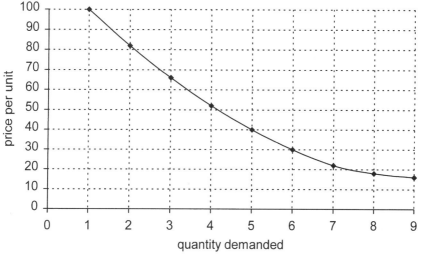

Figure 17.4 Demand curve

Calculating revenue from the demand curve

Once we have drawn the demand curve, we can use it to calculate the business's potential revenue at any given point along it. We learned in the last chapter that:

Total revenue (TR) = Price (P) × Quantity (Q)

At any point on the demand curve, we can calculate the revenue generated at that point simply by multiplying the figure on the quantity axis by that on the price axis. Figure 17.5 uses the data in Table 17.1.

At point P1, the revenue generated will be £40 × 5 = £200. We can perform this calculation at any point along the demand curve to work out the price and quantity that will yield the most revenue.

Question 17.2

Skirozivic is a premium brand of Czech lager and you like it due to its dual qualities as an occasional refreshment and as a rapid intoxicant. You earn a professional salary of £30 000 a year. How many 500 ml bottles of Skirozivic would you buy *per month*, if the price per bottle was as follows. Fill in the table.

Price per 500 ml bottle	Number you would buy per month
30 p	
50 p	
70 p	
£1	
£1.30	
£1.60	
£2	
£2.50	

If possible, add your figures to those of others (e.g. the members of your class) to get the demand for Skirozivic for a bigger group.

Plot the demand curve (when doing this, find the line of best fit rather than just joining the dots).

Answer the following questions:

- How many bottles of Skirozivic would be demanded if the price was £1.10?
- How many bottles of Skirozivic would be demanded if the price was 90 p?

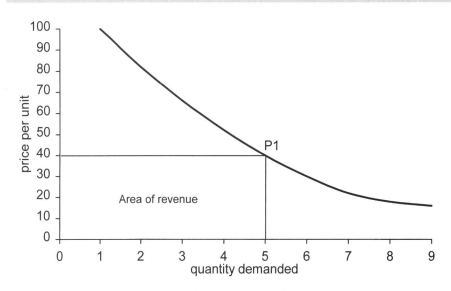

Figure 17.5 Calculating revenue from the demand curve

Extension and contraction of demand

The various points along the market demand curve represent the alternative possible price–quantity situations that the total market will accept. If the actual price of product P, whose demand curve is shown in Figure 17.4 above, is £52, then we can see that four units would be demanded over the time period in question. If the price changes, then the price–quantity situation will move along the existing demand curve. Different terms are used to describe this movement, depending upon its direction:

- A move up and to the left will result in fewer units being demanded at a higher price – a *contraction* of demand.
- A move down and to the right will result in more being demanded at a lower price – an *extension* of demand.

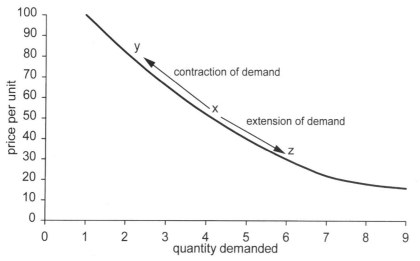

Figure 17.6 Extension and contraction of demand

Let us say that point *x* in Figure 17.6 represents the price–quantity position now. If the price comes down, say to a new price of £30, the quantity demanded would increase to six units (point *z*). Because a higher quantity is the result, it is said that demand has extended. In the event of a move to a higher price (say to point *y*), the quantity demanded would be reduced – hence the term contraction.

Shifts in the demand curve

Under some circumstances, the demand curve itself can move. This happens when more or less quantity is demanded at every price. An example will aid our understanding.

Table 17.2 represents the demand for potatoes in Mr Marrow's small fruit and vegetable shop (a small 'market'). We can now show this schedule as a graph (Figure 17.7).

Table 17.2 Demand for potatoes in Mr Marrow's shop

Price per pound weight	Number of pounds weight demanded per week.
10 p	1000
15 p	850
20 p	700
25 p	550
30 p	400

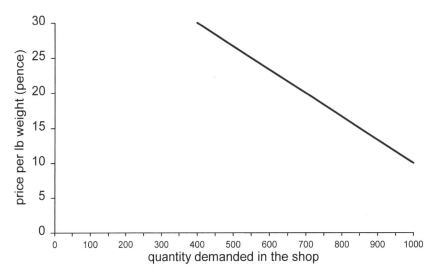

Figure 17.7 Demand curve for potatoes in Mr Marrow's shop

Demand shift scenario 1

Now suppose (hypothetically) that the Department of Health unexpectedly announces that potatoes can act as an aphrodisiac and prevent the development of serious diseases like cancer. This would signal an increase in the demand for potatoes. Because people would want to eat more potatoes, we would expect them to demand more potatoes whatever the price. This means that whereas some consumers may only have been prepared to pay 15 p for a pound of potatoes, the realization that they were so good for you would mean that they would be prepared to pay 20 p in order to secure the benefits of these miraculous tuberous vegetables. In such a circumstance, we would expect a new demand schedule to apply.

Table 17 3 refers to the same shop as does Table 17.2. If we now plot the two demand curves (Figure 17.8) we can see that the curve has shifted as a result of the announcement.

Table 17.3 Demand schedule for potatoes in Mr Marrow's shop before and after the medical announcement

Price per pound	Number of pounds before the announcement	Weight demanded per week after the announcement
10 p	1000	1200
15 p	850	1050
20 p	700	900
25 p	550	750
30 p	400	600

If we take the example of the situation where the price of potatoes was 20 p per pound, we can see that (using the old demand curve) the shop would have sold 700 pounds weight per week (Q1) before the announcement. After the announcement, it can now sell 900 pounds weight (Q2) at that price. This of course also represents an increase in revenue for the shop.

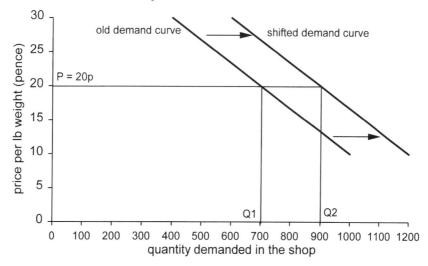

Figure 17.8 Demand curve shift for potatoes in Mr Marrow's shop as a result of the announcement

Before the announcement,

$$TR = PQ$$
$$= 20 \times 700 \text{ pence}$$
$$= 14\,000 = £140$$

After the announcement,

$$TR = 20 \times 900 \text{ pence}$$
$$= 18\,000 = £180$$

The shop in question, in the light of the announcement, theoretically has a happy choice. It can either keep the price the same and sell more potatoes (thus increasing its revenue), or else it can sell the same quantity, but at an increased price (having a similar effect on revenue). Using the demand curve, we can work out how much it could charge for its potatoes if it kept the quantity sold the same (Figure 17.9).

Whereas previously, the market would pay 20p for a total quantity of 700 lbs a week, the shop can now achieve a price of 26p for the same quantity. Again, the shop will enjoy an increase in revenue.

Before: $20 \times 700 = 14\,000$ pence
$$= £140$$
After: $26 \times 700 = 18\,200$ pence
$$= £182$$

A rightward shift in the demand curve can be brought about by anything that causes more of the product to be demanded at every price. Such situations include, as well as the example we have considered, a fall in the price of complementary goods or a rise in the price of a substitute product.

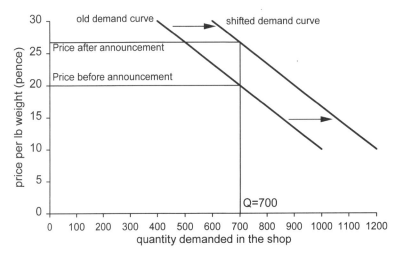

Figure 17.9 Price after announcement at 700 pounds quantity of potatoes per week in Mr Marrow's shop

Demand shift scenario 2

Now suppose that, instead of the previous announcement, the Department of Health actually announces (equally hypothetically) that potatoes are bad for you. Suppose that scientists working on potato biochemistry say that they are linked with male impotence and that they can cause rheumatism and haemorrhoids.

In the case of this announcement, we would expect the demand for potatoes to fall at every price. The demand curve would shift down and to the left. This means that instead of selling 700 pounds a week at a price of 20p, Mr Marrow's shop could now only sell say 500 pounds a week (Figure 17.10).

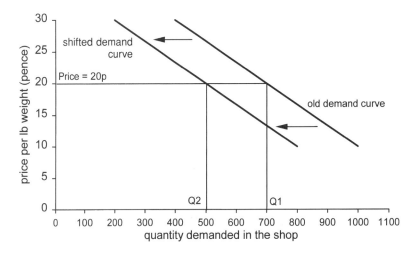

Figure 17.10 Shift in demand after potato health warning, Mr Marrow's shop

If the price was initially 20 p per pound, we know that 700 pounds a week would be demanded (Q1). However, the demand for potatoes would reduce if there was a health scare on them. Hence, at 20 p, the quantity demanded would fall to 500 pounds per week (Q2).

Question 17.3

Which way do you think the demand curve for potatoes would shift (up right or down left), if the following happened?

- the third world rice harvest failed.
- a plague wiped out half of the customers of the shop.

Question 17.4

Mad cow disease and the demand for beef
In a television poll in the Richard and Judy programme in early 1996, 84% of voters stated their intention to stop feeding British beef products to children after the controversy over 'mad cow disease' infected meat. Fears were prevalent that eating British beef products had a link with the onset of the fatal human brain disease, CJD. In what direction would you expect the demand curve to shift as a result of the change in buying patterns?

Mad cow disease and the price of lamb
As a result of the changes to the demand curve for beef, the price of lamb rose by 15%. Which way does the demand curve for lamb shift as a result of the changes in the demand for beef?

Mad cow disease and the demand for horseradish sauce
One of the traditional accompaniments to beef is horseradish sauce. Which way would you expect the demand curve for horseradish sauce to shift as a result of the decline in the demand for beef?

Question 17.5 – The Pope and the price of fish

In the tradition of the Roman Catholic church, Catholics were invited to refrain from eating meat on Fridays. In consequence, many Catholics ate fish instead – 'fish on Friday'. In 1966, however, the Pope announced that Catholics were henceforth allowed to eat meat on Fridays. What do you think happened to the demand curve for fish after the Pope's announcement in 1966? What would happen to the market price for fish, given that the short-term supply curve would remain unchanged?

17.2 Supply

What is supply?

There are two sides to the market system. Having examined the demand side, we turn to supply.

Supply refers to the quantity that producers would want to provide for the market at a given price. In general terms, the higher the price a producer can charge for a product, the more that producers will tend to produce of that product. Conversely, a low market price will tend to stimulate a lower quantity of production. The underlying presupposition behind supply decisions by businesses is that businesses essentially seek to maximize revenues and profits. This presupposition is workable in most situations.

What causes supply?

The decision to supply goods and services to a market depends upon several factors. The quantity of a product supplied will thus depend upon:

- The *price* which the producer can obtain for the product.
- The *prices of other goods*. If, for example, a competitor is producing a substitute product which is expected to be cheaper, this may deter some producers from supplying the market.
- The *costs of producing the product*, which will, in turn, depend upon the wider economic environment, such as labour costs, tax rates, etc.
- *Changes in technology* may reduce the costs of production and stimulate a higher level of supply to the market.
- *Seasonal variations*. Producers of traditionally seasonal products will produce goods in anticipation of increased demand. Ice cream manufacturers will increase production in the early summer months on the assumption that the summer weather will precipitate a higher demand.

The supply schedule

A supply schedule is constructed in the same way as a demand schedule. Information might be gathered about producers collectively on how many units they would supply to the market over a range of possible prices. Equally, a supply schedule can also be constructed for an individual supplier, just as a demand schedule can apply to an individual consumer. The bigger the sample of suppliers represented in the supply schedule, the more informative and meaningful the schedule will be for predicting the nature of the market relationships for that product.

If we return to our earlier example of the potato, the supplier (in this case, Mr Marrow the shopkeeper) makes the decision on how many potatoes to supply depending upon how much money he can get for them. If the market price is high, he may forego stocking carrots and other vegetables to sell more potatoes instead. If the price is low, he would be inclined to dedicate less of his shelf space to potatoes and more to other products which might be expected to yield more profits. The following supply schedule describes the quantity of potatoes that Mr Marrow's shop would offer for sale at each price.

Table 17.4 Supply curve for potatoes – Mr Marrow's fruit and veg shop

Price per pound (pence)	Quantity supplied (pounds) per week
10	400
15	550
20	700
25	850
30	1000

The supply curve

Once we have researched the supply of potatoes for this shop, we can now plot the supply curve from the supply schedule (Figure 17.11). We can see from the graph that it is the converse of the demand curve. At the bottom left, low quantities would be supplied because of the low price. At the top left, higher volumes would be supplied because higher prices are achievable. We described the variables on the demand curve as having an inverse relationship with each other. On a supply curve, price and quantity rising together are said to have a *positive* relationship.

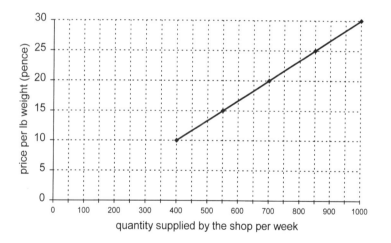

Figure 17.11 Supply curve for potatoes in Mr Marrow's shop

Extension, contraction and shifts in supply

In the same way that we can express changes in price and quantity by moving up or down the demand curve, we can do the same for supply (Figure 17.12). Supply is extended when the price – quantity situation moves up and to the right (more quantity at higher price). It is contracted when it moves down and to the left (less quantity, lower price).

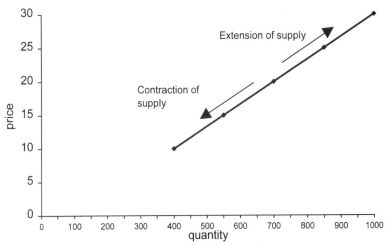

Figure 17.12 Contraction and extension of supply

Similarly, anything that causes more or less to be supplied at every price (such as a good or bad harvest), will cause a shift in the supply curve (Figure 17.13).

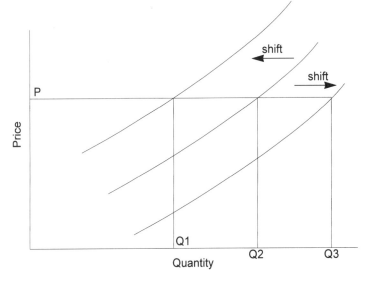

Figure 17.13 Shifts is supply

If Q2 is the initial quantity supplied at price P, then:

- a leftward shift would reduce Q2 to Q1 at the same price – less supply at every price;
- a rightward shift would increase Q2 to Q3 at the same price – more supply at every price.

Supply shifts are brought about by changes in the internal or external environment of the suppliers. To show how this might work, a rightward shift (more supply at every price) could be caused by:

- Decreases in the costs of production. If the supplier can get labour or materials at lower cost, it can produce more for the same cost.
- A fall in the price of other goods. If suppliers receive less revenue by producing some goods, they will tend to produce other goods instead. For example, if the price of baked beans falls, food suppliers may produce more peas. This would signal a rightward shift in the supply curve for peas.
- Technological improvement both reduces the costs of production and can increase production capacity.

Question 17.6

Consider the supply of bus services by bus operators. If more bus services are supplied at every price:

- Which way would the supply curve for bus services shift?
- What might cause this increase in supply at every price?

17.3 Price determination

So far in this chapter, we have looked at the demand side (the quantity that would be demanded over a range of prices) and the supply side (the quantity that would be supplied over a range of prices). The problem is that we don't yet know what the actual price of a good or service will be. Both the demand and supply curves represent a number of possible price – quantity situations, but we do not know at what price the product will actually sell.

The equilibrium point

By comparing a product's supply curve and demand curve on the same graph, we can see that there is one price that both parties (producers and buyers) 'agree' on. This is the point at which both the suppliers and the consumers agree. The noted Cambridge economist Alfred Marshall described the supply and demand curves as two blades of a pair of scissors. Neither blade on its own is enough to 'cut a price'. They must both be present and known before the price can be determined.

We can see how this works by looking again at the supply and demand curves for potatoes at the fruit and vegetable shop we considered earlier (Figures 17.4 and 17.11). If we look at these two curves together, we can see that at a price of 20 p and a quantity of 700 pounds a week, the curves intersect (Table 17.5 and Figure 17.4). This intersection is called the *equilibrium point*.

Disequilibriums

The term *equilibrium* is used in this context for a very deliberate reason. The reason for this is that, whenever the equilibrium is disturbed, the market price will always tend to return to this point.

Table 17.5 Demand and supply schedules for potatoes in Mr Marrow's shop

Price	Supply quantity, pounds per week	Demand quantity, pounds per week
10	400	1000
15	550	850
20	700	700
25	850	550
30	1000	400

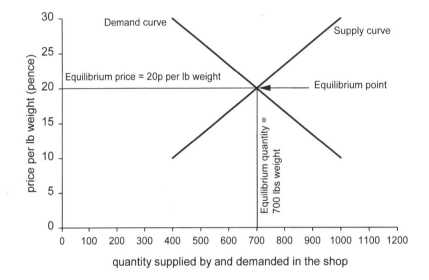

Figure 17.14 The equilibrium point, potatoes at Mr Marrow's shop (per week)

If the supply and demand curves remain approximately in position over a long period of time, the equilibrium price and quantity are likely to similarly remain in a stable position. A condition called *disequilibrium* can occur when, for one reason or another, a price or quantity situation exists which is away from the intersection point of the two curves. The ways in which this can happen are shown in Figure 17.15. The demand and supply curves are those we have previously considered for potato sales in Mr Marrow's small fruit and vegetable shop.

We have seen previously that the equilibrium point is at a price of 20 p per pound at a quantity of 700 pounds per week. By examining Figure 17.15, we can see how two types of disequilibrium can arise.

Disequilibrium type 1: demand exceeds supply
On Figure 17.15, we can see that the price of 15 p intersects the supply curve at a quantity of 550 pounds per week (point A) and the demand curve at 850 pounds per week (point B). This means that at a price of 15 p, 850 pounds per week are demanded, but only 550 pounds are supplied. Hence there is an excess of demand over supply of 300 pounds per week (the distance between the curves at the price in question).

It follows that, if for any reason the price of potatoes is 15 p, there will be a situation of undersupply, or a shortage. In most market situations, the supply side (in this case Mr Marrow, the shop owner) will sense that there is more demand for potatoes than he can supply (he may, for example, sell out of his week's supply of potatoes by Wednesday). His reasonable course of action under such circumstances would be to increase his price, which of course would result in a reduction in quantity sold. Hence, the market situation would approach the established equilibrium position at a price of 20 p.

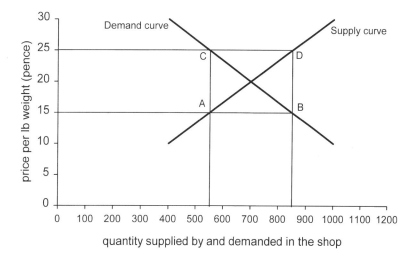

Figure 17.15 Disequilibrium positions

Disequilibrium type 2: supply exceeds demand
The position of supply exceeding demand can be seen in Figure 17.15 at points C and D. If the price of potatoes was 25 p then 550 pounds per week would be demanded (point C) and 850 pounds per week would be supplied (point D). This represents an oversupply of 300 pounds per week – the distance between the two curves at a price of 25 p. Again we see that a substantial disequilibrium exists. In this case, the shop would be left with a glut of potatoes at the end of the week. In order to get rid of the excess potatoes, the supplier is likely to reduce the price of the potatoes, thus encouraging buyers to increase their quantity of purchase. The natural tendency is thus for the market situation to re-equilibrate.

Changes in the equilibrium point

The equilibrium point is not 'cast in stone', and from time to time, it moves. There are two situations that can cause this (Figures 17.16 to 17.19):

- a shift in the demand curve causes an extension or contraction in supply;
- a shift in the supply curve causes an extension or contraction in demand.

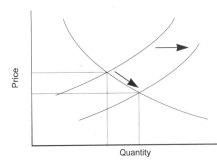

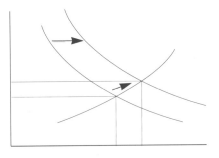

Figure 17.16 Rightward shift in supply curve causing extension of demand – lower price, higher quantity

Figure 17.17 Rightward shift in demand causing extension of supply – higher price, higher quantity

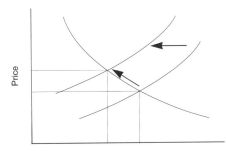

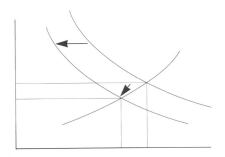

Figure 17.18 Leftward shift in supply curve causing contraction of demand – higher price, lower quantity

Figure 17.19 Leftward shift in demand curve causing contraction in supply – lower price, lower quantity

17.4 The price elasticity of demand

Defining price elasticity of demand

Suppose that a company sales director wishes to increase the value of her sales of company products. She has an idea: to reduce the price of the goods in the hope that, by doing so, more of the company's products will be demanded by the market. She decides to put the idea to the accountant who, being financially minded, asks the question 'Would your proposed reduction in price result in higher or lower total revenues?' Clearly, if the price reduction is not more than made up for in increased quantities sold, the reduction is of questionable economic and business sense. The accountant may well ask the sales director to return to her office and examine the demand curve for the products to seek an answer to the query. The sales director can answer the accountant's question straight away if she knows the *price elasticity of demand* for the product in question.

We have seen that on a demand curve the revenue earned at different points on the curve can vary as the figures for price and quantity change. We can intuitively appreciate that the relationship between price and quantity will be determined by the nature of the curve itself, that is, its slope (gradient) and shape.

The price elasticity of demand measures the relationship between price, quantity and total revenue. It can be calculated mathematically as

$$E_p = \frac{(\Delta q/q)}{(\Delta p/p)}$$

or, by simple mathematical rearrangement, as

$$E_p = \left(\frac{\Delta q}{\Delta p}\right) \times \left(\frac{p}{q}\right)$$

where, E_p is the coefficient of price elasticity of demand, Δp is the change in price, Δq is the change in quantity resulting from the change in price, p is the price prior to the change, and q is the quantity demanded prior to the change in price.

For some calculations, it is easier to use the formula expressed as:

$$E_p = \frac{\text{Percentage change in quantity demanded}}{\text{Percentage change in price}}$$

When the equation is calculated for any given change in price, you will arrive at a number for E_p. We can use this number to tell us the price elasticity of demand for the product:

- E_p is less than – 1 or more than 1, we say the product in question has price elastic demand.
- E_p is less than – 1 or 1, we say that the product in question has price inelastic demand.
- E_p equals exactly ±1, we say that the product has a unitary price elasticity of demand.

The sign (positive or negative) of E_p is usually ignored. In practice, it invariably turns out to be negative, but this is not important in the context of this discussion. For other types of elasticity (see cross elasticity, section 17.6), the sign is very important.

The sales director's decision

The sales director we encountered above is contemplating reducing the price on two of her products. One of them, a premium brand of frozen dessert, currently sells for £2 per unit. By examining the demand curve for the product, she calculated that if she were to reduce the price by 10% to £1.80, she could increase sales from 5000 units per month to 6000.

The other product she is considering is an over-the-counter pharmaceutical. A month's pack of the drug currently sells for £5. She calculates from the demand curve that a 10% price reduction to £4.50 would increase units sold from 10 000 per month to 10 100.

In order to answer the accountant, she calculates the price elasticity of demand for the two products:

	Premium dessert (£)	Pharmaceutical (£)
P	2	5
ΔP	-0.2 (i.e. 20p)	–0.5 (i.e. 50 p)
Q	5000	10000
ΔQ	1000 (i.e. 6000–5000)	100

Hence, using the equation $E_p = (\Delta q/q)/(\Delta p/p)$:

Premium dessert:
$$E_p = \frac{(1000/5000)}{(-0.2/2)} = \frac{0.2}{-0.1}$$
$$= -2$$

A price elasticity of –2 is greater than –1 and is therefore price elastic.

Pharmaceutical:
$$E_p = \frac{(100/10\,000)}{(-0.5/5)} = \frac{0.01}{-0.1}$$
$$= -0.1$$

A price elasticity of –0.1 is less than –1 and is therefore price inelastic.

The sales director returns to the accountant with the figures she has calculated. The accountant, after surveying the figures says, 'We will go ahead with your proposed price reduction on the dessert but not on the pharmaceutical. In fact, I might even increase the price on the drug.'

Price elasticity and the nature of the product

Whether the demand for a product is price elastic or price inelastic depends in large part on the nature of the product itself. Products which have a price elastic demand have a demand quantity which is relatively dependent upon (or responsive to) price. This means that a reduction in price produces a proportionately greater increase in quantity and hence revenue (because TR = PQ). This tends to be true of products which are considered to be non-essential in nature or which your buying decision rests largely upon its price. You might, for example, opt to buy smoked salmon for the weekend if it is on special offer at the supermarket when you wouldn't normally buy it due to its elevated price.

Products that have a price inelastic demand are ones you would buy with relatively little regard to price. In other words, they are items that you place a high value upon, ones that you feel you need rather than want or ones which have such a low price anyway that a slight increase doesn't seem to matter. These are consequently typically necessities, staple goods or products you associate with well-being and health. This category also includes goods and services which are potentially addictive in nature such as tobacco and narcotics. To illustrate using an extreme case, if you are suffering from excruciating toothache, you are likely to ask the pharmacist for the best or most effective analgesic rather than the cheapest. This is because your buying decision is based upon the performance of the product rather than its price.

Question 17.7

Based on the nature of the following products, say whether you think their price elasticity is most likely to elastic or inelastic. Each refers to the general category of goods and not individual brands within the category.

- Toilet paper.
- Motor cars.
- Pain-killing drugs.
- A textbook which you are instructed by your lecturer to buy.
- Caviar.
- Malt whisky.

Perfect elasticity and perfect inelasticity.

We have seen that elasticity and inelasticity refer to the relationship between price and quantity. In the case of a product the demand for which is price inelastic, we expect to see quantity varying proportionately less than price, whilst we would expect the opposite for a product with a price elastic demand. When we take these two ideas to their possible extremes, we arrive at two 'perfect' situations:

- for perfectly demand price elastic products, we would expect there to be no change in price regardless of the quantity demanded;
- for perfectly demand price inelastic products, we would expect there to be no change in quantity demanded regardless of the price charged.

These two extremes are shown in Figures 17.20 and 17.21.

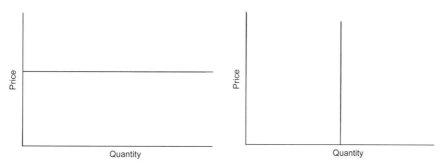

Figure 17.20 Perfectly elastic demand curve

Figure 17.21 Perfectly inelastic demand curve

Price elasticity and revenue

The conclusions that we can draw concerning the relationship to a product's price elasticity and movements in revenue follow logically from what we have already learned. It rests upon the simple mathematical relationship TR = PQ.

For a product with price elastic demand, a reduction in price will produce a proportionately greater increase in quantity, thus more than off-setting the price reduction. E_p, being by definition, more than 1, means that the percentage change in Q will be greater than the percentage change in P.

We can see how this works by inserting notional figures. Product A sells say 5000 units per day at a price of £1. The revenue is thus (TR = PQ), £1 × 5000 = £5000. We then reduce the price of product A to 90 p, a reduction of 10%. Because the demand for product A is known to be price elastic, we expect a proportionately greater increase in Q than the reduction in P, say a 20% increase to 6000 units per day, or

$$E_p = \frac{\text{Percentage change in Q}}{\text{Percentage change in P}}$$

$$= \frac{20}{-10} = -2$$

After the change, the revenue earned per day will have risen from £5000 to 90 p × 6000 units = £5400, an increase in revenue of £400.

For demand price inelastic products, the converse must be the case. An E_p of less than one means that a price change is not offset by a proportionate change in quantity. Again, an example may clarify the point. Product B also sells 5000 units per day at £1, making a total daily revenue of £5000. After a price reduction of 10% to 90 p, sales rose by only 5% to 5250, a figure which does not compensate for the reduction in price. Hence, with a price elasticity of (5–10%) = –0.5, the new revenue becomes 90 p × 5250 = £4725, a reduction in daily revenue of £275.

We can thus draw two conclusions:

- Products which have price elastic demand are relatively *responsive* to price changes:
  - a decrease in price will produce an increase in revenue;
  - an increase in price will produce a decrease in revenue.
- Products which are price inelastic for demand are relatively *unresponsive* to price changes:
  - a decrease in price will produce a decrease in revenue;
  - an increase in price will produce an increase in revenue.

Figures 17.22 and 17.23 show how this works on the respective demand curves.

The price reduction in Figure 17.22 results in a larger 'block' of revenue gained than lost. This is shown by the shallow gradient arising from the elastic nature of the demand. The opposite is true of the inelastic demand curve in Figure 17.23. The price reduction results in a larger 'block' of revenue lost than gained. Although only price reductions are shown on the graphs, readers will appreciate that increases in price simply elicit the opposite response to that described.

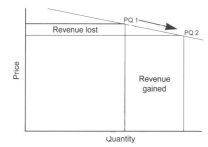

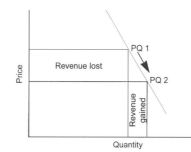

Figure 17.22 Revenue changes on a price elastic demand curve

Figure 17.23 Revenue changes on a price inelastic demand curve

Question 17.8

For the following situations, calculate the price elasticity of demand. For each one, say whether the demand is elastic, inelastic or unitary. (Hint: use the equation $E_p = (\Delta q/q)/(\Delta p/p)$

Original price (£)	Price change (£)	Original quantity (units per month)	Quantity resulting from price change (units per month)
5	–1	1000	2000
600	–60	30000	32000
20	–1	10000	10500
5.40	–0.2	400	400
400	20	2000	1800

Question 17.9

For the following market situations, calculate the price elasticity of demand. For each one, say whether the demand is elastic, inelastic or unitary. (Hint: use the equation E_p = percentage change in quantity demanded/percentage change in price.)

Price change (%)	Quantity change (%)
–2	1
–5	7
8	–8
7	–5

Price elasticities at different points along a demand curve

A feature of demand is that the price elasticity of demand can, in some cases, vary along the length of a given demand curve. If the demand curve is linear (such as some of those we have considered above), the demand will become increasingly price inelastic as demand is extended from left to right. We can see how this works by constructing a simple example. The data in Table 17.6 can be plotted graphically as in Figure 17.24.

Table 17.6

Q	P	TR	MR
1	10	10	
			8
2	9	18	
			6
3	8	24	
			4
4	7	28	
			2
5	6	30	
			0
6	5	30	
			-2
7	4	28	
			-4
8	3	24	
			-6
9	2	18	
			-8
10	1	10	

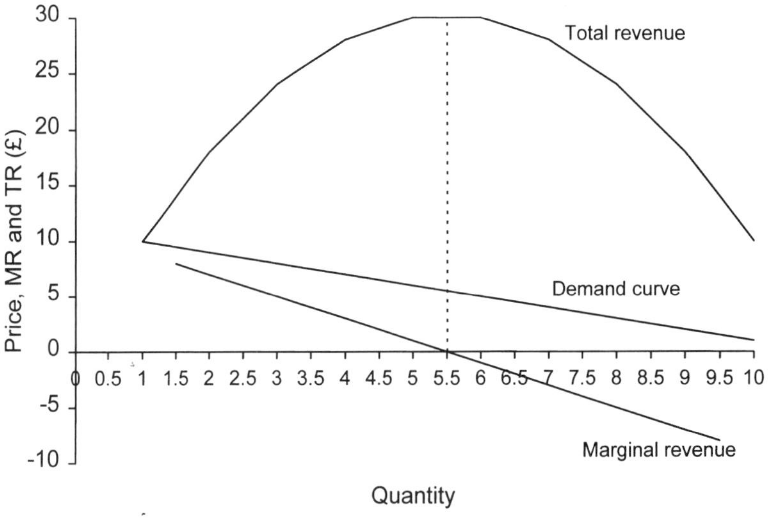

Figure 17.24 How elasticity varies along a demand curve

At all points to the left of Q = 5.5, the positive marginal revenue is testimony to the fact that demand is elastic. We learned earlier that elastic demand is characterized by a decrease in price, resulting in increased revenue. A positive figure for marginal revenue shows that the demand it describes must be elastic.

At Q = 5.5, total revenue is at its greatest. This is the point of transition on this curve between elasticity and inelasticity. An incremental (very small) change in price has brings about no change in total revenue (at the plateau between Q = 5 and Q = 6).

At points to the right of Q = 5.5, the marginal revenue becomes negative. This means that a decrease in price (a downward move on the price axis) results in a fall in revenue, i.e. inelastic demand.

Question 17.10

What would a demand curve look like if the elasticity of demand remains the same along its entire length?

17.5 Income elasticity of demand

The concept of elasticity can be applied to more areas of economics than just price and quantity demanded. The same principles, for example, can be applied to the supply side (the elasticity of supply). In this section, we also consider the relationship between individuals' income and the quantity of certain products demanded.

It is patently obvious that as our incomes vary so does our demand for certain products. During our austere student years, we tend to make economies on such things as food and accommodation as a matter of necessity. Once we graduate and our incomes increase, we tend to increase our expenditures on these goods and many more besides (such as cars, holidays, etc.). There is clearly a link, then, between income and the quantity demanded for some goods. We can analyse the nature of this demand in the same way that we did for prices, by looking at the notion of income elasticity.

The equation for calculating the coefficient of income elasticity involves substituting price for income in the equations we have previously encountered.

$$E_i = \frac{(\Delta q/q)}{(\Delta y/y)}$$

or

$$E_i = (\Delta q/\Delta y) \times (y/q)$$

or

$$E_i = \frac{\text{Percentage change in quantity demanded}}{\text{Percentage change in income}}$$

where E_i is the income elasticity of demand, Δy is the change in income, Δq is the change in quantity demanded resulting from the change in income, y is the income prior to the change, and q is the quantity demanded prior to the change in income.

The rules about the outcome for the coefficient and elasticity hold true for income elasticity:

- If E_i is greater than 1, we say the product in question is income elastic.
- If E_i is less than 1, we say that the product in question is income inelastic.
- If E_i equals exactly 1, we say that the product has a unitary income elasticity of demand.

The same product features apply to elasticity and inelasticity of income as for price. There are clearly some types of product that we must all buy, regardless of income. These are necessities and have an income inelastic demand. Conversely, for some goods, our consumption will be more responsive to our income. These tend to be things we consider to be non-essential goods, for which demand is income elastic. Although Question 17.11 examines income elasticity for an individual, readers should be aware the economists usually examine this principle in the form of *aggregate demand*. Aggregate demand concerns the effects on quantities purchased as the national average income rises or falls.

Question 17.11

You are a business graduate earning £20 000 when, one happy day, your boss calls you in and says that she is so pleased with your performance and that she is awarding you a £10 000 pay rise to £30 000 per year. As a result of your 50% increase in income, how will your spending patterns change?

The following table shows your supposed purchases of certain goods and services last year when your salary was £20 000. Estimate your purchases of the same items for the forthcoming year on your higher income.

	Last year	*This year*
Holidays	1	
Toilet rolls	52	
Pairs of jeans	2	
Cans of beer	500	
Restaurant meals	10	

If possible, add your figures to those of others, such as the members of your class. This will give a figure for the larger indicative market of your class. For each product above, calculate the product's income elasticity of demand. (Hint: Use the equation E_i = Percentage change in quantity/percentage change in income). The change in income obviously remains constant at +50% whilst you can calculate the percentage change in quantity as $(\Delta q/q) \times 100$.

17.6 Cross elasticity of demand

In addition to using the concept of elasticity to examine the nature of the relationships between price and quantity demanded, and income and quantity demanded, we can apply it to the relationship between two separate products. We know that varying the price of a product will have a bearing upon its quantity demanded depending upon its price elasticity, but we do not know whether such a price adjustment will have a bearing upon the sales of other products. Cross elasticity of demand gives us the answer to this question.

The cross elasticity of demand that exists between two separate products can be calculated using the equation:

$$E_c = \left(\frac{\Delta q_A}{q_A}\right) \Big/ \left(\frac{\Delta p_B}{p_B}\right)$$

which can also be expressed as

$$E_c = \left(\frac{\Delta q_A}{\Delta p_B}\right)\left(\frac{p_B}{q_A}\right)$$

or

$$E_c = \frac{\text{Percentage change in the quantity demanded of product A}}{\text{Percentage price change in product B}}$$

where E_c is the cross elasticity between products A and B, Δq_A is the change in quantity demanded of product A, q_A is the original quantity demanded of product A prior to the change, Δp_B is the change in price of product B, p_B is the price of product B prior to the change.

Earlier in this chapter, we encountered the idea of related products. You will recall that there are two ways in which products can be related – they can be complementary to, or substitutes of, each other. It is, of course, possible for two products to not be related at all (e.g. naval submarines and lollipops).

The figure calculated as E_c has two significances:

- Its sign, either positive or negative, tells us the manner in which the two products are related:
  - a negative E_c means the two products are complementary;
  - a positive E_c means the two products are substitutes.
- Its magnitude tells us the degree to which they are related:
  - a relatively large negative figure tells us the two are strongly related as complements;
  - a relatively small negative figure tells us the two are weakly related as complements;
  - a relatively large positive figure tells us the two are strongly related as substitutes;
  - a relatively small positive figure tells us the two are weakly related as substitutes.

Demand for complementary goods will rise in sympathy with each other; for example, a rise in car ownership will produce a rise in the demand for petrol. It follows that an increase in the price of cars which will signal a reduction in quantity demanded for cars will, by association, produce a proportional reduction in the quantity demanded for petrol. We see, therefore, that a reduction in the price of cars produces an increase in the quantity demand for petrol. Hence, the equation for E_c contains a positive figure and a negative figure, which, when divided, always give a negative answer.

Demand for substitute goods will change in opposition to each other. A reduction in the price of butter will encourage consumers of margarine to switch from margarine to butter. This will signal a reduction in demand for margarine; hence both the price of butter and demand for margarine go in the same direction – in this case downwards. Two like signs, either two negatives or two positives, when divided by each other, make a positive, hence a positive E_c demonstrates a substitutionary relationship.

Question 17.12

For the following situations, calculate the cross elasticity of demand. For each one state the manner in which they are related and comment on the strength of the relationship.

- The price of product B is cut by 2% in order to increase sales. The quantity demanded of product A falls by 5%.
- The price of product B is increased by 10% to cover increased operating costs. The quantity of product A demanded decreases by 4%.
- The price of product B is decreased by 5%. The quantity demanded of product A decreases by 8%.

Perform the same tasks on the following:

	Original price of A (£)	Change in the price of A	Original quantity of B	Change in the quantity of B (£)
1	10	−2	5000	−3000
2	25	+2.5	17 000	−15 000
3	56	−5.6	60 000	+500
4	100	+10	1 000 000	+100

17.7 A factor supply and demand market system – the labour market

Supply and demand of labour

So far in this chapter, we have considered micro-economic theories as they relate to the supply and demand of conventional goods and services. The same theory can be applied equally to other sectors of commercial transaction. One such area is the supply and demand in the markets of the *factors of production*. A factor of production is an

---

organizational input which is necessary to produce an output of goods or services. Individuals (private citizens) may buy goods and services because they wish to enjoy them. This motivation to buy contrasts with that of factors, which are purchased by organizations as a matter of necessity to facilitate their normal functioning.

Factors of production

Factors of production are organizational inputs which are necessary in order to enable the organization to produce its output. The factors of production are:

- land and buildings;
- plant and equipment;
- materials and energy for consumption or processing;
- labour.

One of the factors of production is labour. Whereas in many commercial situations, individuals represent the demand side and businesses represent the supply side, the opposite is usually the case in the labour market.

Have you ever wondered why certain things are true of the labour market? A twenty-year-old snooker player can earn more in a single championship match than a nurse earns in a year. Similarly, a university lecturer earning perhaps £25 000 to £30 000 a year earns three times as much as a checkout operator at the local supermarket. On top of all these peculiarities, the chairmen of some of Britain's companies earn well over £1 million per year, whilst somewhere between two and three million people in the UK are unemployed. A skilled manual worker in a European Union country will typically earn in the region of £40 to £60 per day, whereas in India the daily rate is nearer to 40 p.

To some people such features of the labour market might appear unfair, but in studying economics we must remember that the market for labour is like any other market. Nobody would suggest that all goods and services should have the same price, and we intuitively understand why some products remain unsold after the Christmas rush owing to a lack of demand for them.

The supply side of the labour market comprises the sellers of labour – those who have the necessary skills and are available to work. For any given occupation, more people will tend to opt for a job which pays a higher wage rate. Lower numbers will offer themselves for lower paid jobs. This explains the traditional shape of the supply curve in this context. The demand side consists of anybody who wishes to buy labour – employers such as businesses and public sector organizations.

The same shaped demand and supply curves exist for the labour market as for those in the markets for goods and services.

Market price of labour

The general form of the supply and demand curves for labour will be familiar, except that the y axis is the wage rate and not price (wages are the 'price' of labour), and the x axis is numbers employed and not quantity. The general form is shown in Figure 17.25.

The supply and demand conditions will be unique for each job and hence the equilibrium point (the market wage) is similarly unique for each job. For a job with a plentiful supply of labour, the position of the supply curve will be to the right of one for which labour is more scarce. Hence, more will be employed but at a lower wage rate.

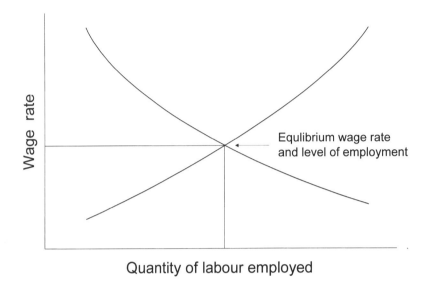

Figure 17.25 *Equilibrium wage rate for a given job*

The supply and demand curves for labour can shift in the same way as they can for goods and services. The demand curve may shift if, for example, a new technology is introduced which requires a certain type of labour or there is a decline in demand for traditional labour such as shipyard welders. The supply for a particular type of labour may shift with changes in population or certain university courses going in or out of 'fashion'. Any of these changes will create a new equilibrium point and hence a new wage rate for the occupation.

Disequilibriums in the labour market

The workings of the labour markets as free markets rests upon the assumption that wage rates are allowed to rise and fall as the two curves shift over time. Disequilibriums can occur, as in the case with any other markets, when one of two situations apply:

- a time lag occurs between a supply or demand shift and the re-establishment of the equilibrium; or
- when, for some reason, there are artificial constraints placed upon the wage rate which prevents it from moving in response to changing supply or demand conditions.

We have already learned that disequilibriums result in either over- or undersupply of the commodity in question (in this case, labour). In the case of the labour market, the most common disequilibrium is oversupply. The scenario is shown in Figure 17.26.

The price P1 and quantity Q1 in Figure 17.26 show the equilibrium values of the labour market for the job in question (which could be any job). The oversupply is shown by supply equal to Q2, but with demand for labour equal to Q1. In this situation, there is an oversupply of labour of Q2–Q1. The situation may have arisen as a result of a shift in either curve but, due to such things as trade union pressure, the wage rate does not re-equilibrate. Labour is thus overpriced, resulting in oversupply – a condition more commonly referred to as unemployment.

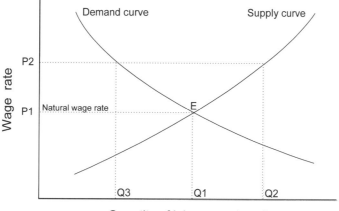

Figure 17.26 Disequilibrium in the labour market

Assignment

Mr Marrow sells more than potatoes in his fruit and vegetable shop. The following information applies to his sales of Brussels sprouts.

Price	Supply quantity, (pounds per week)	Demand quantity, (pounds per week)
5p	500	1400
15p	650	900
25p	800	550
35p	950	300
45p	1100	150

Questions

- On the same graph, draw the demand and supply curves.
- Derive the equilibrium point.
- Calculate the revenue at the equilibrium.
- Calculate the price elasticity of demand between 5 p and 15 p.
- Calculate the price elasticity of demand between 35 p and 45 p.

Demand for Brussels sprouts increases as the result of a bad cabbage harvest. Demand increases by 200 pounds weight per week at every price.

- Draw the new demand curve onto the same graph.
- Derive the new equilibrium point.
- Calculate the revenue at the new equilibrium.
- What quantity would Mr Marrow sell if he kept the price at the old equilibrium.
- Calculate the price at which Mr Marrow would maximize his revenue at the new level of demand.

Further reading

Begg, D., Fischer, S. and Dornbusch, R. (1994) *Economics*, 4th edn. New York: McGraw Hill.

Dobson, S., Maddala, G. S. and Miller, E. (1995) *Microeconomics*. New York: McGraw Hill.

Ferguson, P. R., Rothschild, R. and Ferguson, G. J. (1993) *Business Economics*. London: Macmillan.

Friedman, D. D. (1990) *Price Theory. An Intermediate Text*, 2nd edn. Thomson.

Harrison, B., Smith, C. and Davies, B. (1992) *Introductory Economics*. London: Macmillan.

Harvey, J. (1993) *Modern Economics. An Introduction for Business and Professional Students*, 6th edn. London: Macmillan.

Harvey, J. (1994) *Mastering Economics*, 4th edn. London: Macmillan.

McEachern, W. A. (1994) *Microeconomics. A Contemporary Introduction*. Thomson.

Pashigian, P. (1995) *Price Theory and Applications*. New York: McGraw Hill.

Sapsford, D. and Tzannatos, Z. (1993) *Economics of the Labour Market*. London: Macmillan.

Sutcliffe, M. (1994). *Essential Elements of Business Economics*. London: DP Publications.

Whitehead, G. (1996). *Economics*, 15th edn (Made Simple Series). Oxford: Butterworth-Heinemann.

18

Industry and market structures

Learning objectives

After studying this chapter, students should be able to describe:

- What is meant by the terms 'market' and 'market structure'.
- What factors determine market structure.
- What is meant by monopoly, oligopoly and perfect competition.
- The pros and cons of some of these market structures.

18.1 Introduction to industries and markets

We have seen in earlier chapters that there are two sides to the market system: buyers and sellers. In this chapter, we take a closer look at how these two sides are organized and structured. The market system can be shown by a simple diagram like that in Figure 18.1.

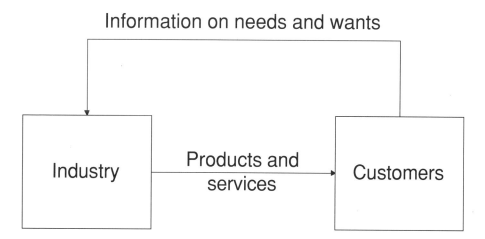

Figure 18.1 A schematic diagram of the market system

We can see from Figure 18.1 that there is a two-way relationship between the two sides of the system. An industry generates products (goods and services) to supply to the customers. Similarly, the industry producing the goods relies on accurate information from the buyers. Information is gathered by monitoring the demand for products and by listening to comments made on product quality and usefulness.

18.2 Market and industry structures

The features of the relationship between the two sides of the market are determined by two important variables. It is these variables that determine which side is the most powerful in any given relationship:

- the number and selling power of sellers of a specific product;
- the number and buying power of buyers of a specific product.

The number of sellers

The markets for some products comprise literally thousands of suppliers. For others, it is just a few suppliers in the entire world, or even just one. If, for example, you want to buy potatoes in the UK, you have the choice of buying from thousands of shops or, if you are a shop, from a very large number of farms or potato producers. On the other hand, if you want to buy a drug to combat the symptoms of AIDS, there is only one major producer of such a drug in the world (Glaxo Wellcome plc), although a US based company is attempting to enter this market to threaten Glaxo Wellcome's supremacy.

The number of suppliers and how they are organized leads us to an important concept, that of *concentration of supply*. In a market with very few suppliers, it is said that supply is concentrated in the hands of just a few large suppliers. In extreme cases, supply can be totally concentrated with just one supplier. The example of potato production demonstrates the opposite case – a very low concentration of supply.

The number of suppliers that a buyer can go to for an essentially similar or identical product will have a significant influence on how the supplier behaves. Producers in markets with a high supply concentration are able to have more power over buyers than those with lower concentrations. The producer of the world's predominant anti-AIDS drug (Glaxo Wellcome plc) is able to charge a relatively high price for it because of its high concentration of supply. A large number of producers who each compete for customers' business are at a pricing disadvantage because of the customers' ability to simply 'shop around' for cheaper prices or better service. An example of this latter situation exists in some high streets which have a large number of similar shops such as the electrical shops in London's Tottenham Court Road or the Asian restaurants in the Rushholme district of Manchester or some areas of other major cities. Suppliers find themselves having to offer incentives to attract customers such as lower prices, better product or service quality.

The number of buyers

The demand side of the market system can be analysed in the same way as for the supply side. In the market for some products, buyers are very concentrated, to the point where, in some cases, there may be just one buyer of a product (a condition known as *monopsony*). For other products, the market contains many buyers, possibly tens of millions of people.

A condition of high buyer concentration puts the buyers in a more powerful position over suppliers than those in a state of low buyer concentration. Two examples will demonstrate this point.

High buyer concentration – Swan Hunter's shipyard

In the market for large shipping, there are relatively few buyers. Whilst the number of suppliers of ships has been significantly reduced over recent decades, the importance of single orders from the very few buyers to the remaining shipyards is often a matter of survival. In the case of the Swan Hunter shipyard in Wallsend, North Tyneside, the major buyer of its ships has traditionally been the British Ministry of Defence.

In the first part of 1993, the Ministry of Defence was preparing to place a large order for a helicopter landing ship, and Swan Hunter, along with other yards, prepared its bid to undertake the work. In the May of that year, it was announced that the work was to go the Vicker's yard in Barrow, Cumbria. The loss of an order from its only significant customer meant that Swan Hunter had literally no orders. This necessitated a large number of immediate redundancies and the eventual closure of the yard – a loss of 2500 jobs in an area of high unemployment.

The case of Swan Hunter shows the difficulties of suppliers depending upon a market with very few or just one buyer. At best, the supplier is in a weak bargaining position with regard to pricing, and, at worst, the monopsonist (single buyer) can precipitate the failure of the supplier.

Low buyer concentration – washing powder

The market for domestic washing powder (as opposed to washing powder for industrial purposes) is an interesting one. The demand side comprises potentially almost everybody, as we all wear clothes and therefore have a need to wash them. Hence, there are tens of millions of washing powder customers in the UK.

The supply side is quite different from the demand side. We have already encountered the concept of concentration of supply and the supply of washing powders is very concentrated indeed. Two very large producers between them control over 90% of the market. The two companies compete vigorously for an increased share of the large but unconcentrated demand side. Individual washing powder customers like you and me have little power over the powerful suppliers inasmuch as we are not in a position to dictate prices or other terms of supply. We are able to choose between brands, but cannot directly influence the powerful suppliers.

18.3 Industry structures

In attempting to understand the way in which markets are structured, we usually divide markets up according to the number of suppliers there are of a product into a given market. This is not to say that the number of customers is unimportant, but that, in practice, a concentration of demand is much less common than a concentration of supply. In most cases, we can assume that demand is relatively unconcentrated, and that market conditions are determined much more by the degree of concentration of the supply side.

The degree of supply concentration can be shown by the use of a simple continuum (Figure 18.2). At the two extremes, monopoly is the case of a single supplier, and perfect competition is the case of an infinite number of suppliers (zero concentration of supply). At the various points along the continuum lie the varying degrees of concentration between the two extremes (markets which are, to a greater or lesser extent, oligopolistic).

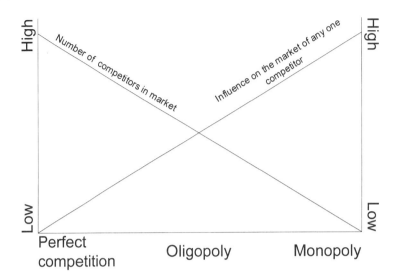

Figure 18.2 *Continuum of market structures*

In the remainder of this chapter, we will examine the various types of supply concentration and their implications for the relationships between suppliers and buyers.

18.4 Monopoly

What is a monopoly?

A true monopoly is said to exist when the supply of a product into a market is totally concentrated in the hands of a single supplier. Note though that it is possible for there to be more than one supplier of a product, but only one supplier of the product into a given market. In other words, monopoly exists when a supplier faces no effective competition in its market and consequently has pricing power in the market. We shall see in Chapter 19 that the legal definition of a monopoly is somewhat broader than this description.

Prior to the widespread privatization programmes of the 1980s and 1990s (see Chapter 19), many of the utilities (e.g. gas, electricity, telecommunications) were state-run monopolies. This meant that consumers had no choice who to purchase their gas from; they could buy from the erstwhile Gas Board or go without gas. In this case, the 'market' in which there was no competition was a very large one – the entire country. On a smaller scale, monopolies can exist in much smaller markets. It may be, for example, that a certain milkman has a monopoly on 'doorstep' milk deliveries in one area of a town or city. There are obviously many milk-round businesses in a large city, but for the few streets in question (the 'market' in this context), there is only one supplier.

An obvious question to ask at this point is why certain markets are monopolies whereas most others are not (i.e. most markets have many suppliers). Monopolies arise when, for some reason, would-be competitors are somehow prevented from entering the market to offer competition to the monopolist. Such hurdles to market entry are called entry barriers. There are a number of possible entry barriers which render market entry either difficult, impossible or undesirable and we shall consider them in some detail in Chapter 20.

Pricing in monopolies

In theory, a monopolist is in a very powerful competitive position. As the only supplier of a product, and unaffected by the pricing of competitors' products, the monopolist is able to charge any price for the supply of its goods. It is effectively able to say to the demand side, 'buy from us or go without'. It is said, therefore, that a monopolist is a *price setter*. In theory, then, monopolists should be able to make exceedingly high profits.

In practice, it is not this simple. Monopolists that can actually make excessive profits are very rare. An effective ceiling is put on prices by one or two mechanisms:

- Regulatory restrictions – when price limits are imposed upon the monopolist by a government body or a piece of legislation.
- Product linked restrictions – products with a relatively high price elasticity of demand will simply experience a reduction in demand with higher prices. This will obviously result in a reduction in revenue. Monopolists trading in products with a highly price inelastic demand will, of course, be in a much more potentially profitable position.

Given that a true monopolist is a price setter, we can see that it may be possible for suppliers to be in this position even although competitors may exist. If a supplier in a competitive market (i.e. one with more than one supplier) has sufficient market share to dictate market prices then the supplier is said to be a *virtual monopolist* because it dominates the market supply. In a virtual monopoly market, smaller competitors are forced to set their prices roughly in line with their much larger competitor (the virtual monopolist is referred to as a *price leader*). They become price followers which results in their profits being more-or-less determined by the virtual monopolist.

Are monopolies good or bad?

We must be careful not to judge monopoly as being necessarily good or bad. However, the prevailing political tide in recent years has been to encourage competition in markets by splitting large monopolies up, thus enabling the parts to compete against each other. One of the key objectives of the Conservative Government's privatization programme (see Chapter 19), was to dismantle state monopolies to introduce competition into such markets as electricity and telecommunications. When businesses are forced to compete, their natural inclination is to reduce costs and increase quality in order to gain market share. This is clearly in the interest of the consumer.

The pros and cons of monopoly can be summarized as follows.

Advantages of monopoly
- Large companies (such as monopolists), tend to be stable and are often able to withstand changes in the economic environment. This is an effective guarantee of ongoing supply.
- If there is only one supplier, potentially wasteful duplication of some activities, such as research and development is avoided.
- The high prices that the monopolist may charge can be used to generate high profits. These, in turn, can be invested to improve product quality and service to the customer.
- Large companies such as some monopolists enjoy increased economies of scale. This leads to lower unit costs. Whilst this is of advantage to the monopolist, increased profits can lead to increased investment, improved products, better service and, sometimes, lower prices.

Disadvantages of monopoly
- If the monopolist charges excessively high prices, the effect on customers can be unpleasant, especially if the monopolist supplies an important product such as gas, electricity or telecommunications.
- Lack of competition can sometimes make the monopolist 'flabby' and inefficient. This may have the effect of further increasing prices as the monopolist attempts to cover higher costs. This was one of the major criticisms of former state-run monopolies such as utility providers.
- The customer is deprived of choice of supplier and hence has no choice of product.
- The total concentration of supply means that if the monopolist cannot supply for any reason (e.g. industrial disputes) then there is no alternative supply to the demand side.

18.5 Monopolistic competition

A variation on the theme of monopoly is *monopolistic competition*. We have already seen that a monopoly is a situation where there is only one supplier of a particular product into a specific market (see Chapter 12). However, monopolies can exist in parts of total markets (i.e. specific segments) and for specific variations and types of products.

Monopolistic competition is said to exist when products have a monopolistic market share in a relatively small part of the market, i.e. a small segment of the total market. When many products each occupy their own 'little monopoly', then they do not directly compete with each other even though the products may be very similar.

A typical way of achieving a situation of monopolistic competition is *product differentiation*. This the practice of making the product unique to enable it to be more acceptable to a specific segment or *niche* in the market. A highly differentiated product which has a high market share in a relatively small market segment enjoys the possibility of commanding a premium ('price setting') price – the same characteristic as a monopolist.

One of the most important mechanisms of achieving differentiation is by product branding. By aggressively promoting a brand, producers of consumer goods attempt to build loyalty to the brand to the exclusion of others. By engendering a brand with unique product qualities (e.g. superior washing power, unique taste or texture), customers remain loyal and thus do not switch to other brands which offer different product benefits. Key technological innovations can also serve the purpose (such as a new format for music recording). As with all monopoly situations, the company's objective is to separate its products to such an extent that the customer has just the one effective choice of product within the sector. The idea of removing customer choice within the sector is key to monopolistic competition. If a company can develop a product to such an extent that customers automatically think of their product, then they have succeeded in this regard.

The competition arises from this scenario because it is the sectors themselves which compete for business. Sellers will attempt to achieve customer loyalty within their sector. If this can be achieved, then their repeat orders will be assured.

18.6 Oligopoly

An oligopoly is the next most concentrated type of market supply after monopoly. In an oligopoly, the majority of supply comes from a relatively small number of relatively large producers.

Within the category of market structure called oligopoly, there is a wide variation of concentration ratios. In some markets, the concentration can rest with as few as two significant suppliers (a situation known as *duopoly*). In other cases, there may be many more companies (say up to twenty) which, between them, control market supply.

Two examples will serve to illustrate the point.

Oligopoly
Example 1: washing powder

We have already seen that the supply of washing powders into the UK market is controlled by two players (hence it is a duopolistic market). The two companies in question are the US based Procter and Gamble Corporation (P&G) and the British Unilever plc (in the form of its subsidiary Lever Brothers Ltd). Lever's brands in this sector include Surf and Persil whereas P&G own Daz, Ariel and Bold. Between the two duopolists, over 90% of supply is controlled – a very concentrated duopoly.

Example 2: food retailing

The food market in the UK is very large; annual food sales amount to around £60 billion. Supply into the market is largely concentrated with the seven largest producers accounting for 50% of the total market – less concentrated than the washing powder market. The remainder of the market is held and fought over by smaller chains and independent 'corner shops' and the like.

The major suppliers are as follows (1994 figures):

Company	Market share (%)	Outlets	Shop names
J. Sainsbury plc	12.3	367	Sainsbury's, Savacentre
Tesco plc	12.2	500	Tesco
Argyll Group plc	7.7	570	Safeway, Presto,
Asda Group plc	6.7	196	Asda, Dales
Somerfield Holdings plc	4.0	465	Somerfield, Gateway, Food Giant
Kwik Save Group plc	3.9	978	Kwik Save, Shoprite.
Marks & Spencer plc	3.4	283	Marks & Spencer
Co-op	3.4	1357	Co-op
Wm. Morrison plc	2.0	72	Morrison's
Iceland Group plc	1.7	743	Iceland, Littlewoods food halls

(Source: Keynotes.)

Pricing in an oligopoly.

Unlike monopolists, big players in oligopolistic markets are rarely powerful enough to be price setters. This means that they are not able to increase their prices to achieve higher profits, because customers are able to simply switch to competitors. If you notice that prices have risen in your regular supermarket, you will be inclined to switch suppliers to another shop. It follows that oligopolists are approximately interdependent upon each other inasmuch as their prices are usually roughly the same.

Price interdependence works by binding all oligopolists, more or less, to the market price. Whilst any competitor could theoretically increase or decrease its price, in practice unilateral price changes are rare.

If a competitor 'breaks ranks' and *increases* its prices, customers will tend to change suppliers. The price increases will thus tend to result in a fall in revenues for the company in question. The company thus has every incentive to reduce its prices back to their original level.

If a competitor unilaterally *reduces* its prices, then a series of events is set in train which adversely affects all of the competitors in the oligopoly. It is called a downward price spiral:

- competitor unilaterally reduces its prices;
- customers switch to the cheaper supplier;
- competitors lose market share to the cheaper supplier;
- competitors reduce their prices to parity with the cheapest competitor;
- customers tend to return to their regular supplier (although their temporary switch of supplier may result in less loyal buyer behaviour).

The result of the unilateral price reduction decision by one supplier is that all the competitors end up making lower revenues and hence lower profits. Of course, such whole-sale price reductions are very welcome to the customers.

As a result of this price interdependence, oligopolists tend to be very careful when it comes to pricing. Price wars benefit none of the competitors in the longer term and competition tends to occur in *non price* areas. The pricing tensions that exist in oli-gopolies usually ensure that prices remain relatively stable.

Competition in an oligopoly

The price interdependence that oligopolists experience means that they must compete with each other for market share on bases other than price. This gives rise to the idea of *non-price* competition. Non-price competition involves the competitors attempting to gain ground on each other by the use of a wide range of measures. Some are designed to increase customer loyalty (i.e. repeat purchases from a supplier) and others are designed to encourage customers to switch suppliers.

The precise non-price measures taken will depend upon the industry and the things that customers value. If the business can give the customers more value (or perceived value), both customer loyalty and increased market share objectives can be served.

Examples of non-price measures include:

- more outlets in key locations;
- more attractive outlets (in retailing, for example);
- better or more professional service;
- loyalty incentives such as loyalty cards (in supermarkets) or money off next pur-chase;
- increases in quality of products and service;
- advertising and other marketing promotions;
- increases in product range offered;
- longer guarantees or warranties.

We can see that many of the markets we come across regularly show evidence of these non-price competition measures. This is because most markets are oligopolistic and so find this the most appropriate competitive strategy. The market for washing powder, for example, is noted for its high dependency on advertising and claims of superior product performance rather than using price to encourage consumers to switch brands.

18.7 Perfect competition

At the other end of the market structure continuum to monopoly is perfect competition. Whereas monopoly represents a situation of total concentration of supply, perfect com-petition is a situation where both the supply and demand sides have zero concentration.

It follows that if there is no concentration of supply, there must be a very large number of suppliers such that no single supplier has the ability to influence the market price.

In its 'pure' form, perfect competition has several distinguishing characteristics:

- a very large number of sellers, each of which occupies a tiny or insignificant market share;
- a very large number of buyers;
- a product which is incapable of being differentiated and where all sellers sell an identical product;
- all buyers have identical cost structures – they all pay the same for materials, rent, labour;
- no single buyer or seller is of sufficient size to influence price;
- there are no innovations or 'secrets' which may give one buyer or seller an advantage over another;
- there are no entry or exit barriers associated with competing in the market.

Like monopoly, 'true' perfect competition is virtually unknown in practice – it represents the extreme at which there is no concentration of supply or demand at all. Some markets, however, exhibit very low supply and demand concentrations and so approximate to perfect competition. Examples include the market for fruit and vegetables in a large town or city market square or the market for bed and breakfast accommodation in a large city.

Because of the features of perfect competition, the market price for any given product is arrived at purely through the economic forces of supply and demand. Because no buyer or seller is big enough to set the price, each supplier must take the market price – they are said to be *price takers*. This tends to lead to medium or low profits for the supplier and relative price stability for the buyer.

Assignment

Bob Lactose has been a milkman in the Eltham area of south London for twenty years. He has traditionally covered a 'patch' of approximately two square miles including some areas of high population density of older people who have been good customers for many years. For all of his twenty years on the territory, Bob has been the only milkman and has consequently come to know many of his customers on familiar terms. He is a popular milkman amongst his customers evidenced in part by the high customer loyalty in the face of cheaper milk at the local supermarket and the number of tips he accumulates at Christmas.

Recently, Bob has heard that Tom Lait, a new milkman, is about to start business on the same territory. The situation is made more worrying by the rumour that the Tom Lait intends to offer milk at a penny per pint cheaper than Bob.

Questions

- What has the market structure been on Bob's territory over the past twenty years?
- What will the market structure be if Tom Lait successfully enters Bob's territory?
- What measures might Bob take to resist the onslaught of Tom?
- Given Bob's relationship to his customers, how would you rate Tom Lait's chances of success in his attempt to enter the market.

Further reading

Begg, D., Fischer, S. and Dornbusch, R. (1994) *Economics.*, 4th edn. New York: McGraw Hill.

Dobson, S., Maddala, G. S. and Miller, E. (1995) *Microeconomics*. New York: McGraw Hill.

Harrison, B., Smith, C. and Davies, B. (1992) *Introductory Economics*. London: Macmillan.

Harvey, J. (1993) *Modern Economics. An Introduction for Business and Professional Students*, 6th edn. London: Macmillan.

Sutcliffe, M. (1994) *Essential Elements of Business Economics*. London: DP Publications.

19

Government and market structures

Learning objectives:

After studying this chapter, students should be able to describe:

- How and why the state influences markets and market structures.
- The key pieces of legislation that affect market and industry structures.
- How regulatory QuANGOs affect market and industry structures.
- What is meant by nationalization and privatization and describe the pros and cons of each.

19.1 Introduction

The matter of whether and how much governments should influence the workings of markets is controversial. Some believe that markets work best, that is to everybody's eventual benefit, if they are left alone to find their own level. Others believe that it is an important duty of government to affect the workings of markets to ensure that excessive profits are not made and that individual consumers are protected from high prices and undersupply.

In one sense, this debate goes to the heart of political ideology. The political right have traditionally leaned more to the 'leave markets alone' position whilst the political left have traditionally argued more for an 'interventionist' approach to markets and industries. In Chapter 24, we shall see that both of these positions can be traced back to a key intellectual 'architect' – a seminal economic philosopher who shaped the two broad strands of thought.

In most modern states, such as the UK, the broadly held opinion is that there is a need for some government influence on markets; the debate is rather on how much and to what extent government should be involved in this.

Why might government want to influence market structures?

If we accept that most governments see some need to influence the operation of markets, we then should ask what the objectives of such influence might be. There are a number of possible objectives:

- to increase competition (and thus give consumers more choice);
- to protect consumers (e.g. from monopoly pricing);
- to make business more competitive and productive;

- to increase the competitiveness of UK businesses abroad (e.g. by forcing businesses to reduce their costs in response to increased competition);
- to make efficient use of a nation's scarce resources (e.g. oil and gas reserves, human resources).

It is generally assumed that one of the purposes of government is to protect its citizens. This duty is in part discharged by ensuring that the citizen's economic interests are not damaged by excessive prices and that there is no undersupply of some key goods and services. In addition, governments usually wish to stimulate business productivity, higher product quality and lower business costs. Many of these objectives can be served by government measures that encourage competition in markets.

How does government influence markets and market structure?

The objectives discussed above can be achieved by governments using a number of measures which are designed to influence market structures:

- introducing legislation that prescribes and limits certain types of business activity;
- setting up regulatory bodies, which are given the power to impose restrictions upon businesses;
- selling and buying businesses to and from the private sector – the processes of privatization and nationalization.

In the remainder of this chapter, we will examine these three instruments of government influence.

19.2 Legislation and market structures

UK legislation

In Chapter 22 of this book, we will look at the various areas of law that apply to businesses. We must, however, be careful to draw a distinction between business law in general and competition and market laws in particular. Competition law is designed to directly influence competition in business and this is typically achieved by influencing market structure.

The most significant piece of UK legislation in this regard is the *Fair Trading Act 1973*. This piece of law, now well over twenty years old, has been very influential in limiting acquisitions and mergers that may lead to a combined business with a high concentration of market supply – a situation that would result in reduced competition in the market in question. The anti-competitive practices provisions of the Fair Trading Act were increased by the *Competition Act 1980* which extended monopolies' regulation to state-owned (nationalized) businesses.

The Fair Trading Act 1973 targets three areas in pursuit of maintaining healthy levels of competition in markets:

- monopoly practices;
- restrictive practices;
- mergers and acquisitions.

Under this Act, a monopoly is defined as a situation wherein a single supplier has in excess of 25% of the supply into a market. This would seem to be at variance to the 'economist's definition' we encountered in Chapter 18. However, given that we also learned that we can define a monopolist as a *price setter*, the Act takes the view that any single supplier with more than a quarter of the total market supply has sufficient 'clout' to significantly influence price and market conditions – a *virtual* monopoly. Clearly, this is potentially against the interests of the consumer.

Restrictive practices are forbidden under the provisions of this Act. If a situation occurs where two or more large competitors 'collude' on prices (i.e. make a formal or informal agreement to set an artificially high price), then the colluders are effectively acting as a monopoly. Customers are deprived of their ability to 'shop around' to get better prices and service from different competitors in the market.

Mergers and acquisitions are also covered by the Act. We saw in Chapter 8 that these are mechanisms by which businesses grow and expand – by buying or merging with others to increase their size. Given that a monopoly is defined under the Act as being a business commanding in excess of 25% of market supply, the Act gives the state the power to block an acquisition or merger which will result in the combined business having in excess of a 25% share (a virtual monopoly) of supply. This power is, however, discretionary; not all cases need to be reviewed, it is usually at the discretion of the Secretary of State for Trade and Industry.

The Treaty of Rome and competition

Legislation such as the Fair Trading Act 1973 apply to competitive practices within national borders (i.e. within the UK). The Treaty of Rome 1957 (the primary legislation of the European Union – see Chapter 22) contains two 'articles' that are relevant to this area of business. Both are designed to stimulate competition between companies in member states and can be used by authorities within the EU to influence the behaviour of business and markets.

Article 85 of the Treaty of Rome addresses the various aspects of anti-competitive practices. It prohibits such things as price collusion, limitations on production output and any other agreements between companies in different member states that would act against 'healthy' competition. Some cases are exempt from Article 85 when such agreements are deemed to be in the public interest (Article 85/3). Article 86 is designed to prohibit the abuse of a dominant market position (i.e. a high market share). It does not prohibit monopoly but seeks to ensure that large business do not use their power against consumer and competitor interests.

The administrative part of the EU – the European Commission – has the responsibility to implement Articles 85 and 86. It can prohibit mergers or acquisitions resulting in a combined national market share of 25% (the same figure as the Fair Trading Act in the UK) or when the combined turnover exceeds a certain financial figure (currently ECU 200 million).

19.3 Regulatory bodies

The government's second mechanism of influencing market structures is to set in place a variety of regulatory bodies. These bodies, as their name suggests, regulate industries on behalf of the government and consumers to ensure that consumer and competitive concerns are not overlooked. In most cases, such regulatory authorities are independent of government and are established as QuANGOs (see Chapter 5) to ensure impartiality. They are usually staffed by people who understand their areas of oversight more thoroughly than politicians – a measure designed to ensure that the best people are in place to make important decisions that protect consumers but do not unnecessarily penalize the businesses in question.

The main bodies that have a bearing on markets and market structures are the Office of Fair Trading (OFT), the Monopolies and Mergers Commission (MMC) and the regulatory bodies set up to monitor the various utilities.

The Office of Fair Trading

Part of the provision of the Fair Trading Act was to set up a body called the Office of Fair Trading (OFT), a QuANGO that came into being in November 1973. The head of the OFT is the Director General of Fair Trading (DGFT) – an individual charged with, among other things, the enforcement of the terms of the Act. The OFT's is also required to act as a central bureau which collects and publishes information on competition and anti-competitive practices in the UK.

The DGFT has six broad areas of responsibility:

- to collect information on business activities that are potentially harmful to competition or the public interest (the DGFT has the power to refer cases to other authorities for review);
- to publish information informing consumers of their consumer rights;
- to encourage trade associations to publish codes of practice which regulate their own activities to the benefit of consumers (i.e. 'self-policing' mechanisms);
- to take legal action against businesses which the DGFT believes may be in breach of competition laws (such as the Fair Trading Act and those listed in detail in Chapter 22);
- to license businesses to grant credit or to hire goods to consumers – and to regulate the credit industry;
- to propose the introduction of new laws that he or she may deem necessary to 'plug loopholes' or to further the interests of consumers.

The Monopolies and Mergers Commission

The MMC is headed by a full-time chairman to whom three part-time deputy chairmen report. This team then draws upon the expertise of specialist members from a range of backgrounds including business, finance, academia and trade unions. All of the members, including the chairman, are appointed by the Secretary of State for Trade and Industry. The MMC comprises a total of 31 members (as at 1995).

The role of the MMC is to look into proposed mergers and acquisitions when instructed so to do by the OFT or by the Secretary of State for Trade and Industry (who is sometimes called the President of the Board of Trade). Whether or not the Secretary of State refers a case to the MMC is a matter of his or her discretion although recent policy changes have increased the assets threshold for merger references from £30 million to £70 million. This means that mergers involving combined assets of under £70 million are not considered to be sufficiently important to trouble the MMC with.

The MMC, like the OFT, acts in accordance with the Fair Trading Act 1973 and is thus concerned with mergers or acquisitions which will result in a combined market share of 25%. The chairman, in the MMC Annual Report of 1994 describes that MMC's role as follows.

We are required under the Fair Trading Act, in accordance with the public interest, to take into account all relevant considerations including:

- *maintaining and promoting effective competition;*
- *promoting the interests of consumers in terms of price, quality and range of goods and services;*
- *promoting efficiency and innovation and facilitating market entry;*
- *maintaining balanced distribution of industry and employment in the UK;*
- *promoting international competitiveness* [i.e. the competitiveness of UK businesses in international markets].

Once a team from the MMC has investigated a proposed merger or acquisition, the findings are published. The findings include the outcome of the investigation, that is, whether the MMC recommends the proposal be permitted or blocked. From time to time, the MMC also undertakes enquiries into whether existing competitive practices are fair and in the public interest.

Utilities' regulatory bodies

Some markets attract particular regulation unique to themselves. When the utilities were privatized in the 1980s (gas, electricity, etc.), supply passed from the state sector to the private sector. In some cases, this meant that rather than having a state-run monopoly, there was a privately run monopoly (or, at least a highly concentrated supply by the new private-sector suppliers). In other privatizations, the privatization process was accompanied by the creation of competition between the various parts of the privatized businesses.

Either way, Parliament at the time deemed it necessary to maintain some level of public control over the pricing and supply of utilities, even though they were now privately owned (i.e. by shareholders). In consequence, the utilities' regulators (or 'watchdogs') were given powers to determine prices for the products as well as controlling the number and type of competitors in each market. The reasons for such a high level of regulation are as follows:

- the fact that in many cases, the *privatized businesses were monopolists*, or at least that they were big businesses with high market shares;

- the fact that *utilities are supremely important* to the well-being of people in the country. They are quite different in significance to other products like luxury goods and even foods.

Each utility has its own independent regulatory body. Like the MMC, the utility regulators are QuANGOs. The principal ones are:

- OFTEL – Office of Telecommunications Regulation (established 1984);
- OFGAS – Office of Gas Regulation (1986);
- OFFER – Office of Electricity Regulation (1990);
- OFWAT – Office of Water Regulation (1989).

19.4 Privatization and nationalization

The issue of who owns business is one of the main determinants of market structure. The selling off of formerly state-owned businesses was one of the key policy areas of the Conservative governments of the 1980s and 1990s.

Privatization is the selling of state-owned assets to private individuals. It is called *privatization* because ownership of the business passes from the public sector (the state) to the private sector (individuals and private businesses). In privatizing a business, the government issues shares to the estimated value of the business and these are then sold through the usual channels of the Stock Exchange. If more than 50% of the issued shares are sold to the public, then state control over the business is lost.

Nationalization is the very opposite of privatization. A business is nationalized when the state takes control of a business that was previously in the private sector. The nationalized business will be run by the government as part of a government department, government agency or state-controlled company (e.g. the erstwhile British Coal). This sometimes involves the creation of a state-run monopoly.

A brief history of privatization and nationalization

The salad days of nationalization were the years following the Second World War. Having led the coalition government during the war, the Conservative prime minister Winston Churchill (1874–1965) was defeated by Labour in the general election of 1945. The war had taken a toll on the country and the electorate saw a need for a wide-ranging economic and social regeneration programme.

The new Labour prime minister, Clement Attlee (1883-1967), set about the task. In addition to significant investment in rebuilding the country's infrastructure (assisted by the United States' *Marshall Plan*), a priority of Attlee's government was to manage the country's key industries directly. Prior to the war, most utilities were operated by private companies, in many cases covering a small area of the country only. In the climate of national regeneration, certain industries were seen as being strategically important to the country's redevelopment. The business categories in the nationalization programme included the utilities, coal, rail and some heavy engineering businesses such as shipping and steel. Over the following decades, other businesses were taken into state ownership, including airlines, motor manufacturing and defence equipment producers such as some military hardware companies and producers of ordinance.

The vast majority of nationalized businesses remained in the public sector until the new Conservative government was formed by Margaret Thatcher in 1979. One of the main thrusts of Conservative policy during the 1980s and 1990s was to privatize the previously nationalized businesses. In consequence, one by one, the government monopolies and other state-owned companies were broken up and sold off to the private sector. By the turn of the decade (in 1990), the government had divested itself of the majority of its direct interests in industry. Privatization was not without its critics. The opposition parties of the time continually argued against each privatization, believing that such businesses should remain under state control.

The principal Conservative privatizations in the 1980s

Date privatized	Company	Value (£)
1979*	British Petroleum plc	7.4 billion
1981*	British Aerospace plc	513 million
1982	Amersham International plc	71 million
1982	National Freight Corp. plc	54 million
1984*	British Telecommunications plc	3.9 billion
1986	British Gas plc	5.4 billion
1987	British Airways plc	900 million
1987	Rolls-Royce plc	1.08 billion
1987	British Airports Authority plc	1.3 billion
1988	British Steel plc	2.5 billion
1989	Water authorities	5.3 billion

*First share issue where other followed in later years.

(Source: *Education Guardian*, 4 June 1991)

The debate over privatization and nationalization

The debate on privatization and nationalization cuts to the core of political ideology (see Chapter 24). The divide in the debate falls approximately along party political lines. The political right (the UK Conservative Party) have traditionally believed in a free-market approach to managing the economy, whilst the left of centre (the UK Labour Party) have traditionally espoused the belief that strategic industries should be under state control.

Prior to the election of Tony Blair as Labour Party leader, Labour's policy with regard to state ownership was summarized in the much-discussed 'clause four' of the Labour Party Constitution, which stated:

To secure for the workers by hand or by brain the full fruits of their industry and the most equitable distribution thereof that may be possible upon the basis of the *common ownership of the means of production, distribution and exchange, and the best obtainable system of popular administration and control of each industry or service'.* [My emphasis.]

Although the wording of this clause has new been replaced, this was the guiding philosophy underpinning Labour's opposition to the privatization programme of the 'Thatcher years'. The Conservatives, in marked contrast, were guided by the philosophical underpinnings of the *laissez faire* school of economic thought mainly attributable to the classical economic school of Adam Smith and the monetarist theories of Professor Milton Friedman of the University of Chicago (see Chapter 24).

It follows that any discussion of the pros and cons of privatization and nationalization must necessarily be incomplete without an enquiry into the underlying philosophies of the two policies. Such a discussion is beyond the scope of this text and so a general examination will suffice. There are strong arguments, in theory and practice, both for and against state ownership of some businesses.

The case for nationalization

Those who argue for nationalization have tended to subscribe to the following arguments:

- It allows the government to exercise control over strategically vital areas of industry. Some industries, particularly the utilities, are arguably too important to be left to the 'vagaries' of market forces and the pursuit of profits by their owners. It also means that market supply can be guaranteed by government, regardless of the movements of market forces.
- By controlling strategic industries, the government is in a position to exercise a wider influence on business activity and consumers' spending in the country. The use of intelligent pricing of key utilities can be used as one of the economic 'levers' used to regulate the economy. Items like energy, communications and transport constitute a significant proportion of both business and domestic expenditure and, by selectively increasing or reducing the prices of such commodities, the government can influence the wider economy. If, for example, the government wishes to stimulate the economy, it could use lower utilities prices as one of the ways of achieving this objective. The converse would be the case if it wanted to slow economic growth.
- Direct control over key industries allows government to ensure that some goods and services are provided which could not be profitably provided by the private sector. Some areas of provision appear not to be able to be provided at a profit and so would not be attractive to private investors. This includes rural bus services and the majority of health provision.
- Nationalization provides government with the opportunity of 'bailing out' companies who could not survive without government assistance. In doing so, it can thus keep such businesses afloat. This is seen as being appropriate when the business is a particularly important employer (such as a large employer in an area of high unemployment) or when the business produces a particularly important product. It ought to be stressed that this is one of the most controversial uses of nationalization, and controversy usually surrounds such an investment of taxpayers' money.
- It provides the government with a means of ensuring that key services are equalized

throughout the country. Those in favour of nationalization argue, for example, that the outlying and rural regions may suffer because it is uneconomic to offer the same level of services (gas, electricity, etc.) to those living in the major cities.

The case against nationalization

The opponents of nationalization have gained much 'ammunition' from the fact that many important businesses were previously nationalized, and so we can learn by observing how they worked in practice. The following are typical arguments against nationalization:

- In many cases, nationalization resulted in state-run monopolies. This was previously the case in each of the utilities. It follows that any of the arguments against monopolies in general are applicable in this context (see Chapter 18), such as a lack of competitive pressure and a restriction in consumer choice.
- In practice, many of the previously nationalized businesses were considered to be 'flabby' and inefficient. Critics argue that, without the commercial pressures upon private companies, nationalized businesses were often overstaffed and overbureaucratic. Management in the businesses could always count on the Treasury (i.e. the taxpayer) to 'bail out' any losses and provide such subsidies as became necessary.
- Again, following on from the previous point, state-run businesses actually ended up costing the Treasury money rather the contributing to it. This obviously is a potentially undesirable situation as it can put pressure on other areas of government finance.

The case for privatization

The underpinnings of the case for privatization are based within the belief that market systems should be allowed to work more or less without governmental interference. It follows that the main proponents of privatization are on the political right wing who tend to espouse the economic theories of such thinkers as Adam Smith and Milton Friedman (see Chapter 24).

The proponents of privatization argue that it has several advantages:

- In many cases, privatizations involved the breaking-up of a state-run monopoly. It follows that in doing so, competition is being introduced into previously monopolistic markets. As we have seen (Chapter 18), an increase in competition tends to result in lower prices and higher quality which is of benefit to consumers.
- The actual sale (by means of share issue) of government assets generates revenues to the Treasury. Receipts can be used by the government for other worthwhile state purposes such as tax cuts or possible investment in government services such as health, education or infrastructure.
- Any subsidies that were previously granted to a business when it was nationalized is saved (by the state) when it is privatized. Any losses are borne by the shareholders rather than by the taxpayer (although it should be borne in mind that in some privatizations, the government 'wrote off' the debt of the business at the time of the

sell-off – effectively a subsidy from the taxpayer).

- The state will receive tax revenues from the privatized businesses whenever they report taxable profits. In this regard, privatized businesses are just like any other private company.
- Privatizations are good for the City of London and for the Stock Exchange in particular. An inflow of investments from overseas in privatized businesses will have a potentially beneficial effect on the capital account of the UK balance of payments account.

The case against privatization

Those who argue against privatization are often the same people who argue in favour of nationalization. In contrast to the free market ideologues who vigorously support privatization, opponents tend to espouse a left-wing political ideology which has traditionally believed in a higher level of state influence on the business sector.

The principal opponents of privatization argue as follows:

- It necessarily reduces the size of the public sector and thus may reduce the government's ability to influence the level of economic activity in the country.
- It involves 'selling the family silver'. This is taken to mean that the state sells off its valuable assets which, at best, is a pity and, at worse, is betraying the trust of those who invested in the 'silver' (formerly state-owned assets) in the first place.
- Privatized business are necessarily concerned with profits in addition to maintaining standards of service. A risk is thus introduced that the profit-seeking companies may overlook some customer groups which it would not be profitable to supply (such as rural communities with gas or bus services).
- In some cases, privatizations have involved the state losing direct control over potentially strategically vital industries, which include some defence equipment manufacturers and electricity generators. There may be times of national emergency when these industries may be (according to some) best controlled by the state, but privatizations have made this legally impossible.
- Some have raised questions as to whether privatization has actually achieved its objectives of increased competition. In some cases a state-run monopoly has simply become a privatized monopoly (or a virtual monopoly). Oft-quoted examples of this include British Gas and British Telecom although recent policy changes in these sectors are expected to increase competition to a certain extent.
- Criticisms have been raised about the high levels of profits that some privatized utilities have made. British Telecom, for example, is capable of making over £3 billion each year in pre-tax profits. Critics argue that instead of making high profits, such companies should charge lower prices to their customers. Similar arguments have been advanced against the allegedly excessive salaries of directors of privatized companies.

Clearly, the arguments both for and against both privatization and nationalization can be compelling. In practice, one's conclusions may be guided more by one's political leanings than by a rational and objective analysis of the arguments.

Assignments

Assignment 1

- From what you have learned about privatization and nationalization, which do you think is the best for managing the country's key utilities? Give reasons for your conclusion.
- The utilities are now in private hands. Under what circumstances, if any, do you think it may be appropriate to renationalize them?

Assignment 2

Over recent years, the MMC has made several important decisions that have influenced the structures of certain industries. Choose a case upon which the MMC has blocked a merger or acquisition and find out the following:

- The market structure of the industry in which the two affected businesses were players.
- The reasons why the merger or acquisition was proposed.

Suggest the reasons why the MMC blocked the proposed merger or acquisition.

Further reading

Armstrong, M., Cowan, S. and Vickers, J. (1994) *Regulatory Reform. Economic Analysis and British Experience*. Cambridge, MA: MIT Press.

Beesley, M. E. (1992) *Privatization, Regulation and Deregulation*. London: Routledge.

Clarke, T. and Pitelis, C. (Eds.) (1995) *The Political Economy of Privatization*. London: Routledge.

Vickers, J. and Yarrow, G. (1988) *Privatisation. An Economic Analysis*. Cambridge, MA: MIT Press.

20

Comparing industries and organizations within industries

Learning objectives

After studying this chapter, students should be able to describe:

- A model that explains differences in company and industry profitability.
- What is meant by the bargaining power of buyers and suppliers.
- What substitute products are and how the threat of substitutes can affect profitability.
- How the threat of new entrants into a market can affect profitability.
- How the intensity of competitive rivalry can affect profitability.

20.1 Introduction

The profits that businesses achieve vary greatly, both from industry to industry and between competitors within industries. Some industries consistently return outstanding financial results, announcing high dividends and pleasing shareholders, whereas in other industries there are tiny profits or even losses. Companies involved in electronics, pharmaceuticals or computer software often make substantial profits, whereas those in coal-mining, ship-building or textiles generally make lower profits.

Even within a given industry, some companies make high profits whilst other companies struggle through, year after year, trying to break even or sustaining losses. This chapter attempts to analyse why these variations exist and the implications of these features for the strategies of companies in the industry context.

20.2 Five forces of industry profitability

An influential American academic, Professor Michael E. Porter of Harvard Business School, has proposed a 'five forces' model of what he termed *determinants of industry profitability*. According to this model, the ability of a company or an industry as a whole to be profitable will depend upon its strength *vis à vis* five economic forces. An industry or company that is in a weak position with regard to these forces will tend to make lower profits, and a strong position will enable higher profits to be achieved. The forces are usually expressed as a diagram (Figure 20.1).

We can see from the diagram that the central force is that of the rivalry between existing competitors. This is very intentional. The profitability of an industry will depend largely upon this single factor. If competition is intense in an industry then there will be a downward pressure on the profitability of each player in the industry. This is because intense competition necessitates cutting prices to retain and gain business or incurring additional costs of supporting a product in the marketplace. Conversely, light competition, or none at all, will enable competitors to make higher profits (the extreme of which, as we have seen, is a monopoly).

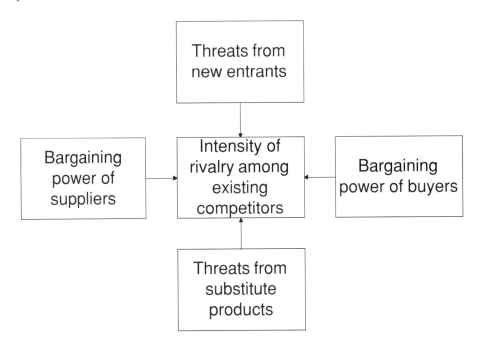

Figure 20.1 Michael Porter's five forces of industry profitability

This central force has, in turn, four major determinants. It is these which determine the intensity of the competitive rivalry in an industry. We will examine the four 'peripheral' forces and then come to the one central force.

20.3 Bargaining power of suppliers

Suppliers are those individuals and enterprises that provide the organization with its inputs. Examples of inputs include:

- materials and operational inputs (e.g. stocks, land, buildings);
- human resources (e.g. employees);
- finances (e.g. from banks in the form of loans).

If an organization is forced to pay a comparatively high price for these inputs, there will be a downward pressure on the potential profitability of the company. If, conversely, the organization can secure the inputs at a favourable price, the opportunity exists for money to be saved, which can increase profits. There are several situations that can affect this force.

- The *market structure* of the industry has a powerful effect. The nearer the organization tends towards monopsony (see Chapter 18), then the weaker the supplier will be. The structures of supplier and buyer bases can vary widely. Some industries have few very large buyers who buy from a highly fragmented supplier base, whereas others have many small buyers who source from a highly concentrated supplier base. Supplying power results from a large supplier selling its output to a small company or when the supplier has a unique product with a price inelastic demand.
- Of course, input need not just be of materials; it can be uniquely qualified *personnel* which cost a great deal of money to secure. Trade unions may also increase the price of labour inputs (powerful suppliers of organized labour) when they insist on a certain level of pay in exchange for continued supply of human resource co-operation. If the organization has a high dependency on employees with rare skills, it follows that a higher price will be attached to this particular input (e.g. highly qualified scientists or uniquely experienced computer programmers).
- The *cost of finance* and its availability may also affect profitability and may even have a bearing on a company's survival. Large companies will generally find it easier to secure long-term loans, debenture capital, etc., than smaller ones. The concentrated nature of the banking industry means that this can be a significant factor for all industries to a greater or lesser extent. The interest rates at which loans are agreed (which can seriously influence net profits) will depend upon the bank's estimation of the risk of loan default and this will vary from company to company and from industry to industry.

A company will tend to have power over its suppliers, and hence will be able to gain savings on unit cost, if:

- it is a large organization which can consequently buy in large quantity;
- it is a monopsonist (or near monopsonist) of a certain input;
- the organization consumes a large proportion of a supplier's output;
- it has a highly fragmented supplier base;
- it uses commodity and undifferentiated material inputs;
- it has a low labour requirement relative to its sales turnover;
- it requires relatively unskilled labour;
- it has an non-unionized labour force;
- it has a labour force with non-transferable skills (who are thus 'locked in' to the employer);
- it is able to sustain debt at negligible risk of default;
- it has low financial gearing (see Chapter 11).

The converse of the above will tend to reduce the organization's power over its suppliers.

20.4 Bargaining power of buyers

The power of an organization over its buyers reflects exactly the previous discussion on the power of suppliers. It follows logically that if a company has pricing power over its customers then it can inflate prices and increase revenue, and, by maintaining costs at existing levels, can increase profits. If a company sells a product which is an important input to a customer's operation *and* it is difficult to obtain elsewhere, then it follows that the supplier will have power in its approach to pricing.

The issue of market structure is as pertinent with regard to this force as it is to the issue of bargaining power of suppliers – it is simply the converse. When the buying power is concentrated then one would expect this to exert a downward pressure on the profitability of suppliers into the market, especially if the supplier base is highly fragmented. There are many good examples of this situation in the UK. As the retail supply of food and DIY goods have become increasingly oligopolistic, suppliers to the retailers have suffered a noticeable reduction in prices chargeable to the retailers coupled with other unfavourable terms of supply such as longer credit periods and demands for shortened lead times. On a more mundane level we can readily appreciate that, as a customer of British Telecommunications plc (BT), the author is a very weak buyer. His annual phone bill of around £280 is negligible to BT (with its annual turnover of over £13 billion) and he would get a short response if he alone were to request a reduction in unit price from the supplier of telephone services. This means that the bill must be paid exactly as BT prescribe or else go without the benefit of a BT telephone.

20.5 Threats from new entrants

A key pressure on profitability arises from a company's competitors. It usually follows that the fewer competitors a business has, the greater the opportunities will be to make higher profits. It goes without saying that new entrants will seek to join an industry that can achieve high profits. What potential new entrants may not realize is that the reason *why* an industry is so profitable might be precisely because it is very hard to enter. Conversely, those industries which have a high turnover of 'joiners' and 'leavers' will tend to return relatively modest profits. The key determinant of the number of competitors is the 'height' of *entry barriers* which present obstacles to would be competitors who wish to enter the industry.

As a rule of thumb, we can say that low entry barriers will encourage new entrants and high entry barriers will deter them. Hence, industries which are hard to enter are generally those which have few competitors (and hence a lower degree of competitive rivalry).

Entry barriers can take several forms. Which are the most important ones will depend upon the sector of industry in question.

- The most important entry barrier in most industries is the *capital requirement*. This can vary from just a few pounds to enter the window-cleaning market (the price of some second-hand ladders, a bucket and a mop) to tens of billions of pounds, which is the price of entering the petrochemicals refinement industry.
- *Legal permission* or *government licences* can be another barrier to entry. Some industries are protected by government legislation inasmuch as competitors must gain a licence to operate within the sector in question. For reasons of ensuring quality in critical sectors, and sometimes for reasons of national security, the government will demand that certain exacting criteria are met before a company will be allowed to operate. As well as being a long and inconvenient process, gaining such approval can be costly and, in this respect, it can also be considered as a capital requirement of market entry. In some sectors of industry, the weight of *government*

legislation can represent a significant investment and source of great inconvenience to new entrants. Laws regarding pollution, health and safety, and employment of individuals can be restrictive and expensive, especially in areas like the chemical industry. In addition, suppliers of the utilities must observe strict pricing limits which are imposed by regulatory bodies (see Chapter 19). These pricing structures put pressure on costs and profitability, and these can be a disincentive for companies to enter the industry.

- Some companies enjoy a *unique access to supply or distribution channels*. When this is the case, new entrants simply cannot do business in the sector. The reasons for unique access to inputs or output channels may be as the result of government restrictions or may have arisen by forward or backward vertical acquisition of an existing player in the industry (see Chapter 8).

- *Intellectual assets* (or intellectual resources) and unique competencies may represent an entry barrier to would-be competitors in some business sectors. If an organization possesses certain intellectual assets which are difficult or impossible to obtain or circumvent, then a significant hurdle exists to new entrants. In this context, intellectual assets can be taken to mean such things as:
  - licences;
  - patents;
  - brand names, logos, registered trade marks and registered designs;
  - uniquely qualified personnel and 'know how';
  - formulations and recipes.

20.6 Threats from substitutes

Substitute products are those that can be used instead of those produced by a given organization. For example, we might frequently substitute margarine for butter or switch between different brands of margarine. A company whose products can easily be substituted for others will naturally find that price increases are more likely to lead customers into having their wants and needs met by substitutes. There are two general types of substitutes:

- *Direct substitutes* are substitutes of essentially the same kind. If you go to the local DIY 'shed' and you find that Dulux white gloss paint is too expensive, you might consider buying Crown paint or the retailer's own brand, both of which are more or less direct substitutes. Substitution by a direct substitute requires no change in the operation in question – you apply the paint in the same way whichever brand you are using. Direct substitutes in, for example, the pharmaceuticals industry include the widely available analgesic (pain-killing) drugs like aspirin, paracetamol and ibuprofen. All of these drugs are available in different substitute forms.

- *Indirect substitutes* are products which are different but which can, under certain circumstances, perform the same role. Over recent years, we have seen more and more parts in cars made out of plastics, whereas at one time internal parts such as dashboards would have been made from metal or wood. Hence, plastic is an indirect substitute for metal in some circumstances. Similarly, margarine is an indirect substitute for butter, in contrast to substituting one brand of butter for another (which would be an example of direct substitution).

Downward pressures on profitability will arise if a company's products are easily substitutable, especially if there are many equivalent direct substitutes (sometimes called *counter* products like two brands of aspirin). The use of indirect substitution in industrial processes usually requires some redesign or adjustment of the process on which it is used. For this reason, indirect substitution sometimes offers less of a threat than direct substitution.

The key manoeuvre to make products or services less substitutable is to *differentiate*. A differentiated product, in this context, is one which is perceived by consumers as being so different from other, similar products, that by substituting it for a counter, the consumer would be losing a key quality. The bases upon which products are differentiated are numerous. Typical examples in the well-known retail sector include claims of higher quality, a distinctive flavour or strongly defined image or a well-trusted brand to which consumers have become loyal. Marketing people often seek to establish a *unique selling proposition* (USP) – a distinctive product feature which separates their product from others.

20.7 Rivalry among existing competitors

The intensity of competition varies greatly from industry to industry. Some industries are composed of competitors which are friendly and genial to one another, whereas others are characterized by aggression, mutual suspicion and dislike. The way in which competitors behave towards one another can have a significant bearing on the profitability of companies in the industry. We must remember that it is the other four forces which largely determine the strength of this force.

It is important to note that the intensity of competition is not usually related to the actual size of the industry (i.e. the *number* of competitors). Rather, it is related to:

- the position of the industry on the industry growth cycle (competitive intensity reaches a maximum at the maturity stage – see Chapter 12);
- the structure of the industry (i.e. the degree of concentration of supply – see Chapter 18);
- the price elasticity of demand of the products supplied by the industry (see Chapter 17);
- the extent of differentiation of products supplied by the different competitors (differentiation reduces substitutability and hence competition);
- the pressures exerted by the other four of Porter's forces.

Companies within an industry can compete with each other in two general ways:

- *Price competition* involves using price to attract buyers. This invariably means *price leadership* – the practice of unilaterally (usually) reducing price in order to increase market share. Such practice results in a short-term gain in business at reduced profit margins, but other competitors may follow the leader downwards in price to win back their lost market share. The result, of course, is that all players in the industry make lower margins, and it is not uncommon for the smaller and weaker competitors to go out of business through not being able to absorb the losses in revenue. Price competition is very rare in oligopolistic industries, as competitors usually recognize their mutual price interdependence.

- *Non-price competition* occurs when competitors seek to gain market share by means other than price adjustment. Non-price instruments include product differentiation, new product launches and a whole battery of above and below line promotions (see Chapter 12). Of course, these manoeuvres are expensive in themselves. Oligopolists can spend as much as 6% of total turnover on marketing promotions, whilst some chemical companies spend as much as 12% of total sales on research and development, continually attempting to gain competitive advantage through new product introductions.

Lower profits are made in industries in which competition is intense, whether on a price or non-price basis.

Table 20.1 Porter's five forces – a summary

Force	Upward pressure on profitability	Downward pressure on profitability
Bargaining power of suppliers	Weak suppliers	Strong suppliers
Bargaining power of buyers	Weak buyers	Strong buyers
Threat of new entrants	High entry barriers	Low entry barriers
Threats from substitute products	Few possible substitutes	Many possible substitutes
Competitive rivalry	Little rivalry	Intense rivalry

20.8 Case study – some simple comparisons

We will now investigate two industries: the British pharmaceuticals industry and the British paint industry. Pharmaceutical companies are primarily concerned with the design and manufacture of chemical compounds which bring about therapeutic, stabilizing or prophylactic (preventative) effects upon the bodies of individuals (drugs). Paint companies are defined as those concerned with the production of paints, liquid surface coatings, powder coatings and varnishes.

As an overview, let us look at a summary of some of the financial results within these industries for the year ending 1995.

Table 20.2 Company profitability in pharmaceuticals and paint. (Note: Trading profit is taken to mean profit before interest, tax and extraordinary items)

Company	Sector	Trading profit on sales (as %)
Glaxo Wellcome plc	Pharmaceuticals	34.2
SmithKline Beecham plc (SB) – pharamaceuticals division	Pharmaceuticals	25.3
Kalon Group plc	Paints	6.15

We can see immediately that there is a difference in profitability between the two sectors: it would appear that pharmaceuticals companies earn higher profits than paint companies. The results reported here are typical of the pharmaceuticals sector. It is rare when a company in this sector makes less than 20% return on sales. Paint companies might dream of these levels of profit. The industry average profit margin in the paint industry is usually between 5–8%. A key strategic enquiry is to ask why these disparities exist.

A further glance at the figures will also show that there are differences in profit between companies in the same sector. Glaxo Wellcome made 34% profit in the period up to 1995, whereas the profit of SmithKline Beecham plc was lower at around 25%. What is the difference between the two companies that results in such a difference in profit? This section examines these questions by analysing both the two sectors and the two individual pharmaceutical companies in the light of Michael Porter's five forces of industry profitability.

From our earlier discussion of the pharmaceutical and paint industries, we might suspect that pharmaceuticals and paint companies would show differing strengths with regard to Porter's five forces.

Porter's five forces – the British pharmaceutical industry

The UK is a very strong player in the global pharmaceutical industry. It boasts the largest pharmaceuticals company in the world and four of the world's ten best-selling drugs (including the 'number one' spot). UK drugs companies produce annual sales of almost £20 billion, making the UK the sixth largest producing nation in the world and accounting for about 6% of the global industry. Employing around 87 000 people in Britain, the UK industry is a large net exporter of drugs, accounting for a trade surplus in this sector of well over £1 billion (i.e. of exports over imports). Growth in the pharmaceuticals sector has rarely been below 10% per year and return on sales is invariably of the order of 20% or higher (often much higher). There are fewer than ten major players in the UK pharmaceuticals industry.

Force 1: Bargaining power of suppliers
Drug companies tend to be large due to the capital investment necessary to get up and running in the first place (SmithKline Beecham plc, in the year to 1995 had total worldwide sales of £7 billion). This factor alone gives the companies in the sector buying power due to economies of scale, as large companies regularly buying in bulk can negotiate cheaper unit prices with their regular suppliers.

Drug companies' strength in regard to this force is further reinforced by the added value of the product itself. Essentially, a drug is a chemical product made by the reactions of other, more simple chemicals. The drug company buys in relatively cheap (unit priced) chemicals, and, by complex chemical processing, adds value to them to produce the final product. The commodity nature of the raw materials also means that supplies could be obtained from several possible suppliers – no single supplier is distinctive enough to exert a threat to a pharmaceutical company. The cost of raw materials bought by a pharmaceuticals company usually represents a relatively small proportion of the total cost structure of the business. Suppliers have little power over a pharmaceutical company.

Force 2: Bargaining power of buyers
Most drugs have highly price inelastic demand. For some drugs, the coefficient of elas-

ticity will be almost perfectly inelastic. We must begin by asking who the buyers of drugs are. There are three broad categories:

- direct sales to National Health Service (NHS) pharmacies;
- prescription sales from retail pharmacies (where the doctor prescribes the drug);
- 'over-the-counter' (OTC) sales of non-prescribed drugs to members of the public.

The simple fact is that none of these customer groups is very price sensitive when it comes to the purchase of drugs.

The NHS is a part of the government, and recent years have seen many advances in the complexity of medical treatment in the NHS. Such developments have required more complex pharmaceutical preparations, which has necessarily meant higher drugs bills for the NHS. The drugs bill for this department rose substantially over the 1980s and early 1990s, and is currently of the order of £3.5 billion (about a tenth of total NHS spending). The increased drugs spending by the NHS is shown in Figure 20.2.

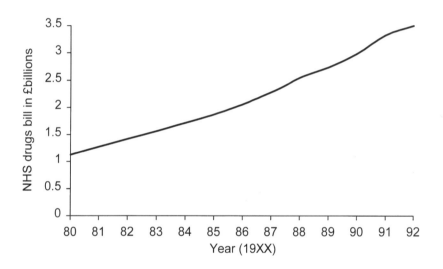

Figure 20.2 Drug spending in the British NHS. (Source: Keynotes)

The increased spending over time is, in large part, due to the expectation of the NHS patient that every and all necessary drugs for their treatment will be supplied free of charge and when needed. The government in the form of the NHS may be unwilling (although this may change in the future) to risk the unpopularity of refusing medication to a patient on the grounds that the price of the drug is too high (there are, however, efforts to reduce the NHS drugs bill).

The doctors who prescribe drugs are professional people who have the well-being of their patients as their highest professional objective. They will therefore tend to prescribe the most appropriate medicament, regardless of the price (the doctor may not even know the price). As, in the UK, there is a fixed charge for prescriptions, the actual cost to the NHS of the drug (over and above the prescription charge), will usually be of little concern to the patient. Recent changes in the status of GP practices (assuming 'fund-holder' status) may be modifying GPs' approaches to drug prescription.

The relief of pain and discomfort, and the desire to be cured are extremely strong motivators for individual consumers. Put simply, individuals are usually prepared to pay a high price, if necessary, for the means to ensure the continuity of life or for the relief of pain. Highly differentiated drugs for the treatment of life-threatening illnesses can command a particularly high price.

In essence, purchasers of drugs buy them because they *need* them and this explains the highly price inelastic nature of the demand. When the choice is 'Pay the asking price or suffer' (or 'Pay the asking price or see your patients suffer'), the choice becomes something of an academic one. We all know what it is like to be in pain, whether it is toothache, migraine or something more serious. In such unfortunate circumstances, we will have experienced an intense need for a medicament, usually with little regard for the price. This fact in itself exerts an upward pressure on profitability for the drug companies.

Force 3: Threat of new entrants
The entry barriers that apply to the pharmaceutical industry are very high.

- The *capital costs* of setting up a pharmaceutical plant are very large. The complexity of the chemical processes and the technology that must be installed mean that minimum capital investment is of the order of hundreds of millions of pounds. Glaxo Wellcome plc, the UK's (and the world's) largest pharmaceuticals company, has assets of around £5 billion – a lot of money to find for would-be new entrants.
- *Research and development* costs, both of introducing new products and of maintaining the market share of existing ones, are very high. Spending on new product development, longer term research and related activities is typically around 16% of total sales – a figure significantly higher than other sectors of the chemical industry. We have already encountered Glaxo Wellcome plc, which employs 7000 scientists and spends well over £1 billion a year in this activity. R&D personnel in this area of science must be highly qualified and highly skilled (and consequently highly paid). In addition, new drugs in the UK must gain an individual entry in the 'official' listing of drugs – the *British Pharmacopoeia*. It is estimated that the full cost of bringing a new drug to the market is of the order of £90 million and can take up to twelve years.
- A great deal of *expertise* is necessary in order both to develop pharmaceutical products and to make them safely and efficiently in a factory. A company tends to learn and develop its procedures over time and to modify and improve things over years and decades.
- The *selling process* for drugs is very expensive, predominantly because the customer base is so diverse. Competitors in the industry employ a large number of representatives, who, due to the nature of the products and the initial customers (doctors and pharmacists), must be individuals well versed in biochemistry and medicine. In consequence, the majority of these representatives are science graduates or qualified nurses. Whilst it may be said that all sales representatives are expensive, with their salaries, expenses and cars, it may be said that pharmaceutical 'reps' cost more than most. More are needed per area of territory (compared to other industries) as a sales call is usually to just one doctor (or one practice), and there are a lot of doctors to call on.
- Intellectual resources play an important role in the pharmaceuticals industry. Many

drugs have *brand-names* that patients and doctors have learned to respect over time. New entrants would have to overcome this barrier in order to ensure their new products are prescribed in preference to established products. Some drugs have international *patents* that prevent competitors from manufacturing a counter or similar product.

The clear conclusion that can be drawn from this discussion is that the entry barriers in the pharmaceuticals industry are exceedingly high. These represent a strong deterrent to would-be new entrants to the industry and they serve to maintain the market in its existing form and structure. The fact there hasn't been a serious new entrant into this industry for many years is testimony to the height of these barriers. This is a source of upward pressure on potential profitability.

Force 4: Threats from substitute products

There are few substitutes to pharmaceuticals, when considered as a general group of products. The very low price elasticity of demand reflects the difficulty (or inability) to substitute. One might argue that 'alternative' medicines, and such practices as acupuncture, homeopathy and others may be substitutes, but these are practised in a minority of cases of illness. The clear fact is that it is very hard to substitute effectively for a drug. This is a source of upward pressure on potential profitability for pharmaceutical companies.

Within the sector itself, companies can, to a certain extent, substitute each others' products. Each drug has what is called a *generic* name. This describes the chemical nature of the product. Some companies attach brand names to generic drugs in an attempt to differentiate them in their favour (for example, the generic drug paracetamol (or *para*-acetyl *ami*no phen*ol*), is sold under such brand names as Anadin paracetamol, Panadol and Hedex). The most common way by which companies avoid the threat of generics is to patent the formulation, but this only applies to new products.

Force 5: Intensity of competition between existing competitors

The intensity of rivalry varies in the pharmaceuticals sector according to product type. In the OTC market, competition among some products (e.g. analgesics or painkillers) is quite intense. This results in lower profits than in the prescription medicines market. The area of least intense competition is that of pharmaceuticals protected by patent. This is because competition is not possible due to legal barriers.

The contributory effects of the other four forces means that competition in this industry is much less intense than in most other industries. Most serious competitors in the industry make reasonable profits, which tends to mean that the need to step up the rivalry is usually absent.

Summary

All five forces, to a greater or lesser extent, act in favour of the industry. Some, such as the threat of new entrants, act strongly in favour of companies in the sector. This is what Porter himself would call a 'five-star' industry. We would rightly expect it to return high profits.

Glaxo Wellcome and SmithKline Beecham – why the profitability difference?

We saw in Table 20.2 that in the year to 1995, Glaxo Wellcome plc made a much higher profit margin than SmithKline Beecham plc (SB). We know that they are both in the pharmaceuticals industry, so such a difference in performance might come as something of a surprise.

The two companies differ, however, in the range of products they produce. The majority of Glaxo Wellcome's products are within the prescription pharmaceuticals market – many of which are protected by patent. SB has a powerful presence in this sector but also has sizeable interests in the OTC market with its brands Phensic, Tums, Night Nurse, Ribena, Nicorette, Horlicks, Lucozade, Macleans and Hedex (to name but a few). It is this difference – the breadth of their respective product ranges – that is the key to the differences in profitability. SB's significant participation in the OTC market means that profits are lower owing to competition in this sector. Glaxo Wellcome's concentration in the prescription medicine's market has reduced the ability of competitors to substitute its products.

Glaxo Wellcome produces a number of important prescription medicines. Two of them, Zantac and Retrovir are among the most profitable drugs in the world owing to two factors: both are in significant demand and both are protected by international patent (making demand very price inelastic). Throughout the 1980s and early 1990s, Zantac has been the major drug for treating gastrointestinal ulcers. Retrovir is the world's major treatment, to date, for treating the symptoms of HIV and AIDS. Both of these products eliminate the legal threat of direct substitution and make indirect substitution difficult. The fact that the two drugs account for a large proportion of the company's output (Zantac 28%; Retrovir *ca.* 12%) means that this factor (a reduced threat of substitution – one of Porter's five forces) is *the* principal cause of Glaxo Wellcome's superior performance. It should be borne in mind, however, that although its profitability is higher, Glaxo Wellcome's portfolio is narrower than SB's, making it potentially less well able to withstand threats to any of its major products. Unless it can provide replacements, we might expect Glaxo Wellcome's profitability to decline after the patent expiry of these two products.

Porter's five forces – the UK paint industry

The UK paint industry is composed of over 250 companies. Even though there are more competitors than in the pharmaceuticals industry, the sales are much lower. The total UK paint industry is worth around £1.5 billion (the NHS alone spends around £3.5 billion on drugs). It follows that many of these paint companies are small businesses – typically with annual total sales of under £10 million and employing fewer than 100 people (there are a few big players in the market). Hence, it is a fragmented industry composed of many small to medium sized companies.

Force 1: Bargaining power of suppliers
The raw materials from which paint is made are largely sourced from a number of large chemical intermediate manufacturers who supply many other industries besides the paint industry. Many of these suppliers are multinationals whose sales to paint companies represent a relatively small percentage of their total sales. This suggests that the suppliers might be able to exert some power over the paint companies and, whilst this is true in part, the power is partly offset by the oligopolistic nature of the supply industry. Furthermore, most raw materials in the paint industry are relatively undifferentiated

(e.g. white spirit), and paint companies may have a choice of several companies from which they can buy.

Force 2: Bargaining power of buyers

The markets for paint products include tradespeople (via trade distributors), the DIY retailers, local authorities and a whole range of industrial concerns. For relatively undifferentiated paint products, such as decorative paints, the principal outlets are the retailers and trade distributors – both of which are relatively concentrated. The large paint companies, who have a large proportion of their outputs going to this area, have had to endure a downward pressure on prices resulting from the high buying power of the large DIY 'sheds' (e.g. Focus, B&Q). Differentiated products supplied into more fragmented markets can maintain higher margins, but these products have lower volumes than the decorative 'white gloss' markets.

Force 3: Threat from new entrants

The capital costs of entering the paint industry are relatively low, typically under £10 000, presuming reconditioned equipment is purchased and a minimum amount of raw material stocks. A chemistry graduate with a few years' experience in the industry would have sufficient know-how to operate a small paint company, so the intellectual resources requirement is not prohibitive. There is some mandatory legislation that applies to the industry, but these are not expensive for small companies. Formulations for paint products are widely available from raw material suppliers. (For example, the formulations for a simple white gloss or emulsion paint are decades old and can be obtained from any resin or pigment supplier. Most paint chemists could scribble such a formulation down on the back of an envelope.)

Force 4: Threat from substitute products

The fact that there are over 250 UK manufacturers of paint, all producing essentially similar products, means that there are many direct substitutes for most paint products. Some differentiated products (e.g. anti-graffiti paints) have fewer substitutes and these usually command a price premium. The non-essential nature of the product (compared to pharmaceuticals) means that there are a number of indirect substitutes such as tiling, cladding, plastic coating, PVC plastisol, and in some cases, wallpaper. In addition, architects are skilled at designing buildings which do not need to be painted at all, such as by using non-corroding metals such as aluminium.

Force 5: Intensity of competition between existing competitors

There is necessarily some degree of competition in the paint industry. It is a very mature industry (i.e. the total demand for paint grows either slowly or not at all) and, in consequence, growth can only be achieved at the expense of a competitor's market share. Price competition is rare, largely due to the fact that margins are already relatively low (but price reductions are occasionally brought about by powerful buyers). Competitive advantage is often brought about by advertising and a range of below-the-line promotions, and most companies also provide a free on-site technical service to customers.

Summary

We can see that paint companies face something of a 'mixed bag' with regard to

Porter's five forces. There is no single force which acts strongly in favour of the individual paint manufacturer, and some (e.g. threats from new entrants) act strongly against the industry. We would consequently expect competitors in the industry to return low to medium profits.

Assignment

John Trout has decided to set up a company called Illegal Nuclear Weapons Limited. He will specialize in intercontinental ballistic missiles and believes he has a ready market of potential buyers among developing nations and those national leaders who have been censured by the West for alleged state-sponsored terrorism.

Questions
- Which entry barriers is the company likely to encounter in seeking to enter this market, bearing in mind that John has no knowledge or experience in nuclear technology or rocketry?
- Use Porter's five-force model to explain the type of competitive position that such a business might encounter if the entry barriers could be somehow dealt with.
- What levels of profitability might the company expect to return (you should be able to derive this from your five forces analysis).

Further reading

Porter, M. E. (1980) *Competitive Strategy: Techniques for Analysing Industries and Competitors.* New York: Free Press.

Porter, M. E. (1985) *Competitive Advantage: Creating and Sustaining Superior Performance.* New York: Free Press.

Part Three
The External Business Macro-environment

21

The political environment

Learning objectives

After studying this chapter, students should be able to describe:

- The meaning of the term 'state'.
- The composition of the British state at national level.
- The structure and responsibilities of sub-national government.
- The history of the European Union (EU) and its objectives as a source of supranational political influence.
- The institutions of the EU.

21.1 The political 'state'

The actions and policies of political institutions have a profound effect on the way in which businesses operate. All businesses must act within legal and regulatory conditions which are set by the state in which the business is located.

Each autonomous region of the world is composed of a *state*. The various parts of the state set out the conditions in which both its citizens and businesses exist. Hence, to be a part of the state system carries with it certain privileges (or rights) and responsibilities.

The *privileges* available to members of a state include access to the goods and services that the state provides. We expect to benefit from, for example:

- national security (ensured by the state's provision of armed forces and a nuclear deterrent);
- health provisions (hospitals, etc.);
- educational establishments (schools and universities);
- law and order (police and the judiciary);
- good transport links;
- social security provisions (e.g. child benefit, unemployment benefit).

In exchange for enjoying the state's provisions, citizens must also accept certain *responsibilities*. The principal responsibility of the citizens of a state is a legal one. Citizens' legal responsibilities include our agreement to abide by the laws that the state puts in place. We agree to pay taxes, to obey the laws and to allow others their rights to live peaceably and unmolested. Failure to observe our responsibilities in this area will result in the state bringing a sanction against us (such as fines or imprisonment). Political philosophers like John Locke (1632–1704) and Thomas Hobbes (1588–1679) have proposed the notion of a *social contract* that exists between the government of a state and its peoples. This concept means that those who observe their responsibilities have a right to enjoy its privileges. Conversely, those who wish to enjoy the benefits of a state must also accept their responsibilities. Continued order in society depends upon the vast majority accepting their responsibilities, and the order in a state system would soon become untenable if this were not the case.

21.2 Levels of political influence

The effects of political institutions upon a business come from three quite separate 'levels'. These levels exist in an approximate hierarchy, but it is not the case that each level automatically can claim authority over the lower one. The authority and influence of each level varies between different policy areas and over time.

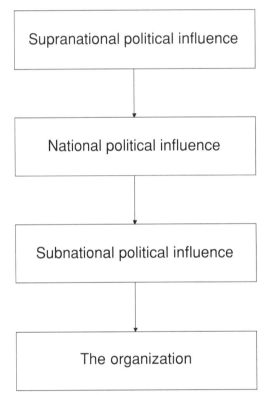

Figure 21.1 Levels of political influence

Subnational political influence arises from the actions and policies of the local authority that exercises power in the immediate vicinity of the business. In the UK, local authorities are subject to national government, based in Westminster. National government determines the policies that affect every business and each local authority. Supranational political influence is political policy that can affect many countries at the same time. For the UK, the principal supranational influence comes from the European Union (EU). The EU has certain powers over the UK state, but in other matters the national government remains pre-eminent over national affairs.

21.3 What is the 'state'?

A state (not to be confused with a 'government') is a self-governing, autonomous geographical region comprising a people with (usually) a common recent history. The state has the right to raise tax revenues from its people and exert the force of law over them. As a concept, a state has four distinct and separate components and states differ in how these 'organs' are set in place and how they are structured. The four organs are present in all cases. The components of a state are:

- The *executive* – responsible for overseeing all other parts of the state, for policy making and for proposing legislation to the legislature.
- The *legislature* – responsible for drafting, debating and passing laws which will apply to the people of the state.
- The *judiciary* – an independent (by varying degrees) part of the state, responsible for enforcing both statute laws (passed by the legislature) and common law (law that is generally accepted but not recorded in statute).
- The *secretariat* – responsible for carrying out the administration of the state through a number of departments, authorities and government agencies. (*Note*: Some textbooks subsume the secretariat into the executive.)

21.4 The state at national level in the UK

The state in which the majority of readers of this book will reside or study is correctly called the (or Her Majesty's) United Kingdom of Great Britain and Northern Ireland. This is shortened, for obvious reasons, to the United Kingdom or the UK. It is often the case that the full name is slightly different from the common name. Germany, for example, is formally referred to as the Bundesrepublik Deutschland (the People's Republic of Germany). Let us look at the role of the various organs of state, paying particular attention to their composition in the UK.

The executive

The executive is that part of the state which is empowered to oversee all other parts and to make policies and actions that determine its direction. In a democracy, such as the UK, the composition of the executive is determined by those over whom they will exercise power – the people of the country. More commonly called *the government*, the executive has powers, given by the people, to execute policy based on a *manifesto* – a statement put out by a political party in advance of a general election. The period of time that an executive is mandated to serve varies from country to country. In the UK, there is an upper limit of five years, whilst in the USA the president (and his or her cabinet) is elected after exactly four years.

The UK executive is primarily made up of the prime minister and the members of the cabinet, although it also includes a number of ministers below cabinet level. As the senior members of the party commanding a majority in the House of Commons, the cabinet contains the politicians who head each of the government's departments. This facilitates the enactment of policy through the departments.

Democracy

The prevalent system of government in the western world is called *democracy*. The meaning of the word can be seen in its construction from the ancient Greek language. *Demos* means 'the people', and *cratos,* means 'rule by'. The clear implication is that government is installed by those over whom it will govern.

Democracy is in contrast to the so-called *authoritarian* forms of government, most notably *aristocracy* and *autocracy*. Aristocracy (*ariston* is the ancient Greek word for 'the best') is a form of government first propounded by the Greek philosopher Plato. According to the theory of aristocracy, individuals who are superior in intellect and judgement should be identified early in life and trained to govern. In autocracy (*auto* means 'the self'), a single powerful ruler, sometimes a dictator, exercises supreme executive power. In both of these philosophies, the opinions of the people are not sought. In aristocracy, the underlying supposition is that the opinions of the normal citizens are not reliable, or are inferior to those of the informed and intelligent rulers. Autocracy, in practice, is based on the view that the opinions of the people simply do not matter.

The earliest stirrings of democracy were the city states of ancient Greece. Realizing that government worked more smoothly with some degree of involvement of the people, the leaders of the day invited the opinions of the men of the state in open forums. The idea was refined in the seventeenth and eighteenth centuries with a number of philosophical theorists, notable amongst whom were the English thinkers John Locke (1632–1704) and Thomas Hobbes (1588–1679) and the French philosopher Jean Jacques Rousseau (1712–78). By proposing that the state should be governed by elected commoners (ordinary people) with a number of 'checks and balances' to prevent excessive abuses of power, these philosophers were among the key intellectual architects of modern democratic government.

Modern democracy has a number of features which are found in most democratic states.

- There is an *electoral system* wherein the people elect part (sometimes all) of the legislature and executive.
- There are a number of *competing political parties* with differing agendas, offering alternative political emphases to the voters.
- There is an *independent judiciary* which interprets and enforces the laws passed by the legislature.
- There are usually a number of *groups which legitimately bring pressure on elected representatives* in order to further their own agendas (e.g. the anti-abortion lobby, environmental pressure groups and the press). It follows that a democracy allows, within the bounds of libel law, freedom of speech and expression.

The British system ensures that the government is opposed as a matter of constitution. When the leaders of Her Majesty's loyal opposition oppose the government in the House of Commons and in the media, they are simply doing what is rightly expected of them – providing a potential alternative government and demanding the government defend their policies and actions. This system of checks and balances is designed to prevent an abuse of government power and policy excesses.

The power vested in the executive varies from country to country. The same is true of the role of the chief executive (who in the UK is the Prime Minister). The nature of democratic government ensures that the head of the executive does not have excessive powers which can be exercised without an endorsement of the legislature. In the UK, the Prime Minister must gain the support of a majority in Parliament for any changes in legislation, but does have a good deal of power as a result of his or her rights to (albeit with the nominal consent and agreement of the reigning monarch):

- appoint and dismiss the members of the cabinet;
- appoint and dismiss other members of the government below cabinet level;
- appoint senior civil servants and senior bishops in the established church (the Church of England);
- nominate the date of a general election within the term of a five-year parliamentary session;
- appoint those who chair cabinet committees;
- confer titles and recommend people for honours (e.g. knighthoods).

In order to remain as Prime Minister, the incumbent must continue to enjoy the support of his or her party in the House of Commons as without this, he or she would be unable to enact legislation or policy. The downfall of Prime Minister Thatcher in 1990 was directly due to a fall in the support for her in the Conservative parliamentary party. As part of the democratic system of executive accountability, the Prime Minister (or a deputy) must answer questions twice a week in a formal sitting of the House of Commons. During Prime Minister's Questions, any Member of Parliament can ask the Prime Minister any question about government policy or any other relevant matter about which the Member may be concerned.

In other states, the remit if the head of the executive differs slightly. The chief executive in the USA, for example (the President), has specific executive powers set out in a written constitution. Among the President's unilateral powers is a right to veto (overturn) legislation passed by the United States legislature unless the legislation has been passed by Congress by a two-thirds majority. The British Prime Minister does not have this power, but such a situation would not usually be necessary owing to the fact that he or she is the head of the largest party in the British legislature.

The legislature

The legislature is that part of the state which is responsible for the drafting and passing of laws. In the UK, the composition of the legislature is slightly more complex than in most other modern democracies. Whereas in other countries, such as the USA, the legislature is entirely elected, the UK has an elected component and two unelected parts that may be considered as quasi-aristocratic. The British legislature therefore has three components.

- The *House of Commons* is composed of 655 *Members of Parliament* (which include the prime minister and most of the members of the cabinet), each of whom represents a section of the population known as a *constituency*. Elected as members of a political party, the Commons is divided into the *government benches* and the *oppo-*

sition benches the latter being made up of all those parties which are not part of the government. The elected nature of the House of Commons ensures that, even though it is only a part of the legislature, it assumes the prominent role in all matters that pertain to the other parts of the state.

Question 21.1

There are several political parties represented in the House of Commons. How many can you name?

- The *House of Lords*, or the *upper house*, is an unelected body composed of *Peers of the Realm*. Peers include those who, it is believed, bring a seniority and/or expertise to the process of law-making that the state will and should benefit from, even though they are not elected. Some members are *hereditary peers*, where membership is automatic by virtue of parentage whereas others are *non-hereditary*. This latter category includes some retired senior politicians (e.g. Baroness Thatcher) and bishops in the established church (the Church of England).
- The *monarchy* is the oldest institution of the British state and goes back well over a thousand years. As the Head of State, the king or queen is responsible for signing all legislation passed through parliament (comprising the Houses of Commons and Lords). Unlike the other two parts of the legislature, the monarchy does not take any part in the debating of legislation. The monarchy is said to be 'served' by parliament, but such an assignation doesn't actually mean very much in practice. The king or queen is strictly 'above' the squabbling of party political controversy.

The divine right of kings

In modern times, it is taken for granted that the reigning monarch assumes no part in the active policy-making government of the state. The king or queen, as the nominal head of state, is considered an important but impotent member of the legislature as the office of monarch carries with it little power to influence or debate political or legislative issues. This has not always been the case.

In the first half of the second millennium AD, the kings and queens of England, Scotland and Wales (and their medieval predecessors), assumed executive powers. In other words, the monarchy was the unelected power which could execute absolute power over the citizens of the state. The ancient doctrine of the *divine right of kings* held that the monarch, as head of state, was answerable only to God. Whilst the monarch must therefore accept that he or she would be judged by God according to the manner in which they governed, ordinary people, including Parliament, had no right to challenge the decrees of the monarchy. This all changed in the 1640s.

Oliver Cromwell was a senior parliamentarian at this time, who became increasingly concerned at the autocratic manner in which the king of the time – Charles I – was exercising his power. The matter came to a head in 1645 with the conclusion of the *English Civil War* when the parliamentary forces, led by

Cromwell, defeated the forces of Charles I at Naseby Field in modern day Leicestershire.

Believing that the right to govern was gained by a mandate from the people rather than by a monarch accountable only to God (although Cromwell was a Christian and a Puritan), Cromwell consented to the execution of Charles I in Whitehall in 1649. After a period during which the monarchy was abolished (and Britain was consequently a republic), it was restored in 1660 when Charles II was crowned after Cromwell's death. However, the outcome of the civil war had signalled a major readjustment in the English political constitution – that the most important policy-making body is the elected part of the state and that the monarchy is effectively subject to it. This remains the case today.

How laws are made

A law begins its life as a draft document called a *Bill*. A Bill can be put forward by the government, by the opposition parties, by ordinary Members of Parliament (in a so-called *Private Member's Bill*) or occasionally by a member of the House of Lords. The bill then passes through the following stages in both Houses of Parliament:

- First reading, where the Bill is published with no debate.
- Second reading, where the general merits of the Bill are debated.
- Committee stage, where the Bill is examined in detail by a cross-party Parliamentary Standing Committee of about 20 members. The Committee can propose amendments to the Bill before it returns to the House.
- Report stage, where the amended Bill is reported to the House for approval.
- Third reading, where verbal amendments may be made in debate and the Bill is finally approved by the House.

When the Bill has received its three 'readings' in each House, and assuming it has received a voted majority at each reading, it then goes to the monarch. The king or queen must sign the Bill because it has been duly passed by Parliament. Upon receiving *Royal Assent*, the bill becomes an *Act of Parliament* and eventually passes into British law.

The secretariat

What is the secretariat?

The secretariat or administration of the state is by far the largest of the four 'organs'. It comprises the various government departments and the large part of the economy which is commonly called the *public sector*. This part of the state, which employs, directly or indirectly through government agencies, around six million people, serves whichever party is in government (theoretically) without partiality.

There are a number of types of people in the secretariat. Central government departments are staffed largely by *civil servants*, whilst local governments employ *local government officers*. Professionals are well represented in the public sector, notable among whom are health professionals such as most doctors and dentists, educators like teachers and university lecturers, public sector accountants and administrators.

Central government includes around twenty departments many of which are based in Whitehall, London, although much of the main activity of these departments occurs in the regions.

Government Departments

- Department for Education and Employment.
- Department of Health.
- Department of National Heritage.
- Department of Social Security.
- Department of the Environment.
- Department of Trade and Industry.
- Department of Transport.
- Foreign and Commonwealth Office.
- Her Majesty's Treasury.
- Home Office.
- Law Officers.
- Lord Advocate's Office.
- Lord Chancellor's Department.
- Ministry of Agriculture, Fisheries and Food.
- Ministry of Defence.
- Northern Ireland Office.
- Privy Council Office.
- Public Services and Science (Office of the Chancellor of the Duchy of Lancaster).
- Scottish Office.
- Welsh Office.

Question 21.2

Suggest reasons why central government might locate much of its activities in areas other than London.

The secretariat and the executive

We have seen that the actions of the secretariat are determined by the policies of the executive. Cabinet members are placed in charge of government departments, but each department is also staffed by a hierarchy of permanent managers who remain in place as their political 'masters' come and go. The job-titles of these senior managers varies from department to department, and each department usually has a senior civil servant in Whitehall in addition to a chief executive who oversees the activities of the department on a day-to-day basis. We can see the relationship between the executive and the secretariat in Figure 21.2.

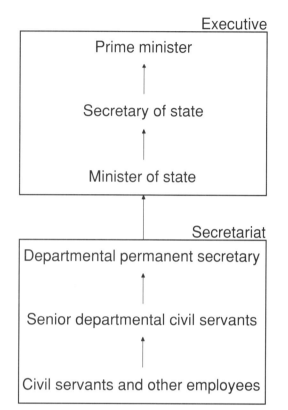

Figure 21.2 Relationship between the executive and the secretariat

The judiciary

There would be little point in having a legislature to make law if the state did not also have a means by which it could be powerfully enforced. This is the explicit role of the judiciary. Although the head of the judiciary is a member of the cabinet (the Lord Chancellor, who is also a member of the House of Lords), the part of the state which executes justice is largely independent of the executive and the legislature in practice.

Question 21.3

Find out the following things about the judiciary:

- What is the name of the current Lord Chancellor?
- A senior member of the legal system is the *Attorney General*. Find out what this person's role is and how it differs from that of the Lord Chancellor.

The judiciary is composed of the various levels of courts. These vary in significance from the local magistrates' court to the highest court; the House of Lords. Different courts specialize in different types of law and there are strict legal rules which govern which cases are heard at which courts. They all have in common one thing – the decisions made in them are on behalf of the state. It is thus the state and not the judge which sends a convicted person to prison, because the judge is empowered to act for the people of the state as a whole.

There are two ways in which the judiciary can act on behalf of the state. Firstly, in *civil cases* – disputes between two parties – the judiciary acts as an *umpire*. An umpire or referee ensures that fair play occurs. The state is thus empowered to award damages against an offender in much the same way as a football referee awards a free-kick to the offended team after a foul is committed. Secondly, in *criminal cases*, the judiciary sits as an *executioner*. Criminal cases are those wherein, even though the offence may have been committed against an individual, the offence is sufficiently serious for the state, and not the individual, to bring a case against the accused. The judiciary has a much wider range of measures it can bring to criminal cases, including imprisonment and, in some countries, the death penalty. We will examine the composition and role of the judiciary in more detail in Chapter 22.

Figure 21.3 shows the passage of a successfully prosecuted criminal case passing through the legal process. We can see how only the 'deciding' part of the process is the judiciary. The other 'administrative' roles in the judicial process are discharged by the secretariat.

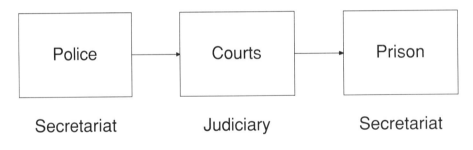

Figure 21.3 The secretariat and the judiciary

21.5 Subnational government

Local government

In addition to the influences upon the business sector exerted by the policies and structures of central government, a second 'layer' is also worthy of study. Each area of the UK is controlled locally by a local authority. The geographical area and population over which a local authority governs varies from region to region and also changes over time, as central government makes changes to this provision.

Whilst central government in the UK has legislative power over all local authorities, it is deemed helpful to devolve some powers to the arm of government at local level to enable it to be 'nearer to the people' in the hope that it will be more responsive to local needs. The fact is that the needs of communities vary across the country and by having a local layer of government, such differences can be accounted for.

Unitary and federal local government

The constitutional basis of local government varies greatly depending upon whether the state operates a unitary or a federal constitution.

A *federal* system is operated in many democratic states including Germany and the USA. A federation of any kind is an agglomeration of independent bodies who have chosen to merge together. In doing so, they allow the federal government certain powers but retain some for themselves. The federal government does not have the right to overrule individual states in matters which are of local concern. The federal government is therefore a 'servant' of local government and not the other way round. In the USA, for example, the federal government in Washington, headed by the President with two legislative houses (the *House of Representatives* and the *Senate*), is responsible for economic policy, defence, foreign policy and other areas which are best dealt with at the national level. The individual 'states', headed by a *state governor*, retain responsibility for, among other things, education, policing and some local judicial matters (e.g. some states have the death penalty whilst others have not).

A *unitary* local authority system is the converse of the above. According to the constitution of a unitary state, central government exercises, more or less, total executive power over local government organization. Local authorities in a unitary state must act according to the frameworks set for them by central government. From time to time, central government amends the responsibilities and powers of local government. Over recent years, central UK government has restructured local government by scrapping some authorities whilst instituting others. When a British local authority carries out local education policy it is only because it has been instructed to do so by central government – this duty could be taken away from it or additional duties added to it.

Local government in the UK is based in town halls, civic centres and county halls, depending upon the nature of the area over which the authority governs. The nature of regions controlled by the various types of local authority varies. Some oversee a large area of mainly rural population (e.g. Northumberland County Council), whereas inner-city areas – areas of small geographical area but high population – are controlled by metropolitan or borough councils (e.g. Enfield Borough Council is one of the many councils in Greater London).

How is local government controlled?

In a democracy such as the UK, local government is controlled in the same way as central government – by elected representation. At the local level, representatives are called *councillors* and each one represent a small part of the local region called a *ward*. Councillors are local people who have offered themselves to serve on the local authority and have been duly elected by popular ballot in a local election. Whereas national politicians will generally campaign on national issues (such as national unemployment, the National Health Service and the national economy), local candidates are uniquely concerned about local issues. Typical among these will be local transport infrastructure, local schools and local authority services and spending.

Question 21.4

Find out the following about the local authority in the locality in which you are studying:

- The name of the local authority.
- The political party which controls the authority.
- The name of the leader of the council (the leading councillor in the majority party).

The same system of competing political parties operates, for most councils, at the local level, so most candidates who stand for a seat on the local authority will represent one of the main national political parties. The party which has the majority of local councillors in any given authority is said to have *control* of the council as, by voting as one, their policies cannot be overturned by the opposition of all other councillors.

	Name of representative	*Area represented*
Central government	Member of Parliament	A constituency
Local government	Councillor	A ward

Collectively, councillors in a local authority constitute the *executive* of local government. They sit on various council committees which have power over a range of local provisions. In the same way that executive policy in central government is carried out by a national secretariat, at local level, *local government officers* are responsible for carrying out the decisions of elected councillors.

Representatives and delegates

Astute readers will notice that the word *representative* has been used in this chapter to describe the roles of councillors and Members of Parliament. This term is in marked contrast to the role of a *delegate*. Both representatives and delegates operate on behalf of an organization; the difference lies in the autonomy given to the person in their responsibilities.

A *representative* is appointed on the basis of his or her abilities to represent the organization or constituency. The importance of appointing the right person is seen when one realizes that, once appointed to represent, he or she acts in whatever way they see fit. They do not need to refer back to the constituency in order to be instructed how to act. It is said that a representative is mandated to represent the constituency on the basis of his or her pledges at the time of selection. A Member of Parliament is a representative.

A *delegate* acts on behalf of an organization or constituency according to a brief. He or she has no authority to act on his on her own volition. Delegates are appointed to attend such things as conferences, where they are instructed how to vote on various issues and what to say on behalf of an organization. This principle is used in the management practice of delegation, when a manager passes work to a subordinate with a brief as to the subordinate's instructions, limits of authority, time limit on the job, etc.

How is local government funded?

Local government is charged with the provision of local services. These are managed at the local level, for the benefit of the local population and must usually be funded in part by local people. The cost of running local services and the administration of local government is met in several ways:

- Some money is allocated to each local authority from *central government funds*, via (in the case of authorities in England and Wales) the Department of the Environment. As central government funds, this money is raised through general taxation.
- The local authority can raise a relatively small amount of money from *fees and charges*. An example of this revenue is the entrance fee at the swimming pool or the amount you pay for the local authority employee to come and clear your drains.
- Any other money that the local authority needs in addition to that raised from these first two sources must come from *local taxation*. This is money paid directly to the local authority by residents and businesses located within the area covered by the authority. The mechanism by which local revenues are raised has been the subject of much debate over recent years. When the old 'rates' system was replaced with the ill-fated 'community charge' (or *poll tax*) in the late 1980s, political pressure forced central government to scrap it in 1991, introducing in its place the 'council tax' – a system where the amount paid depends upon the value of the resident's home.

Each year, a local authority will prepare a spending budget. Similarly, the Department of the Environment will prepare a *standard spending assessment* (SSA), based on the previous year's spending, whilst taking into account any changes to the authority's duties. The local authority budget will work like this (greatly simplified):

	£
Standard spending assessment	XXX
minus central government grant	(xxx)
minus other sources of local revenue	(xxx)
Shortfall	XXX

The shortfall, a figure of many millions of pounds, must be made good by local taxation. The figure is divided up by the number of local taxpayers, accounting for 'banding' according to house value, and each home and business receives an invoice for the amount, usually collected as a monthly payment.

Central government in a unitary state, such as the UK, retains the right to 'cap' local authority spending. If the local authority's budget exceeds the SSA, central government can block a local authority's council tax level, insisting it be brought down to a lower amount. Such a move is usually very unpopular with the local authority in question as it must make cuts in services to account for the shortfall in funding (although the council tax payers are usually more appreciative).

The duties of local government

Because the UK is a unitary and not a federalist state, the responsibilities and duties of local government are determined by central government. Moreover, they change from time to time as different governments implement differing policies regarding local government.

Change in the responsibilities of local government over the years of the Thatcher and Major Governments tended to focus on contracting out certain local authority contracts to private businesses. Such a process, such as the invitation of tenders to provide the authority with its refuse clearing services, was designed to provide the local taxpayer with optimum value for money as the local authority accepts the lowest quote for the contract. Some services are subject to a process called *compulsory competitive tendering* (CCT). This means that services covered by CCT must (in law) be offered to tender to outside contractors, although the authority's *direct labour organizations* (DLOs) may also apply for the tender to supply the service.

The statutory duties (set out in legislation) of local government include at least a partial role in:

- the maintenance of local *transport infrastructure* (e.g. local roads, pavements);
- the provision of local *education services*, which includes non-grant-maintained schools but not universities;
- *environmental services* (e.g. hygiene and licensing of pubs and clubs);
- *social services* (care of the less economically unfortunate and others considered as vulnerable);
- collection of household *refuse* and its disposal;
- the provision of local authority *housing* and homes for senior citizens;
- adequate care of *homeless persons*.

21.6 Supranational political influence – the European Union

A business can experience some degree of influence from political institutions at a level above its national government. Such institutions are ones which affect many countries and, in some cases, all countries. The major supranational influence on UK businesses is the European Union, although others do exist (such as the United Nations).

The beginnings of the EU

That which we now call the European Union (EU) began life in 1957 as the European Economic Community (EEC). After the Second World War ended in 1945, there was a general mood among the European nations that the countries should become progressively closer and that formal links should be instituted to secure a 'friendly', peaceful and prosperous future.

The initial idea of the EU almost certainly came from the war-time British prime minister, Sir Winston Churchill who, in 1945, made an important speech on the theme of unity among European nations in the French city of Strasbourg where a plaque now 'marks the spot'. The first successful attempt at European co-operation came in 1952 with the establishment of the European Coal and Steel Community (ECSC) under the *Treaty of Paris, 1951*. The ECSC was set up between France, Italy and the Benelux countries (Belgium, Netherlands and Luxembourg), although West Germany joined later. It served to abolish trade restrictions between the member countries on coal and steel imports and exports and to co-ordinate production levels and pricing policies.

The success of the ECSC prompted political leaders to investigate the possibility of closer co-operation on a much wider scale. After much negotiation, the various proposals were formalized in *The Treaty of Rome 1957* – one of the most significant international accords of the twentieth century. Resulting from this legal document, two Communities came into existence on 1 January 1958: the European Economic Community (EEC) and the European Atomic Energy Community (Euratom). Notwithstanding the seminal influence of Churchill in the vision behind the EEC, the UK declined to participate in both the ECSC and the initial EEC organization.

The name of the EEC has changed since its inception, causing some confusion among observers. The EEC was the community of nations which was primarily concerned with closer economic ties. The changing perceptions and roles of the various parts of the Community prompted the heads of state and government to approve the name to be changed to the European Community (or EC), dropping the narrower 'economic' part, as part of the *Maastricht Agreement of 1992*. The term European Union (EU) was later introduced to describe the 'umbrella' organization of nations which includes the EC, the ECSC and Euratom. For most purposes, our discussion will use the term EU.

Membership of the European Union

The membership of the EU has grown to include more and more European nation states since its beginnings in 1958. Some of the countries that joined subsequent to its formation would not in fact have qualified in 1958 owing to the fact that they were not, at that time, democratic in their form of government. Spain, for example, was effectively a dictatorship until Franco died in November 1975, after which a democratically elected government was installed. Portugal and Greece, similarly, are relatively recent democracies.

- Founder members (1958): West Germany (Germany was divided into East and West prior to 1989), France, Belgium, Netherlands, Luxembourg, Italy.

- 1972: Great Britain, Republic of Ireland, Denmark.
- 1981: Greece.
- 1986: Spain, Portugal.
- 1995: Sweden, Finland, Austria.

The current (1996) membership of 15 countries contains a total population of 370 million people. It is consequently the largest single trading block in the world. The EU is expected to increase in size in future years as applications to join have been received from, among others, Turkey (in 1987), Cyprus (1990), Malta (1990), Norway (1992) and Switzerland (1992). Some formerly Communist Eastern European states are also expected to be admitted eventually.

The European 'organs of state'

The Treaty of Rome 1957 set in place institutions that would enable the EU eventually to operate as a single federal state. Whilst these establishments have their place in the various stages of the development of the EU, the founders had in mind that they could facilitate the coalescence of nations into a European federal state if the political will of the member states wished this to happen.

The European Union's executive

The European executive is called the *Council of Ministers* (or the European Council). The Council is made up of a government minister from each member state. It follows that any meeting of the Council comprises 15 ministers. Because the members of the Council are elected ministers in their respective countries, they have the elected authority to make policy on behalf of their own and other member states.

When the Council meets to discuss European financial matters, the finance ministers from each member state assemble (the representative from the UK will be the Chancellor of the Exchequer). On agricultural issues, the Council will comprise the agriculture ministers, on health matters, the health ministers and so on. From time to time, the heads of state or government meet (the Prime Minister, the German Chancellor, the French President, etc.) in a summit. Such meetings tend to be called to discuss high level strategic matters such as the development of the EU and political changes in the EU structure, such as moves towards political union. The European heads of state or government meet at least twice a year in the context of the European Council.

The presidency of the Council rotates, with each member state assuming oversight for a period of six months. The minister at the Council representing the presiding country assumes the chairman's role in Council meetings. When Britain last held the presidency, in the latter six months of 1992, Prime Minister Major also held the title President of the Council of Ministers of the European Union. He used his influence during his presidency to, among other things, hold a heads of state summit in Edinburgh to discuss the future of the EU.

The European executive has supreme influence over the policies of the EU although it also has a pivotal role in the legislative process. A building is reserved for meetings of the Council in Brussels, although some meetings take place in Luxembourg. The Council is served by a committee called COREPER (the Committee of Permanent

Representatives). COREPER comprises the member states' permanent ambassadors to the EU and it prepares the work of the Council, in addition to acting on the decisions of the Council, such as setting up committees to make preparations or to study particular matters of interest.

Decisions are passed by the Council on a democratic voting system. However, ministers from different member states carry more or fewer votes depending upon the population they represent (i.e. the population of their country).

The total vote of 87 is composed of the following vote weightings in the Council (as at 1996):

- France, Germany, Italy, the UK: 10 votes each.
- Spain: 8 votes.
- Belgium, Greece, Netherlands, Portugal: 5 votes each.
- Austria, Sweden: 4 votes each.
- Denmark, Finland, Ireland: 3 votes each.
- Luxembourg: 2 votes.

The matter of voting in the Council is further complicated by the fact that very few matters are decided simply by a simple majority of 51%. For some votes, a *qualified majority* of 62 votes is required for the motion to be passed, whereas in other, very important issues, unanimity is required – one country can defeat the motion by the use of its veto.

The European Union's legislature

The principal forum for debate in the EU is the *European Parliament*. The Parliament usually sits in Strasbourg, France, although sometimes it meets in Brussels. Its administration is based in Luxembourg. Although it is called a parliament, it does not have the same functions or procedures as the Westminster Parliament in that it does not have sole responsibility for the legislative process within the EU (the EU legislative process is discussed in Chapter 22).

The first elections to the Parliament were in 1979 and its size has grown as new member states have joined the EU over the intervening years. As at 1996, the European Parliament comprises 626 *Members of the European Parliament* (MEPs), each of whom is elected for a period of five years. Each member represents a constituency, although the size of a European constituency is obviously larger than its domestic equivalent.

Although the members come from different countries, they sit in party groups rather than national groups in the Parliament. In this respect, it is like Westminster, in that members sit with their political parties regardless of which part of the EU they represent. There are nine major political groupings in the Parliament with an additional 31 members who are non-affiliated. Parliamentary sessions are guided in the various debates and discussions by a president and 14 vice-presidents – one from each member state, one of whom is appointed to be the overall president. The issues debated are prepared for the Parliament by 20 committees, each comprised of MEPs.

The powers and responsibilities of the European Parliament have changed and increased, most notably since the passing of the *Single European Act 1986*. Its principal powers and responsibilities are as follows:

- to generate initiatives for the political and economic development of the EU;
- to supervise and appoint the European Commission and, if necessary, to dismiss it (the Commission is the European secretariat);
- to debate and vote upon initiatives put forward by the Commission;
- to monitor the day-to-day management of the various other parts of the EU;
- to examine petitions and requests addressed to the Parliament by ordinary European citizens;
- together with the Commission, to agree upon and adopt the annual budget of the EU (the amount of money required to facilitate the normal functioning of the EU – a figure of about 80 billion ECU in 1995);
- to confirm the accession of new member states to the EU.

The European Parliament by national representation

Country	Number of MEPs
Germany	99
France	87
Italy	87
UK	87
Spain	64
Netherlands	31
Belgium	25
Greece	25
Portugal	25
Sweden	22
Austria	21
Denmark	16
Finland	16
Ireland	15
Luxembourg	6
Total	**626**

(Source: *The Institutions of the European Union*, ECSC-EC-EAEC, Brussels & Luxembourg, 1995.)

Question 21.5

Find out the following:

- The name of the European Parliamentary constituency in which you are studying.
- The name of your MEP.
- The political party to which your MEP belongs.
- The European Parliamentary party grouping in which your MEP sits.

The European Union's secretariat

The administrative arm of the EU is the *European Commission* and is based in Brussels, Belgium, and in Luxembourg. The Commission is headed by 20 European Commissioners but it also contains around 15 000 officials divided between 30 senior administrative officers called Directors General. One of the Commissioners is chosen by the member states to occupy the office of President of the European Commission, whose task it then is to guide the policy of the Commission. The 20 Commissioners are appointed by their domestic governments to serve the EU as a host national of their home country. There are two each from France, Germany, Italy, Spain and the UK, and one from each of the other EU countries.

The duties of a Commissioner are to the EU and not to their home countries – they are there to serve the EU and not to represent their respective home governments. Each Commissioner is given oversight over an area of EU policy such as transport, trade, etc., but decisions are taken on the basis of collective responsibility.

The Commission has three broad areas of responsibility. The primary *raison d'être* of the Commission is to be the 'guardian' of the various European Treaties. In this responsibility, it ensures that each member state fully implements the provisions of each treaty, such as the terms of the Maastricht Treaty 1992. It has powers to impose fines or to initiate proceedings against any country for failure to enact the provisions of a Treaty, referring the country, if necessary, to the European judiciary. Secondly, the Commission has the sole right to initiate legislation. It has the power to bring its influence to bear on each stage of the law-making process in negotiation with the European Parliament, the Council and the 15 member states. Thirdly, the Commission has the responsibility to issue rules for the implementation of EU Treaties and to administer the financial budgets. The majority of EU expenditure falls within four major funds:

- the European Agricultural Guidance and Guarantee Fund;
- the European Social Fund;
- the European Regional Development Fund;
- the Cohesion Fund.

Each fund is an effective redistribution of the total EU budget, with money raised from each member state as a condition of membership of the Union.

Question 21.6

- Who is the current President of the European Commission?
- What nationality is he or she?
- Britain has two European Commissioners. Who are they?
- What are their areas of oversight?

The European judiciary

There are two courts which comprise the legal arm of the EU: the *European Court of Justice* and the *European Court of First Instance*, which is a relatively recent development, having been established in 1988. Both courts are overseen by fifteen independent judges (one from each country) who serve the judiciary for a period of six years although the judges in the Court of Justice are assisted by nine Advocates General. Both courts are located in Luxembourg and each, being part of the supranational political structure, has supremacy over national courts.

The European Court of Justice and the Court of First Instance differ in their jurisdictions (i.e. areas of legal responsibility and oversight). The Court of First Instance can only hear trial (or First Instance) cases, whereas the Court of Justice can also hear appellate (or appeal) cases, usually from senior national courts. The Court of First Interest hears cases brought by businesses and private citizens of the Community and does not have the wider powers of the Court of Justice.

The Court of Justice enforces the Treaties and legislation of the EU. It can find member states guilty of failing to comply with European law and impose fines for contravention. The Court can also give preliminary legal rulings or interpretations of the various European laws when parties are engaged in a dispute as to the extent or meaning of a certain piece of law. Between 1952 and 1994, the Court heard more than 8600 cases, many from private individuals, which included 2900 references for preliminary rulings or legal interpretation.

Other European Union bodies

In addition to the four main bodies we have so far discussed, there are others of which we should be aware.

The *Court of Auditors* is located in Luxembourg. It acts as the EU's internal auditor and checks that all revenues are collected from member states and that expenditure is incurred in a lawful and regular manner. The Court consists of fifteen members appointed with the unanimous decision of the European Council after consultation with the European Parliament. It submits an annual report to the Council and Parliament to confirm that the Commission has correctly managed the Community's budget.

The *Economic and Social Committee* (ESC) is a body of 222 members which sits in Brussels. Its *raison d'être* is to express opinions on matters of business, economics and social affairs, and is consequently composed of those able to comment on such matters, i.e. representatives of European employers, employees and other economic stakeholders. It is consulted prior to any major European decision on economic and social matters and may submit opinions on its own initiative. It typically submits about 170 opinions per year. A similar body is the ECSC Consultative Committee, which comprises 108 members and acts in a similar capacity to the ESC in matters concerning the coal and steel industries.

The *Committee of the Regions*, like the ESC, has 222 'permanent' members and an equal number of 'alternate' members who represent local and regional authorities throughout the EU. Both types of members serve four-year terms on the Committee, which was established in March 1994. The Committee of the Regions must be consulted by the other European institutions in relation to a number of areas concerning regional interests (such as the provision of aid to a region of the UK such as rural South Wales). It is assumed that representatives of the various regions can reliably inform the EU institutions on such matters as local education, youth, culture, public health, etc. The main Committee meets in plenary session five times a year, although its work continues with eight commissions and four subcommissions.

Finally, there is the *European Investment Bank* (EIB), which was set up by the Treaty of Rome to help finance investments which will help towards the EU's objectives. The EIB, which is based in Luxembourg, like any other bank is independent, and thus must organize its own financial affairs without subsidy from the EU, although it can make use of loan capital from the EU. Its priority is to help to facilitate a 'balanced development' of the Union which involves supporting EU interests outside as well as inside Europe itself. There is also a a major proposal to institute a *European Central Bank*. In the event that EMU (see later in this chapter) comes about, this Central Bank would manage EU-wide monetary policy as well as managing a European single currency.

Objectives of the European Union

The debate

The intensity of political debate which surrounds so many European issues may serve to confuse observers as to the EU's essential objectives. The broad spectrum of political opinion within the fifteen member states contains a plethora of varying attitudes regarding how the EU should grow and develop. The two extremes of opinion are:

- That the EU member states should eventually converge to become a single federal political state ('the United States of Europe'). There should be a single European currency and each member country should be the same as a USA state, such that the UK would act in essentially the same way as, for example, Texas or California.
- That the EU should be disbanded and all overtures to increased European integration should be immediately discontinued. The individual European nation states have long histories and unique peoples. To try to mix such disparate cultures and economies would not only be a coarse and artificial effort, it is also unnecessary and undesirable.

Within these two extremes lie many positions and attitudes to the EU. In reality, the *raison d'être* and objectives of the EU have evolved and changed over the years. Whilst, initially, the majority saw the EU primarily as a trading block, the debate over recent years has centred around the possibility of moves towards federalization. Perhaps the only EU objectives which are more or less common to all member states are those which are detailed in the various Treaties and European Acts although many of these have been the subject of heated debate within the various member states.

Recent amendments to the Treaty of Rome 1957 have included the *Single European Act 1986* and the *Treaty on European Union 1992* (Maastricht Treaty). Both of these treaties concern a closer union of the EU nation states, not only as a single market, but also politically and economically.

The European Union's stated objectives

The broad themes of the EU's objectives are expressed in the metaphor of a single roof resting on three 'pillars'. It follows that the EU 'roof' is held up by the three pillars. This is shown in Figure 21.4

The EU's various publications give us a clearer picture of its stated objectives. The following extracts are taken from an EU publication in 1992, when the EU was composed of 12 states and not 15 as now. Readers should be aware that many of the objectives stated are rather more open to discussion and debate than the publication implies.

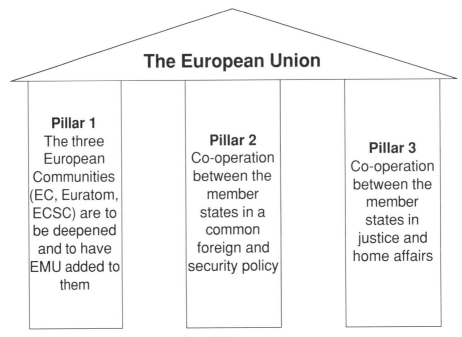

Figure 21.4 The three pillars of the EU

Europe in the year 2000: an extended Community of more than 20 countries? Private citizens and businesses – no longer checked at border crossings – from the North Cape to Sicily and from Warsaw to Lisbon using a common currency, the ecu, to make payments? Over 370 million Europeans whose interests are represented at international level by common institutions?

Europe has come a good deal closer to these goals. At the Maastricht Summit (9 to 11 December 1991) the Heads of State or Government of the 12 Member States agreed on a Treaty on European Union. This Treaty is intended to facilitate the development of the European Community into a political union and an economic and monetary union (EMU). It is intended that by 1999 at the latest the European currency, the ecu, will replace the currencies of the Member States. A common foreign and security policy will be introduced, followed later by a common defence policy.

Reproduced from *Europe on the Move*, ECSC-EC-EAEC, Brussels & Luxembourg, 1994.

The same document then goes on to give a more detailed description of its objectives as 'The objectives of the European Union'.

- *To promote economic and social progress which is balanced and sustainable, in particular through the creation of an area without internal frontiers, through the strengthening of economic and social cohesion and through the establishment of economic and monetary union, ultimately including a single currency.*
- *To assert the European identity on the international scene, in particular through the implementation of a common foreign and security policy including*

the eventual framing of a common defence policy which might in time lead to a common defence.

- *To strengthen the protection of the rights and interests of the nationals of Member States through the introduction of a citizenship of the Union.*
- *To develop close co-operation on justice and home affairs.*
- *To maintain the acquis communautaire and build on it with a view to considering to what extent the policies and forms of co-operation introduced by this Treaty may need to be revised with the aim of ensuring the effectiveness of the mechanisms and institutions of the Community.*

(ibid.)

A discussion of European Union objectives

A European single market

The creation of a single European market was the objective upon which the EEC was founded in 1958. A single market is one which comprises several separate nation states which act, in matters of trade, as though they were the same country. Within any given country, there are no restrictions on trade and the same benefits and restrictions apply to all businesses. In the objective of a European single market, principles are applied that enable business to take place between countries without restriction. Much of the Treaty of Rome and subsequent EU legislation has prepared the Union for the accomplishment of this objective.

There are several conditions which must be in place before a single trading block can be created (trading blocks as a feature of international business are discussed in Chapter 28):

- the abolition of internal tariffs and quotas (tariffs, or duties, are taxes charged on goods upon their importation; quotas are maximum limits placed upon the amounts of imported goods);
- the application of a common external tariff, enabling quotas and tariffs to be uniformly applied to goods imported from countries outside the Union;
- the harmonization of laws helping or hindering business activity in each member state of the Union;
- the harmonization of economic conditions in each member state, such as similar monetary conditions and closer fiscal regimes.

The single European market has, in recent years, become a partial reality. The passing of the Single European Acts of 1986 and 1992 brought about some of the conditions necessary. In 1993, internal EU quotas and tariffs were abolished and a common external tariff was partially imposed. There has been more difficulty in meeting the objectives of harmonizing legal and economic matters.

Single markets such as the EU are designed to advantage businesses by allowing them to grow and expand without the limitations of national borders. Whilst allowing businesses to export goods without restriction offers the opportunity of expansion, importing materials without having to pay duties on them reduces the costs of a production process. Both of these features are potentially good for business. The converse of this, of course, is that as well as UK businesses gaining access to markets in other

EU states, businesses from other EU states gain access to the UK. For some businesses, this is a threat.

Economic and Monetary Union

It follows that if EU member states are truly to act in matters of trade as though they were one country, then as well as enjoying trade without tariffs and quotas, they will also share more or less identical economic conditions. This means that they will share identical levels of monetary pressure (i.e. the same interest rates and rates of monetary growth) and exchange rates which do not vary against each other.

This objective of the EU has given rise to the idea of economic convergence. The fifteen member states of the EU have traditionally had widely differing economic conditions and some politicians and economists have consequently expressed serious doubt over the feasibility of this objective. However, a first step towards EMU was taken in 1978 with the establishment of the *European Monetary System* (EMS). A key plank of the EMS was a mechanism of attempting to stabilize the variations in the exchange rates between the currencies. The *Exchange Rate Mechanism* (ERM) of the EMS commits member countries to maintaining parity of their currencies within strict limits of each other.

In its implementation, the maintenance of exchange rate parity has actually caused problems with other features of EMU (e.g. convergence of monetary regimes). This is due to the fact that such things as interest rates are a key determinant of exchange rates. In order to maintain the exchange values of the various currencies, countries found that they needed to increase or decrease interest rates significantly as other factors influence the value of the currency (such as the level of exports). In some cases, the costs of maintaining parity (the 'pegged' value of the currency against the others) in the ERM has proved rather too high. Some countries left the ERM after it became effectively impossible to keep the exchange rate within the parity range. The difficulties with the ERM have made some politicians sceptical about its long-term prospects as a vehicle of monetary union.

A European single currency – the 'Euro'

If we examine the objectives of EMU, we can see how a common currency became an economic objective within the EU. If all EU states shared the same currency, then all member states must, by definition, share the same interest rates (see Chapter 23 for a discussion of the links between interest rates and currency exchange values). It is this feature of EMU that is the most controversial as it necessitates all member states sharing a central bank and hence a centralized control of monetary policy.

The EU has a currency unit already in place – the *European Currency Unit* or ECU. This unit has an economic role as a means of measuring other currencies against it, although it can be used by businesses in some international trading activities. The ECU is a notional 'basket' of all the EU currencies where its value is a composite of the relative contributions of the member currencies. It therefore represents the weighted average of all the European Union currencies. Its value as a means of comparison is widely used to indicate the strength of national currencies. If, for example, the pound sterling rises against the ECU, it indicates a relative strengthening of sterling against the average of other EU currencies. This is sometimes more useful than comparing sterling against single currencies such as the French franc or the deutschmark.

How the ECU is made up

The ratio of currencies in the ECU varies from time to time. The following is the case since 6 March 1995.

Currency	Country	Percentage of ECU
Deutschmark	Germany	32.68
French franc	France	20.79
Pound sterling	UK	11.17
Florin	Netherlands	10.21
Belgian franc	Belgium	8.38
Lira	Italy	7.21
Paseta	Spain	4.24
Krona	Denmark	2.71
Punt	Ireland	1.08
Escudo	Portugal	0.71
Drachma	Greece	0.49
Franc	Luxembourg	0.33

Source: Eurostat, *ECU-EMS information & Central bank interest rates*, 9, 1995.

It should be stressed that, whilst the ECU may be a forerunner, it is not the same as a single currency. The single currency as conceived by its proponents requires the discontinuation of all national currencies such as sterling and a 'hardening' of the ECU into a usable currency in both cash and non-cash forms (i.e. it will then perform all of the normal functions of money). On 15 December 1995 the European Council announced that a single currency would to be called the *Euro*. The perceived pros and cons of a single European currency can be summarized as follows.

Advantages of EMU
- Other conditions, necessary as a prerequisite for the single currency, will have already been met, such as the abolition of internal tariffs and quotas and the imposition of a common external tariff. These conditions are generally considered to be conducive to business growth.
- Uncertainty and fluctuations in currency exchange values will have been eliminated. Hence there would be total confidence among importers and exporters that the exchange value of currencies would not change within the EU.
- The commission that must usually be paid upon cash transactions between different currencies would be eliminated. This is seen as being good for holidaymakers and others who deal in cash.
- The trans-European mobility of people and capital will be enhanced, as spending and cash transfers between and within member states is greatly simplified.

Disadvantages of EMU

- The fact that the currency must be centrally managed means that national governments lose control of it. Hence, whereas previously the UK Government may choose to adjust its currency exchange value to benefit UK businesses, this option would be closed.
- National governments must give up a large slice of their sovereignty, particularly that over monetary policy, to the European central bank. The UK government thus becomes unable to adjust its own interest rates to help such groups as UK based homebuyers or businesses who have debt.

The ERM was seen as an essential step on the way to the creation of a single European currency. If exchange rates could be stabilized within a few percentage points of each other, then it would be a relatively straightforward task to merge each into a currency fixed at the stable exchange value of each currency. In practice, the ERM became a little 'unstuck' owing to the pressures of maintaining currency exchange values at their 'pegged' levels against other currencies. The UK Government withdrew the pound sterling from the ERM in September 1992 owing to its inability to prevent market forces from forcing a devaluation. This story has been repeated in some other countries.

Political union

The objective of political union is probably the most controversial of those held by participants in the EU. According to the proponents of political union, once full EMU has been successfully accomplished, then in many respects the EU is already operating as one country anyway. Full EMU would mean that all EU states would share the same currency, the same central bank controlling monetary policy, and previous national borders would become irrelevant as far as they concern the passage of people, trade and capital. It is thus a small step to create a federal European 'superstate' much like the models adopted in the USA and some other federal countries like Switzerland.

The federalization debate has become one of the most fractious over recent years and any number of opinions have been put forward *vis-à-vis* its possibility and desirability. In the UK, there are elements in all of the main political parties that see it as desirable, but the UK has emerged as one of the main voices in the EU who see the loss of sovereignty of the British Parliament as unacceptable. Proponents see federalization as the logical extension of the many moves to closer co-operation that have taken place over the past forty years, whereas the opponents see a richness in the diversity of different European histories and cultures that may be lost if they were all submerged into one big superstate.

Certainly, the instruments are in place in preparation for political union. We have seen that the EU has each of the 'organs' of state and, by devolving more and more power to these organs, political union may become increasingly realistic over time.

Assignments

- If you are using this textbook as part of a class or group, organize a debate comprising two sides presenting arguments before an audience (the rest of the class). Eight to ten volunteers should divide into two sides. One team should prepare a case in favour of the contention: *European federalization would be good for the UK*. The other side should prepare the case against (i.e. that federalization would be bad for the UK). The debate itself should comprise both sides presenting their cases to an equal time limit (say 20 minutes each), beginning with the case in favour. The class then should have the opportunity to question each team. After a final summing up of both arguments by the two teams, the class should vote on the contention based on the arguments put forward.
- Discuss the proposition that local government is unnecessary and a waste of local taxpayers' money. Do you agree that all of its functions could be managed either by private companies or direct from central government?
- In August 1996, President Clinton announced that he intended to reclassify nicotine as an addictive substance, thus bringing about the possibility of increased restrictions on the sales and consumption of cigarettes. 'The tobacco industry has no right to peddle cigarettes to children or encourage them directly or indirectly to smoke. It is immoral', the President said. Accordingly, the share prices of the major tobacco companies fell, thus damaging the investments of shareholders. Discuss the extent to which a senior politician has the right to damage private and institutional investments in this manner. State whether you agree with the President's actions, and give reasons for your answer.

Further reading

Dinan, D. (1994) *Ever Closer Union? An Introduction to the European Community*. London: Macmillan.

Dyker, D. (Ed.) (1992) *The European Economy*. London: Longman.

Goodman, S.F. (1996) *The European Union*, 3rd edn. London: Macmillan.

Gros, D. and Thygesen, N. (1992) *European Monetary Integration. From the European Monetary System to Monetary Union*. London: Longman.

Maidment, R. and Thompson, G. (1993) *Managing the United Kingdom. An Introduction to Its Political Economy and Public Policy*. London/Milton Keynes: Sage. Open University.

Nugent, N. and O'Donnell, R. (1994) *The European Business Environment*. London: Macmillan.

Nugent, N. (1994) *The Government and Politics of the European Union*, 3rd edn. London: Macmillan.

Wilson, G. K. (1991) *Business and Politics. A Comparative Introduction*, 2nd edn. London: Macmillan.

22

The legal environment

Learning objectives

After studying this chapter, students should be able to describe:

- The nature of law and legal rules.
- The nature of and difference between civil law and criminal law.
- The nature of and difference between common law and statute law.
- The purpose and structure of the British and EU judiciaries.
- The types of EU law and the EU legislative process.
- The key areas of business law and the relevant legislation.

22.1 What is law?

When we consider how legal matters affect businesses and other organizations, we should consider it to be essentially a part of the political environment. However, its complexities and importance necessitate a more detailed discussion. This is the objective of this chapter.

Definition and purpose of law

A system of rules

In any society, the complex interrelationships between legally responsible parties (such as people and companies) need to be regulated. It is generally understood that limits must be placed upon activities to prevent miscreants and other irresponsible people from abusing their freedom in a democratic state. Such acceptance leads to the enforcement of 'rules'. However, not all rules carry the same weight. A distinction needs to be drawn between legal rules and other types of rules. We sometimes use the term 'rules' to describe norms of behaviour in society. We may consider ourselves to be breaking 'social rules' if we act in an antisocial manner, such as dressing in an unconventional way or if we are rude or insulting to others. Within organizations, rules are imposed to facilitate normal functioning and may take the form of rigid procedures and limits of behaviour (such as a rule that receipts must be provided to support all expense claims).

Legal rules are different from social and other rules. They are characterized by the fact that they are enforceable by the judiciary, which acts on behalf of the state. So, whereas the *de facto* rule 'do not swear in the office' is not enforceable by the state, the rule 'do not steal cars' is. It is a matter of legal and philosophical debate at which degree of seriousness a rule becomes enforceable in law by the state. The rule 'do not walk on the grass' in a public park may, for example, be a rule which some individuals feel should be enforceable in law, while others may consider it a matter of utter inconsequence.

Because the law is primarily designed to *serve* the citizens of a state, it is reasonable to expect that legal rules should vary according to differing national customs and societal expectations. In traditional Islamic law, for example, adultery is considered to be illegal (breaking a legal rule) as it is in contravention of the *Qu'ran* (Koran). In consequence, the act, if discovered, is (theoretically) punishable by the Islamic state. In contrast, the sensibilities of citizens in western nations like the UK renders adultery an act which may contravene most people's social or ethical code, but is not considered to be punishable by the state. This is not to say that adultery may not lead to indirect legal action in the event that the offended spouse elected to seek a divorce.

The purpose of law

Legal rules serve essentially the same purpose as other types of rules. It does not take a lot of imagination to conceive of the chaos that would arise if football was deprived of its rules, and the same is true of society at large. Laws serve three broad purposes:

- to *permit* individuals to engage in lawful activities without apprehension or molestation by others;
- to *restrict* unlawful or otherwise disturbing individuals and behaviour;
- to *constrain* individuals to comply with legally required activities, such as the payment of taxes.

The normal functioning of society rests upon the assumption that the majority of people agree to comply with the law, in the same way that the normal functioning of a football match relies upon each player complying with the rules. It follows that the majority must view the laws that affect them as reasonable and fair – a situation theoretically guaranteed by having a democratically elected legislature.

Important distinctions in law

When we consider the general area of laws and legal rules, we must be aware of two important ways of dividing law. The first concerns the seriousness of offences and the second concerns the source of law (Figure 22.1).

Civil law and criminal law

At their simplest, matters of civil law and criminal law can be distinguished according to the perceived seriousness of the offences. Civil and criminal law are two distinct areas of legal practice and are overseen by separate parts of the judiciary.

In matters of *civil law*, individuals can bring other individuals (or legal entities such as companies) to the judiciary in order to have disputes settled. A civil matter is one in which a legal entity feels that they have a legitimate grievance against another, but the 'offence' is a matter which is not serious enough for the state to bring the case to a criminal court. The nature of the 'offence' is not considered to be a threat to society as a whole. In civil cases, the judiciary therefore acts as an umpire, ensuring that wrongs are redressed and that fairness is enforced. Once a civil court has made a judgement, the ruling carries the authority of the state.

Some of the most common civil disputes concern matters of *tort*. The Law of Torts concerns legal wrongs against an individual which gives the plaintiff (the party that brings the complaint – see later) a right of civil action for damages, but which do not arise over matters of breach of contract or trust. It is a broad expectation in society that individuals should have the right to pursue their lives without personal offence to their persons, property, etc., and to enjoy their possessions and property without unreasonable intrusion by others. Tort concerns such things as trespass, nuisance, negligence and defamation of character. It gives individuals the right of legal redress when they have been offended against in these matters.

A *criminal case* is one in which the offence is viewed as being of sufficient seriousness that, even though it may be an individual that has been 'wronged', the case against the alleged offender is brought by the state (or *the Crown*) in the form of (in England and Wales) the Crown Prosecution Service (CPS). In criminal cases, the successful prosecution of an offender is assumed to be in the interest of the state and society as a whole rather than just the individual who may have been offended against. In contrast to the judiciary acting as an umpire (as in matters of civil law), the courts act as an executioner in criminal cases in that they have power to execute (carry out) punishment.

Civil law and criminal law – simple (fictional) examples

The author has a next-door neighbour who decides to remove the fence separating the two adjoining gardens. In erecting his new fence, the next-door neighbour 'steals' half a metre of the author's garden by fixing the fence in a new position within the former boundaries of the author's garden. After pointing out the misplacement of the new fence, the neighbour refuses to replace his fence. The author takes the matter to his solicitor, who recommends that he brings a civil case against the neighbour. In this case, the author has been offended against, but not in such a serious manner that the state would entertain bringing a case against the neighbour. Apart from the neighbour's theft of a small piece of land, he is a law-abiding, tax-paying citizen. The law acts as umpire, looking at the two conflicting cases and awarding 'victory' to the party who has been offended.

After a sharp exchange of opinions over the newly replaced garden fence, the next-door neighbour produces a gun and proceeds to shoot the author. By fortunate happenstance, the bullet penetrates the author's leg, which, whilst painful, is not a life-threatening wound. After the police had been summoned to the scene and reported back, the Crown Prosecution Service decides to bring a criminal case against the neighbour. The state considers a shooting to be of sufficient seriousness that it (the state) should bring the case against the neighbour, even though it is the author who has been shot.

The legal system employs different terminology to describe the various people and processes involved in these two areas of law (Table 22.1).

Statute law and common law
The difference between statute and common law is their respective origins. We saw in Chapter 21 that some laws are made in the state's legislature, which in the UK comprises Parliament (the Houses of Commons and Lords) and the monarchy. Laws

produced by this mechanism are called statute laws. As Acts of Parliament, they are written down *in statute* in documents called legislation or statutory instruments.

Table 22.1 Criminal and civil law terminology

Criminal law	*Civil law*
• Cases are referred to as *R v. Smith* (or the Crown v. Smith)	• Cases are referred as *Smith v. Jones* (two private parties in dispute)
• The *Crown* initiates the proceedings	• The *plaintiff* initiates the proceedings
• The Crown *prosecutes*	• The plaintiff *sues*
• The *accused* is prosecuted	• The person sued is the *defendant*
• The accused is *convicted* of a crime	• The defendant is found *liable*
• If convicted, the accused is *punished* or *penalized*	• If found liable, the defendant is required to *remedy* or to *make reparations*

In contrast, common laws, which are no less enforceable than statute laws, are not written down as such. Common laws, which comprise the majority of laws in most modern democracies, are the result of (in the case of UK common laws) over 800 years of legal interpretation by the learned members of the judiciary. Unlike statute law, common law tends to evolve and change over time as members of the judiciary reinterpret ancient *forms of action* in the light of changing social and legal environments. It is generally understood, for example, that murder is highly antisocial behaviour. For this reason, it need not be enshrined in statute – it is a matter of common law. When murder was first punishable by the British judiciary in the dark recesses of medieval history, the most frequent mechanism of the crime was probably by the use of bare hands, clubs or bows and arrows. When however, the gun was invented, the judiciary would extrapolate the spirit of the common law of murder and find gun murderers guilty in the same way as those who had killed by more primitive methods. If murder was the subject of statute law, the statute would have to be revised by the legislature to account for the introduction of a new means of carrying out the offence. Under common law, the fact that murder had been punished in earlier legal cases meant that the judiciary merely had to refer to these, and adapt the law to account for a new means of carrying out the crime.

This brings us to an important principle in common law – that of *judicial precedent*. According this principle, current cases in matters of common law can be assessed in the light of previously decided cases. If, for example, a case concerned a civil matter where two people disagree over whether a tree should be chopped down, they could scour the annals of previously decided cases and, upon finding a precedent, could appeal to that precedent to decide their disagreement.

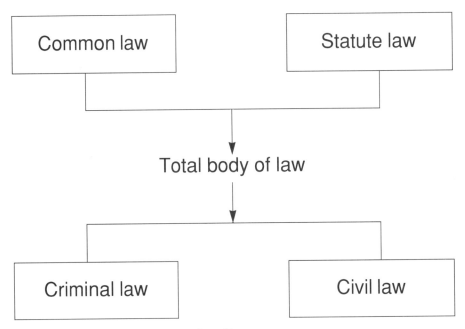

Figure 22.1 Sources and categories of law

22.2 The judiciary

Distinctions in the judiciary

The British judiciary, comprising the complicated system of courts, is divided up according to two broad distinctions. It is thus important that we appreciate the difference between *trial* and *appellate* courts, and between *civil* and *criminal* courts.

Trial and appellate courts
The distinction between trial and appellate courts is straightforward. Trial courts hear cases 'at first instance' or first time around. Appellate courts (or appeal courts) are able to hear cases on appeal that have previously been heard in trial courts. Both trial and appellate courts are used in both civil and criminal cases.

The rules which govern the progress of cases from trial to appellate courts can be very complicated. It is by no means an automatic right for anybody who loses a trial to appeal. Furthermore, the grounds on which appeals are permitted are equally complex. Appeals are usually allowable if, for example, new evidence comes to light that was not available at the time of the initial trial. The basis of jurisprudence in the UK, that is that a person is innocent until proven guilty, means that the appeals procedure is available in order to give people every opportunity to demonstrate that they are not guilty.

Civil courts and criminal courts
These two areas of law demand very different legal procedures. This is due to the respective content of civil and criminal cases. Different skills are required by profes-

sionals who operate in these two legal areas, and this necessitates that they be separated by the courts system.

In order to demonstrate that either a civil or criminal offence has been committed, evidence is offered. The ways in which evidence is heard and weighed varies according to the area of law and the court in which it is heard. It must be the case, for example, that the weight of evidence required to convict an alleged murderer must be greater than that required to settle a civil case concerning an allegedly broken employment contract. Hence, whilst some types of evidence may be perfectly acceptable in civil cases, the same evidence may not be admissible in a serious criminal case. The judiciary is thus divided into courts intended for different legal purposes.

Structure of the courts system

A general structure of the courts system is shown in Figure 22.2. Some textbooks incorrectly represent the court structure as a hierarchy, indicating that some courts have automatic seniority over others. This is not the case, as there are complicated rules which govern the passage of a case through the various types and levels of courts.

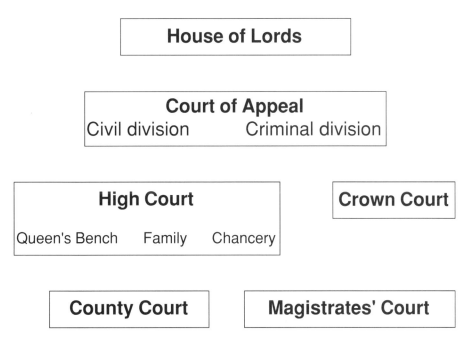

Figure 22.2 The system of courts in England and Wales

The House of Lords
The House of Lords is the most senior court in England and Wales. Its legal purpose is appellate only; that is, it only hears appeals and is not a trial court. Its appeals come almost entirely from the Court of Appeal, but can, under certain circumstances, be referred from the High Court.

Cases in the House of Lords are heard by five 'Law Lords' more formally known as

Lords of Appeal in Ordinary. The seniority of the Lords of Appeal means that they have final jurisdiction over both civil and criminal appeals. Their workload is low compared to other branches of the courts system – usually around 100 cases a year. Appeals only reach the House of Lords in special circumstances, when all other judicial appeals have been exhausted and the qualifications for a case to be heard by the Lords are stringent. In addition to the considerable cost of bringing an appeal to the Lords, the Law Lords will only hear an appeal if it is considered to be 'of general public importance'. This means that there must be a significant degree of doubt regarding the operation of the rule of law in regard to the case. Such cases are few, hence the relatively low workload of the Lords compared to other courts.

The Court of Appeal

The Court of Appeal, which, as its name suggests is appellate only, is divided into two divisions: the civil division which hears civil appeals, and the criminal division which accordingly hears criminal appeals.

The civil division hears appeal cases which have been referred by the High Court and County Court. Presiding over the civil division only is the country's senior civil judge who carries the title *Master of the Rolls*. The criminal division hears cases that have been referred by the Crown Court and take the form of appeals against sentence or conviction. It is headed by the *Lord Chief Justice* who is also considered to be Britain's most senior judge (who is considered to be senior to the Master of the Rolls). Both civil and criminal cases are heard in the court by (normally) three judges called *Lord Justices of Appeal*. Civil cases are heard only by Lord Justices of Appeal whilst criminal cases are heard by judges drawn from among the Lord Chief Justice, the Lord Justices of Appeal and the Judges of the High Court.

Question 22.1

Find out the names of the current Master of the Rolls and the current Lord Chief Justice.

The High Court

The High Court has the most complicated structure of any of the courts and has both trial and appellate functions. It contains three divisions:

- The *Queen's Bench* deals with the main areas of common law such as the law of contract.
- *Family* deals with matrimonial disputes (e.g. divorces), the wardship of children and matters of adoption.
- The *Chancery* division is concerned mainly with property, corporate (business) and tax matters.

Each division is concerned with first instance (trial) cases, but in the form of a Divisional Court can also hear appeals. The Divisional Court of the Queen's Bench division, for example, has appellate function inasmuch as it exercises 'supervisory jurisdiction' over the quality and legality of decision-making in inferior courts and tribunals.

Crown courts

These courts, which are located in major towns and cities, have trial and appellate functions, but their area of jurisdiction is purely criminal, i.e. they do not hear civil law cases. Most of the crown courts' work is first instance, concerning serious criminal offences such as murder, physical and sexual assaults and property offences resulting in a high value of loss or damage. The normal method of trial is by a judge sitting with a jury. The jury – a committee of selected members of the public – hears evidence from both prosecution and defence counsels (legally qualified professionals) and decides, on the balance of evidence, if guilt has been demonstrated beyond reasonable doubt. In the event of a guilty verdict being returned, the judge delivers a sentence consistent with the seriousness of the crime. A lesser part of the purpose of a crown court is to hear appellate cases referred from Magistrates' Courts.

Magistrates' courts

Magistrates' courts are presided over by magistrates or Justices of the Peace – lay persons of notable local standing who usually have no legal qualification. They are advised on legal matters by a legal specialist called the Justice's Clerk. The jurisdiction of the magistrates' court is purely first instance and in practice, is almost exclusively criminal with a small civil jurisdiction over such matters as liquor licensing. Their normal case load comprises less serious criminal cases; more serious cases are tried at the Crown Court.

County courts

County courts have a purely civil jurisdiction, similar to that of the High Court. Whereas the High Court deals with any value of civil claim, the County Court is concerned with smaller claims, usually up to a value of around £5000.

Other courts

Whilst the vast majority of legal cases are heard at one of the above courts, others do exist for occasional or special purposes such as industrial tribunals and matters concerning the constitution of the state. These include the *Judicial Committee of the Privy Council* which tries some Admiralty cases and a number of *Administrative Tribunals* which have a range of jurisdictions such as employment disputes and social security entitlements.

22.3 European Union law

In addition to the complexities of the English legal system, a study of the legal environment would be incomplete without examining how European legal institutions and instruments can affect UK businesses and individuals. The European legal system is of importance to the UK because the UK is a member of the European Union. Upon joining the EU in 1972 (when the EU was called the EEC or European Economic Community), the UK became (voluntarily) subject to both primary and secondary European legislation, and, in doing so, effectively surrendered part of its sovereignty over legal matters. In most matters, European law is superior to domestic law in that rulings in the European judiciary take precedence over rulings in UK courts, and laws passed by the EU must have their effect on individuals and businesses in the UK.

Types of European law

European laws are divided into two main types: primary and secondary legal instruments.

The *primary* legislation of the EU is the *Treaty of Rome, 1957*. This is a lengthy legal document which was drawn up as the time of the EU's inception and was the document which legally created the EU. The term *primary* is applied to the Treaty of Rome because all other legal instruments of the EU are subject to it. It sets out the structure of the EU and many of the pivotal legal matters that characterize the EU, such as equal pay for men and women for equal jobs. From time to time, the Treaty of Rome is amended as new ideas come to the fore that member states believe should form part of the EU's primary law. The most notable recent example of such an amendment is the *Treaty on European Union 1992* (Maastricht Agreement), in which the member states agreed to pursue closer political and economic union, eventually leading to, among other things, a common European currency (see Chapter 21).

Secondary European law is subordinate to the primary Treaty of Rome. As such, no secondary legal instrument can in any way contravene any part of the primary law. There are three types of secondary European Union law.

- *European Regulations* are said to be directly applicable to each member state as they enter national law without being debated and passed by national parliaments. Hence, when a Regulation is passed, it becomes law in each member state and has precedence over any conflicting provisions of domestic (i.e. national) legislation.
- *European Directives*, like regulations, are binding upon each member state, but their mechanism of implementation is different. Whereas regulations pass into national law automatically, directives are required to be passed into national law after they have first been debated by national parliaments. Hence, a European Directive is implemented in UK law as an Act of the British Parliament. All parts of the provisions of a Directive must pass into national law, and there is usually a period of time within which it must be enacted.
- *European Decisions* are narrower in scope that both Directives and Regulations as they are specific to certain member states only. A Decision may be binding upon just one member state as a means of corrective action in, for example, one area of national policy. Decisions are binding upon the 'targeted' state from the date on which the addressee is notified of the Decision.

The EU legislative process

The procedures by which European law is made are significantly more complicated than that for laws made by the UK legislature. This is partly because of the complex structure of the EU and partly due to the wide consultation and amendment procedures that must be undertaken before any law is enacted.

Membership of the EU necessarily means that member states surrender part of their sovereignty over legal matters to the Union. This does not, however, mean that individual member states simply surrender European law-making to centralized authorities – each state takes an active part in the legislative process alongside their fellow members. The central European institutions also play an important role as they are empowered to do so (by Treaty) by the governments of the member states.

There are four stages in the European Union legislative process.

The *proposal procedure* involves the ideas for new laws being proposed, together with a draft of the provisions and limits of the proposed law. This task falls to the Commission only, as it acts upon its *right of initiative*. In some areas of legislation, the Council must be advised and the Council has the power to overturn a proposed law at the proposal stage.

The *formulation stage* occurs after the proposal has been accepted in principle by the Council. The task of actually drafting the law falls to the European Commissioner with oversight of the area within which the law will operate (e.g. trade, transport). He or she may consult widely with experts in the field at this stage in order to ensure that all necessary provisions are covered. Once drafted, the law returns to the European Commission (the twenty Commissioners), where a simple majority is required to enable the draft to go forward to the next stage. As a newly created 'Commission proposal', the document goes to the Council (a right guaranteed by the principle of 'compulsory consultation'), together with a detailed explanation of the grounds for the proposal.

The *consultation stage* is the third procedure in the law's passage. Several EU bodies must be apprised of the proposal. Whilst the Council, as the executive body has the final say, the European Parliament must also be allowed to debate it. The Parliament, acting on behalf of the citizens of the EU, submits a formal written opinion to the Commission and the Council together with any amendment recommendations. The Economic and Social Committee is also invited to express an opinion which, again, is delivered to the Commission and the Council. The Commission may, on the advice of the various opinions, decide to amend the proposal before passing it again back to the Council.

The fourth and final procedure in the formation of a European law is the *enactment stage*. The final (and possibly amended) proposal, once in the possession of the Council, is scrutinized by specialist working parties on behalf of the Council and then by the Committee of Permanent Representatives (COREPER). Once these committees are satisfied with the proposal, it goes before a full session of the appropriate committee of the ministerial European Council. Once adopted by the Council, it is signed by the President of the Council. The proposal becomes a law and is published in all nine official European languages in the *Official Journal of the European Communities*.

The European Union judiciary

We learned in Chapter 21 that the European judiciary comprises two courts, both based in Luxembourg.

The European Court of Justice

The European Court of Justice is overseen by fifteen independent judges – one from each member state – one of whom is appointed as president. They are assisted in their duties by nine senior legal officials called advocates-general, who serve terms of six years. It is Europe's most senior court and assumes supremacy over all national senior courts and has both trial and appellate functions. In addition, the Court of Justice has a special role in the independent enforcement of EU treaties and legislation. The EU describes the Court's judicial functions as follows:[1]

- Actions for failure to fulfil obligations under the [EU's] Treaties. These are civil actions brought (usually) by the European Commission against a member state.
- Actions for annulment against the Council or Commission.
- Actions on grounds of failure to act (against the Council or Commission in the event that either body fails to fulfil its responsibilities).
- Claims for damages against the Community.
- References from national courts for preliminary rulings to clarify the meaning and scope of Community law (the Court's appellate function).

The Court of Justice combines several legal functions in one whole.

- It is a *criminal court* in that it can impose fines upon other parts of the EU, such as the Commission, for failing to discharge its responsibilities.
- In is a *civil court* in that it can settle claims for damages. A key part of this role is the interpretation of a legal document called the *Brussels Convention on the Enforcement of Judgements in Civil and Commercial Matters*.
- It is a *constitutional court* in that it can review and settle disputes between Community institutions or review the legality of legislative instruments (a constitutional court is one which has powers to decide the legality of the structure of the European Union).
- It is a *labour court* and an *industrial tribunal* in that it can settle cases concerning the freedom of movement of workers in the Union, social security matters and equal opportunities issues.

The European Court of First Instance
The European Court of First Instance, as its name suggests, is concerned with trial cases only and has no appellate jurisdiction. It is a more recent development than the Court of Justice, having been set up in October 1988 (the Court of Justice was instituted at the same time as the EEC itself). Like its neighbour, the Court of First Instance consists of fifteen judges.

Its areas of jurisdiction include the following:

- actions relating to the various Staff Regulations of the European Communities (the EC, the ECSC and Euratom);
- competition law (relating to rules of business competition in member states);
- coal and steel disputes;
- all direct actions brought by citizens and businesses against Community institutions except in anti-dumping matters.

22.4 Business law

The legal regulation of business in the UK has increased over recent years. Whilst some aspects of law that affect business are ancient, such as the ancient common laws concerning contract, others have arisen from such factors as employees' increased expectations from employers and the UK's supranational influences, particularly the EU. The result of increased regulation is a complex legal environment which, some have argued, imposes an inconvenient cost burden upon businesses. There is an active political debate regarding the extent to which business should be regulated, particularly with regard to the regulation of employment policies and employers' obligations towards employees. The political right have tended to oppose greatly any increased regulation, whilst the European left have tended to espouse a contrary philosophy.

All areas of law that we have considered can affect business – both civil and criminal laws apply to business. Furthermore, the tranche of laws that we need to consider includes both common laws and statute legislation. Recent trends have seen an increase in statutory legislation. In considering this area of law, we will discuss it as it affects the various aspects of business practice. No discussion of this nature can possibly be exhaustive, but it is hoped that readers will gain an appreciation of the types of law that can influence and regulate business practice.

Company law

This area of law affects the legal status of limited companies and hence has no direct bearing on unincorporated organizations such as sole proprietors and partnerships. The conditions placed upon limited companies and their prescribed legal *modus operandi* are enshrined in a raft of Companies Acts – statutes of Parliament.

Company law has tended to evolve and change as the activities and situations which needed to be legislated for changed over time. The earliest pieces of company law were introduced in the nineteenth century. The *Companies Act 1844*, the *Limited Liability Act 1855* and the *Joint Stock Companies Act 1856* established the notion of a non-human business entity comprising many investors and members and introduced the important concept of limited liability (see Chapter 4).

A new Companies Act is passed by Parliament when it feels the need to update the law to account for changes in business activity or in the business environment. Each one builds upon the provisions of the previous Acts, but unless it is a *Consolidated* Act, does not replace or repeal earlier Acts. The interpretation of Companies Acts is made rather more complex by a number of important common law precedents – decided cases which amend the meanings of the Acts.

The tranche of company law is necessary because of the privileges and responsibilities associated with holding limited liability. Accordingly, all limited company activities are regulated by either statute or common law including:

- the constitution and nature of limited companies and limited liability;
- rules governing the issuing of shares and responsibilities towards shareholders;
- responsibilities of directors and the company secretary;
- procedures in the unfortunate event of insolvency.

Contract law

Businesses use contracts in a wide variety of contexts. Examples include employees' contracts of employment and sales and purchases being subject to contracts of sale and supply. Contracts, which are a matter of common law, contain four legal components. The law cannot enforce a contract unless all four components are evident. The four components are as follows:

- There must be an *offer*. This is a declaration that the offering party intends to be legally bound by the terms of the offer. The offer may be in writing, or, importantly in the case of some contracts, the offer may be verbal (spoken rather than written). In some cases, an offer may be implied by conduct. The law accepts many types of offer, but in all cases they must be clear and unambiguous. An offer can be cancelled at any point up to the time that it is accepted.
- There must be an *acceptance* of the offer. The acceptance of the offer must also be clear and unambiguous and must be on the same terms as the offer (i.e. it does not contain any amendments or additions). The combination of an offer and an acceptance constitutes an *agreement*, but this is not yet a contract.
- There must be *consideration* – the legal term for payment. It should be understood that payment need not necessarily be financial, it can be an exchange or swap of payment in kind.
- There must be an *intention to create legal relations*. This is an agreement to be legally bound by the contract. This is the key difference between informal agreements and contracts. In order to create a legally binding agreement, both parties in the contract must have legal *capacity* – that is, they must be entities which are legally able to make contracts, such as individual people or businesses. In the case of a limited company, the company has legal capacity, whilst for non-incorporated businesses the proprietor is recognized as having capacity.

The law recognizes contract as a matter of civil law. A plaintiff who believes that he or she has been unfairly treated under a contract must usually demonstrate that one of the components of the contract is defective or that the other party has failed to honour it in terms of the substance of the offer or acceptance.

The law, personnel and employment

The area of laws as they affect the employment and management of people cover a wide range of activities and practices. Included in this category are laws which cover:

- terms and conditions of employment;
- sex and racial discrimination;
- employment of ex-offenders;
- employment of disabled workers;
- maternity rights;
- equal pay for 'equal jobs';
- dismissal and redundancy.

Some of the most important pieces of employment legislation are discussed below.

The most significant piece of employment law in recent years is the *Employment Protection (Consolidation) Act, 1978*, a wide ranging piece of legislation that provides that, among other things, employees be furnished with written terms and conditions of employment within two months of starting. This document should contain the general details of the employment agreement, such as the identity of the two parties, rate of pay, holiday entitlements, job title, etc. Other important employment law issues are discussed below.

Discrimination

Sex and race discrimination are covered in law by three Acts of Parliament. The *Sex Discrimination Acts* 1975 and 1986, the *Equal Pay Act 1970* and the *Race Relations Act 1976*. The overall effect of these laws render it unlawful to discriminate against anybody on sex or race grounds in respect of selection, redundancy, pay, promotion, training or dismissal.

Employment of ex-offenders

Practices relating to the employment of ex-offenders are covered by the *Rehabilitation of Offenders Act 1974*. This Act is designed to enable ex-offenders to gain employment by selectively declaring their previous prison sentences. In terms of declaring their offences when applying for jobs:

- sentences up to 6 months become 'spent' after 7 years (i.e. there is no requirement to declare the sentence on applications 7 years after release);
- sentences between 6 months and 30 months are spent after 10 years;
- sentences over 30 months are never spent.

Some types of occupation are excepted from the provisions of this Act. These are jobs which are by nature sensitive to any previous criminal involvement and include doctors, teachers and accountants.

Employment of disabled persons

The law attempts to facilitate fair treatment for disabled workers in three pieces of legislation. The *Disabled Persons Acts 1944* and *1958* impose a 'quota' on organizations, which states that employers of over 20 employees must employ registered disabled people at a rate of 3% of the workforce. Further provisions are added by the *Disability Discrimination Act 1995,* and the *Companies Act 1985*, which provides that companies of more than 250 employees must include a formal statement in their annual reports (i.e. annual accounts) describing how they have acted towards disabled people over the year under review.

Maternity

Maternity rights are provided for by the *Trade Union Reform and Employment Rights Act 1993*. Women are permitted to take time off work, mostly at the employer's expense, to give birth and be with a child for as long as 29 weeks after birth and still retain the right to return to work. A number of qualifying conditions apply for maternity leave, such as length of service, level of pay and hours per week worked (some types of leave, such as time off for ante-natal care are not dependent on length of service). Pay during the time off takes the form of a percentage of salary for a fixed number of weeks (depending upon the length of previous service) followed by a lesser sum called *statutory maternity pay* (SMP).

Termination of employment

The various pieces of employment legislation place limits upon the conditions under which employees may be forced to leave employment. It goes without saying that legal complications would not be expected when an employee voluntary leaves a job (unless the employee is subject to a fixed term under a special contract). The law makes provisions to protect both employers' and employees' rights. The anti-discrimination laws apply to unfair dismissal and redundancy in the same way as they do for recruitment and promotion. It is consequently illegal to select people for redundancy on the grounds of race, gender, trade union membership (or non-membership) or the revelation of a spent conviction (or on grounds of pregnancy, although exceptions do exist for this).

The *Employment Protection (Consolidation) Act 1978*, which we encountered above, makes provisions for both unfair dismissal and redundancy. Section 54 of the Act states that, 'every employee shall have the right not to be unfairly dismissed by his employer'. The grounds for unfair dismissal include those mentioned above (on grounds of race, gender, etc.). Redundancy is covered by Section 81 of the Act. It is stated that *'every employee who is dismissed by reason of redundancy shall receive from his employer a redundancy payment'*. Redundancy occurs when the employer's need for a particular employee's labour is discontinued or reduced. The level of redundancy payment upon redundancy is dependent upon the employee's age, length of service with the employer, and level of weekly wage.

The law and trade unions

The regulation by law of trade unions was one of the key planks of the Conservative legislative programmes throughout the 1980s. During the so-called 'winter of discontent' (a phrase borrowed from Shakespeare) of 1978–1979, the UK was subjected to a large number of strikes by trade unions seeking improved pay and conditions. In some areas of life, these disputes caused a great deal of inconvenience to the public. When the Conservative Margaret Thatcher succeeded Labour's James Callaghan as Prime Minister in 1979, a reform of trade unions assumed a prominent place in her thinking. In practice, this meant reducing unions' power over employers to cause disruption and to assist businesses to maintain normal activity for as much time as possible.

Accordingly, a number of Acts of Parliament were passed which gradually limited the activities of trade unions. Over time, laws in this area gradually increased the regulation of unions. The major laws in this respect are described below.

The Employment Act 1980 had two major provisions:

- the banning of secondary picketing (the practice of union action by employees not in dispute with their employer in sympathy with a set of employees that are);
- the banning of a closed shop unless it is supported by 80% of the workforce (a closed shop is an organization in which trade union membership is compulsory for all employees – quite common for some organizations prior to this Act).

The Employment Act 1982 provided that trade unions themselves could be subject to fines and prosecuted if they were found to be in breach of the law, including, of course, the Employment Act, 1980.

The Trade Union Act 1984 addressed issues of democratic control in internal union matters. Included in the provisions of this were the following:

- an insistence that any political contributions made by unions (e.g. to the Labour Party) must be mandated every ten years by a secret ballot of the members;
- full-time executives employed by a union must be re-elected by secret ballot every five years;
- that any proposed strike action by the union be mandated by a secret ballot of the union's membership which could take place at the workplace – this was designed to prevent 'wildcat' strikes where a shop steward calls employees out on strike without a vote.

The Employment Act 1988 included two major provisions:

- it strengthened the rights of union members who disagreed with the actions of their union;
- it added to the provisions of the Trade Union Act 1984 by insisting that secret strike ballots should be conducted by post (postal ballot) rather than at the work-place.

The Employment Act 1990 made the unions themselves legally responsible for any unofficial actions (i.e. against the provisions of previous Acts) of their members. In addition, the Act provided that employers could not discriminate against anybody on the grounds of trade union membership or non-membership.

In 1992, all of the above laws were brought together in a new consolidated Act of Parliament. The *Trade Union and Labour Relations (Consolidation) Act 1992* covers the same provisions as the above Acts.

The law, sales and consumers

The most significant consumer laws
Consumer law is primarily designed to protect the interests of consumers (of products and services) against the unfair actions of business in making transactions. The existing set of laws in this area are both civil and criminal in nature.

The *Trade Descriptions Act 1968* has provisions to protect consumers from producers or sellers that deliberately misdescribe goods and services in an attempt to persuade consumers to buy. Under the provisions of the Act, sellers may be found guilty of a criminal offence for:

- making a false description of goods offered for sale;
- making a false description of services offered for sale;
- making a false statement of price.

Penalties for contravention of the Act include fines and imprisonment. The emphasis of the Act is on practices that mislead consumers and, in consequence, the Act provides that advertisements and other sales presentations must be truthful. Claims that prices have been reduced must, similarly, be accurate. Goods and services must be on sale for 28 consecutive days at the higher price before a seller can claim that the price has been reduced to the lower, more attractive price.

The *Consumer Protection Act 1987* concerns the liability of sellers arising from the sale of defective goods and services. This is a piece of civil law under which, a plaintiff must demonstrate beyond reasonable doubt that a loss or injury has 'product liability' caused by the producer's (or, in some cases, the seller's) defective goods or services. Because this Act was introduced as part of the implementation of an EU Directive (85/374), its provisions apply to sellers and producers throughout the EU. It also contains provisions for taking actions on producers outside the EU if necessary.

There are a number of defences that a seller or producer can put forward against a civil case under this Act. Under Section 4, these include defences based upon the contention:

- that the defendant did not actually supply the allegedly defective product;
- that the defect did not exist at the time the product was sold (e.g. a fault that develops in a car through the negligence of the owner rather than through bad workmanship);
- that a defect is attributable to a requirement to comply with other existing laws;
- that the level of scientific or technical knowledge at the time of the product's supply was not sufficiently advanced for the defect to be recognized (a rather controversial provision in the case of products such as pharmaceuticals).

The *Sale of Goods Act 1979* protects consumers by imposing restrictions upon the contracts of sale used by sellers. It imposes three conditions of sale upon all sellers:

- that the goods sold must match the description of the goods presented to the consumer (Section 13 of the Act);
- that the goods supplied must be of 'merchantable quality' (Section 14);
- that the goods supplied must be fit for the purpose indicated to the consumer by the seller (also Section 14).

It is worth noting that the terms 'merchantable quality' and 'fitness for the purpose' have been the subject of some debate. Such terms are usually interpreted in the light of the nature of the product. The *Sale and Supply of Goods (Amendment) Act 1995* amended the term 'merchantable quality' to *satisfactory quality*. The terms of the Sale of Goods Act 1979 were extended to services in addition to goods under the *Supply of Goods and Services Act 1982*. This means that consumers of services (e.g. house and car repairs) have the same rights as consumers of goods.

The *Unfair Contract Terms Act 1977* and, more recently, the *Unfair Terms in Consumer Contracts Regulations 1994* prohibit the use of clauses or statements in sales contracts that seek to circumvent the terms of any of the other pieces of consumer protection law. A seller is committing a criminal offence under these Acts if unfair 'exclusion' clauses are inserted which seek to deny a consumer his or her consumer rights. These Acts therefore rule out the use of statements such as 'no refunds given' when such refunds may be required by consumers under the terms of other consumer Acts.

More specific consumer laws
Other pieces of consumer protection legislation address specific areas of the relationship between consumers and business. These include the following:

- The *Consumer Credit Act 1974* regulates businesses that provide credit facilities to consumers. Its provisions include the requirement that lenders state the annual percentage rate (APR) of the loans, and to limit, in some cases, the amounts that consumers can borrow.

- The *Weights and Measures Act 1985* requires manufacturers to use suitably reliable equipment when packaging goods which specify a weight or volume (e.g. a 50 g bar of chocolate or a 5 litre tin of paint). The goods must not weigh less than the amount specified or comprise a lower volume (as appropriate).

The law, factories and offices

The regulation of activities in offices and factories is a long-standing feature of the business legal environment. The *raison d'être* of this area of law is to provide legal protection from harm for employees whilst they are actually at work.

Early legislation

The earliest significant laws in this area were in the nineteenth century – the various Factory Reform Acts. In the modern era, the most significant laws are the *Factories Act 1961* and the *Offices, Shops and Railway Premises Act 1963*. These Acts broke new ground at the time by placing the majority of the responsibility for health and safety in the workplace onto the employers. This was not to say that employees did not need to be mindful of potential hazards, but that once the employees had fulfilled their obligations (such as wearing the requisite protective clothing, etc.) responsibility for accidents rested with the employer. The *Fire Precautions Act 1971* extended the general principles of the two earlier Acts to issues concerning fire safety. Two years later, the *Fire Precautions Act 1973* made it a legal requirement for all premises to carry a valid fire certificate showing that it conforms to the requirements of the local fire authorities. Such requirements may include the provision of suitably marked fire escapes, appropriate fire extinguishers placed in key locations, limits on the numbers of people allowed into the premises at any time and the training of certain employees in emergency evacuation procedures.

The Health and Safety at Work Act 1974

The *Health and Safety at Work Act 1974* (HASAWA) was a key development in health and safety policy. The provisions of this Act were strongly influenced by the Robens Committee of Enquiry on Health and Safety at Work. The provisions of the Act brought together the contents of earlier laws whilst expanding them to apply to all places of work except domestic employment. Among its most important provisions are descriptions of the roles of both employers and employees in ensuring health and safety in the workplace.

Section 2 of HASAWA states that: 'It is the duty of an employer to ensure, so far as is reasonably practicable, the health, safety and welfare of all his employees'. In particular, this involves:

- The provision of a working environment and equipment that are both safe and appropriate to the work in question. There should also be an appropriate level of maintenance of such equipment.
- The provision of safe access into and exit from the working premises.

- Minimizing the risks associated with working procedures.
- Training employees in procedures with a view to reducing the risk of injury.
- Providing adequate levels of supervision.
- The provision of adequate facilities at work to ensure the welfare of employees whilst at work.

In addition to prescribing (albeit in rather general terms) the duties of the employer, HASAWA also sets out the requirements made of employees. Accordingly, employees are made responsible for:

- taking reasonable care at work, both of their own health and safety and of those with whom they work;
- co-operating with the employer to facilitate the employer's conformance to his duties under health and safety legislation.

Trade unions are also apportioned some responsibility under HASAWA. They were given the right to appoint a health and safety representative on a business site to engage in discussions with employers, on behalf of union members, on health and safety matters.

HASAWA is enforced in the UK by the *Health and Safety Executive* (HSE) – a government body established by the Act. The HSE employs inspectors who visit and inspect employers' premises for compliance with the terms of the Act. Continued failure to comply with HASAWA is a criminal offence which is punishable with a fine or imprisonment.

Recent developments

There are a number of legislative influences that have come to bear upon business workplaces since HASAWA. The UK's membership of the EU has brought with it a number of directives. Most notably, an *Approved Code of Practice* became effective on 11 January 1993 together with a set of regulations known as the *Management of Health and Safety at Work Regulations* (MHSW).

Meanwhile, the UK Parliament passed the *Control of Substances Hazardous to Health Regulations 1989* (COSHH). This is a set of regulations that tightens the law pertaining to the handling of materials in the workplace and thus COSHH particularly affects those businesses that are engaged in areas such as chemicals and engineering. Its provisions also technically apply to all substances used, including office chemicals such as correction fluid. COSHH provides that all substances used in a business be appropriately labelled, stored and used so as to minimize the risk of harm or injury.

Assignments

- After his secretary became pregnant, the Chief Executive Officer (CEO) of a small engineering company decided to dismiss her. He told a friend, 'I can't afford to give her time off for ante-natal appointments and maternity leave. Money is tight enough as it is. Better to get rid of her now and replace her with someone who is likely to stay for a few years without disruptions such as this'. Advise the CEO of the legal implications of his decision.
- You have bought a mechanical alarm clock from a major high street retailer and, on getting it home, you find that it has no internal workings. Naturally you take the clock back but you are surprised to hear the shop manager say that you bought the clock in good faith and the lack of internal components is a matter you should take up with the clock manufacturer, not the shop. In what respects is the shop acting illegally and what recourse to law might you legitimately make to have the dispute settled?

Reference

1. Borchardt, Dr Klaus-Dieter. (1994) *The ABC of Community Law*, 4th edn. Luxembourg Office for Official Publications of the European Communities. Brussels and Luxembourg: ECSC-EC-EAEC.

Further reading

Abbott K and Pendlebury N. (1995) *Business Law*, 6th edn. London: DP Publications.

Judge, S. (1995) *Business Law*. London: Macmillan.

Kadar, A., Hoyle, K. and Whitehead, G. (1996). *Business Law*, 4th edn. Oxford: Butterworth-Heinemann.

Price, T. (1995) *Mastering Business Law*, 2nd edn. London: Macmillan.

Smith, D. and Lawson, R. D. (1996) *Business Law for Business and Marketing Students*. Oxford: Butterworth-Heinemann.

Stirk, I. and McFarquhar, H. (1996) *Business Law*. London: Longman.

23

The economic environment 1: Macro-economic management

Learning objectives

After studying this chapter, students should be able to describe:

- The difference between micro-economics and macro-economics.
- The complex nature of macro-economic decisions.
- The generic types of national economy.
- Who manages the national economy.
- The meaning and components of fiscal policy.
- The meaning and the components of monetary policy.
- The role of the central bank in monetary policy.
- The significance of the major macro-economic indicators:
  - economic growth;
  - inflation;
  - exchange rate;
  - unemployment;
  - balance of payments.

23.1 The macro-economic environment

Micro- and macro-economics

In Chapters 16 and 17 we examined micro-economics – the theories behind business costs and revenues, and the theories of product supply and demand. In this chapter, we extend our discussion to consider how the macro-economic environment can influence a business.

The terms 'micro' and 'macro' are both derived from the ancient Greek language. *Micro* means 'small', so micro-economics is the economics of individual buying and selling decisions and the economics of individual businesses (Figure 23.1). It addresses the questions concerning the volumes of production of individual businesses and price and wage levels.

Macro-economics, borrowing from the Greek '*macro*' for large, is the study of the 'global' or collective decisions that are made by millions of individuals and businesses rather than individual buying and selling decisions. It examines the national and international aspects of economics and how national economic policies affect individual households, consumers and businesses. Macro-economics is also concerned with the ways in which the state manages the economy by using the range of economic 'levers' or 'weapons' at its disposal.

Figure 23.1 Different branches of economics

Micro- and macro-economics – an imperfect metaphor

If you look at a picture from a great painter, you can appreciate it on two levels. From a distance you can enjoy the totality of the painting, its spatial arrangements, the configurations of the figures, the blends of light and shade, the colours, and so on. If you then approach the painting and examine it in detail, possibly with a magnifying glass, you can analyse the intricate individual brush strokes, the textures and the individual colour amalgams.

Whilst we mainly see the big picture, we can readily appreciate this would not exist without the intricate, painstaking work invested in each stroke. The quality of the painting comprises both levels of appreciation.

We can view macro-economics as our view of the total painting, and micro-economics as our examination of the intricate strokes and textures. Macro-economics concerns the effects of thousands or even millions of individual micro-economic decisions.

The macro-economic 'environment'

Given that macro-economics concerns the 'big picture' of economics, it is reasonable to ask what the components of the macro-economic environment are inasmuch as they can affect businesses (which, after all, is the subject of this book). The macro-economic environment includes such national and international concerns as:

- levels of tax levied by the government;
- levels of public expenditure (i.e. spending by the state);
- the price of borrowing money (i.e. interest rates);
- the rate of growth of the money supply;
- the size and rate of growth of the economy as a whole;
- the rate of inflation in the national economy and how this compares to other countries;

- the value of currency when it is used to exchange for foreign goods and services;
- the rate of unemployment (i.e. the number of people unemployed compared to the total labour force);
- the pattern of business and capital transactions that a country carries out with foreign countries (expressed in the balance of payments statement).

Changes in the macro-economic environment are very important to both businesses and individuals. This is principally because they can affect their income and (in the case of businesses) profitability. Changes in any of the macro-economic *indicators* (see later) can affect an individual business in either or both of two ways. Let us consider a simple example: an increase is announced in the basic rate of tax.

- The company itself will be required to pay more of its profits to the Inland Revenue. This means that there will be less money left over (profit) to reinvest in the future of the business or to pay dividends to shareholders. This is a *direct influence* from the macro-economic environment.
- Individuals who buy a business's products, because they must pay more tax on their incomes, will have less money to spend. This means, when taken as a whole, that a downward pressure is exerted on business revenues (although the relationship between tax and consumer expenditure is not, in reality, as straightforward as that indicated). This is an *indirect influence* on the business from the macro-economic environment. Put simply, by having a lower level of disposable income, consumers may delay or cancel plans to make purchases from businesses.

The complexity of the macro-economic environment

Differences of economic opinion
One of the most noticeable features of this area of economics is the considerable disagreement over what are the best courses of action in any set of economic circumstances. You may hear one politician or economist say that interest rates should be increased, whilst others will advocate the opposite view. One businessman may want to see the value of the pound sterling devalued, whilst others will argue strongly that it should be maintained or strengthened. Why is there such disagreement amongst the informed on how macro-economic policy should be conducted?

The reason is this: any change in the macro-economic environment will, to a greater or lesser extent, usually work to the advantage of one part of the economy whilst causing harm to another. Some businesses will be pleased with a change whilst others will be very displeased. Let us consider a simple example.

Wednesday. Was it 'black' or 'white'?
Wednesday 16 September 1992 was an important day for the UK economy and for British businesses. At the close of business on the previous day, one pound sterling was worth 2.95 deutschmarks (the German currency, abbreviated to 'DM' or D-mark) when exchanged for goods, services or cash. During that Wednesday, for a number of reasons, the value of the pound fell rapidly against the deutschmark, so that by the close of banking business on the day, the pound had fallen 17% to DM 2.45. By any standards, this was a major change in the macro-economic environment. The opposi-

tion Labour Party saw this change as a bad day for Britain and coined the term 'Black Wednesday' to describe it.

But was this change all bad for UK businesses or was it in part beneficial? It was both. The lower value of the pound would have a great influence on any business that dealt directly or indirectly with foreign suppliers or customers. Exporters, by and large, were pleased with the devaluation because it meant that their goods and services would be cheaper to foreign customers. This is because less foreign currency would need to be exchanged into sterling to meet the British company's asking price, which would be set in sterling because the exporter is a UK company. Exports could be expected to increase – good news for companies like ICI, British Aerospace and Glaxo Wellcome, who are amongst Britain's major exporters. Conversely, the devaluation was bad news for importers. If goods were purchased from Germany, then more pounds would have to be found to exchange for deutschmarks to pay for the German goods. Hence, the price of imported goods like French cars and Japanese consumer goods rose after the devaluation of the pound sterling. Businesses therefore had to either absorb higher costs or pass the increased cost on to the customer in the form of increased prices – equally undesirable outcomes.

The principle of any change 'cutting both ways' applies to all the components of the macro-economic environment, and it is this feature which makes its management so difficult and sometimes controversial.

Generic types of national economy

The balance between state control and the market system varies across the world. It is this balance that is a major characteristic of the generic types of national economy. We can view this as a continuum (Figure 23.2).

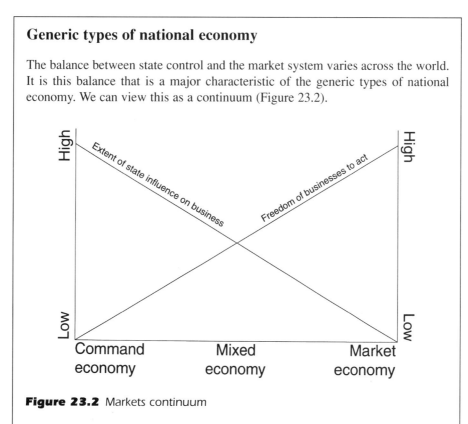

Figure 23.2 *Markets continuum*

A *command economy*, in its purest sense, is one wherein all of the commercial activity in a country is controlled directly by the state. There are no private businesses in a command economy and the state ensures an acceptable level of employment and economic activity by its direct control. In a true *market economy*, there is no state control at all – everything in the economy happens through the natural workings of the market mechanism. The state, in a market economy would adopt a completely *laissez faire* approach, and would allow all business to proceed unregulated. The *mixed economy*, as its position on the continuum suggests, is a mixture of the two. There is a large private business sector and a sizeable state influence which regulates, to a greater or lesser extent, the activities of private business. Mixed economies can vary according to the degree of state influence. Some are very close to the market economy whilst others have higher levels of state intervention.

Question 23.1

- Which type of economy best describes the UK?
- Which countries, either in the past or present, best resemble the command economy?

23.2 Who manages the national economy?

The management of this important aspect of the country's fortunes is the responsibility of a number of important people employed by the state, although their decisions are greatly influenced by the activities of business in general. The principal 'officer', who is empowered by the state to make the most important economic decisions, is the *Chancellor of the Exchequer*. The Chancellor is an elected individual who is accountable to Parliament and who, along with the foreign secretary and the home secretary, occupies one of the three 'great offices of state' (reporting to the Prime Minister). He or she has the power to pull several 'levers' which can influence the general economic climate in which businesses must operate. Each year in the autumn, the Chancellor sets out the 'budget'. This is a statement of projected taxation and spending plans for the forthcoming financial or *fiscal* year (from April to April), although the Chancellor can also make any number of other adjustments to the economy throughout the year.

A second important person is the *Governor of the Bank of England*. The Governor works closely with the incumbent Chancellor and is appointed by the Prime Minister. He or she advises on monetary policy (see Section 23.5) and implements some changes in this area. The Governor exercises control and regulation over the British banking system, which in turn has great influence over the business sector in the country.

Question 23.2

- What is the name of the current Chancellor of the Exchequer?
- Where is the official residence of the Chancellor?
- To what political party does he or she belong?
- Who is the current Governor of the Bank of England?
- Where is the Bank of England located?

The *Chief Secretary to the Treasury*, like the Chancellor, is a Cabinet position and as such, is accountable to parliament and is an elected Member of Parliament (although the Chief Secretary has not always been in the cabinet). The Chief Secretary is responsible for regulating government spending through the various government departments and agencies which, in turn, influences the level of employment in the public sector. The decisions of the Chief Secretary can have a profound influence on some businesses as they directly affect companies who supply government departments. Such private sector businesses include manufacturers of pharmaceuticals, aircraft, military equipment, paint, construction and many others. In addition, because government spending determines the public sector pay increases of around six million people, an influence can be exerted on the demand side of the economy (the spending power of six million people is significant when it represents around 25% of the working population). Government spending is also one of the key regulatory influences on the economy as a whole.

The 'markets' as an influence in the macro-economic environment refer to the stock exchanges and other capital markets across the world, principally those in the world's main financial centres of London, New York, Tokyo, Hong Kong and Frankfurt. It would be untrue to suggest that the markets, which deal in millions of international financial transactions every day, actually 'manage' national economies. However, it is the aggregate (i.e. collective) influence of these transactions in shares, bonds and currencies which can profoundly influence or even determine government policy in regard to the macro-economy. The Chancellor and the Governor carefully monitor activity in the markets and sometimes take action in response to trends in the buying and selling of currencies, shares and other 'commodities' by the markets.

23.3 Businesses in the macro-economy

In an ideal world, the conditions in the macro-economic environment would always be favourable to the business sector. Let us examine what these conditions might look like.

Low tax levels (or low *fiscal pressure*) would be the first and most obvious condition. If the government allows businesses and consumers to retain more of their incomes for themselves, it follows that companies could grow and invest and that consumers (you and me) would spend more money with businesses – another source of business growth. Because business growth would be strong, a downward pressure would be exerted on unemployment as businesses took on more people to meet the increased demand from consumers.

Low monetary pressure would act in a similar way to low fiscal pressure. If the banking sector (at the command of the Chancellor and the Governor) lends money at a low rate of interest then:

- businesses would pay less on loans used to invest in growth and development;
- consumers could afford higher loans and thus would spend more with businesses.

These factors, taken together, would exert a significant influence on favourable business growth, although we will see later that such conditions may have longer term effects which might damage businesses.

23.4 Fiscal policy

Surpluses and deficits

The fiscal part of macro-economics centres around the government's financial revenues and expenditures. Each financial year, the government receives income from a number of sources (e.g. taxes) and it also spends so much through the various departments and government agencies. Government spending, in some respects, is very much like our normal household situation. Each year, an individual earns a certain amount and also spends a certain amount. If we spend less than we earn we are left with a cash surplus, and if we spend more than we earn we must find some way of financing the deficit (e.g. by approaching the bank manager for an overdraft). The same is true of government spending, but on a much grander scale.

If, in any given financial year:

- the government spends *less* than it makes in revenues, the difference is referred to as a *budget* (or fiscal) *surplus*;
- the government spends *more* than it makes in revenues, the difference is referred to as a *budget* (or fiscal) *deficit*.

A fiscal surplus enables funds to be set aside for reserves or tax reductions, whereas a deficit must be financed by borrowing (i.e. the country goes into debt).

The amount of money that the government must borrow in a given fiscal year is called the *public sector borrowing requirement* (PSBR) (Figure 23.3). In the event of a fiscal deficit, the PSBR will be a positive figure, whilst in the happy event of a fiscal surplus the PSBR will be negative. It follows, of course, that borrowed money must be repaid. The amount of money that the government puts aside each year for this purpose, the *public sector debt repayment* (PSDR), constitutes a sizeable part of government cash outflow (especially with the interest payments that must be paid on the debt).

Where does government money come from?

The state has many needs for money. We saw in Chapter 21 that it provides many services through its various departments and the total cash requirement for these is very substantial indeed. Government money is raised through a number of channels.

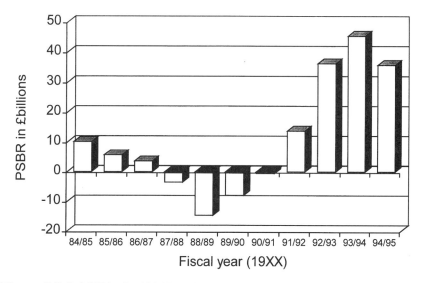

Figure 23.3 PSBR in the UK. Note that a positive PSBR means the government is borrowing. (Source: Annual Abstract of Statistics, No. 132, 1996, CSO, London: HMSO.)

Taxation

The major source of revenue is, as we have seen, taxation. There are two types of taxation: direct and indirect.

Direct taxation is tax paid on taxable income. The rates at which tax is payable on income change from time to time and according to how much income is made (higher rates apply to higher incomes). Individuals pay direct tax on their personal incomes, whilst businesses pay it on their profits. Direct tax is collected by the Inland Revenue.

Indirect taxation is tax levied on some of the things we buy. It is sometimes called expenditure tax or turnover tax. Unlike direct tax, the payment of indirect tax is, to a certain extent, optional in that if, for example, you choose not to buy alcohol, then you won't pay alcohol tax. The price we pay for many goods and services includes an element of tax which is collected by Her Majesty's Customs and Excise. There are various types of indirect taxation.

- The most important is *value-added tax* (VAT), which involves a fixed percentage being added to the price of a good or service. All goods and services are classified in one of three ways with regard to VAT:
  - *VAT rated*, where VAT is levied on the price of the good or service;
  - *VAT exempt* – goods and services that are not subject to VAT;
  - *zero rated* – goods and services are subject to VAT, but upon which, VAT is not currently applied.
- *Hydrocarbon tax* is the indirect tax levied on some products derived from oil. A substantial percentage of the price of petrol, diesel and industrial solvents (e.g. white spirit) is tax.
- *Tobacco tax* is paid, as the name suggests, on tobacco products like cigarettes and cigars.

- *Alcohol tax* is paid on beer, wine, spirits and liqueurs.
- *Import duties* are taxes paid on some goods imported into the UK. Since the creation of the single European market in 1993, no import duties (sometimes called import *tariffs*) are payable on goods bought and sold between businesses in European Union states. If, though, you were to import a car from South Korea or Japan, the UK would require a payment to be made which would be a fixed percentage of the price paid for the car from the Far Eastern exporter.

Question 23.3

The rates of indirect tax vary from time to time. Find out the following:

- Who determines the rate of VAT.
- The current rate of VAT.
- Three examples of VAT-exempt products or services.
- The current level of indirect tax payable on a packet of 20 cigarettes.
- The current level of indirect tax payable on a pint of beer.

Sources other than taxation
Whilst the bulk of government money is gained from taxation, the government receives revenue from some other sources:

- *National Insurance* is paid by individuals and employers and is 'earmarked' for use specifically by the Department of Social Security (DSS).
- *Rents* from property and land owned by the state.
- *Incomes from licences,* which include those granted to extract oil from British coastal waters.
- *Dividends from shares* held by the state.
- *Capital injections* of cash may arise from such things as privatizations of previously state-owned businesses.

Question 23.4

Find out the current:

- Basic rate of income tax.
- Highest rate of income tax.

Are the current rates historically high or low?

Figure 23.4 shows the sources of government income for the financial year 1993–1994. The total government revenue for 1993–1994 of £242.723 billion is shown in Table 23.1.

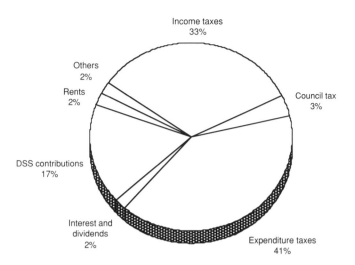

Figure 23.4 Fiscal revenues – UK general government, 1993–1994. (Source: Annual Abstract of Statistics, No. 132, 1996. London CSO/HMSO)

Table 23.1 Government revenues, 1993-94. (Source: Annual Abstract of Statistics, No. 132, 1996. London: CSO/HMSO)

	£ billions	Percentage of total
Income taxes (direct)	80.554	33.2
Expenditure taxes (indirect)	96.950	40.0
DSS contributions	41.977	17.3
Council tax	8.465	3.5
Rents, etc.	5.397	2.2
Interest and dividends	4.837	2.0
Other revenues	4.54	1.9

How is government money spent?

The government has many calls upon its financial resources. The majority is spent through its various departments, although, in the event of a fiscal deficit, some must be reserved for debt repayment and interest payments (Figure 23.5). Table 23.2 shows the expenditure in more detail. The total expenditure of £285.736 billion is more than the sum of the list in Table 23.2, due to measuring errors and difficulties in reporting.

The management of fiscal policy presents many problems to the Chancellor. Whilst, on the one hand, he or she wants to provide quality services, such as education, he or she knows that high taxes to pay for them are bad for both businesses and consumers. Hence, the Chancellor's decisions on fiscal matters are invariably criticized by somebody. This is often the basis of party political argument.

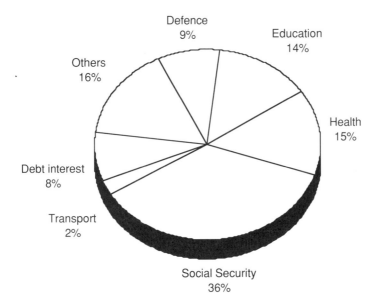

Figure 23.5 Government spending, fiscal year 1993–1994. Percentages shown approximate and are for indication only. (Source: United Kingdom National Accounts (The Blue Book), 1995. London: HMSO)

Table 23.2 Government expenditure by function of government, 1993–1994

	£ billions	% (approx.)
Defence	23.815	8.3
Education	36.057	12.6
Health	38.657	13.5
Social security	98.236	34.4
Recreation and culture	4.476	1.6
Fuel and energy	0.6	0.2
Agriculture, forestry and fishing	3.28	1.1
Mining, construction, etc.	1.632	0.6
Transport	6.441	2.2
Other economic affairs	6.32	2.2
Other expenditure (including debt repayment)	27.901	9.8

23.5 Monetary policy

What is monetary policy?

We have seen that one way in which the government can regulate the economy is by the use of fiscal measures. If the Chancellor increases tax, for example, he or she will slow down inflation by taking spending power out of the economy, but at the same time economic growth may be slowed. Fiscal measures are very powerful tools that can be used to great effect.

The second set of levers that the government can pull to regulate the economy are monetary measures. Whereas fiscal policy concerns the use of taxation and government spending to regulate the economy, monetary policy concerns controlling the *price* and *supply* of money.

The price of money

The price of (borrowed) money, sometimes called the rate of interest, is the price paid to gain the use of somebody else's money. Varying the price of money can be used to powerful effect as a tool to regulate and control activity in the macro-economy.

The price of money – a simple example

Bob McRobert wanted to buy a house, but he didn't have sufficient funds for the full purchase price of the property. He approached a well-known national building society with the question 'Can I have £55 000 to put towards the price of a house please?' After surveying Bob's financial situation, the manager of the building society branch said, 'Yes, but you will have to pay the current market price for the money I lend you.'

He continued, 'As long as you have use of our money, you will pay 8% interest on the outstanding loan so long as you enjoy its benefit. The figure of 8% may go up or down depending on the decisions of the Chancellor.'

Hence, the mortgage on Bob's house is somebody else's money which must be paid for at the current rate of interest – an example of paying the price of borrowed money.

The price of money therefore only applies to a situation where borrowed money is involved. It follows that, whilst individuals and businesses must pay the rate of interest on loans from banks and building societies, so financial institutions must pay interest on money they use which doesn't belong to them – savers' deposits.

The growth in the use of debt to finance investment and spending over the past twenty years or so has meant that varying the rate of interest has become a powerful tool for the Chancellor. Most students know all about overdrafts and credit card debts which are subject to interest, whilst most businesses make extensive use of the bank's money in the normal conduct of their business. Reducing the interest rate can introduce spending power into the economy (because you are likely to spend more if you have lower pay-back charges), whilst an increase has the opposite effect. Consumers and businesses with large debts (e.g. a family with a large mortgage and a car loan) are particularly sensitive to changes in this type of *monetary pressure*, whereas it has less impact on those who are 'cash-rich'.

Money supply

The money supply is about the amount of money in circulation in the economy. If there is a lot of money in circulation, there will be a higher aggregate spending than if money supply is limited. The issue of money supply is more complicated than it appears when we take into account the fact that the word *money* includes more than just cash. Cash is only a part of the money used by consumers and businesses. Money supply also includes the growth in total credit and changes in the amount of foreign currency that people in the UK make use of.

Measures of money supply growth

The problem with measuring how much money is circulating in the economy and how fast the money supply grows, is that defining 'money' is not as straightforward as it may seem. Money, in its broadest sense is anything that can be exchanged for goods and services. We can, for example, use money from our pockets (notes and coins), cheques from a current account, cheques made out from a deposit account, credit and, in some cases, foreign currency. To account for the breadth of definitions, the government uses several measures of money supply growth (Table 23.3 and Figure 23.6).

The broad/narrow distinction refers to the breadth of the types of money included. Clearly, M0, as it only includes actual notes and coins, can be seen as a narrow definition. M4 is considered to be broad because it also includes money that doesn't actually exist in the form of notes and coins. The deposits held in savings accounts are said to be *notional* in that their full paper value does not exist in the form of notes and coins. If everybody withdrew their deposits at the same time, not all depositors could be paid as the banks would run out of notes and coins. The banking system acts upon certain assumptions, one of them being that there will be a certain amount of stability in people's financial situations, causing approximately the same amount of money to be withdrawn as is deposited.

Table 23.3 Monetary growth measures in the UK, 1992

Measure	Broad or narrow	Definition
M0	Narrow	The total value of notes and coins in circulation
M2	Narrow	M0 plus all 'sight' deposits (e.g. in current accounts)
M4	Broad	M2 plus deposits in savings accounts
M3H	Very broad	M4 plus foreign currencies held by UK banks and residents

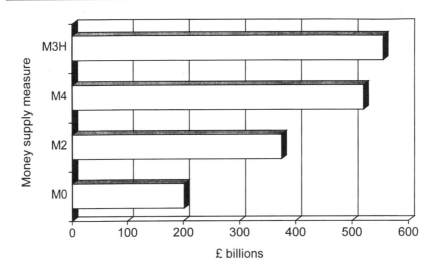

Figure 23.6 UK monetary growth measures – fiscal year to 1992

Monetary volume and velocity

In measuring the use of money in the economy, we need to be aware of two important principles: the *volume* of money circulating and its *velocity* of circulation.

We can see from Figure 23.7 that money circulates between consumers, businesses and banks. Consumers like you and me usually obtain our cash from a bank, either across the counter or through a cashpoint. We then spend it with a business in exchange for goods and services. The business then deposits the cash with its bank. We then get more cash from the bank and the cycle goes round again.

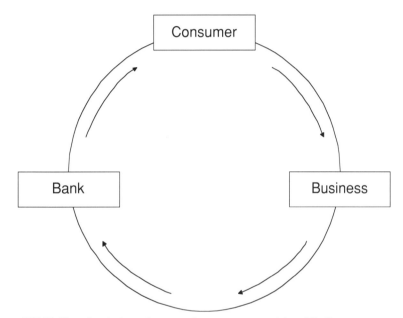

Figure 23.7 *The circulation of money in an economy (simplified)*

If we consider the simplest measure of money, M0, the volume of money in an economy is the total number of notes and coins in circulation. If the government reduces the volume of M0 (i.e. takes cash out of the economy by destroying more notes than it currently prints), then it might be thought that spending would go down, but this isn't necessarily the case. Let us imagine a simple example – there is a reduction on the volume of M0. We extract our cash from the bank as usual and we then take our cash and spend it at Marks and Spencer. Lots of other people do the same until the bank gets low on its cash reserves due to the reduction in volume. In order to avoid running out of cash, the bank rings Marks and Spencer and asks if it can deposit its day's takings earlier than usual. Marks and Spencer obliges and delivers its cash (which we spent earlier in the day) to the bank for recirculation. Hence, the velocity of money has increased because the volume has been reduced.

Thus, in simple terms, there is an inverse relationship between volume and velocity, i.e. *if volume is reduced, velocity tends to increase,* and, *if volume is increased, velocity tends to (but does not necessarily) decrease* (see the notes on the quantity theory of money in Chapter 24).

This model holds true only up to a point. The picture becomes more complex when the cycle we encountered above is no longer a closed system. If extra cash is introduced into the cycle or if cash is taken out of the cycle, then the volume – velocity relationship may no longer hold.

Cash injections into the money cycle can occur, for example, when:

- Savers spend some of their savings.
- Foreign currency is changed into sterling (effectively a cash injection from abroad). This happens, for example, when a UK business exports goods.
- The government releases reserves into the economy in the form of government spending (e.g. by building hospitals, roads or increasing the funding to your university).
- Individuals or businesses borrow money to invest and thus keep their cash for immediate spending (borrowed money from a bank doesn't exist as cash).

Cash 'leakages' from the cycle occur when:

- People put cash into the bank as savings rather than spending it.
- People pay tax to the government (money which cannot be recycled immediately).
- People make investments using cash. For example, by buying shares or government bonds.
- Money goes abroad, for example, to pay for imported goods or services, foreign bank deposits or foreign holidays.

Hence, a more accurate money cycle will be as shown in Figure 23.8.

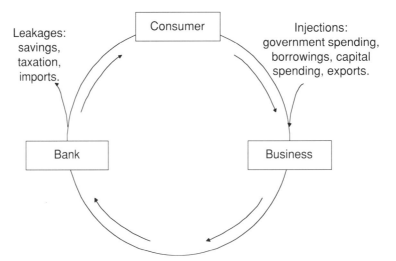

Figure 23.8 *Money cycle showing leakages and injections. Note: Leakages and injections can occur at any point in the cycle, not just at the points shown*

The role of the central bank in monetary policy

The UK has a central bank – the Bank of England – which has certain unique functions that other banks do not share. Based in Treadneedle Street in the City (London's financial centre), the Bank of England's functions include:

- acting as the government's bankers (handling the huge public sector finances);
- acting as a central banker to the main clearing banks (e.g. Barclays, National Westminster);
- managing the country's foreign currency reserves (foreign currency which the country keeps to influence the value of sterling as the need arises);
- managing any debts which the country has with foreign countries or other banks (or, of course, any surplus which the country may have);
- issuing of notes and coins for general circulation, overseeing the printing and minting of money and the destruction of used notes and coins;
- implementing monetary policy (varying interest rates and the supply of money – of all types – in the economy).

An independent central bank?

There has been some debate over recent years as to who should have the final say in the management of monetary policy (the final point in the above list). Some argue that it should be firmly within the area of responsibility of elected politicians (which in the UK would be the Chancellor of the Exchequer), whereas others contend that it should (at least in part) be implemented by an independent bank without reference to the elected government.

The case for having monetary policy carried out the elected executive is as follows:

- All economic decisions would be made by those who are democratically accountable. The electorate can thus, via their MPs, call on the Chancellor to account for the state of the economy. This would not be the case if some of the key decisions were made by senior civil servants.
- The government may have a broader political strategy than the central bank may be aware of. Hence, whilst the central bank may not agree with the Chancellor in some of his or her short-term decisions on monetary policy, such manoeuvres could be seen as coherent in the context of the government's overall strategy, which would include using monetary policy in conjunction with fiscal management.

Conversely, the case for taking some monetary policy matters away from the elected executive and placing it with the central bank is as follows:

- The central bank would make its policy decisions independently and on purely economic grounds. There would consequently be no risk of the government using monetary policy as a short-term 'fix' for its ailing political unpopularity, which may not be in the best long-term interests of the national economy.
- It would take a sizeable burden of responsibility off the Chancellor's shoulders. Some groups of people, for largely ideological reasons, would like to see less power vested in elected people and more in the independent secretariat.
- It could be argued that the senior members of the central bank, as career bankers, have more experience and expertise in managing such an important part of the economy than a Chancellor who is likely to only be in post for a few years. It follows from this argument that, by and large, the banker's views are likely to be more reliable than a politician's who is not by profession a banking or economic specialist.

In the UK, the central bank is not independent. The Governor and the Chancellor have regular meetings to discuss the various parts of the economy, but it is the Chancellor who makes all the key decisions on both monetary and fiscal matters – sometimes against the advice of the Governor.

The opposite is the case in Germany. The Deutsche Bundesbank is entirely independent of the German federal government and is charged with the primary task of protecting the value of the currency – the deutschmark (DM). Accordingly, the Bundesbank has the power to vary interest rates and monetary supply without reference to the government in order to meet the economic objectives of the country as a whole. Because the deutschmark is a leading world currency, the decisions of the Bundesbank on monetary matters can have implications in many other countries of the world. It is common, for example, for an increase in German interest rates (made to protect the value of the deutschmark) to be immediately mirrored in France, the UK and the USA. Such a response would be made to prevent other currencies (e.g. the pound sterling) from falling in value against the deutschmark. There has been some resentment expressed that the decisions of 'bureaucrats in Bonn' (the German capital) can have effects on the price of mortgages and loans in the UK, but such a situation is unavoidable given the complex interrelationships between the world's major currencies.

23.6 Economic 'indicators'

When observers want to assess the strength of a national economy, it is unusual to look at the levels of fiscal or monetary pressure. It is more common to look at other parts of the economy which are largely determined by fiscal and monetary policies. By examining the figures and trends in these 'indicators', the strength of an economy can be assessed.

Economic growth

Growth and inflation
If we were to plot the totals of all business transactions in the UK over a long period of time, we would see that the graph would show a definite upward trend. This is because each year the total (aggregate) sales in the country are usually greater than in the previous year. There are two causes of for such increases:

- Demand in the economy increases. Each year, we spend more than the previous year. This could be due to the fact that we earn more in real terms, or that the prices of goods and services have fallen in real terms, making them more affordable. By becoming richer, we spend more as time passes.
- Prices have risen over the previous year. Hence, we must spend more just to maintain the same level of business activity and quality of life that we did last year. This is growth resulting from inflation.

A key objective of both government and businesses is that of *non-inflationary growth*. This is growth brought about entirely by increased production and consumption with no element of increased prices causing the year-on-year increase. A key term in measuring growth is that of 'real' growth. Real growth is the rate of increase in the economy's output minus the prevailing rate of inflation over the same period. This, in turn, can be measured by one of two aggregate figures.

- The *gross domestic product* or (GDP) which is the total output of a domestic economy from within the borders of that country.
- The *gross national product* (GNP), which is the GDP plus any net overseas income received by UK based individuals and businesses (after allowing for outgoings). Overseas income includes profits from foreign investments and interest and returns on bank deposits and other financial investments.

We can also use GDP and GNP to measure the wealth in a country in the form of the *real income per capita*. This is the GDP or GNP divided by the number of people in a country. It is seen as a measure of the increasing or decreasing economic wealth of the population. We must be careful not to assess the wealth of a nation purely by looking at the GDP or GNP figure, as this tells us little about the economic standard of living enjoyed by its citizens. In terms of GNP or GDP, the UK is the sixth richest country in the world (Table 23.4). When we examine the income per capita, we see that the UK is only the 18th 'most comfortable' nation (although some of those above the UK are very small states and the comparison is thus not very meaningful) (Table 23.5).

Table 23.4 *The world's seven richest nations by GDP (the G7 countries). (Source: Datastream)*

Country	GDP 1994 (US $ billions)
USA	6638.2
Japan	4651.1
Germany	2041.5
France	1318.9
Italy	1020.2
UK	1013.6
Canada	541.5

Positive and negative growth

The expectations of economic growth are part of our business and societal culture. Most consumers and businesses expect to become richer and more comfortable as they progress through life, not less so. If, however, we look at a graph of economic growth over recent years (Figure 23.9) we can see that upward growth is not constant. There are times when growth is strong and times when it is slow or even negative. Such variations are due in large part to the fact that economic activity is approximately cyclical. There are sustained periods when both spending and investment are high and businesses enjoy growing, buoyant conditions. It seems, though, that from time to time economic activity slows down. Slow economic growth is obviously bad for business. On some occasions, an economy's GDP actually falls against the previous year and this is called negative growth or *recession*.

Table 23.5 The world's richest countries by GNP per capita. (Source: The Guinness World Data Book, 2nd Edn, 1993)

Country	GNP per capita (US$, 1992)
Switzerland	35 500
Japan	32 018
Luxembourg	31 080
Sweden	29 600
Denmark	28 200
Norway	28 200
Finland	24 400
Belgium	22 600
Iceland	22 580
USA	22 520
Canada	21 710
Netherlands	21 400
Liechtenstein	21 020
Italy	20 200
United Arab Emirates	19 680
Singapore	18 143
Australia	17 320
UK	17 300

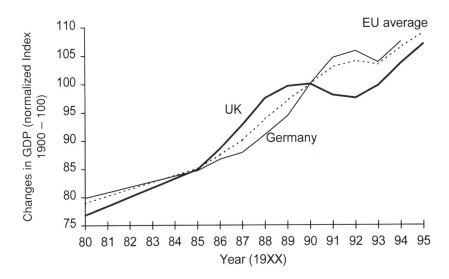

Figure 23.9 Growth in GDP in the UK, Germany and the EC. (Source: Economic Trends, No. 509, March 1996. London: HMSO)

An examination of Figure 23.9 shows both strong growth and a UK recession. The period from 1985 to 1989 shows strong growth in GDP for both the UK and for Germany. In 1990, the UK growth begins to turn downwards – an unhappy situation that continued until 1992, when GDP began to climb again. From the graph, we can tell that both the UK and Germany experienced a recession around this time, but that the

UK entered and emerged from the downturn before Germany. Furthermore, the downturn was deeper in the UK.

Whilst the actual value of economic growth is important to domestic consumers and businesses, perhaps more important is the value of the UK's growth compared to that of its main industrial competitors. If the UK experiences an outstanding year of real growth, say of 10%, but both Germany and France enjoy a rate of 12%, then in international terms the UK has shrunk in relative terms against the competitors by two percentage points. We will find that this comparative analysis applies to most of the economic indicators.

Inflation

What is inflation?
Inflation is defined as the year-on-year overall (aggregate) rise in prices. It can also be defined as the year-on-year reduction in the value of money, because a £1 coin will be worth less in spending power this year compared to last year by an amount equal to the rate of inflation.

Question 23.5

Some economists say that inflation is robbery. Explain what they might mean by this description.

The most commonly used measure of inflation is the *Retail Prices Index* (RPI) – a notional 'basket' of consumer products, the prices of which are monitored each month. The percentage change in the price of this basket over the course of a year is defined as the rate of retail inflation over that period (Figure 23.10). The *underlying rate* of inflation is also often used, and this describes the RPI with the effects of mortgage repayments taken out, thus nullifying the direct effects of monetary policy. There are other measures of inflation other than retail prices such as the rise in industrial costs – *factory gate prices* inflation. These are of less direct concern to consumers but tend to be indicative of future movements in the RPI because business cost increases are usually passed on to consumers eventually.

What causes inflation?
The major causes of inflation are two-fold. The two causes can work independently of each other, but it goes without saying that inflationary pressures are at their most when both factors are at work simultaneously.

- *Cost-push inflation* occurs when the costs to industry are increased. These can be due to increased energy prices, increased import prices (which may be linked with a fall in the value of the domestic currency), increased labour costs or any number of other input price changes. Whilst businesses may be able to absorb cost increases in the short term, any sustained increases in industrial costs must be 'passed on' to the consumers, and eventually lead to retail prices inflation. This effect has been termed *supply-side inflationary pressure.*

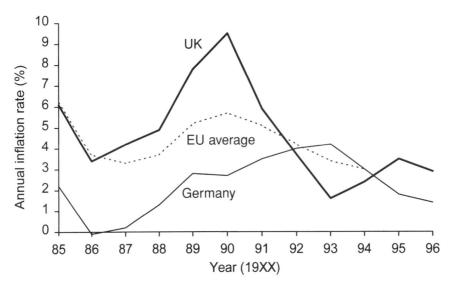

Figure 23.10 Consumer price inflation in the UK, Germany and the EU (average). (Source: Economic Trends, No. 509, March 1996. London: HMSO)

- *Demand-led inflation* is brought about by an excess of spending power in the economy over the economy's ability to meet the demand. Producers will tend to increase their prices when they are confident that there is an excess of demand. This type of inflation can be stated simply as 'too much money chasing too few goods' and has two equally obvious causes. Firstly, demand-led inflation can be caused by anything that causes aggregate spending power in the economy to grow. Such factors will include cuts in the rate of tax, cuts in monetary pressure, high wage rises, increases in government spending, falling unemployment, etc. Such changes are said to come from the *demand side* of the economy. Secondly, it can be caused by anything that prevents the business sector from meeting demand, such as higher fiscal and monetary pressure, high wage demands, low investment, etc.

Question 23.6

For the following changes in the economic environment, say whether each of the changes are most likely to be inflationary or deflationary:

- A cut in the basic rate of income tax (reduced fiscal pressure).
- An increase in interest rates (increased monetary pressure).
- An increase in unemployment.
- A cut in government spending (increased fiscal pressure).
- A devaluation in the domestic currency.

The effects of inflation
The reduction of inflation is an objective which is shared by all businesses and political parties. It is generally accepted that low inflation is good for the majority of people

and businesses in an economy. Its management consequently forms a major plank of government economic policy, whichever party happens to be in power.

The effects of inflation in an economy are summarized below.

- If the UK rate is higher than those of its major competitors, it will, over time, make British businesses less price competitive in international business transactions. This is the most important of the negative effects of inflation.
- It tends to exert an upward pressure on wage demands. This increases company costs, and, through the increased prices to cover the increased labour cost and through increased spending power, it can make inflation worse. This is referred to as a *wage–price inflationary spiral*.
- Variable or erratically increasing prices add to the uncertainty of the economic environment. This can have a negative effect on business confidence and may delay investment and spending.

Inflation in international trade

Both the UK and France export motor vehicles to other European states. Suppose that this year, the price of the French car, say a Peugeot, is £20 000 (in French francs, obviously). The British built car, say a Rover, also costs £20 000. This price parity means that a car buyer in Belgium would choose between them using non-price criteria (such as appearance, handling, style, 'feel', etc.). The two cars are equally price competitive.

Over the course of the following year, the UK and France experience different rates of inflation. In the UK, the rate is 10%, but in France, it is only 5%. This means that costs in the two countries will have increased by these percentages (the respective rates of inflation). If the full effects of these cost increases are passed on to the customers then, for the French Peugeot the new price would be

£20 000 + 5% = £21 000

and for the British Rover, the new price would be

£20 000 + 10% = £22 000

Hence, the British car is less price competitive because of the higher rate of inflation. Rover's other choice, instead of passing on the price increase, is to set their price equal to the price of the Peugeot and absorb the lower profit margin. Either way, the results for Rover are unpleasant.

Value of currency

The value of a currency refers to its value against other (foreign) currencies. At any point in time, the pound sterling will have a value against all other currencies. The most important exchange rates are those of the countries with which Britain does most business – the German deutschmark, the Japanese yen, the US dollar and the French franc.

The exchange rate of the pound will be of vital interest to any business in the UK that deals with foreign companies – as a supplier, a customer or a partner.

The value of currency, like any other economic commodity, is determined by the demand for the commodity. An increase in the demand for bananas would cause their market price to rise, and the same is true for currency.

What determines the exchange rate?
What, then, would cause an increase in the demand for sterling which would in turn increase its value against other currencies (Table 23.6)?

- *An increase in the demand for British goods* and services. When a UK based business exports a product (e.g. a car) or a service (e.g. an insurance policy), then foreign currency must be changed into sterling to pay the British company. The demand for sterling goes up and so, therefore, does its value. Customers will only buy British goods if they are more competitive than foreign ones – if they are higher quality, cheaper or both. There is therefore an important link between the exchange rate and the competitiveness of British business.
- *High interest rates.* The amount of interest that international investors can obtain by putting money on deposit will influence the country in which they place their cash. If the British interest rate is higher than it is in other countries, then the UK will attract investment capital. Again, the investors (who manage vast sums of money on behalf of banks, insurance companies and other financial institutions) will have to buy sterling in order to place it in UK banks. Hence, its value will increase.

Table 23.6 The effects of interest rate changes on bank deposits

Interest rate	Bank deposits	Value of sterling
Increases	Increased	Higher
Decreases	Decreased	Lower

Question 23.7

Find out the current exchange rate of the pound sterling against:

- the deutschmark.
- the French franc.
- the US dollar.

For each one, try to identify the trend – is it on an upward or downward trend against the pound?

The effects of a high or low exchange rate
The matter of exchange rates is quite complicated as we cannot say that a high or a low exchange rate is particularly favourable or unfavourable. It all depends upon the par-

ticular circumstances of the business. In summary though, we can say the following of a *high value of sterling* (relative to other major currencies):

- Will make *exports relatively uncompetitive* (i.e. expensive). This is because more foreign currency will have to be changed into sterling to meet the British asking price. Conversely, a lower value of sterling will make exports more price competitive.
- Will make *imports relatively cheap*. Less sterling will need to be exchanged to meet the foreign seller's price. Whilst this may be good for company costs, it may not be good for British businesses if foreign goods are cheaper. This will also increase the value of visible imports (see section on balance of payments later in this chapter), which will have the effect of reducing the exchange rate for reasons we will see later. Again, a low exchange rate will have the opposite effect.

The one objective in regard to exchange rates which most businesses do have in common is that they should be relatively stable. We have seen that high or low exchange rates will please some organizations and displease others (depending, for example, on whether they are mainly importers or exporters), but very few like to see frequent and erratic fluctuations. Stability of exchange rates increases the certainty of carrying out international business transactions and this tends to increase the volume of business across national borders.

Unemployment

Definition

The official unemployment figure is defined as the number of people who are out of work and are claiming benefit from the Department of Social Security (DSS). We learned in Chapter 17 that unemployment is caused by a disequilibrium between supply and demand in the labour market – an excess of supply (of labour) over demand.

Unemployment is measured, like most of the economic indicators, on a monthly basis. Observers often analyse unemployment in terms of its upward or downward trend, rather than the actual figure itself. Governments tend to analyse the level of unemployment as a percentage of the total labour force, often making comparisons with other 'competitor' countries.

We can see from the graph in Figure 23.11 that the trends in unemployment are quite marked. In 1991, for example, much of the European Union, including the UK, was beginning to experience an episode of negative economic growth (see Figure 23.9). As a consequence of this, there was increasing unemployment in both the UK and in the EU average. Germany was fortunate enough not to feel the effects of the recession in terms of increased unemployment until the following year (1992).

Note also from Figure 23.11 that, notwithstanding fluctuations in unemployment levels, Germany has performed well compared with the EU average. The UK has historically been more-or-less around the EU average – Germany has consistently (historically) done much better than the rest of the EU.

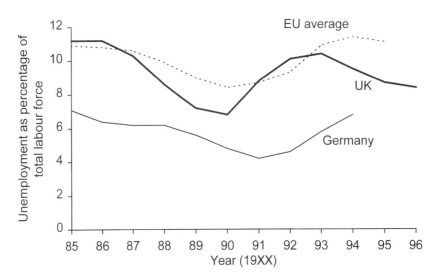

Figure 23.11 Unemployment in the UK, Germany and the EU (average) as a percentage of total workforce. (Source: Economic Trends, No. 509, March 1996. London: HMSO)

Types of unemployment
The total unemployment figure is made up from a number of 'types' of unemployed people. The type is linked to the respective cause.

- *Frictional unemployment* is caused by friction in the labour market. In this context, 'friction' means a difficulty in matching job-seekers with employers. It takes some time for peoples' skills to be matched up with employers who are seeking those skills. It may be that there is a shortage of teachers in London, but an excess in Scotland. This is overcome in some cases by migration to areas where the skills are in demand. Frictional unemployment is necessarily temporary in nature, representing a period of transition for job-seekers from one job to the next.
- *Seasonal unemployment* occurs as a result of varying labour demand at different times of the year. The tourism and building industries take on more labour in the summer, whilst postal services and retailers increase their labour requirements towards Christmas. As a result of seasonal unemployment, the overall rate can fluctuate over the year.
- *Structural unemployment* arises as a result of changes in the structure of industry and the commercial sector in general. Recent years have seen a decline in traditional industries like ship-building and mining. Many businesses which once employed thousands of people simply no longer exist. Unemployment arising from such closures, often regionally concentrated, has been the major contributor to the national unemployment total since the 1970s.
- *Cyclical unemployment* is unemployment that arises as a result of cycles in the state of the economy. In times of rapid economic growth unemployment falls as businesses take on more labour, whilst in recessions unemployment will increase as businesses shed labour.

- *Technological unemployment* is seen by some as being a type of structural unemployment. The increased use of technology in all areas of business life has reduced the need for labour. The increased use of robots, for example, has reduced the need for workers on production lines, whilst the computerization of banking and accounting systems has reduced the need for book-keepers and clerical staff. Motor car manufacturers once employed tens of thousands of people to perform simple engineering tasks. Extensive automation of motor car plants means that they now produce more cars with a fraction of their former labour requirement.

Seasonal, frictional and cyclical causes of unemployment will tend to be short term. Structural and technological unemployment are more worrying to governments, due to their long-term effects.

Figure 23.12 shows the trends in UK unemployment since 1971. The coming to power of Prime Minister Thatcher in 1979 coincided with an increase in structural unemployment as the result of a general 'modernization' of the economy away from heavy industries towards less labour intensive businesses. This increase also contained a strong element of technological unemployment, coinciding as it did with some key developments in microcomputer technology. Such an increase, it should be understood, also occurred in other industrialized countries. In the late 1980s, the economy as a whole enjoyed a boom and, accordingly, the rate of unemployment fell. Subsequently, in the early 1990s, a recession signalled an increase in cyclical unemployment.

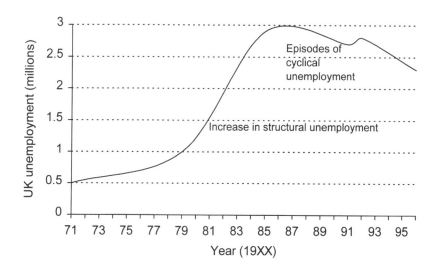

Figure 23.12 Unemployment in the UK (simplified to show general trends)

Effects of unemployment

The effects of unemployment on a community and in the country are complex. In regions of the country that have suffered high rates of unemployment for sustained periods, it seems that the unemployment has engendered effects other than just the personal misery that it can involve. We can consider the effects of unemployment as falling into three categories:

- The *primary effects* are the experiences of the people being made unemployed and of the businesses that have been forced to close or lose some of their employees. Redundancy or the closure of a large employer can have the effect of reducing the affected people's confidence, increased stress, depression and even despair. The loss of earnings to a family and the enforced idleness can engender a number of social and domestic problems.
- The *secondary effects* of unemployment arise as a result of the closure of large employers or of a large number of employers in a region. Secondary effects extend to the suppliers to a closed business, its contractors and customers. Suppliers may be forced to close as a result of the closure of the business buying its output. A significant loss of employment in a locality can also have the result of reducing spending power, which can lead to the closure of other local businesses such as shops and pubs.
- The *tertiary effects* include demographic migration away from areas of high unemployment and the deterioration of such localities as a result. Some semi-rural areas in the UK which formerly depended upon employment from mining have suffered declining population and a reduction in local services as a result. Young people tend to leave the locality to gain work, and hence local populations get progressively older.

Most governments have come to the conclusion that a situation of 'full employment' is essentially unachievable. Some argue that it is not actually desirable as the spending power created by full employment would potentially be very inflationary (see the discussion of the Phillips curve in Chapter 24). Notwithstanding this, governments often make concerted efforts to reduce unemployment, as it is known to have several undesirable effects.

The disadvantages of unemployment to the various affected parties are as follows:

- The *costs of state assistance* to the unemployed can be very significant, especially in times of recession when unemployment is high and tax revenues are relatively low. The UK government has, over recent years, sought to monitor unemployment assistance carefully as it is not only expensive to the taxpayer, but also, if overgenerous, can act as a disincentive for the unemployed to return to work. Coupled with the fact that unemployed people do not contribute income tax, the costs to the state can be seen to be significant.
- Unemployment, especially structural unemployment, can result in a *loss of human skills* to the economy. The closure of many heavy engineering operations signalled an increase in structural unemployment and many skilled workers began to lose their skills through periods of prolonged unemployment. Whilst for some skills this may not be very significant (i.e. those which the economy has decreasing demand for), for other skills the costs of retraining may be significant.
- Unemployment represents an underutilization of one of the main factors of production. Put simply, human resources add value to goods and services in a business, so unemployed people are not being used for this economic purpose. It is thus said to be a *waste of human resources*.
- There is much debate regarding the *links between unemployment and a number of social disorders* such as increased crime, ill health and deteriorating race relations. Whilst some dispute such links, the majority of observers concede that unemployment is one of the factors that contributes to such disorders. It is argued, for example,

that if people are in work, they not only have less time on their hands to be a menace to society, they also have less financial reasons for being so.

The level of unemployment is generally taken to be an indicator of the economic health of a country. Rising unemployment, in most cases, is generally assumed to indicate that businesses are shedding jobs or curtailing recruitment – not things that are typical of behaviour in times of rapid economic growth. Whilst the level of unemployment may not be of direct concern to businesses, it could be contended that a large pool of available labour, which can often be bought in at favourable cost (i.e. lower wages) is of some advantage. The negative effects of unemployment, particularly the inclination of the Chancellor to maintain fiscal pressure (to facilitate the payment of unemployment benefits), probably outweigh any benefits the business may enjoy from a wider choice of recruits.

Balance of payments and trade

The balance of payments statement is a record of a country's transactions with the rest of the world. It records all cash movements in and out of the country. Although the statement is issued monthly, most interest revolves around the annual statement, which is the sum of all the monthly statements for a one-year period.

There are two parts of the balance of payments account. The *current account* records all payments that result from trade in goods and services, whilst the *capital account* records movements of capital for investment purposes and the currency transactions which make trading (shown in the current account) possible. The two parts of the balance of payments statement must, therefore, by definition, balance. There tends to be a statistical error resulting from inaccuracies in recording cash movements, and this figure is termed the *balancing item*.

The current account
The recording of transactions that arise through normal trading activities are naturally split into two categories: goods (visibles) and services (invisibles).

Visible transactions record trade in physical goods:

- Imports occur when goods enter the UK. British businesses, in paying for the goods, send money overseas, causing a cash outflow from the UK.
- Exports occur when a UK business sells goods to foreign customers. Cash flows into the UK to pay for the exported goods.

The difference between the values of visible imports and exports is called the *balance of trade*. This figure (especially whether it is positive or negative overall), is thought to be a good indicator of the competitiveness of British manufacturing. If the balance of trade is a negative figure for the year, it means that the UK has imported more goods (in value terms) than it has exported. This is taken to mean that, for reasons of quality and/or price, foreign goods are more attractive to buyers than British goods, although this can also be affected by the value of the currency. The UK government is keen to see increased exports and reduced imports, not least because of what this would say about the desirability of British goods.

Constructing the balance of payments account – two simple rules

The balance of payments account records movements of cash, not goods or services. Hence, the following rules apply when constructing the account:

- All money flowing into the UK, for any reason, is entered as a *positive* figure in the account. The UK has become 'richer' by the amount of money coming into the UK.
- All money flowing out of the UK is entered as a *negative* figure in the account.

It therefore follows, for example, that exports, inward investment and inward bank deposits are entered as a positive figure. Imports, overseas investment by UK companies and money we take on holiday to France are entered as a negative figure. In the UK balance of payments statement, all figures are entered in pounds sterling. Foreign currencies held in the UK are converted into pounds value at the current exchange rate for the purposes of the statement.

Invisible transactions mainly comprise movements in cash to pay for services. Also included are dividends and interest from investments. When a Spanish shipping company takes out insurance with Lloyd's of London, cash flows into the UK. Conversely, a British student going to study abroad is benefiting from an education service, causing money to flow out of the UK in course fees. The *invisibles balance* is the difference between all invisible inflows and outflows and it can be a positive or negative figure.

Over recent times, Britain has witnessed several years of balance of trade deficits (Figure 23.13), but this is partly compensated for by relatively healthy invisibles balances. The message from such figures would seem to be that Britain is competitive in its supply of services, but less so in its manufacturing sector.

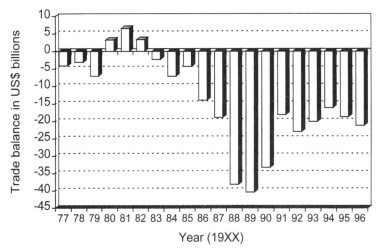

Figure 23.13 UK trade balance. (Source: OECD Economic Outlook, No. 57, June 1995)

The *current balance* records the overall surplus or deficit arising from all trading activities with overseas parties. Calculated simply by adding together the balance of trade (the visibles balance) and the invisibles balance, a positive current balance is obviously better than a negative figure (Figure 23.14).

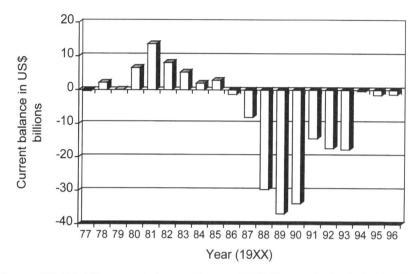

Figure 23.14 UK current balance. (Source: OECD Economic Outlook, No. 57, June 1995)

Question 23.8

If the balance of trade is a good indicator of the competitiveness of British manufacturing, describe the significance of the invisibles balance and the current balance overall. Comment on the performance of the UK as shown in Figures 25.13 and 25.14.

The capital account

The capital account is more correctly called the *transactions in external assets and liabilities*. It records financial movements across the national borders which are not linked directly with trading relationships.

The various components of the capital account are predominantly as follows.

- *Foreign investment in the UK* occurs when foreign businesses either buy British businesses or build plants in the UK to carry out business. Foreign acquisitions include the purchase of Rover Group by BMW, whilst Toyota's greenfield investment in Derbyshire is an example of a 'new-build' (these are both discussed in Chapter 28). The inward flow of funds to pay for foreign investments means that this is a positive figure on the statement, although the positive figure is partly offset by transfers back to the foreign country of returns on the investment.
- *UK investment overseas* represents funds that have left the UK to pay for overseas investments, although the negative outflow figure can be offset by returns to the UK

on foreign investments such as dividends. An example of inclusions in this category is UK companies buying shares in overseas companies. If Hanson plc buys a company in North America or if ICI builds a chemical plant in Asia, the values of these investments would be entered as UK investment overseas. On a less grand scale, this entry also includes UK residents who buy holiday homes abroad.

- *Currency transactions* show the movements in sterling as it is exchanged to or from other currencies which occur whenever one currency is exchanged for another. Imports and exports both involve changing money from one currency to another. Bank deposits to and from the UK will also involve a currency transaction.
- *Inward and outward bank deposits* show the values that are moved across the sea for the purposes of banking deposit.
- *Changes to the 'official reserves'* refers to the Bank of England's reserves of currency. This is a sum amounting to billions of pounds and is held in both sterling and a range of foreign currencies. It is used, among other things, to influence the exchange rate of sterling.

The Balance of Payments Statement (1994 – simplified)

Current account	*£million*
Visible trade	
exports	134 611
imports	(145 349)
Visible balance	(10 738)
Invisibles balance	8 910
Current balance	*(1 828)*
Transactions in external assets and liabilities	
UK investment overseas	2 140
Overseas investment in the UK	38 513
Foreign currency transactions of UK banks	(8 846)
Sterling transactions of UK banks	6.553
UK dealings with foreign banks	(10 686)
Net borrowings from banks abroad	2 118
Other transactions (net effect of)	(28 070)
Changes in official reserve	(1 045)
Net transactions in assets and liabilities	*(3 581)*
Balancing item	5 389

(Source: *Annual Abstract of Statistics 1996*, No.132, London: HMSO).

Question 23.9

For the following items, say:

1 where they would be entered in the balance of payments account, and
2 whether they would be entered as a positive or negative item.

- Glaxo Wellcome, the British company, buys a US based company.
- The government of Saudi Arabia buys aeroplanes from British Aerospace plc.
- Siemens invests £1.1 billion in a microchip factory on Tyneside.
- You buy a French Peugeot car.

Different parts of the balance of payments statement signify different things. We have seen that the current balance is an indication of the competitiveness of the UK's trading sector. The balance between inward and outward investment is an indicator of the attractiveness of the UK as a place to invest whilst the difference between inward and outward bank deposits is usually influenced by monetary policy over the year.

Assignment

During the period 1992–1996, the UK enjoyed a period of declining interest rates from around 10% to about 6.5%. At the same time, the annual rate of inflation was stable at between 2.5% and 3.5%.

Questions

- Explain the theoretical link between interest rates and inflation.
- Discuss the reasons why inflation might remain stable despite declining interest rates.
- What other changes might occur to other economic indicators as a result of falling interest rates.

Further reading

Abel, A. B. and Bernanke, B. S. (1992) *Macroeconomics*. New York: Addison Wesley.

Barro, R. and Sala-i-Martin, X. (1995) *Economic Growth*. New York: McGraw Hill.

Begg, D., Fischer, S. and Dornbusch, R. (1994). *Economics*, 4th edn. New York: McGraw Hill.

Cole, K., Cameron, J. and Edwards, C. (1991) *Why Economists Disagree*, 2nd edn. London: Longman.

Curwen, P. (1994). *Understanding the UK Economy*, 3rd edn. London: Macmillan.

Dornbusch, R. and Fischer, S. (1993) *Macroeconomics*. 6th edn. New York: McGraw Hill.

Greenaway, D. (Ed.). (1989) *Current Issues in Macroeconomics*. London: Macmillan.

McEachern, W. A. (1994) *Macroeconomics. A Contemporary Introduction.*, 3rd edn. Thomson Publishing.

Staff authors (1995) *Business Basics – Economics*, chs 9–17. London: BPP Publishing.

Sutcliffe, M. (1994) *Essential Elements of Business Economics*. London: DP Publications.

Whitehead, G. (1996). *Economics*, 15th edn. (Made Simple Series). Oxford: Butterworth-Heinemann.

24

The economic environment 2: Competing economic philosophies

Learning objectives

After studying this chapter, students should be able to describe:

- An 'ideal' set of economic circumstances.
- The effects of pulling fiscal and monetary 'levers'.
- The classical economic philosophies of Adam Smith.
- The economic philosophies of John Maynard Keynes.
- The monetarist theories of Milton Friedman.

24.1 A review of economic objectives

The 'Nirvana' scenario

Can you imagine a situation where a government had the national economy exactly as it wanted? Let us look at this ideal 'Nirvana' situation.

- *Interest rates* would be low enough to stimulate industrial investment and consumer spending, but high enough to give savers an acceptable return on their deposits and to support an acceptable exchange rate.
- *Monetary growth rates* would exactly match the rate of inflation.
- *Taxation* levels would be low enough to stimulate investment and consumer spending, but high enough to maintain an acceptable level of public spending.
- *Government spending* would be high enough to provide quality public services, but low enough to enable tax levels to be maintained at acceptable levels.
- *Inflation* would be lower than competitor countries, but high enough to meet the expectations of some stakeholders, such as homebuyers who like to see the price of their homes appreciating.
- The *foreign exchange value of the currency* would be high enough to avoid excessive costs to importers, but low enough to favour a high level of exports or to necessitate an increase in monetary pressure.
- *Unemployment* would be low enough to obviate the need for government spending on unemployment support, but high enough to enable employers to acquire labour as they needed it.
- The *rate of economic growth* would be high enough to stimulate high levels of busi-

ness activity, but low enough to offset the threat of inflation.

- The *balance of trade* would be sufficiently in surplus as a result of a high excess of exports over imports, but not so high as to put too much upward pressure on the foreign exchange value of the currency.
- There would be a sizeable *fiscal surplus*.

We can see that each 'indicator' is finely balanced. Furthermore, as we explore the complex interrelationships between the various factors (see Chapter 23), we can see that a change in any of them precipitates changes in others. The hard fact of economic management is that the 'Nirvana' scenario is impossible. Governments must, it seems, accept some good and some bad at any time in their management of the economy. Any change in the economic environment will have some welcome effects and some unwelcome ones.

Question 24.1

Suggest some advantageous and some disadvantageous effects of the following hypothetical changes in economic conditions:

- The Chancellor of the Exchequer announces a cut in interest rates.
- Inflation falls to less than 1% a year – the lowest figure ever.
- The pound gains 10% against all other major world currencies.
- The Chancellor announces that VAT is to be completely scrapped.
- The indirect tax on petrol is trebled.
- Unemployment rises by 25% over the year.
- Britain declares war on France.

Pulling economic levers: a summary of causes and effects

We examined the various aspects of macro-economic management in Chapter 23. The senior managers of the economy have two primary economic levers they can 'pull' – the matters of monetary and fiscal policy. Changes in any part of such policies have a 'knock-on' effect in other parts of the economy (Table 24.1).

24.2 Government and economic strategy

Whilst it may be the case that the objectives of economic management remain broadly the same (the 'Nirvana' scenario), governments of different political persuasions may not agree on how to manage the economy to bring about the most favourable outcome. Furthermore, the way that governments have managed the economy has changed over time as different approaches have gone in and out of fashion.

Let us consider a simple example. We saw in Chapter 23 that economic growth is not always as strong as governments would like. Sometimes the rate of growth slows and it can even decrease – a recession. Nobody likes recessions. Unemployment increases, and therefore Department of Social Security (DSS) spending goes up, tax revenues fall, companies 'go bust', consumers feel 'the pinch' as their disposable incomes decline, and so on. The question is this: how should the government act with regard to economic policy in times of recession? There are a number of possibilities (Table 24.2).

Table 24.1 Effects of pulling monetary and fiscal 'levers'

Lever 'pulled'	Effects of change
Increased monetary pressure	• Inflation – downward pressure • Investment – downward pressure • Value of currency – upward pressure • Unemployment – upward pressure • Economic growth – downward pressure
Decreased monetary pressure	• Inflation – upward pressure • Investment – upward pressure • Value of currency – downward pressure • Unemployment – downward pressure • Economic growth – upward pressure
Increased fiscal pressure	• Inflation – downward pressure • Investment – downward pressure • Public spending – may increase • Unemployment – upward pressure • Economic growth – downward pressure
Decreased fiscal pressure	• Inflation – upward pressure • Investment – upward pressure • Public spending – may decrease • Unemployment – upward pressure • Economic growth – downward pressure

Table 24.2 Options in a recession

Action	Advantages	Disadvantages
Do nothing	Saves the bother of worrying about what to do next! Allows a 'natural' development of the economy without government interference	Government spending and unemployment continue to rise, tax revenues and business confidence continue to fall
Increase taxes	Offsets the increased spending on unemployment benefits – may avoid or reduce a budget deficit	May have the effect of making business confidence even lower than it is and of reducing consumers' spending power. Increases unemployment
Reduce taxes	Stimulate spending and investment. Reduce unemployment	Inflationary, and may bring about a budget deficit
Increase government spending	Invests in public services, stimulates spending through public sector jobs and projects	Bound to cause a budget deficit as tax revenues will be falling at the same time. Exert an inflationary pressure
Reduce interest rates or increase monetary supply	Stimulate spending and investment	Inflationary and would put downward pressure on the foreign exchange value of the currency

Table 24.2 offers only some of the possibilities open to the Chancellor in times of recession. We can see that each possible action has finely balanced pros and cons, and that any decision made will be both praised and criticized.

In practice, economic decisions tend to be made along broadly ideological lines. Politicians tend to have certain underlying beliefs which guide their views on how to manage the economy. In consequence, the economic decisions of any political party in government tend to be relatively predictable, and it is usually possible to trace a common intellectual thread over time.

Traditionally, the divisions in economic philosophy have tended to fall along party political lines. This has been the case in many countries in addition to the UK, a notable example being the changing governments in the USA. Left-of-centre parties such as the British Labour Party and the Democrats in the USA have broadly tended to follow one economic philosophy, whilst right-of-centre parties, the UK Conservatives and the USA Republicans, have traditionally adopted a contrary philosophy.

In terms of the major intellectual economic philosophies, it can be said with justification that Britain has made by far the most substantial contribution. The work of the two prominent British thinkers we shall consider in this chapter, have, between them, heavily influenced the macro-economic activities of the major industrialized countries for over two centuries.

24.3 The 'classical' economic philosophy of Adam Smith

Who was Adam Smith?

The Scotsman, Adam Smith (1723–90) has been called 'the father of modern economics'. His now classic work, *An Inquiry into the Nature and Causes of the Wealth of Nations* (shortened to *The Wealth of Nations*), was published in 1776 – coincidentally the same year as the initial foundation of the USA. The book, considered a seminal influence on politico-economic systems, was the first major contribution to economics as an intellectual discipline.

Professor Adam Smith was born and brought up in the small port of Kirkcaldy, just across the Firth of Forth from Edinburgh. After being educated at the University of Glasgow, Smith held academic positions at Glasgow and Oxford Universities as well as carrying out some work abroad. His contemporaries regarded Smith primarily as a political philosopher, and his early writings were in that area. His first major work, *The Theory of Moral Sentiments*, published in 1759, was essentially a philosophical work.

Smith's economic philosophy

Arising from his earlier work, *The Wealth of Nations* set out Smith's economic theories. Although he was not primarily an economist (one could argue that economics was not defined as an academic discipline prior to Smith), his penetrating and incisive analysis of economic systems in the book has been applauded by countless observers since its initial publication.

The 'invisible hand'

According to Smith, macro-economic systems work best when the individuals and businesses in the economy are allowed to behave according to their own economic best interest. In other words, individuals behave in a way that they believe will bring them the greatest personal wealth, thus increasing their quality of life. If we wish to increase our quality of life, we spend our income to benefit from the goods and services which offer us the best value for money and utility. The collective actions of many such people acting on the same level of self-interest will, Smith argues, ultimately benefit everybody by creating a buoyant economy.

To explain how this works, he put forward his theory of the 'invisible hand'. In a market economy – one in which the government plays only a minimal role – individuals are guided by an invisible hand in pursuing their own self-interest, which, when taken together, leads to the benefit of the economy as a whole.

Consumers act in own best interest → Optimal performance of the total economy

The invisible hand is a mechanism which links individual economic decisions and the aggregate benefit derived from them. Each of a consumer's decisions is led by the invisible hand which 'mystically' acts to maximize the wealth of the macro-economy as a whole.

The invisible hand idea does not guarantee an equal distribution of wealth or income. It acknowledges that some will be better off than others. Rather, it states that *given* a nation's social and political conditions, and its relative wealth of resources (financial, material and human), the invisible hand will guarantee an optimal economic well-being of the citizens as a whole.

Smith's assumptions

A key underlying assumption of classical economics is that economic systems work entirely freely. They are not in any way impeded or skewed by government interference – in short, it assumes market economy conditions. It follows that any government interference will in some way undermine or distort the market mechanism and hence render the nation's wealth sub-optimal. Classicists argue, for example, that government attempts to redistribute wealth in an economy, by 'robbing the rich to give to the poor' or by subsidizing certain industries, ultimately work to the disadvantage of the total economy. In markets where demand exceeds supply, prices must be allowed to rise to equilibrium notwithstanding any perceived inequalities of the price rise decision. All changes in market conditions must be allowed to rapidly readjust without government involvement in order to maintain the efficiency of each market in the economy.

Classical economics in different markets

Classical economics can apply to all parts of the economy, not just the markets for goods and services. The same principles apply in the markets for financial assets and for labour. In the same way that the price for goods and services can rise or fall in line with changing conditions of demand and supply, so can the price of money and the price of labour. Lenders of money are free to increase or decrease their rate of interest on loans in line with the effective demand for loans. The more controversial point is that wage rates, along with prices, can fall as well as rise to meet equilibrium market conditions. Furthermore, just as we might expect the prices of money and goods to respond rapidly to changes in demand, the same is true of labour.

Wage and price flexibility is crucial to the invisible hand concept. It must be possible for wages and prices to be infinitely variable as the forces of demand and supply drive them up and down. Measures such as a statutory minimum wage or interest rate ceilings would undermine the invisible hand's operation. In a market with perfect information, price changes would be brought about as soon as there is a change in the equilibrium, i.e. it would readjust immediately. In practice, there is necessarily a time-lag as the market adjusts to new economic circumstances.

Neo-classical economics

A softening of the classical approach
Since Adam Smith's initial theories were published, his ideas have been developed and refined as the macro-economic situation has changed over the years. Whilst the theory has been developing, all classical and neo-classical economists have held two doctrines as axiomatic:

- that people do and should pursue their economic self-interest;
- that market prices will adjust reasonably quickly to balance quantities supplied and demanded.

There has been some dilution of Smith's 'pure theory' in order to accommodate the complexities of the political environment. It is simply impractical, given the powerful stakeholder coalitions in most democracies, to have literally no government involvement in the workings of an economy, so much of the debate has centred around *how much* involvement there should be. Neo-classicists argue that, whilst some government involvement may be necessary (say to redistribute a small percentage of the wealth to obviate extremes of poverty), it should be kept to an absolute minimum.

The 'laissez faire' school
In recent years, this neo-classical approach to macro-economic management has been dubbed the *laissez faire* approach. The term *laissez faire*, French for *let it be*, implies an economic strategy directed by an ideology that business should be 'left alone' as far as possible, to manage itself, with government influence only being exerted reluctantly. The prominent political proponent of this idea in recent years was Prime Minster Margaret Thatcher in the 1980s, strongly influenced by her close political allies, Sir Keith Joseph and Enoch Powell. The politico-economic doctrines which have become known as *Thatcherism*, are primarily characterized by a neo-classical economic approach to the management of the economy. In the USA, President Ronald Reagan also employed a *laissez faire* approach to a lesser extent. However, the macro-economy in both of these countries already had a sizeable public sector, so the objectives of latter-day neo-classical economics is to reduce as far as possible the influence of the state over commercial activity.

Traditionally, the neo-classical economic philosophy has been embraced by right-of-centre political parties. The British Conservative Party, for example, have had a number of policies which clearly mark it out as broadly neo-classicist. Its underlying view is that the tax levels should be reduced, and its huge privatization programme of the 1980s are testimony to this. The opposition Labour Party – a left-of-centre party – has traditionally criticized these particular Conservative policies. Whilst some of its opposition can be put down to the fact that it is constitutionally bound to oppose the government, the underlying reason is that left-of-centre parties have traditionally espoused a contrary economic philosophy to neo-classicism (Keynesianism – see later in this chapter), one which favours relatively more government influence.

Classical economics and business cycles
In Chapter 23, we examined the effects of cycles upon business activity and consumer spending. The fact that economic downturns are an unpleasant experience for all parts of the economy might tempt us to think that government should take any measures possible to reduce the impact of recession. Classical economists say that, even when recessions occur, governments should not be tempted to intervene.

Recessions, according to classicists, are times of readjustment in demand, supply and prices in an economy. They can be seen as an opportunity for the economy to lose uncompetitive companies and to gain efficiency by shedding surplus labour along with other superfluous costs. Such a process of 'purging the dross' ultimately strengthens a country's economy. Downward troughs in an economic cycle also serve to defeat inflation, as the downward pressure on wages and prices takes effect.

Criticisms of classical economics

Most economists, even non-classicists, agree that Smith's economic theories can work – in theory. The problems with it have mainly arisen because of the political restrictions on an economy, preventing businesses and consumers from trading in true market economy conditions. Classicists would argue that, if a classical economic system is allowed to run its course, it would eventually benefit almost everybody in society. However, some stakeholders have prevented this from happening owing to their contrary economic and political persuasions. This section is concerned with the criticisms of Smith and the reasons why his economic theories have broadly failed to be implemented in a true market economy setting.

It overlooks the necessity of a state sector
The social and political changes that have taken place since the work of Adam Smith have signalled significant changes in citizens' expectations. It is broadly assumed, across the political spectrum, that certain public and merit goods are not only desirable, but necessary. Such things include the state provision of national defences, education, health services and many others. The costs of such services necessitates the state making tax demands of individuals and businesses. Furthermore, direct state influence on business, through such things as grants and indirect taxes, have further moved the economy away from a market situation to mixed economy status.

It ignores inequalities in society
Classical economics is an economic theory. It is used by politicians, but it cannot be said to be a politico-economic theory *per se*. In consequence, it has been modified by

neo-classicists to include the main elements, but with many concessions designed to make it more politically palatable. Critics have said that Smith's ideas are unworkable and even uncaring because they offer no direct solution to economic inequality. Smith, writing in 1776, was doubtless used to seeing a great deal of poverty in society, but assumed that by the country as a whole growing richer the poor would indirectly benefit through increased employment, etc.

Political sensitivities bear upon this issue in the present day. When the Conservative Government privatized the utilities in the 1980s (a gesture underpinned by a neo-classical economic ideology) it was criticized by the opposition parties owing to the perceived risks of the removal of price protections enjoyed by the less economically fortunate. The government sought to address this criticism by appointing regulators (see Chapter 19). One of the roles of the utilities' regulators is to determine pricing levels such that competition is encouraged and pricing is 'fair'.

It underestimates the time-lag in price and wage adjustment
The limitations on the speed of information travel means that a change in the state of supply or demand is not immediately disseminated to all players in any given market. Whereas in a perfect market, price and wage adjustments would be immediate, the imperfections in markets usually mean that a time-lag occurs between a change in supply and demand and the concomitant price adjustment.

24.4 The economic philosophy of John Maynard Keynes

Who was Professor Keynes?

If it has ever been suggested that academics are closeted in their ivory towers with no influence on the real world, then the life work of Keynes (usually pronounced 'kanes') is testimony to the fact that one man's work can significantly influence the economic activity of two entire First World continents for a generation. His economic doctrines were not only highly influential, they were practised for over forty years in the world's major economies.

Professor John Maynard Keynes (1883–1946) was an Englishman and a Cambridge academic. He set out his economic ideas most clearly in his noted work *The General Theory of Employment, Interest and Money*, first published in 1936 – one of several books which Keynes published. The point at which his seminal book was written is salient to its contents – after the experience of the First World War, which was immensely costly in both human and monetary terms, and in the middle of the Great Depression, a time of great economic slow-down when national unemployment reached around 20% of the working population.

In addition to his academic writings, Keynes also acted as an important advisor to several politico-economic initiatives. His economic projections were used by the UK government in both World Wars, but his most notable 'non-academic' achievement was probably his input to the Bretton Woods conference on international exchange rates in 1944. As well as having a profound influence on the world's exchange rate systems, the Bretton Woods conference also established the World Bank and the International

Monetary Fund. His well-publicized membership of the esoteric 'Bloomsbury group' in the 1920s and 1930s brought him into close contact with some of the most notable artists and philosophers of his day.

His economic doctrines were not considered by governments when his *General Theory* was first published. After the Second World War, his ideas came to the fore and were, for almost forty years, considered to be almost axiomatic.

Keynes' economic doctrines

Keynes' economic ideology (termed *Keynesianism*) is in stark contrast to the classical doctrine of Adam Smith. Whereas Smith argued that government should adopt a 'hands-off' approach with regard to economic regulation, the very essence of Keynesianism is a belief that the government has a crucial role to play in the management and regulation of the macro-economy.

It is probable that uppermost in Keynes' mind when writing *The General Theory* were the economic problems facing the country in the Great Depression. Seeing the misery caused by the severe downturn in an economic cycle, he proposed that, rather than allowing markets to rule the economy, with its unpleasant effects in times of recession, the government should adopt a much greater role in its management. Whilst the primary purpose of government influence should be to reduce the intensity of economic downturns, Keynes continued in *The General Theory* to describe a much wider economic philosophy embracing all aspects of macro-economics.

Keynes recognized that one of Smith's most important assumptions, namely, that wages and prices respond rapidly to changes in supply and demand, is not usually the case in imperfect markets. He contended that it is simply a fact that there would be long periods of time when prices and wages would be out of equilibrium with actual market conditions. Hence, whereas a downturn in the demand for labour ought to signal a reduction in the price of labour (lower wages), the existence of unemployment was testimony to the fact that labour was overpriced – a disequilibrium. If demand for labour falls but its price remains the same, it is inevitable that unemployment will result. The same is true of the prices of goods and services – time lags between changes in supply and demand and the response of the market price rendered Smith's theories, in the opinion of Keynes, unworkable.

The problem of unemployment
According to Keynes, unemployment was a double evil, having two highly negative effects:

- it was a source of great misery to its sufferers;
- it significantly reduced the spending power (and hence the total level of demand) in the economy.

So not only is unemployment bad for the individual, but a high rate of unemployment is bad for the economy because unemployed people do not have the spending power necessary to maintain a buoyant economy. In times of recession, unemployment is also one of the main features which holds an economy back from recovery.

Keynes argued that, if unemployment could be held to a minimum or even eliminated, the result would be a robust economy with continually high spending power, which in turn would benefit the citizens.

The Keynesian role of the government

According to Keynes, a classical economic approach could not guarantee a high level of employment. On the contrary, in a classical system, unemployment is likely to fluctuate in sympathy with wages and prices, as market prices continually change according to market forces. Professor Keynes argued that, due to its sheer size and its huge spending power, the state should use its economic muscle to maintain employment and hence aggregate spending power.

When an economic cycle was in a 'boom', unemployment would be naturally low and hence the state need only assume a supervisory or 'back-seat' role. However, at the point at which the economy begins to show signs of slow-down in preparation for a recession, the government should increase its spending to maintain a high aggregate level of demand in the economy. This may take the form of such things as capital investments such as road-building, or revenue expenditures such as increased industrial grants or procurement (say of ships or equipment for the health service).

By maintaining demand in the economy, employers would have no need to shed labour. No upturn in unemployment means no reduction in spending power. No reduction in spending power means no recession.

Astute readers will have realized that increased government spending has obvious implications for the budget situation and fiscal policy. A feature of Keynesianism is a belief that short-term fiscal deficits brought about by spending to obviate recessions would soon be repaid by revenues from taxes from individuals and businesses benefiting from the avoidance of recession.

Criticisms of Keynesianism

Like classical economics, Keynesianism has its critics. Economists have the advantage, in assessing this philosophy, of having seen it in action. This gives the opportunity of seeing how the economy responds, over the longer term, when Keynesian principles are applied. The criticisms centre around the implications of Keynesianism for inflation and for the long-term competitiveness of the economy once it has been practised for some period of time.

It sees unemployment as the pre-eminent economic indicator

Critics argue that the Keynesian focus on unemployment as the major determinant of demand is too simplistic. The effects of high levels of unemployment upon other economic indicators are significant (see Chapter 23). Working in 1958, twenty years after the publication of *The General Theory*, A. W. Phillips discovered that there was an inverse relationship between unemployment and inflation over a longer time period. In other words:

- the lower the rate of unemployment, the higher the inflationary pressures;
- the higher the rate of unemployment, the lower the inflationary pressures.

It follows from Phillips' work, that the price of high or full employment may be high inflation. Similarly, low or reducing unemployment will usually be deflationary.

According to the Phillips curve (Figure 24.1), a level of employment to the left of the point at which the line intersects the zero inflation line will be inflationary. Unemployment can be set at a point at which there will be no inflationary pressure in the economy and a figure of unemployment to the right of the intersection will actually be deflationary.

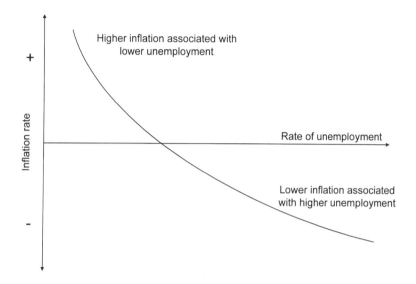

Figure 24.1 The Phillips curve

Critics of Keynesianism argue from Phillips' work that maintaining employment at high levels regardless of other conditions in the economy will precipitate inflation. The question then must be asked, 'Which is worse, high inflation resulting from low unemployment, or a recession resulting from a fall in aggregate demand?' This question is something of an imponderable and arguably rests in the purview of politicians rather than economists.

It discourages competition and thus acts against competitiveness
Critics of Keynesianism believe that a high level of government intervention in the economy prevents markets from operating efficiently. In order to maintain employment in the economy, it may be the case that the government 'bails out' a large employer which would otherwise become insolvent and close. The effect of such support over time is an economy comprising many inefficient businesses which could not effectively compete were it not for government assistance. Such a state of affairs does not encourage increased efficiency, and may even positively encourage complacency and wasteful bureaucracy.

Similarly, whereas classical economists see recessions as a vehicle for disposing of uncompetitive competitors, a Keynesian system which minimizes the effects of economic downturns would not facilitate the demise of such businesses. Such a short-termist approach measure, say the critics, makes for an inefficient business sector.

It increases the size of government.

There is something of a debate amongst politicians and economists about how much of a nation's wealth the government should account for. The UK is typical of most western nations, with its state sector accounting for around 45% of national wealth (calculated as a government budget of *ca.* £260 billion against a GDP of *ca.* £600 billion: 1993).

In order to have the financial ability to influence the economy through Keynesian policies, the state sector must be at least a certain size. Consequently, governments which have exercised a Keynesian approach over a period of time tend to be larger than otherwise. This is, of course, a predictable criticism of Keynesianism by classicists.

In the opinion of some, the ideal is to have a small state sector which allows businesses to operate with a minimum of state 'interference'. In order to have the financial 'clout' to be able to spend to obviate recession, the state must levy sufficient in tax and other revenue earners and, accordingly, exert its influence through spending.

This issue is a matter of intense political debate. The political right-wing tends to contend that government should be smaller in order to pursue a neo-classical economic philosophy. The left have argued that the state has a responsibility to maintain a certain level of spending in order to provide services and influence. Rather than stating such objectives explicitly, the underlying economic persuasion is often shown up by proposed policies. In the USA, a prominent theme of the office of President George Bush was to 'get government off our [the normal American peoples'] backs'. This theme was continued after the right-of-centre Republicans gained a majority in the 1994 elections to the US legislature. In the UK, the broad Keynesian beliefs of the left-of-centre Labour Party have engendered such policies as proposals for a statutory minimum wage and its opposition to privatizations.

24.4 The economic philosophy of Milton Friedman

Who is Professor Friedman?

Milton Friedman (1912–) has probably been the most influential economist of the latter third of the twentieth century. His ideas began to assume greater prominence among academics and politicians after Keynesianism, with its apparent inflationary effects, began to be questioned . He was appointed Professor of Economics at the University of Chicago, Illinois, in 1946. His published works have reflected his *laissez faire* approach to economic theory. In *Capitalism and Freedom* (1962), Friedman argued for the decentralization and replacement of traditional welfare services. Other books have expatiated his theories of monetarism, such as *A Monetary History of the United States 1867–960* (1963) and *Monetary Trends of the United States and the United Kingdom* (1981). Professor Friedman led the economic research of what became known as the 'Chicago school' of economic thought and was awarded the Nobel Prize for economics in 1976.

Friedman's economic doctrines

Monetarism

Friedman's major contribution to economic thought was through his development of what has become known as *monetarism* or 'new classical' economics. He and his colleagues at the University of Chicago, working from the 1950s onwards, concluded that economic management should be primarily geared to the control of inflation. Having had the benefit of observing Keynesianism in action for some years, the monetarists believed that the fiscal management which characterizes Keynes' philosophy was not only inflationary but acted against the best long-term interests of the economy.

The essence of monetarism is a belief that the best way to regulate the economy is by the careful use of monetary rather than fiscal instruments – particularly the use of monetary supply as a means of controlling inflation. In practice, such an emphasis is coupled with a belief that the state should assume a less influential role with regard to its fiscal policy, i.e. that it should adopt a *laissez faire* approach. According to most monetarists, economic management should be 'hands-off', except for a minimal influence in order to implement monetary policy. In this respect, monetarists eschew Keynes and his 'big government' notions, preferring instead to identify with a neo-classical approach.

The quantity theory of money

The intellectual basis of monetarism goes back to an economic formula first put forward early in the twentieth century. Known as the *quantity theory of money*, it is expressed as follows:

$$MV = PQ$$

where, M is the rate of monetary growth (i.e. the *nominal money supply*), V is the velocity of circulation of money in the economy, P is the price of goods and services, Q is the total quantity of goods and services sold in the economy.

Put simply, this theory shows a direct causal relationship between the rate of monetary growth (M), and the price of goods and services (P; the growth in which is inflation). It follows from this relationship that a restriction in the rate of monetary growth should enable inflation to be controlled, with all the benefits that low inflation affords. If, for example, the government or central bank (whichever has the responsibility for monetary policy) wishes to limit the annual rate of inflation to 3%, then it should restrict the main indicators of monetary growth to approximately the same figure. For M0 (see Chapter 23), this restriction is straightforward, as cash minting and printing can be controlled directly. For other elements of monetary growth, e.g. bank deposits and loans, monetary measures such as the varying of interest rates can be used to restrict the money supply.

The monetarists' use of this theory led to them being labelled, quite reasonably, as 'neo-quantity theorists'.

Assumptions of the quantity theory

In order for monetary growth to be used as a means of controlling inflation, two important assumptions must be made. Both are linked to the mathematical form of the equation itself. The first assumption is that the velocity of circulation (V) is relatively constant notwithstanding any changes in the money supply. The second is that the aggregate quantity of goods and services produced by an economy (Q) will not expand in sympathy with any increases in prices. The importance of these assumptions can be shown by rearranging the equation.

If $MV = PQ$, then it follows that (by simple rearrangement),

$$P = \frac{MV}{Q}$$

or

$$P = (V/Q)M$$

If we wish to control the growth in P (inflation) by varying M, then there should be no (or almost no) change in V or Q – i.e. they must, together, form a constant. If the term V/Q can be shown to be constant, then we can say that P is proportional to M, or

$$P \propto M$$

or

$$P = kM$$

where k is constant and equals V/Q.

The quantity theory of money no longer holds if either V or Q varies when there is a change in either of the other two (P or M). Economist *Michael Stewart* discusses these assumptions as follows:[1]

> *What the quantity theory does is to assert a particular causal relationship. Put crudely, it says that V does not change very much (or changes in a steady and pre-dictable way), and therefore there is a close correlation between M and PQ; and that it is changes in M that causes changes in PQ, and not the other way round.*
>
> He continues, '... *the fact that increases in M generate increases in PQ is not the end of the matter: the question now arises of how far the increase in PQ takes the form of an increase in P, and how far of Q. In other words, how far does an increase in the money supply lead to a rise in output [Q], and how far does it simply lead to a rise in prices? At its very simplest, the monetarist theory says that it cannot lead to a rise in output because the normal condition of the economy is one of full utilization of resources and hence maximum output; therefore it simply leads to a rise in prices.*
>
> (Reproduced with the permission of Penguin Books Ltd)

Hence, the monetarist theory rests upon the assumptions that velocity of circulation adapts slowly and predictably, and that the economy is operating at more-or-less full capacity (thus eliminating the possibility of a rapid change in Q). In some circumstances, these assumptions hold true, but the outcomes of other (such as when there is spare manufacturing capacity in the economy) circumstances are less predictable.

Monetarism and unemployment

Like the classicists, monetarists believe in the idea of a self-regulating economy. This means that, if left alone (except for the implementation of monetary policy), wages and prices will adjust to find their natural equilibrium. Hence, when all wages are in equilibrium, supply balances demand in the labour market and there will be what the monetarists term a *natural rate* of unemployment. The monetarists' natural rate is quite different from Keynes' notion of full unemployment. Monetarists accept that when supply in the labour market exceeds demand, and wages consequently fall, some people will prefer not to work, believing their labour to be worth more than the low wages on offer. This, in a sense, is voluntary unemployment, as potential workers elect not to work, considering the wages on offer to be unworthy of their time and effort. Whilst such a natural level is unfortunate if historically high, the government should not be tempted to intervene to reduce unemployment by 'artificially' increasing wages (such as by the imposition of a statutory minimum wage). Such interference would lead to inflation – the very thing that a government is trying to purge from the economy.

Governments which have pursued monetary policy have attempted to reduce unemployment by effectively making it as unpleasant as possible. By reducing the level of unemployment benefit and state support, the motivation to accept a job on low wages is increased. Reductions in unemployment benefits thus meet two economic objectives in concurrence with monetarist theory: to encourage people to accept work and as part of a neo-classical wish to minimize state influence.

Assignment

During the political season 1992–97, the Labour Shadow Chancellor, Gordon Brown, announced that 'full and fulfilling employment' would be an objective of a future labour government.

Questions

- What would the implications of such a policy be if it were to be realized?
- What measures might the government need to put in place to achieve full employment?
- The Labour Party, at the same time as espousing full employment, also intended to implement a statutory minimum wage. Discuss the compatibility of these two policies.
- How would a proponent of classical economics respond to the policy of a minimum wage?

Reference

1. Stewart, M. (1986) *Keynes and After*, 3rd edition. London: Penguin.

Further reading

Aspromourgos, T. (1995) *On the Origins of Classical Economics*. London: Routledge.

Blaug, M. et al. (1995) *The Quantity Theory of Money from Locke to Keynes & Friedman*. Ashgate.

Cagan, P. (1965) *Determinants & Effects of Changes in the Stock of Money, 1875–1960*. National Bureau of Economic Research, Incorporated.

Hobson, J. A. (1973) *Gold, Prices & Wages: With an Examination of the Quantity Theory*. New York: Augustus M. Kelley.

Kenway, P. (1993) *From Keynesianism to Monetarism. The Evolution of UK Macroeconomic Models*. London: Routledge.

Keynes, J. M. (1965) *The General Theory of Employment, Interest, & Money*: London: Harcourt Brace.

Laidler, D. (1991) *The Golden Age of the Quantity Theory*. Princeton NJ: Princeton University Press.

Mankiw, N. G. and Romer, D (Eds) (1991) *New Keynesian Economics*. Vols 1 and 2. Cambridge, MA: MIT Press.

Moggridge, D. E. (1995) *Maynard Keynes. An Economist's Biography*. London: Routledge.

Rider, C. (1995) *An Introduction to Economic History*. Thomson.

Smith, A. (1984) *The Theory of Moral Sentiments*. Indianapolis, IN: Liberty Fund.

Smith, A. (1982) *An Inquiry into the Nature & Causes of The Wealth of Nations*. Vols 1 and 2. Liberty Fund.

Stewart, M. (1986) *Keynes and After*, 3rd edn. London: Penguin.

25

The sociological environment

Learning objectives

After studying this chapter, students should be able to describe:

- The nature of the sociological environment.
- The nature of demography and how it can affect organizations.
- The fashions and trends in opinion and preferences that can affect organizations.

25.1 What is the sociological environment?

In one sense, sociological influence on an organization can come from any internal or external source involving *people*. This clearly includes a wide variety of possible stakeholder influences such as customers, employees, suppliers, opinion leaders and trade unions.

The sociological environmental presents two important facets which are relevant to business:

- the features of the population, including its size, distribution, composition and changes (demography);
- the opinions, beliefs, cultural norms and preferences of the population.

We will examine these two components in turn.

25.2 Demography

What is demography

Demography is the study of populations. The scope of the subject includes:

- the size of the population in the country (or a region) as a whole;
- growth or decline in the population;
- the composition of the population by location and distribution;
- the composition of the population by skill and education level;
- the composition of the population by concentration and density;
- the composition of the population by age and gender profile;
- the composition of population by its economic activity (e.g. the size and structure of the working population);
- changes in the population distribution by migration.

Why is demography important to business?

The size, composition and distribution of the population is not just a matter of academic interest. Businesses take account of demography in a number of areas of activity. Its importance is linked to both the demand and supply sides of the market 'equation'.

On the demand side, demography informs a business as to how to organize its location or the distribution of its products. A business is more likely to locate its distribution outlets where there is a high concentration of the key segment of its market. We examined the factors that inform business location in Chapter 6 when we learned that, for some businesses, the concentration of specific types of people is the key determinant of where the business is set up. For retail outlets (shops), for example, the number of 'targeted' people (i.e. those within the market segment boundaries – see Chapter 12) within convenient travelling distance of the shop is of prime importance to the success or failure of the business.

On the supply side, an organization will take account of demography in its access to key inputs. Perhaps the most obvious input in this regard is that of the supply of labour. All businesses must be aware of demography in their search for appropriate labour. One of the key reasons, for example, why motor car manufacturers establish their sites around large centres of population is due to their need for several thousand employees of all types of skill. Clearly, such a demand for labour could not be so easily met in a rural area of lower population density.

Population

'Population' simply refers to the number of people that inhabit a given geographic area. In terms of global demography, the world's total population has shown a significant increase.

The total world population is estimated to have been around 300 million in the year 1000 AD. Between the turn of the first millennium AD and the beginning of the industrial revolution in 1750, it grew relatively slowly to 728 million. Changes in migration, bringing about areas of high demographic concentration since then, has precipitated a significant acceleration in population growth. By 1962 the world population had reached 3000 million (3 billion), and by 1994 it had reached 5.6 billion. Reputable authorities project that the world's population will reach 8.5 billion by the year 2025. Such a marked population increase has given rise to the coining of the phrase 'population explosion'. The concerns associated with such a population explosion include worries about food supply, the implications for the redistribution of wealth and the potential effects on the environment.

In contrast to the rapid increase in the population as a whole, the populations in most of the world's wealthiest countries have remained relatively manageable. This means that the key areas of growth are the poorer and less-developed regions like Africa, India, South and Central America (the Third World). In any country, the determinant of population growth is the disparity between the birth rate and death rate. In developed countries, the death rate has fallen with advances in such things as medical knowledge and healthier living conditions. However, a stable population is more or less maintained because the number of births per year has also fallen as couples have greater access to contraception, are less concerned about infant mortality and more certain of prosperity in old-age.

The population of the UK rose significantly in the first part of the twentieth century. The rate of increase has slowed over time and the population is actually expected to begin to decline mid way through the twenty-first century (Figure 25.1). Table 25.1 describes the changes in more detail.

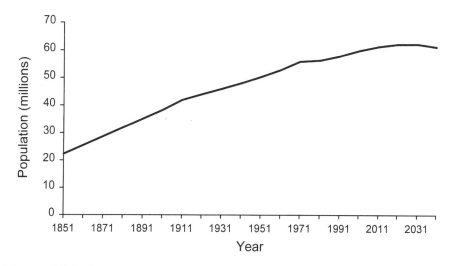

Figure 25.1 Changes in the UK population including projections (Sources: Social Trends, 1995, London: HMSO, and Annual Abstract of Statistics, No. 132, 1996, London: HMSO)

Table 25.1 The UK population, 1901–2051. Source: Social Trends, 1995, London: HMSO, amended from Table 1.3 from the Office of Population Censuses and Surveys; Government Actuary's Department; General Register Office (Scotland); General Register Office (Northern Ireland)

Decade	Population at start of period (thousands)	Live births (thousands)	Deaths (thousands)	Annual change (thousands)
1901–1911	38 237	1,091	624	385
1911–1921	42 082	975	689	194
1921–1931	44 027	824	555	201
1931–1951	46 038	785	598	213
1951–1961	50 287	839	593	252
1961–1971	52 807	963	639	312
1971–1981	55 928	736	666	42
1981–1991	56 352	757	655	145
1991–1993	57 808	779	637	192
1993–2001	58 179	776	623	203
2001–2011	59 800	716	614	146
2011–2021	61 257	718	635	89
2021–2031	62 146	703	693	9
2031–2041	62 241	666	767	−102
2041–2051	61 223	656	819	−163

The twentieth century has witnessed some quite marked variations in birth rate, whilst the death rate (expressed as births and deaths per thousand of the population) has fallen marginally (Figure 25.2). The period from around 1920 to around 1950 showed a marked downturn in the birth rate. This period coincided with a severe economic downturn (the 'depression') in the 1930s, followed by the Second World War (1939–45). Rising prosperity in the 1950s signalled a significant rise in what has become known as the 'baby boom' before falling away again in the 1970s.

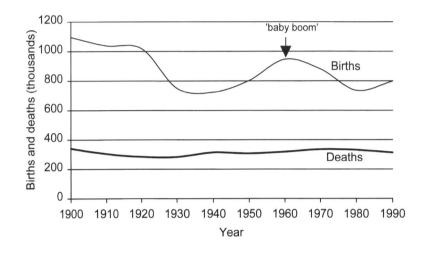

Figure 25.2 Births and deaths in the UK (Source: Social Trends, 1995, London: HMSO)

Age distribution of the UK population

An examination of the death rates for the UK population show an interesting trend. The number of deaths per thousand per year (for men) has fallen from 17.1 in 1900, to 12.6 in 1961, to 11.1 in 1993. The obvious outcome of such statistics is that people are living longer and that the average age of UK residents is becoming higher.

In addition, we have seen that birth rates have tended to be a bit 'lumpy'. Some periods of time seem to engender a higher than usual number of births per thousand (such as the post-War 'baby boom'), whilst other periods show a downturn in births. The result of variations in these two variables means that the age profile is both change-able over time, and at any point in time, is irregular in nature (Figure 25.3).

The broad trends show an overall reduction in people under 16 years and in the next band (16–39 years). At the other end of the age range, the number of older people is increasing. These trends have a number of implications including some important ones for the state. The disparities that are forecast between these age groups indicate that the numbers available to take part in the workforce may fall whilst the numbers of older people will increase. This is expected to become a significant problem, as the older population will require more healthcare and pensions, whilst those available to pay for these provisions through tax will become fewer – one reason why the government may have to take these provisions outside the public sector.

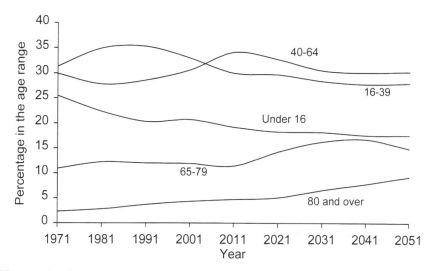

Figure 25.3 Age range distribution of the UK population (1971–2051). (Source: Social Trends, 1995, London: HMSO)

Population density

The population density refers to the number of inhabitants per unit area of land (usually expressed in *persons per square kilometre*). In more common parlance, this means how 'tightly' people are packed together. We can analyse this both across the different parts of the UK and by comparing the UK with other countries (Table 25.2).

Table 25.2 Population densities of selected EU countries. (Source: Eurostat tourism figures)

Country	Population density persons per square kilometre)
EU average	141
UK	238
Germany	228
France	106
Belgium	255
Netherlands	371
Ireland	51
Finland	15

The UK itself has a very wide distribution of population by density. The average for the country (*ca.* 240 per square kilometre) conceals very broad disparities. The area of highest density (Greater London) has a density over 500 times that of the area of lowest density (the Highland Region of Scotland). Greater London contains 4400 people per square kilometre whilst the Highlands of Scotland average only 8 people in an equivalent area (but a much higher concentration of sheep, salmon, otters, etc.).

The bulk of the UK population is concentrated in seven major *conurbations* or centres of particularly high density:

- Greater London;
- Birmingham and the West Midlands;
- Leeds, Bradford;
- Liverpool and Greater Manchester;
- Tyne and Wear (Newcastle and Sunderland);
- Scottish Central Lowlands (Glasgow and Edinburgh);
- South Wales (Cardiff, Swansea, Bridgend).

It is not surprising from such a distribution of density that we find most businesses and social facilities to be similarly distributed. Hence, the centre of the UK's financial and service industry is in London, whilst the West Midlands is particularly known for its high proportion of manufacturing industry. Similarly, facilities like hospitals and universities also show a higher concentration in these conurbations. The distribution of density by region is shown in Figure 25.4.

The population, skills and education

The success or failure of businesses depends in large part on the availability of people with appropriate levels of skills and education. The demographic trends in this respect contain some good news and some not-so-good news for the UK in comparison to its international competitors.

Firstly, the UK has witnessed a marked increase in enrolments in further and higher education and, accordingly, an increase in the number of students pursuing study beyond the age of 16 years. Figure 25.5 shows this increase in one form of post-school education – higher education. The increases are evident in both men and women in higher education, but the largest increase is amongst women. In the years between 1970 and 1992, female enrolments increased by two-and-a-half times. Trends of this nature are considered to be very encouraging for business in the UK. In short, it can be taken to mean that the UK is becoming better educated and more highly skilled. However, the upward trend conceals within it some not so good indicators; for example, a decline in the number of applications to study science and engineering in higher education. This trend has triggered some of the UK's major employers of scientists to run science workshops in schools in an attempt to stimulate pupils' interest in science with a view to increasing the number of quality science graduates in future years.

Question 25.1

Although there are more men than women in higher education, growth in enrolments since 1970 has been slightly higher for women than for men. Suggest reasons for this.

Population density: by area, 1993

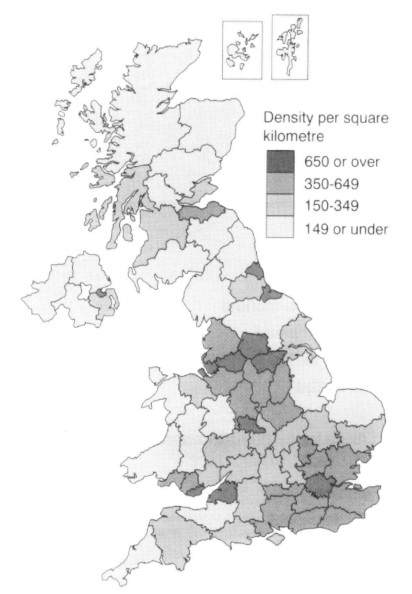

Source: Office of Population Censuses and Surveys;
General Register Office (Scotland); General Register
Office (Northern Ireland)

Figure 25.4 Population density in the UK. (Source: Social Trends, 1995 London: HMSO)

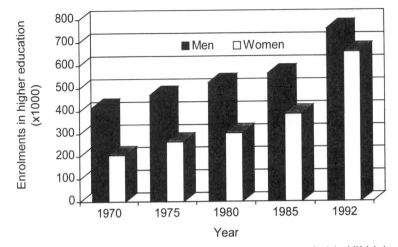

Figure 25.5 Full and part-time course enrolments (by gender) in UK higher education institutes (universities, etc.). (Source: Social Trends, 1995, London: HMSO)

Secondly, although the UK has witnessed an increase in post-school education and training, the same is true of Britain's international competitors. If the education and skill levels of young people is an indicator of how competitive businesses in a country are likely to be (e.g. how many well-educated scientists a country has), then the UK is not doing quite so well as some other countries. As at 1991, 18% of all 18 to 21 year olds in the UK were in some form of higher education (e.g. on HND or degree courses) (Figure 25.6). The figure was twice this in the USA (36%), but half this (9%) in Germany. Since these figures were published, the numbers have continued to rise and are projected to expand further in future years.

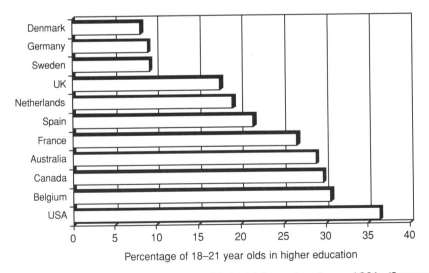

Figure 25.6 Percentage of 18–21 year olds in higher education – 1991. (Source: Social Trends, 1995, London: HMSO)

The changes in the educational level of the population are not, however, restricted to higher education. Notwithstanding the increase in higher education enrolments, graduates still form a relatively small proportion of the population (Table 25.3).

Table 25.3 Education levels in the UK – all categories. (Source: Social Trends, 1995, London: HMSO; from the Office of Population Censuses and Surveys)

Highest qualification held	% of population
Degree	12
Higher education (non degree)	13
GCE A level or equivalent	12
GCSE, grades A-C or equivalent	22
GCSE, grades D-G, apprenticeships or equivalent	10
Foreign	3
No qualifications at all	28

The working population

The size of the working population in a country is important for two reasons:

- Labour, as a factor of production is one of the determinants of the country's ability to add value to goods and services, thus affecting the prosperity of the country.
- The number of people either in work or available to work determines how much money the government can raise in tax revenues. This, in turn, influences the quality of life and the ability of the state to provide public and merit goods and services.

We might expect the size of the working population roughly to reflect the size of the population as a whole and, whilst this is broadly true, a number of factors have introduced complications in the relationship between the two (Figure 25.7). The fact that the UK's residents are living longer means that there are more old (i.e. retired and therefore economically inactive) people in the population. When this is combined with a more or less falling birth rate, the result is a complicated picture with, as we have seen, some potentially worrying consequences.

25.2 Fashions and trends in society

In addition to changes in the size and structure of the population (demographics), it is also true that populations change in their preferences. In some cases, fashions and trends are linked to demographic trends (such as an increased demand for baby clothes during a period of increased birth rate), but at other times preferences change seemingly 'by themselves'. Some types of preference seem to change often, whilst others show a consistent increase or decrease over time. This is the nub of the difference between fashions and trends.

- A *fashion* is generally taken to mean a relatively temporary increase in preference. Fashions may also be roughly cyclical and are difficult to predict.

- A trend is a longer-term change in consumer preference. Consumers sometimes demonstrate a long-term increase or decrease in their preferences.

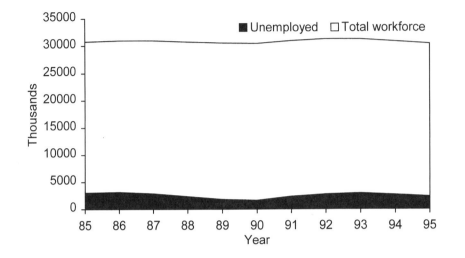

Figure 25.7 Composition of the workforce. (*Source: Annual Abstract of Statistics, 1996, No, 132, London: HMSO.*)

Questions 25.2

Fashions and trends can apply to product preferences. Suggest three product types that are currently in fashion and three that are currently showing a trend in increased popularity.

It is important to appreciate that fashions and trends do not refer just to products. Opinions, beliefs and forms of behaviour are also subject to change. In some areas of opinion, such as political polling, opinion changes form the basis of entire industries. Some areas of human preference are notoriously fickle, such as many things associated with health. The changes in opinion in March and April 1996 associated with the concerns over the 'safety' of British beef is an example of how rapidly human opinion can be influenced.

Fashions and trends with an economic cause

Over the past twenty-five years or so, one of the key underlying economic trends has been an increased prosperity for the majority of the population. This trend alone has been the cause of many changed preferences in consumption.

Increased 'real' disposable income per capita has engendered a number of key changes in both preferences and spending patterns. The most obvious change resulting from increased disposable income is an insistence on higher quality and of generally being more selective in many matters of purchasing. In the case of some products, increasing prosperity has coincided with falling product prices. This category includes most types of consumer electronic goods and food.

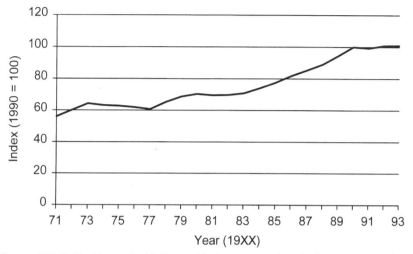

Figure 25.8 Real household disposable income per head of population (after taking inflation into account). (Source: Social Trends, 1995, London: HMSO)

The food industry is an interesting case (Figure 25.9). The combination of increasing real wages and lower real (after inflation) prices has brought about a plethora of changes in the food supply industry. In the early 1970s, the first supermarkets in the UK were known for their 'pile 'em high, sell 'em cheap' philosophy with the general belief that price was the most important buying decider for customers. Increased buying power coupled with cheaper food real prices has precipitated a general trend in higher quality foods, more choice and a much wider choice of food products.

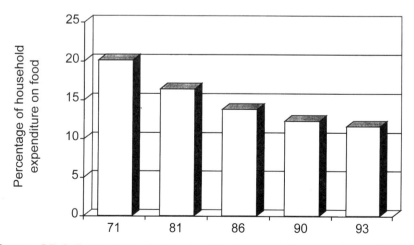

Figure 25.9 Percentage of total household expenditure on food, 1971–1993. (Source: Social Trends, 1995, London: HMSO)

A similar trend can be seen in other consumer products. Expenditure on alcohol has fallen from 7.3% of average household expenditure in 1971 to 6.1% in 1993. This downward trend is, like food, the result of increasing real spending power and a reduction or stabilization in the real price of alcoholic beverages. The case of food is reflected in the alcohol markets – more choice, more exotic products, more competition and an insistence on higher quality.

We might reasonably ask what the average household has done with its increased real income. If expenditure on food and alcohol has fallen, what areas of household expenditure have risen? The answer is, perhaps predictably, complicated. One outlet for increased spending power is on housing, where spending has risen from 12.4% of household expenditure in 1971 to 15.7% in 1993. Part of this increase is due to an increasing trend in the amount we spend on our homes, part on the increase in home ownership and part on increases in mortgage costs. The most marked increase in expenditure is, however, in the areas of transport and leisure. This increase, perhaps more than any other, is indicative of the increased standard of living enjoyed by UK citizens over the past twenty-five years. Over this time, we have collectively increased our expenditure on motor cars (because car ownership has grown) and on leisure activities like holidays, sport and entertainment.

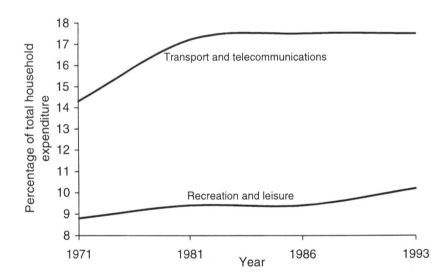

Figure 25.10 Expenditure on transport and communication, recreational activities as a percentage of household expenditure. (Source: Social Trends, 1995, London: HMSO)

Changes in human opinion

In addition to changes in wealth and preferences in expenditure, the population also collectively changes its opinion. Unlike changes resulting from economic changes, opinion changes tend to be less predictable due to their more complicated cause. We have the space to look at only a small sample of 'opinion' issues.

Environmental opinion

One area in which opinion has changed quite dramatically is in concern over the Earth's environment (see Chapter 26). Within this area, however, the collective opinion of the population has shown itself to be relatively volatile. Table 25.4 shows changes in environmental opinion over the four-year period 1989–1993. We can see from this table that a handful of issues seem to attract more public concern that others. Over half of the population are 'very worried' about river pollution, toxic and radioactive waste and beach pollution. It is also interesting to note that, in many of the areas of concern listed, the percentage of people 'very worried' has fallen over the period in question. For example, less people are concerned about ozone layer depletion, global warming and acid rain than they were previously.

Table 25.4 People who were 'very worried' about various environmental issues – England and Wales (Source: Social Trends, 1995, London: HMSO)

	% of population	
Issue	*1989*	*1993*
Chemicals in rivers/seas	64	63
Toxic waste: disposal/import	–	63
Radioactive waste	58	60
Sewage on beaches/bathing water	59	56
Oil spills at sea/on beaches	53	52
Tropical forest destruction	44	45
Loss of plants/animals in UK	–	43
Ozone layer depletion	56	41
Traffic exhaust fumes/urban smog	33	40
Drinking water quality	41	38
Loss of plants/animals abroad	–	38
Use of insecticides/fertilizers	46	36
Loss of trees/hedgerows	34	36
Losing Green Belt land	27	35
Fumes and smoke from factories	34	35
Traffic congestion	–	35
Global warming	44	35
Acid rain	40	31
Litter/rubbish	33	29
Fouling by dogs	29	29
Using up United Kingdom's natural resources	–	27
Decay of inner cities	22	26
Household waste disposal	–	22
Need for more energy conservation	–	21
Vacant/derelict land/buildings	16	19
Not enough recycling	–	19
Noise	13	16

Notwithstanding the variable indicators in the wide variety of environmental matters, there has been an increase in the recycling of all types of materials. This may be indicative of a more broadly based change of opinion toward environmental concern (Table 25.5).

Table 25.5 Recycling levels in the UK. (Source: Social Trends, 1995, London: HMSO)

	% of material recycled			
Material	*1990*	*1991*	*1992*	*2000 (target)*
Paper and board	31	34	34	
Waste paper used in news	27	28	31	40
Glass	21	21	26	50
Aluminium cans	6	11	16	50
Steel cans	9	10	12	–
Plastics	2	–	5	–

Other selected areas of opinion

The large number of changes that have occurred over recent decades in demography and in economic prosperity have precipitated many changes in attitude in their wake. When we add in factors such as global communications, which make us all much more aware of the world, we can see that there are many potential influences upon our attitudes and actions.

Many people have become much more health-conscious than they were (or than their parents were). Things that fifty years ago would not even been heard about can now change customer buying patterns in quite drastic ways. A large number of people have taken to activities like jogging and aerobics, whilst 'unhealthy' products like polysaturated fats have been on the decline. The number of people in the UK who smoke cigarettes has declined from 41% of the population in 1970 to 28% in 1992.

Some may argue that we have also become increasingly isolated we tend to spend more of our leisure time watching television and playing computer games and less time than we used to in more social pursuits. This is beneficial for television advertisers, but some have expressed concern that such trends may pose an eventual threat to the cohesion of society. In addition, increasing numbers choose to travel alone, evidenced by the increase in car ownership from 277 cars per thousand people in 1981 to 367 per thousand in 1992.

Changing leisure pursuits are also in evidence in the ways in which we choose to take our holidays. Whereas at one time the typical family holiday comprised a week at the nearest seaside resort to the family home, increased prosperity and increased leisure time have signalled the growth of important industries. In 1970, UK residents took a total of 4.2 million foreign holidays. By 1992, this figure had increased to over 23 million – good news for the airline and holiday industries, not such good news for hotel owners in Bognor, Bridlington, Blackpool and Bexhill.

Assignment

- Some have argued that increased prosperity has given rise to the phenomenon of consumers giving greater emphasis to the ethical behaviour of those from whom they buy. Discuss the possible links between rising prosperity and ethical awareness and indicate whether you feel that such a link exists.
- The next fifty years are expected to witness a rise in the number of retired people and a relative decline in the number of younger people. Discuss the implications of these changes for the National Health Service, the university system and the government's finances.

Further reading

Auster, C. J. (1996) *The Sociology of Work. Concepts and Cases*. Thousands Oaks, CA: Sage.

Weeks, J. R. (1994) *Population. An Introduction to Concepts and Issues*, 5th edn. Thomson.

See also further reading at the end of Chapter 26.

26

Environment and ethics

Learning objectives

After studying this chapter, students should be able to describe:

- The ways in which businesses respond to social concerns.
- The range of ethical and environmental concerns.
- The nature of environmental concern, with examples.
- The nature of ethical concern, with examples.

26.1 A changing cultural and societal environment

A significant change has taken place in business over the past twenty years or so. Whereas at one time for-profit organizations operated on the principle that, as Milton Friedman said, 'the business of business is business', recent developments have focused on the wider social responsibility of organizations which may not directly be in the pursuit of purely profit aims. The change centres around the question of the extent to which the business has some degree of responsibility to the other members (corporate and individual) of society and the extent to which a business should account for the opinions of the wider public.

In once sense, this change in thinking is testimony to the power of an organization's stakeholders. In purely economic terms, shareholders have traditionally viewed profitability as the only legitimate objective business, but this has been modified in the light of a number of key concerns among the wider stakeholder community.

The increased concerns have encompassed a wide variety of issues, and most readers will be able to list many of them from their own experience. In this chapter, we deal with the various issues under two broad headings:

- concerns over the physical (natural) environment; and,
- concern over a range of ethical matters.

Sociologists may argue over how this cultural change was initially brought about. Certainly our awareness of wider issues has been heightened by the spectacular rise in global communications. The events in a famine-stricken country are brought directly into our living-rooms through television, whilst scientists ruminate before millions of viewers about the effects of global warming and acid rain. Pictures are broadcast of calves in veal-crates or dogs in scientific experiments, presenting us with a graphic illustration of some people's concerns. Coupled with these features has been an increasing sense that business and government has a responsibility to hear the concerns of interested parties and that stakeholders collectively, can 'make a difference'. Figure

26.1 shows how three of the major conservation societies in the UK have grown in membership over the past twenty or so years, reflecting the increased concern among individuals over environmental and ethical issues.

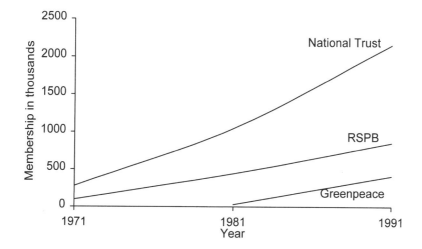

Figure 26.1 Trends in membership of three selected voluntary conservation organizations. (Source: *Social Trends*, 1995, London: HMSO)

26.2 Business and social responsibility

As we have seen, there is an implicit assumption that for-profit businesses exist primarily to make a profit before all else. However, given that a business benefits from society (e.g. from its provision of skilled employees and customers), the question arises as to how much businesses should take account of wider social issues in their policies and decisions.

In practice, the social responsiveness of an organization depends upon its various stakeholder influences and the personalities and convictions of its management, much as it might do for an individual. Some individuals take great care to buy goods with minimal packaging, to recycle all their glass, paper, etc., and to avoid animal products which have been produced through alleged 'cruelty' to the animal. Others adopt an altogether more indifferent or cavalier approach to wider environmental and ethical issues, not giving a moment's thought to such matters.

It is important to appreciate, however, that many of the areas of concern in environment and ethics are covered by a wide range of (mainly) statute laws. There are therefore some issues that are not open to interpretation by individual businesses – a 'minimum' standard of corporate behaviour is required by the legal underpinning. In this context, laws cover such things as industrial pollution, fish catches in the sea, employment practices (the way the organization treats its employees), disclosure of some information and advertising statements (which must be legal, decent, honest and truthful). Such a regulatory regime clearly reduces the scope of an organization to be guilty of environmental and ethical 'sin', but in large part still leaves some room for debate and voluntary restraint over and above the legal minimum.

We might expect, therefore, a wide range of opinions and practices amongst businesses to their wider role in society. We can divide business responses to social responsibility by considering four broad categories:

- Some businesses are actively *socially obstructive*. This description can be applied to organizations that actively resist any pressures or attempts to modify pure business objectives in the light of social concern. Such organizations may resist attempts to make them abide even by the minimum legal standards of behaviour – behaviour which may be followed by denial and an attempt to keep 'interfering' bodies out of their business. Some have argued that tobacco manufacturers fall into this category as in order to protect their sales of cigarettes, they may effectively deny that tobacco causes as much harm as some health professionals have indicated.
- Some businesses observe no more than their minimum *social obligations*. This description can be applied to organizations that are prepared to abide by whatever restrictions are placed upon them by governments, in other words, the legal minimum. They are unwilling to give credence to any pressure or lobby groups which, in the opinion of the organization, do not have any statutory influence over them.
- The third group are those that are *socially responsive*. These organizations submit to minimum legal standards for corporate behaviour towards society and the environment, but go further than socially obligative organizations. The difference is that socially responsive organizations will do more to address people's concerns if pressurized to do so by stakeholders such as pressure groups.
- The final group are those organizations which seek to make a *social contribution*. This description can be applied to organizations that willingly do all they reasonably can to extend their social and environmental involvement. In this sense, such organizations seek to make a positive contribution to the communities they serve, to help protect the natural environment and to avoid any unethical business practices. Some social contribution organizations may exist primarily for the purpose of promoting social responsibility and ethical business practice.

26.3 A taxonomy of concern

In order to examine the issues that businesses must face, we can consider the two broad categories of *environment* and *ethics*, and the various concerns that are subsumed under each one (Table 26.1). Some thinkers in this area would consider environmental concern to fall under the broad heading of ethics, but for the sake of our discussion, it will be clearer if we view them separately.

We can see from the taxonomy (classification) given in Table 26.1 that environmental concern has two subcategories: concerns over the Earth's resources and concerns over the pollution by individuals and businesses of the natural environment. Both of these are of potentially great interest to businesses because:

- It is primarily businesses that extract materials from the Earth and use them as a factor of production.
- Much of the criticism that surrounds the pollution debate has been made against

businesses. Examples of this include bad engine design in cars and emissions from chemical plants into the environment.

Table 26.1 A taxonomy of concern

Key area	Subsidiary concerns	Examples of personal opinion areas
Environmental concern	Resource issues	• Energy resources and conservation • Mineral resources and conservation • Extinction and overfishing
	Pollution issues	• Global warming • Ozone depletion • Health concerns (e.g. skin cancer, asthma) • Industrial emission • Rubbish and waste (including nuclear) • 'Acid' rain
Ethical concern	Arising from the nature of markets	• Third World debt management • Fair Trade • Multinational company 'exploitation'
	Arising from the business's responsibility to society	• Community involvement • Marketing practices (e.g. corporate sponsorships and advertising) • Animal 'cruelty' issues • Product health and safety • Compensation and reparations (e.g. drugs, oil spills)
	Arising from the internal and industry activities of the business	• Employment practices • Health and safety in the workplace • Treatment of women and minorities • Treatment of suppliers, customers and other stakeholders

The ethical debate is slightly more complicated than the environmental one. Whilst there is a broad agreement that 'something should be done' about the environment, there is a wider spectrum of opinion in matters of ethics and morals. Some First World consumers actively campaign for higher ethical standards, whilst others adopt the opinion, either stated or unstated, that whilst global warming may in time affect them the plight of the Third World or the experiences of farm animals do not. This approach, slightly cynically labelled the 'I'm alright Jack' philosophy, is present to a greater or lesser extent in all First World societies. The issue is also complicated by the plethora of different religious and cultural convictions held by individuals in the various parts of the world.

Different 'worlds'

The terms First and Third World are used a great deal by groups concerned about environmental and ethical matters.

The *First World* is generally taken to mean the sector of the world comprising the wealthy industrialized nations of Western Europe, North America, the Pacific Rim (e.g. Japan), Australia and New Zealand. The temperate climates and stable democratic government in these countries has, over time, provided a business climate which encourages industrial investment, increasing wealth and a high quality of life for its citizens.

The *Second World* is less industrialized than the First World, but still enjoys some degree of industrial development. It comprises Eastern Europe, the former USSR and some regions of Asia and South America. In many cases, Second World countries fall behind First World countries due to centralized economic planning and a state regime that does not encourage private industrial investment.

The *Third World* comprises predominantly most of Africa, and parts of South America and Asia. Such countries are characterized by a low income per capita resulting from relatively poor agricultural output and low industrial development. Third World economies tend to be simple in nature with a currency of low exchange value. In practice, Third World countries often have high levels of debt and high inflation accompanied by a lower standard of living than those in other parts of the world.

26.4 The nature of concern 1: environmental issues

We have seen that environmental concern has two parts: concern over the Earth's resources and concern over pollution.

Resource issues

There can be no doubt that the Earth contains only a finite amount of material. The supply of oil, coal, minerals, etc., is therefore not inexhaustible. It is also the case, therefore, that as time passes and as we use up resources, that fewer and fewer reserves are left to extract.

The problem of diminishing resources has two prominent causes. Firstly, the economic growth across the world over the past century or so has meant that resources have been used in order to produce goods that are in turn used by consumers. By their very nature, manufactured goods require a material input which must be obtained, ultimately, from the Earth. Similarly, industrial growth needs energy to turn raw materials into manufactured goods – another requirement for the Earth's resources. Secondly, the growth in population – one of the main causes of increased economic growth – has accelerated the consumption of resources. At the turn of the nineteenth century, the world population was not a cause for concern but, as it has grown (see Chapter 25), the rate of resource consumption has grown accordingly.

Energy resources

In the context of our current discussion, energy is taken to mean the materials that are used to make energy. These are (principally):

- natural gas;
- oil;
- coal;
- nuclear materials.

The first three of these (gas, oil and coal) are known as fossil fuels, due to their having an organic origin (formerly living matter). Materials used in nuclear power generation, on the other hand, are minerals that are mined. There is some confusion as to the precise quantity of energy resources left in the Earth, mainly because oil companies, who spend a lot of time and money prospecting, frequently come across new oil fields which can supply future demands. In consequence, estimates of future reserves are continually being revised.

Opinion is split as to how concerned we should be about energy reserves. Some contend that, because they are bound to run out eventually, we should be making investments now to find alternative sources of renewable energy. Others say that, because the problem of running out is not immediate, there is no need to be too concerned for the foreseeable future (i.e. for the next century). The economics of the energy business make it difficult to allocate too much money to the development of renewable sources (sources which do not use up finite resources, such as solar, wind and wave power). Like all businesses, they must provide a return to their shareholders, so the incurrence of excessive development costs would make the companies less attractive to investors. Notwithstanding this, there has been an increased level of interest in renewable energy among some parts of the academic community.

The fuels that cause the most concern are those which are in shortest supply, which, as may be expected, are also those in greatest usage. Estimates of the 'number of years' left of these fuels varies according to the source of the information and the assumptions made regarding the level of consumption and price. The figures given in Table 26.2, from British Nuclear Fuels Limited (BNFL), are typical.

Table 26.2 Energy reserves – world (BNFL, 1993)

Fuel	Years left – (approx.)
Oil	50
Gas	50
Coal	220
Nuclear	1000

Of course, in addition to the 'world' estimates given in Figure 26.2, the UK has its own oil and gas reserves, mainly in the shallow continental shelf waters in the North Sea and, to a lesser extent, the Atlantic. It is difficult to estimate how much is left to be

exploited in British waters, as there are fields still to be fully exploited. The best estimates in 1993 suggested that 44% of the UK's oil reserves and 32% of the UK's gas
have been extracted. The worst estimates suggest a rather more serious picture, with
perhaps as much as 73% of oil reserves having been exhausted and as much as 60% of
gas.

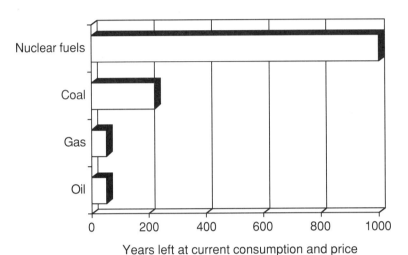

Years left at current consumption and price

Figure 26.2 Projected energy reserves (approximate) at current usage and prices.
(Source: BNFL, 1993)

It is interesting to note that nuclear fuels, possibly the most controversial form of
energy, are also the most abundant. Nuclear generators would also be keen to point out
that, whereas fossil fuels contribute to pollution in the process of power generation,
nuclear fuels do not. This is not to say that the storage of used nuclear fuel is without
its problems.

Mineral and forestry resources
Minerals are those materials which form the basis of many important manufactured
products. Prominent minerals are metal ores (from which metals are extracted), materials used in building (e.g. lime, silicates) and chemicals. The importance of these
materials as industrial inputs is beyond dispute and various parties have expressed
concern over these reserves.

It is as difficult to arrive at accurate estimates of the actual world reserves of many
minerals as it is for energy reserves. Whilst it is obvious that reserves are finite, known
reserves for some materials actually rise over time as more are discovered in different
parts of the planet. Notwithstanding this, extraction is usually expensive, especially if
the mining takes place in remote parts of the Earth. For reasons of their cost and their
finiteness, recycling of some materials has become increasingly common. Whilst recycling is possible for materials like metals, it is not possible for many non-metallic
resources such as talc and gypsum.

Forestry attracts similar concern to minerals. Most of us will have heard of concern
over the equatorial rain forests. This are vast areas of natural hard-wood forests which
are important for two reasons. They not only provide a natural habitat for a huge range

of plants and animals, but the trees themselves collectively play an important part in the Earth's eco-system. Over recent decades, the equatorial forests have been subject to clearance at a rate faster than they can regrow. On a more local level, moves have been made to increase tree coverage in many non-equatorial parts of the world, including in the UK. This is an attempt partly to redress a potential ecological imbalance and partly to support *sustainability*. This is a term applied to forestry that is replaced at least as rapidly as it is harvested.

What is an ecosystem?

The initial observation that all life on Earth exists in a type of balance was made by Professor Arthur Tansley in 1936. We should understand that the concept is very complicated.

For our purposes, we can define an ecosystem as follows:

An eco-system is a self-sustaining complex of interdependent organisms (both animals and plants) and a range of physical environmental factors which exists within a sustainable equilibrium.

The key themes of an ecosystem are that animals and plants are interdependent with each other and with their environment. This means that each organism is dependent upon and is turn, depended on for the normal continuance of life. Each species of organism, as well as being interdependent on other life, is in equilibrium with 'external' environmental factors such as chemical nutrients and energy from the sun. The totality of the ecosystem takes account of all organisms on Earth and even influences beyond the Earth, that is energy from the sun. In practice, to make the study of ecosystems easier, they are sub-divided into regional ecosystems such as that which exists in a desert, in a rainforest or even in the duck pond in the local park. Eventually, all of these 'mini' ecosystems are part of the global picture and none exist truly in isolation.

The delicate balance of an ecosystem can be upset when any single part of it is interfered with. For example, an increase in the intensity of the sun may cause plants to disappear in some areas of the world. In turn, herbivorous (plant-eating) animals will also die out. Next, the carnivorous (meat-eating) animals that eat the herbivores will die out. The fact that such animals do not live on the land will, in turn, make the deficiency of plants even worse – there will be no animal waste and decomposing animal matter to feed the soil on which the plants grow. The 'knock-on' effects of any disturbance in any part of an eco-system demonstrates the complexity of the balance.

Extinction and overfishing

A discussion of species extinction and stock shortage involves extending our definition of 'resources' beyond material resources in the Earth. Concern over these matters rests upon the supposition that a balance of species on the Earth is an essential requirement to maintain the stability of the Earth's ecosystem. From time to time, we see on television a report on a species in one part of the Earth that is in danger of extinction. Such reports can generate strong feelings among viewers and have been known to influence business practice such as advertising campaigns.

One of the more topical and close to home 'life stock' issues pertains to fish in the seas in and around Europe. Although few of the major species of fish are threatened with global extinction, their numbers in some key localized regions has given cause for concern. The decline in fish stocks can be seen by examining some simple figures. In 1970, it was estimated that the North Sea contained 263 000 tonne of breeding cod and 403 000 tonne of breeding haddock. By 1990, both of these had been reduced to around 64 000 tonne each.

The problems of overfishing has been of concern for some time. It is estimated that fish stocks in the Baltic Sea (in northern Europe) are now so depleted that fishing must completely stop immediately if stocks are not to be irreparably damaged. The European Union (EU), in partial response to this problem, has introduced quotas – maximum limits placed upon member states' catches per year. There is some evidence that reduction in quotas does allow stocks to recover. Fishing for herring in the North Sea was banned in 1977 for a period of five years. During this period, breeding stocks recovered from 300 000 breeding-tonnes to the more sustainable level of 1.2 million breeding-tonnes.

Pollution issues

As economic growth, population and consumption have increased over the course of the twentieth century, so the waste arising from consumption has increased. Physical waste, by definition, unless it can be reused, is defined as pollution. The concerns over pollution are two-fold:

- Some concern exists that *certain pollution exists at all*. This occurs when the pollution represents a visual 'eye-sore' (e.g. slagheaps) or when it is potentially hazardous (e.g. nuclear waste).
- The second area concerns the *effects of pollution on other things*. It is thought, for example, that pollution is a major contributor to global warming, ozone depletion and ecological imbalance. On a more local level, rubbish put into a landfill may pollute local water courses.

Refuse and waste
Physical refuse and waste is an unfortunate result of almost all consumption. Industry produces waste, whether it be in the form of empty containers or piles of burnt coal from a power station. Consumers produce waste from households in the form of used packaging, etc.

The problems from refuse arise mainly from decisions concerning its treatment or disposal. The simple choices of burn it or store it are both equally undesirable in their own ways. Burning thousands of tonnes of refuse each year would itself be a major contributor to atmospheric pollution, whilst storing it makes significant demands on space. The favoured method in the UK is to use refuse as a form of land fill – a process of burying refuse and then covering with a layer of topsoil. In other countries, refuse is systematically dumped into shallow sections of coastal seawaters. The result of this is that new 'islands' of rubbish are eventually created.

Some forms of refuse that cannot be stored must be burned. This includes clinical waste (e.g. human tissues, pharmaceuticals and used medical consumables such as hypodermic needles) and some industrial by-products. The process of incineration of such materials also presents its own unique problems. It is often the case that such materials release toxic or pungent chemicals on incineration which, as well as constituting an atmospheric pollutant, is unpopular with local residents.

One form of waste which is of unique concern is spent material from nuclear power generation. Notwithstanding the benefits of nuclear power, nuclear waste has two major drawbacks:

- It is associated with the causation of several serious health hazards. Notable among these are concerns over fears that nuclear waste is:
  - carcinogenic – (causing cancers);
  - teratogenic – (causing birth defects);
  - mutagenic – (causing genetic defects in sex cells).
- It remains a health hazard for a very long time. Some forms of nuclear waste can remain radioactive for as long as 20 000 years.

Although some nuclear fuels can be reprocessed and used again, it follows that all nuclear materials must eventually be stored as waste. Some pressure groups have led vocal campaigns to reduce or eliminate the use of nuclear fuels, mainly for the reasons outlined above.

Industrial pollution

Whilst in one respect the causes of pollution rest with increased consumption as populations have increased, some sectors of industry are viewed by many as being particularly culpable of environmental irresponsibility. The most frequently criticized sector is the chemicals industry. There are two principal causes of 'industrial' pollution.

Firstly, and by far the most important are the *intentional emissions* (by design) that some chemical plants produce as a result of the chemical processes carried out. It is an unavoidable fact that most chemical reactions produce by-products which are of no commercial interest to the business, and these are usually discharged from the plant. Gaseous waste is discharged into the atmosphere whilst liquid waste is often discharged into local water systems (e.g. rivers). The precise method of disposal of industrial by-products will, of course, depend on the chemical nature of the material. Local authorities grant permission for some materials to be discharged, and so a certain amount of policing occurs.

The second type of industrial pollution is that which happens *by accident*. Although, by volume, spillages and leaks account for less than that produced by emissions, they are often more serious in the short term owing to a high concentration of a chemical 'nasty' in a localized area. The concern over such accidents is heightened by the facts that they are invariably well publicized and that they can wreak havoc on local environments, and in some circumstances can affect human life in the locality.

Industrial accidents – two notable chemical cases

Union Carbide – Bhopal, India.
Union Carbide Corp. (UCar) is a multi-national chemicals group based in the USA. Like its major international competitors, UCar is very widely spread geographically, owning as it does plants and outlets in many countries throughout the world. The UCar plant in Bhopal, a town in northern India, was just one of its plants in the Asian continent.

The Bhopal plant was geared up to make a pesticide called Sevin. This product contained several chemicals, a major constituent being a highly toxic material called methylisocyanate (MIC). The MIC used to make Sevin was stored on the Bhopal site.

An accident occurred on 3 December 1984, when water entered a tank containing MIC. This caused a rupture of the MIC container and a cloud of the toxic gas leaked out into the atmosphere. The prevailing wind at the time unfortunately carried the cloud across the town of Bhopal. Within a few hours, the gas had killed 2600 local people and its effects left an estimated 300 000 people with long-term respiratory problems. By 1991 it was estimated that one person per day was still dying in Bhopal as a result of the MIC leakage.

The Exxon Valdez oil spill – Alaska
Exxon is one of the world's largest companies. As a multi-national oil company, it operates all over the world and in the UK, is usually known by its Esso brand-name.

Like all major oil companies, Exxon ships massive quantities of crude oil around the world in large tankers. One of its ships, the *Exxon Valdez* was involved in an accident in March 1989. The tanker ran aground in a particularly environmentally sensitive waterway in Alaska and spilled its load of crude oil into the surrounding sea. The 11 million gallons of crude oil caused significant damage to the wildlife in and around 1100 miles of coastline in Prince William Sound. Fatalities of the spill were half a million birds, 5500 sea otters, in addition to the loss of fish and flora in the Sound. Ecologists surveying the scene considered it one of the worst industrial accidents ever as far as its environmental implications are concerned.

'Global' effects of pollution
Whilst the above concerns about pollution are prevalent, there is more concern about the effects of pollution of the global eco-system than the other two, although all factors in this category are more or less interlinked. It has been suggested that the aggregate effects of all sources of pollution are having an effect on the eco-system of the Earth as a whole. Experts differ on the extent of the threat, but there seems to be an increasing convergence of opinion on some matters.

The 'global threat' causing most concern is that of *global warming*. According to holders of this concern, the effects of continual build-up of certain pollutants in the atmosphere cause the Earth's atmosphere to act a bit like a greenhouse (it has been labelled 'the greenhouse effect'). This means that, whilst the sun's rays enter the atmosphere and heat the Earth, some of them are prevented from leaking away into space by pollutants in the atmosphere. The effect of this is that the average temperatures on the ground rise over time. The main pollutant causing this effect is thought to be carbon dioxide – a gas produced by burning fossil fuels such as coal, gas and petrol, and by animal life itself in the form of exhaled air. If the average temperature on the Earth rises then, it is believed, a major climatic change will result over the longer term. Although the problem of global warming is (as its name suggests) global, its effects may be felt at a local level. Adverse effects of such a change would be include rising sea levels as polar ice caps melt. This would have the effect of increasing the area of desert in equatorial regions and of flooding large areas of low-lying land such as parts of Holland and areas of England like Lincolnshire and East Anglia. Crop production would be reduced and a number of health problems would be in greater evidence.

A second effect of global proportion is that of *ozone depletion*. The ozone layer is a thin layer of triatomic oxygen molecules high in the Earth's atmosphere. Its effects include the ability to deflect harmful (e.g. carcinogenic) ultra-violet (UV) solar rays away from the Earth. British research societies which monitor the ozone layer report that the problem of the disappearing ozone layer is most marked around the poles, but that the trend is very much towards expansion of these holes. An increased incidence of UV rays on the Earth, as well as adding to global warming, also represents a hazard to health owing to the ability of UV rays to increase the risk of skin cancers in susceptible people. Pollutants thought to contribute to ozone depletion include carbon dioxide, but most particularly a group of chemicals called chlorinated fluorocarbons (CFCs). Traditionally, CFCs were used as propellants in aerosols, as refrigerants and as industrial gases (e.g. for inflating foam plastics). The concern over the effects of CFCs has meant that, in most applications, they have been replaced (Figure 26.3). It is thought, however, that the effects of CFCs on the ozone layer will continue to be negative for some time after their complete removal (owing to the nature of the chemical reaction they bring about).

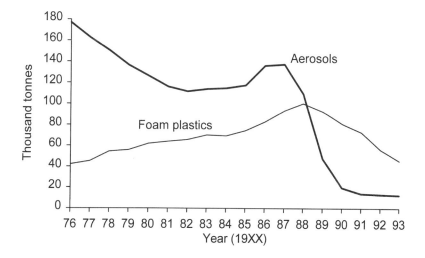

Figure 26.3 *Sales of CFCs in the EU in thousands of tonnes per year for two of their main uses. (Source: Social Trends, 1995, London: HMSO)*

The third major concern, although lesser in significance, is over *'acid' rain*. The increased concentration of gases resulting from fossil fuel combustion, particularly carbon dioxide and sulphur dioxide, is predominantly to 'blame' for this effect. Sulphur dioxide, emitted from coal power stations, rises and reacts with water in the atmosphere to form precipitated sulphurous acid. The acid causes damage to plants and water systems when it eventually falls as rain.

26.5 The nature of concern 2: ethical issues

Ethics as a business issue is considerably more complex than concern over the environment. The variety of opinions held over ethical issues can be attributed to the wide spectrum of systems of belief that people hold. Some individuals have a deep sense of concern for almost all ethical issues, some focus on one area of concern (e.g. animal use by business or Third World issues), whilst others don't seem too concerned about any of it.

The variety of opinions held also makes it much harder to circumscribe the issues that might fall into this category. There are many issues that are not of major concern but are strongly held by some consumers in some societies, for example for a specific religious reason.

In the taxonomy outlined at the beginning of this chapter, we saw that the ethical debate can be distilled into three areas, each of which has a number of subsidiary concerns. We will briefly examine each in turn.

Ethical issues arising from the nature of markets

One of the problems with the nature of markets is that they are concerned with rationing. We learned in Chapter 17 that the market mechanism serves to bring buyers and sellers together at a price that provides an economic return to sellers whilst at the same time satisfying the needs of the buyers as a collective group. One of the problems with this approach is that a market price necessarily prohibits some individual consumers from enjoying the benefits of the product. The market system thus inevitably results in inequalities. Some consumers have a great deal more than the 'average' consumer, whilst others have much less. In many areas of life and business, we freely accept this in that we realize that we cannot all afford certain items, such as BMW motor cars. In other cases, however, the nature of markets results in inequalities that appear to some to be a little unfair.

Part of the inequality of both the demand and supply sides of the market system arises due to the fact that factors of production are not evenly distributed. Some countries and regions of the world, for example, have inherently better land, better resource reserves and national cultures that are apparently more conducive to business success than others. In consequence, it is an unavoidable fact that some countries are richer and more economically powerful than others.

Countries that are wealthy – those in the First World – have the opportunity to exert influence over poorer countries who have weaker currencies and sometimes intense economic problems. Concern has arisen over some business practices that rest upon this disparity of wealth and currency value. The award of a contract or a sale from a

First World based company to a Third World supplier results in an inflow of 'hard' (high exchange value) currency, and this represents an opportunity for powerful First World multinationals to 'exploit' the weaker Third World producers (using the 'bargaining power of buyers and suppliers' we encountered in Chapter 20 – Porter's five-force model). This can result in the producer acting unethically to meet the order (such as by employing child labour) or by otherwise acting irresponsibly. Alleged irresponsibility arises when, for example, food crops which could provide food for local people are replaced with 'cash-crops' to sell abroad to gain foreign currency.

Ethical issues arising from the responsibility of business to society

The second area from which ethical concern arises is in the way in which businesses respond to the opinions of their external stakeholders in society. In Chapter 2 we learned that an organization has a wide range of potential stakeholders, often with conflicting aspirations for the organization. The manner in which an organization should respond to its stakeholders is often a matter of controversy. We also learned in Chapter 2 that there are two models to explain the organization–stakeholder relationship.[1] The normative model suggests that an organization responds to its stakeholders because they have legitimate rights over the affairs of the organization and that the organization sees stakeholders as ends in themselves. Conversely, the instrumental approach argues that organizations observe stakeholder aspirations only inasmuch as they are consistent with maximizing profits.

There is often a tension between the wishes of shareholders who have an economic interest in the business's profits, and the wishes of 'community' stakeholders who tend to exhort the business to behave in a more 'responsible' way even although this may result in suboptimal profits.

Underpinning the idea that businesses should behave responsibly towards society is the belief that businesses, like individual people, are *citizens* of society. Citizens are members of society who have both rights to benefits from society and responsibilities towards it. It is self-evident that businesses benefit from society as a supplier of labour and customers. Accordingly, advocates of the normative model subscribe to the belief that businesses have a moral and ethical responsibility to behave as responsible citizens. In many situations, serving the social responsibilities (to society) of a business may result in short-term costs, but it is nevertheless believed that ignoring its responsibilities can result in long-term losses (the instrumental model).

Predictably then, an organization interprets its responsibility to its stakeholders in a variety of ways. Concerns which are often considered in this area of business ethics include:

- the extent to which a business is involved in the communities in which it is located;
- honesty, truthfulness and fairness in marketing activities such as advertising and the statements and images used in marketing communications;
- the use of animals in product testing (although for some products, animal testing is required by law);
- agricultural practices such as intensive methods of crop growing and the 'battery' farming of some animals (particularly chickens and pigs);

- the degree of safety built into product design and manufacture (e.g. the extent to which suspect meat is used in human food products);
- the extent to which a business accepts its alleged responsibilities arising from mishaps, spillages negligence and leaks (e.g. oil spills, pollution leakages and compensation claims from employees suffering bad health as a result of asbestos or coal dust);
- the amount of money that the company donates each year to charitable causes (this is shown in the company's annual accounts).

Ethical issues arising from the internal and industry practices of business

In addition to an organization's responsibilities to its external stakeholders, it also has responsibilities towards those inside the organization and in its micro-environment – its employees, suppliers, customers, etc. Again, much of this area of business practice is regulated by law (see Chapter 22), but some issues are open to debate and interpretation by individual businesses. It is, for example, illegal to discriminate against anybody on the basis of gender or race, whilst safety in the workplace is covered by a raft of laws including the Health and Safety at Work Act 1974 (detailed in Chapter 22).

Common concerns in this area of ethics include:

- the way in which a powerful company treats its customers, for example honouring the spirit (in addition to the 'letter') of warranties and the quality of after-sales service;
- the way in which a powerful company treats its suppliers, such as the payment of bills on time and honouring verbal agreements to take stock over a period of time;
- the number of women and members of ethnic minorities in senior positions in the company (some organizations actively try to engage women and minorities at all levels in the organization);
- the number of disabled workers in the organization over and above the legal quotas for such and their positions within the organization;
- the organization's loyalty to its employees in difficult economic conditions (i.e. how hard it tries to *not* make employees redundant in difficult trading climates).

26.6 Responses to the concerns

So far in this chapter, we have examined the various concerns that people have over environmental and ethical matters as they relate to business. In this section, we look at the ways in which the interested parties have responded to these concerns.

Political responses

Government legislation
The most obvious way that government can respond to people's concerns about environment and ethics is by legislating (making laws). Businesses in the UK are affected

by a range of environmental laws from both Westminster and from the EU (although it should be borne in mind that Westminster Acts tend to be in response to European Directives).

One of the most influential Acts over recent years has been the *Environmental Protection Act 1990* (EPA) which regulates environmental pollution into land, water and air. This was followed by the *Water Resources Act 1991* which, as its name suggests, focuses on water. The EPA includes the concept of *integrated pollution control* (IPC) which aims to:

- prevent pollution happening (as opposed to clearing up the mess afterwards);
- ensure that businesses act in such a way that minimizes risk to human health and to the environment;
- encourage the adoption by businesses of the best environmental processes (i.e. those which will cause the least harm to the environment);
- assess how much pollution the environment can take without causing irreparable damage;
- ensure that the polluter pays for any clear up.

The *Waste Management and Licensing Regulations 1994* were introduced into English law in response to an EU directive. This set of regulations distinguishes between waste disposal and waste management. They seek to encourage businesses to manage their waste more responsibly so as not to harm the environment or increase human health risk. Specifically, the Regulations seek to encourage businesses to:

- prevent or reduce waste production;
- develop products that will not cause harm to the environment;
- develop techniques for effectively disposing of dangerous substances and materials;
- consider recycling all or part of their waste;
- explore the possibility of using waste as a source of energy.

Responsibility for the enforcement of environmental laws is the responsibility of a QuANGO called the *Environment Agency*. This has the responsibility to monitor activity as it may threaten the environment and to bring charges against offenders according to the provisions of the various environmental laws.

EU influence

The EU has put forward a number of measures in an attempt to influence business and consumer activity in respect of social responsibility. Its methods of persuasion include both legislation and codes of practice.

On the legislation front, Directives have been passed which concern (for example) Europe-wide emissions, manufacturing practices and pollution control. One of the most publicized measures over recent years has been the European law that insists upon the fitting of catalytic converters to all new cars sold in the EU. These are devices fitted to car exhausts that reduce exhaust fume emissions by recirculating part of the emission back into the engine.

Environmental sustainability is encouraged by EU policy frameworks. The *5th EC Environmental Action Programme 1993* prescribed policies to encourage responsible practice in a number of key areas of business; manufacturing, energy, transport, agri-

441

culture and tourism. In agriculture, for example, the framework prescribes a decrease in the use of chemicals, the protection of biodiversity (the breadth of animal and plant life) and natural habitats. In manufacturing, the framework prescribes the reduction of waste, pollution prevention and control, and research into refuse and recycling technology.

The Brundtland Report

Environmental sustainability was the subject of the Brundtland Report of 1987. Chaired by the Norwegian Prime Minister (Mrs Brundtland), the Committee reported on ways in which business could consume the world's resources in such a way that allows them to be replenished at the same rate at which they are used. Its broad investigation included aspects of the implications of population growth, resource conservation, food supplies, ecosystem preservation and urban development. The Brundtland Committee proposed a number of key recommendations, including:

- recognizing people's right to a healthy environment and to protection from environmental deterioration;
- the preservation of environmental resources, ecosystems and biological diversity for future generations;
- the assessment of the environmental effects of economic and business activity;
- the provision of information on the environmental effects of economic activity and resource consumption;
- international co-operation on the use of resources that cross national borders;
- the implementation of environmental protection measures;
- the planning of how environmental (behaviour) standards will be set and put into practice;
- working out responses to environmental 'disasters';
- the limiting of general environmental damage.

Local Agenda 21

One of the most influential governmental responses to environmental concern has been the Local Agenda 21 initiative (LA21). This initiative arose out of the Earth Summit, held in Rio de Janeiro, Brazil, in 1992. Its *raison d'être* is to provide principles for the implementation of environmental conservation measures at the local level. LA21 was thus designed to be carried out by local authorities and, although it is wide in its scope, has been criticized by environmental lobbyists as allowing too much interpretation at local level. The implementation of LA21 varies according to the views of local citizens, local organizations and private enterprises in the locality. The timetable set out at Rio specified that a programme for local action should be in place by 1996 on six broad policy areas:

- energy;
- recycling;
- pollution monitoring and minimization;
- transport and planning;
- environmental protection and enhancement;
- health.

In the UK, many local authorities have failed to meet the 1996 target for these policy proposals. One of the problems expressed by local authorities in respect of LA21 is that no new financial resources were made available to them for its implementation.

Persuasion

In addition to legislation and the issuing of voluntary codes of practice, governments and other political institutions have undertaken a programme of gentle and not so gentle persuasion. The objective of such tactics is to try to make business behaviour more responsible without the need to impose the burden of legislation. In many matters of environmental concern, we have seen that legislative and regulatory frameworks exist that influence the behaviour of businesses. In ethical matters, such frameworks are much more problematic: how do you legislate that businesses should be 'nice' or 'ethical?'

In consequence, governments and other political bodies have attempted to influence ethical business behaviour by exhortation and persuasion. There is, of course, a difference of opinion on many issues and this gives rise to an element of debate in the country as a whole in respect of such matters as animal experiments. Politicians have been known to agree on some areas of ethical business on such things as the way in which large businesses treat their smaller suppliers and the time taken to pay invoices. On many issues, however, the differences of opinion that exist mean that individuals are often left to make their own minds up with regard to ethical issues.

Corporate (business) responses

As we have seen, much of the activity of business in respect of corporate responsibility is underpinned by law. The question is thus to ask what organizations do to address environmental and ethical concerns over and above the legal minimum.

Many businesses have appreciated that an *appearance* of social responsibility is good for business. Very few businesses exist for charitable purposes only and so it is generally understood that commercial businesses adapt their behaviour with a view to increasing customers' confidence in both the company and its products.

Marketing practices

One of the most important ways in which organizations have responded to concern is by making changes in its marketing activities. All aspects of the marketing process (see Chapter 12) can be affected by environmental and ethical concern. Examples include:

- changes in product design and R&D have resulted in products being designed to increase energy efficiency, to be eco-friendly and to use materials from sustainable sources (e.g. by using wood from sustainable forest areas);
- using product packaging that is less lavish than it might be and an increase in the use of materials that can be recycled;
- informing consumers of the background of a product by a creative use of labelling, such as the 'keep Britain tidy' logo, the use of the recyclable logo, or stating explicitly that the product is made without cruelty to animals;
- making advertising statements that are fair, honest and true;
- responding rapidly and appropriately to any complaints or expressions of grievance

by any of the organization's stakeholders (including customers).

One model put forward for 'green' marketing is that of the 'four Ss'. When we examined marketing in Chapter 12, we learned that a conventional marketing process comprises four Ps. The four Ss place a different emphasis on marketing activity:

- satisfaction of customer needs and wants;
- safety of products and the production processes;
- social acceptability of the products, their production and of the behaviour of the business;
- sustainability of the products and production processes in respect of materials used and the method of production.

Conforming to standards

A relatively recent development is the establishment of environmental standards. The main standard in this context is British Standard (BS) 7750: 1994 in environmental management systems. In the same way that BS 5750: 1987 specifies systems for the assurance of product quality, BS 7750: 1994 requires a conforming organization to comply with standards with regard to its responsibility to the environment.

Organizations that conform to the standard undergo the following procedures:

- undertaking a preliminary environmental review of the organization's processes and outputs;
- documenting the organization's environmental policy (which is usually the subject of some consultation and debate);
- setting out an appropriate management structure to implement the environmental policy;
- keeping records and registers of wider environmental regulations and their effects;
- establishing specific objectives and targets which must provide for continual environmental improvement;
- formulating an appropriate environmental management programme including a description of the procedures adopted to achieve the targets;
- writing an environmental management manual and accompanying documentation;
- keeping records to show that the procedures are being consistently followed;
- establishing a system whereby environment management systems are regularly audited (checked) for conformance to the system adopted;
- periodically assessing that targets and procedures are appropriate and modifying them as is required to meet the aim of continual improvement.

The award of the BS 7750: 1994 kite mark enables an organization to demonstrate to its stakeholders that it takes its environmental responsibilities seriously and that it is acting consistently in respect of its environmental management programme.

Changing corporate behaviour

Some organizations have made some significant changes to their activities to address environmental or ethical concerns.

Some organizations formalize their responses to concern by modifying or re-writing their *mission statements*. They may include phrases such as, 'within the constraints of environmental responsibility' or 'to show respect to our suppliers, customers and employees'. The Body Shop's mission statement begins with the words, 'To dedicate our business to the pursuit of social and environmental change,' and continues, 'To passionately campaign for the protection of the environment, human and civil rights, and against animal testing within the cosmetics and toiletries industry'. Such a top-level expression of commitment is designed to influence behaviour throughout the organization and to signal to stakeholders the organization's desire to respond to concerns.

Some organizations go a step further than modifying their mission statement by issuing a *code of business ethics*. This is a document which states how the organization intends to act towards its stakeholders. Many of the UK's largest companies have issued such a document, including British Airways, Barclays and Lloyds Banks, Whitbread, British Aerospace, Phillips Petroleum and United Biscuits. The *Institute of Business Ethics* in London is a body promoting, among other things, such codes of ethics. Its patrons include senior religious leaders in the UK including the Archbishop of Canterbury and the Chief Rabbi and its council includes some leading business people. The Institute recommends that organizations issue statements in respect of ethical practice regarding:

* relations with customers;
* relations with shareholders and other investors;
* relations with employees;
* relations with suppliers;
* relations with the government and the local community;
* the environment;
* taxation;
* relations with competitors;
* issues relating to international business;
* behaviour in relation to mergers and take-overs;
* ethical issues concerning directors and managers;
* compliance and verification.

The third way in which organizations have changed their practices in the light of concerns is by the compilation of *social accounts*. This is a document which is compiled and published voluntarily by an organization – unlike its financial accounts which are required by law. Social accounting or social auditing is the recording of the impact the organization has made upon its stakeholders. The objective of such an exercise is to test how well or badly the organization has measured up to its mission statement and/or code of business ethics. Organizations who pursue this option tend to have the audit carried out by an independent body in much the same way as a financial audit is carried out by independent auditors. Social accounts are relatively new to the world of business ethics. Early adopters included several alternative trading organizations (ATOs – businesses which exist to pursue ethical purposes like 'fair' Third World trade), although the idea may be gradually catching on with more conventional business organizations.

In addition to the broad measures mentioned above, many organizations have taken specific measures in particular parts of their activity. Some businesses involving non-essential animal experiments have discontinued such activities to reflect customer concerns. Chemical companies have made a number of non-mandatory changes, including the phasing out of CFC production and the introduction of processes to profitably use by-products as a means of partly reducing waste. Supermarkets have changed their stocking policies to include a range of eco-friendly products such as special washing powders, free-range meat and egg products and unbleached paper products.

Consumer responses

Consumers are the cause of most of the other changes – governments and organizations care largely because consumers (ordinary people) care. Popular opinion is thus the engine of change.

Product preferences
The most obvious way in which consumers respond to their concerns is to change the choices of the types of products they buy. A number of changing buyer preferences include the following:

- a trend towards smaller cars and more efficient car engines;
- increasing sales of organic produce and free-range meat products;
- increasing sales of products with reduced levels of packaging;
- buying lower packaging 'refills' of products which are used to replenish permanent containers;
- deliberately avoiding buying products from companies who are believed to be guilty of environmental or ethical irresponsibility (boycotting).

Recycling
Many consumers have established the practice of segregating their refuse between that which is recyclable and that which is not. Tins, glass, paper, cloth, and some plastics can be recycled and used again, thus requiring less 'virgin' material to be used in future manufacturing. Recycling centres are frequently set up by local authorities (e.g. adjacent to municipal rubbish tips) and in supermarket car parks. Although the UK currently recycles less consumer waste than some other countries such as Germany and the USA, the LA 21 initiative is expected to increase recycling levels in most countries over the longer term.

Assignment

If you are using this textbook as part of a class or group, organize a debate comprising two sides presenting arguments before an audience (the rest of the class). Eight to ten volunteers should divide into two sides. One team should prepare a case in favour of the contention:

The business of business is business.

or alternatively,

Stakeholders should only be considered by a business insofar as their demands are consistent with the maximization of profit.

The other side should prepare the case against. The debate itself should comprise both sides presenting their cases to an equal time limit (say 20 minutes each), beginning with the case in favour. The class then should have the opportunity to question each team. After a final summing up of both arguments by the two teams, the class should vote on the contention based on the arguments put forward.

References

1. Donaldson, T. and Preston L E. (1995) The stakeholder theory of the corporation: concepts, evidence and implications. *Academy of Management Review*, **20**(1), 65–91.

Further reading

Cannon, T. (1992) *Corporate Responsibility*. London: Pitman.

Cannon, T. (1994) *Corporate Responsibility. Issues in Business Ethics, Governance, Roles and Responsibilities*. London: Pitman.

Chryssides, G. and Kaler, J. (1996) *Essentials of Business Ethics*. New York: McGraw Hill.

Cline, W. R. (1992) *The Economics of Global Warming*. London: Longman.

Collins, D. and O'Rourke, T. E. (1994) *Ethical Dilemmas in Business*. Thomson.

Daly, H. E. and Townsend, K. N. (Eds) (1992) *Valuing the Earth. Economics, Ecology, Ethics*. Cambridge, MA: MIT Press.

Drummond, J. and Bain, W. (1994) *Managing Business Ethics*. Oxford: Butterworth-Heinemann.

Freidman, M. (1970) The social responsibility of business is to increase its profits. *New York Times Magazine*, 13 September.

Houlden, B. (1988) The Corporate Conscience. *Management Today*. August.

McInerny, P. and Rainbolt, P. (1994) *Ethics*. London: Harper Collins.

Murray, D. (1996) *Ethics in Organizations*. London: Kogan Page.

Nordhaus, W. D. (1994) *Managing the Global Commons. The Economics of Climate Change*. Cambridge, MA: MIT Press.

Shrivastava, P. (1995) *Greening Business. Sustaining the Corporation and the Environment*. Thomson.

Sorell, T and Hendry, J. (1994) *Business Ethics*. Oxford: Butterworth Heinemann.

Taylor, B., Hutchinson, C. and Tapper, R. (Eds) (1994) *Environmental Management Handbook*. London: Pitman.

Weiss, J. W. (1994). *Business Ethics. A Managerial, Stakeholder Approach*. Thomson.

Welford, R. (1993) *Environmental Management and Business Strategy*. London: Pitman.

27

The technological environment

Learning objectives

After studying this chapter, students should be able to describe:

- The advantages that technology offers to an organization.
- How a business uses technology.
- What is meant by information technology and how IT is used by a business.
- What is meant by operational technology and how it has affected business activity.
- How technology has influenced product research and design.

27.1 Business and technology

The growth of technology

The growth and expansion of technology has been one of the key characteristics of the twentieth century. Although the scientific heritage goes back many hundreds of years, the development and application of technology and its effects on social and business life have been enormous since the early years of this century. In the year 1900 the world was very different than it is today. It was a world that had never conceived of flight, television, antibiotics, anaesthetics or computers, and in which the telephone and the motor car were in their infancy.

Such a massive set of changing circumstances has had a profound effect on almost every part of personal and business life. Technological change has brought about the possibility of global communications, interplanetary transport, the world-wide development of businesses and the greatly increased speed (manufacturing and distribution) and quality of manufactured products. In this chapter, we will consider the ways in which businesses use technology and how its development has changed organizational life and may continue to do so in the future.

What advantages does technology offer a business?

The starting point of our discussion is to examine the benefits that the various types of technology has brought to business.

Technology can help a business to *reduce costs*. One of the most obvious ways in which this has been done is to replace manual tasks with automation. Much of the work that was previously performed by armies of line workers in a factory or by teams of clerical workers in an office can now be carried out by machines of various types.

Technology offers the business an opportunity to *increase quality* through the removal of human error and the introduction of more consistent procedures. The reduction of errors by increased automation offers the possibility of greater customer confidence and lower costs through reduced error corrections.

Technology enables business to make significant *increases in productivity*. Productivity refers to the business's ability to produce output with a specific level of resource. The employment of technology renders the business more efficient – machines can work longer hours with no breaks; they never 'ring in sick' or go to the bathroom. In short, more work output can be produced for the same cost, or less, than if the work was performed by humans.

Technology can help businesses to *speed processes up*. The more rapid transmission of information coupled with the mechanization of many tasks means that decisions can be made faster and goods can be produced more rapidly than previously.

Technology facilitates the making of *better and more accurate decisions*. We know from our own experience at home that we are more informed about complex issues than ever before through such media as radio, television and other electronic means of communications. In business, the rapidity and accuracy of information transmission has enabled managers to have possession of the information they need to make informed decisions.

How does a business use technology?

The ways in which technology has pervaded business life is not dissimilar to how we encounter it in our personal lives. We use it in the kitchen, in our cars, for entertainment, to communicate, in education and in countless other areas of life. It is thus a difficult task to distil the effects of technology on business into a few key areas.

One way of subdividing technology in business is to categorize it by its use. Although the technology used in different parts of organizational life may be similar, we can nevertheless consider technologies as essentially separate according to where it is employed within the organization. Accordingly, we can identify three ways in which businesses use technology:

- business uses technology in communications and in information management;
- business uses technology in operations, for example in manufacturing;
- business uses technology in product design and in research.

In the remainder of this chapter, we will examine these three broad areas of technological usage.

27.2 Information technology

What is IT?

Information technology (IT) is a term which encompasses many new types of technology and pervades an even wider range of applications in business. We can define IT as: *technology that is dedicated to the generation, transmission, storage, organization or management of information.*

We can immediately appreciate that such a definition can include a lot of things. We might use a calculator, for example, to generate information and then use a computer to manage it. Then we might use a telecommunications network to transmit the information. All of these technological vehicles are part of IT.

There have been a number of trends in this area of technology. The key trends are:

- the trend towards increasing speed of processing and transmission;
- the trend towards increased accuracy and more 'user-friendly' forms of information;
- the trend towards miniaturization (that is, the components used in IT become smaller).

When taken together, it would not be an exaggeration to say that IT has transformed many areas of home and business life. Information and its technology has grown to become the core activity of a number of very large industries, as well as having a substantial impact on almost all of us.

Why is information important?

Information has a number of important functions, both in business and in our domestic lives. The communication of information is a major factor in maintaining cohesion in society and a vital factor in the normal functioning of business and the state.

Firstly, information facilitates *control*. When we examined control systems in Chapter 7, we learned that information is needed throughout the process to communicate standards and to provide feedback.

Secondly, and linked to the use of information for control, is the use of information to *influence attitudes and actions*. The influence upon actions can be either instructive (prescriptive) or restrictive. The former influences what we do, or should do, and the latter, what we do not do, or what we believe we should not do.

Thirdly, information is essential to enable those in business to *make decisions*. Intelligent decision-making rests upon the notion that those who make decisions are in possession of all relevant information. Organizations often put formal communications channels in place for this purpose although in many cases, decisions are taken using information gathered by more informal means (e.g. by word of mouth).

Fourth, information is used to *educate and to entertain*. The book you are currently reading is an example of educational communication, whilst one of the purposes of television is to entertain.

How is IT used in business?

The applications of IT in business are many and varied. In one sense, IT is used in all areas of business, but it has found particular use in a few key areas.

Firstly, IT is used in *administration*. Included in this area of application are:

- office uses such as word-processing and graphic design;
- numerical analysis by the use of spreadsheets;
- accountancy uses such as computerized report generation and electronic ledger compilation;
- banking uses such as electronic funds transfer;
- salary and personnel administration.

Secondly, IT is used in *business communications*. This category includes:

- television and radio communications;
- telephone and fax systems;
- electronic mail;
- satellite systems;
- the Internet.

Thirdly, IT is used in *information gathering*. This area may make use of other types of IT such as communications systems. This category includes:

- library information systems;
- databases (computerized systems which contain a lot of information in a readily accessible form);
- electronic point-of-sale systems which enable a business to rapidly accumulate information on its sales;

The 'ingredients' of IT

Although, as we have seen, the uses of IT in business are many and varied, there are two key 'ingredients', i.e. two core areas of technology that comprise IT systems. These two ingredients are computers and telecommunications technologies.

IT and computers

Computers form such a significant part of organizational life that it is difficult to imagine how organizations ever coped without them. Furthermore, nowhere is the progress of technology more marked than in the speed of innovation in this area. In addition to the importance of computers to business, they have come to form an important element in many other parts of life as well, from usage in our motor cars and video recorders to controlling medical equipment and burglar-alarm systems.

We use the term *computer* in more than one way. The most usual meaning of the term is to describe a programmable device which is designed to perform a wide range of data-processing tasks. However, we also speak of computers controlling equipment, parts of cars and domestic appliances like microwave ovens. The part that both types of computer share is called a *processor*. In most appliances, the processor is a small semiconductor chip and is therefore called a *microprocessor*. The ways in which processors are used leads us to distinguish between two essential types:

- *programmable processors* are found in devices that we would recognize as computers. They can be programmed to perform many different tasks;
- *embedded processors* are sometimes called *dedicated* processors and cannot be reprogrammed. They are designed to perform a predetermined task and are embedded in an appliance as a mechanism of control. They have no useful purpose if they are removed from the appliance for which they are designed.

Both types of processor are accompanied by components that support the processor's designed purpose. A programmable processor is surrounded by components that assist the processor (usually called a central processing unit, or CPU) in its purpose. This includes memory that can both be written to (such as random access memory (RAM), and storage memory such as a hard or floppy disk), and memory that cannot be written to and is permanent (read only memory or ROM). It will also include mechanisms of both inputting data to the CPU and a means by which outputs from the CPU can be read. A dedicated processor will not usually contain memory but will provide input and output capabilities, although these may be inaccessible to the user.

Computers (using programmable processors) are often subdivided into types according to their size. Three types have traditionally been identified:

- *Mainframe computers* are very large and have a central processor that can support many users at the same time. Each user is located at a terminal which is linked to the main CPU; terminals may be located either locally (e.g. in the same building) or remotely via telecommunications links. Remote terminals may be located anywhere in the world. Mainframes usually demand specialist personnel to manage them and are typically housed in rooms which are subject to controlled environmental conditions. Large computers of this type are used by organizations that have the need to process large amounts of data simultaneously such as banks, universities and insurance companies.
- *Minicomputers* are smaller than mainframes but can nevertheless be of a considerable size and power. They work on the same principles as a mainframe except that can support a lower number of users. Minicomputers are used in organizations that have a need for several rather than many users simultaneously such as office complexes or scientific laboratories.
- *Microcomputers* are stand-alone machines. They have a CPU that can only be accessed from one input device – that is, one keyboard, a floppy disk drive or similar. For this reason, microcomputers are always 'stand-alone' machines. They contain their own data storage capability, usually in the form of an 'on-board' hard disk, and have output devices in the form of monitors and printer terminals. The use of a microcomputer gives the user autonomy that other computer types do not. This, coupled with their growing ease of use and reducing price (in real terms) have made this the key growth area in computer usage.

In some organizations, microcomputers are connected together in the form of a *local area network* (LAN). A LAN is used to connect stand-alone microcomputers together in an office locality. The central point of the LAN is a *file server* from which users access programmes and information. The file server can also be used as a point for interconnecting users for the use of electronic mail (Email) and as a link to external information sources such as the Internet.

IT and telecommunications

If computers in their various forms are responsible for managing information, then telecommunications systems are responsible for transmitting information. Like all other areas of technology, telecommunications has been the subject of rapid innovation and change in recent decades. The word *telecommunication* means communication over a distance (the prefix *tele* means 'distance' and appears in other words where *tele* means the same thing: *tele*phone, *tele*kinesis, *tele*pathy, *tele*vision, etc.). At its simplest, there are only two ways in which information can be electronically transmitted from one place to another:

- along physical wires or optoelectronic links;
- through the air by means of electromagnetic transmission.

The innovation underlying the key developments in telecommunications is that of a widespread switch from old analogue transmission to modern digital information. This has resulted in much faster and more accurate telecommunications and, importantly, has facilitated the connection of computers (which are also based on digital technology) together over a distance.

There are a number of key trends in respect of business and telecommunications. An increase in real incomes coupled with a fall (in real terms) of the prices of telecommunications services has stimulated much higher usage and ownership of telecommunications appliances. Whilst the telephone has been a feature of some domestic homes for many years, ownership has increased quite markedly over the past three decades. Other developments are much more recent.

- The *facsimile* or fax, a device for transmitting images became popular in the 1980s replacing the telex, which involved communicating a typed message. Faxes are now a part of every office in organizations in the First World.
- The *mobile telephone* (and mobile fax) also came to the fore in the 1980s. Initially the domain of senior executives and travelling sales representatives, mobile telephones have become increasingly commonly used by members of the public for social and domestic purposes. Mobile telephones are connected together by land-based receivers, each of which has a receiving range of several kilometres. The receivers then transmit the message to other parts of the mobile and trunk network.
- *Electronic mail,* or Email, is telecommunication between computers or between local area networks. Network users have their own unique identifier ('address'), whilst home users must usually subscribe to a service provider who allocates an identifier to each user. Email enables messages to be left for people at a fraction of the cost of speech-based telephony.
- The *Internet* is a world-wide network of computer users, including individuals, universities and other organizations, including many businesses. Until relatively recently, the Internet was mainly of interest to academics who used it to keep in touch with a view to keeping up to date with each other's research work. Internet users can now access sites all over the world to gain information from well over two million databases and many more news groups and general information sites. It also acts as a vehicle for the transmission of Email.

McFarlane and McKenny

It is self-evident that the extent to which organizations use and rely on technology in their normal operations varies widely. In attempting to understand these variations, McFarlane and McKenny developed a grid comprising two intersecting continua. The *y* continuum describes the organization's *current* dependence and the strategic importance of IT and systems in normal operations. The *x* continuum (the horizontal) describes the *future* dependence that the organization is likely to have on IT given the nature of the industry, customer requirements and competitor behaviour. When it is constructed, McFarlane and McKenny's grid is like the one shown in Figure 27.1.

Figure 27.1 McFarlane and McKenny's IT grid

For some organizations, information technology is of *strategic* importance. This is said to be the case when the organization's dependence on its information systems is already very high and when its future is also expected to be very highly impacted by developments in IT. Accordingly, the head of IT may well be a member of the organization's board of directors. Examples of organizations for which IT is strategic include banks, insurance companies and telecommunications companies. It will usually be the case that the business simply cannot operate if the information systems (on computer) 'go down'.

For other organizations, dependence on their IT systems is currently relatively low, but changes in the environment means that IT will eventually become very important. These are organizations in the *turnaround* category of McFarlane and McKenny's grid. Most of the major supermarket multiples have just recently undergone this stage by moving from a state where IT was used to help control stock and assist with accounting to the current state where IT systems are crucial for the logging of sales and many other parts of the retailing process. Supermarkets have, however, some significant investments still to make in IT, such as fully implementing systems to facilitate electronic funds transfer at the point of sale and in stock ordering (although many chains are well down this road). For turnaround organizations, IT is expected to become strategic in the medium term.

Organizations which McFarlane and McKenny describe as *factory* currently have a high dependence on IT for their competitive performance, but future developments in IT are not expected to significantly add to their ability to compete in markets. Some airlines fall into this category, where there is a high dependence on IT systems for booking and recording of passengers but where future changes in IT are not expected to increase their competitive edge.

Finally, McFarlane and McKenny identify a category which they refer to as *support*.

These are organizations whose current use of IT does not significantly contribute to their ability to compete and where IT is not expected to affect competitive performance in the future. Such organizations may find IT useful for support purposes such as accounting, word-processing and work scheduling, but have not found IT to be a source of leverage over competitors. Organizations in this category may be those performing relatively simple services or manufacturing businesses in low-technology sectors of industry. A company involved in landscape gardening may find a personal computer useful, but its competitive edge will be primarily down to the care and skills of its designers and gardeners. Furthermore, it is unlikely that landscape gardening will ever become so impacted by IT that it becomes a matter of competitive importance.

27.3 Operational technology

Introduction

In the 1970s and 1980s, business and engineering students learned of technologies called CAD and CAM. These are acronyms for computer-aided design and computer-aided manufacturing, respectively. At the time, CAD and CAM represented a new way of gaining the advantages of technology in their operations departments. In the 1990s, however, the use of computer technology in operations has become so widespread that CAD and CAM have become the norm rather than the exception. It is only a few businesses that have not, at least in a small way, automated parts of their operations department since the advent of a range of new operational technologies.

Broadly speaking, operational technology borrows heavily from the areas and types of IT that we have already encountered. In addition, though, operations departments also employ technology based on innovations in electrical, electronic and mechanical engineering which have combined to automate many of the tasks that were previously performed manually.

IT in operations

Almost all types of organization (with the possible exception of monasteries) have found computer systems to be of immense value in their operations systems. The university or college at which you are studying most likely manages its student recruitment, marks and awards on a database system – an innovation that means that, at the touch of a button, all the information about you can be accessed immediately and displayed on a computer monitor.

In other operational contexts, computer systems are used in all parts of the process. Just-in-time (JIT) manufacturers (see Chapter 15) use computer linkages with their suppliers to order directly the appropriate amount of incoming raw material. Systems also exist for scheduling jobs or batches through a production facility in the most optimum way. Production managers usually have a computer terminal on their desks which enables them to find out up to the minute information on their department such as the batch schedule, the levels of raw materials and finished goods stocks (see Chapter 14) or what is currently happening on the 'shop floor'.

Some computer systems offer a comprehensive approach to managing the operations function. Manufacturing processes based on assembly (e.g. cars, electrical goods) sometimes employ a system called MRP II – manufacturing resource planning. The 'II' indicates that MRP II replaces a previous regime called MRP – materials requirement planning – a system which only took into account the stock requirements of a job or batch. Once the 'order book' has been inputted, MRP II calculates not only the precise stock requirements for a job or batch, but also the best way to schedule work through manufacturing to enable all orders to be met with the minimum of slack and delay. The system can be modified so that the computer actually orders the precise amount of raw materials stocks, thus saving the organization time and money previously needed for a purchasing manager to perform the ordering task.

One area of business that has benefited significantly from innovations in IT is the supermarket. Whilst the most obvious and visible change has been the recording of sales by the use of bar-codes (as opposed to the assistant typing in the individual prices), other developments have been equally important. Electronic point-of-sale (EPOS) systems have enabled managers to gain immediate information on product sales which guides decisions on such things as product discounting and stock ordering. EPOS systems can also generate 'checkout savers' – discounts vouchers which are generated in response to specific purchases and paid for by competitors to the brand purchased (e.g., a purchase of a six-pack of Coca Cola may generate a checkout saver for a six-pack of Pepsi).

Engineering technology

Although highly dependent upon IT, innovations in engineering are worthy of separate consideration. We need look no further than our own homes to see the advances in engineering and how they have changed our lives. Most of us have appliances such as washing machines, televisions, hi-fis, microwave ovens and dishwashers, and we can testify as to the extent to which they have made our lives easier.

In business, the automation and mechanization of procedures has engendered similarly beneficial results. Some of the earliest mechanized procedures involving ravelling cotton and wool in the eighteenth century have given way in the latter part of the twentieth century to a situation wherein automation has reached new heights of refinement and accuracy. The work that was previously done by hundreds of human workers has, in many work-places, been replaced with machines that work with greater accuracy and quality than humans and with greater productivity at lower cost.

The complexity of factory automation varies widely. Some machines are designed to perform relatively simple, repetitive tasks, such as paint jets continually spraying paint at products passing on a single conveyor line. There has, however, been a marked trend in the increasingly complex tasks that machines are made to undertake. More advanced machines make use of microprocessor technology in the forms of both programmable and embedded processors. In the engineering business, computer numerically controlled (CNC) technology has been used for many years. CNC machines are machine tools which use coded computer information to produce batches of precisely matched components from such things as CNC lathes and milling machines.

Among the more complex automations are those used in industries like motor manufacture and the production of silicon chips and printed circuits. Machines used in these processes must usually be capable not only of exceptionally minute movements but also of intricate movements through three dimensions. Nissan Motors in Sunderland reports that it uses:

> *a family of more than 200 robots provid[ing] an automation level in excess of 80%. Six high-speed tri-axis transfer presses – one 5000 tonne, two 3200 tonne and three 2700 tonne machines – mean the Sunderland plant has the highest concentration of these advanced presses in Europe.*

27.4 Technology in research and design

We must be careful not to define the term *technology* too tightly. We may tend to think of technology purely in terms of electronics and sophisticated machinery, but the term as it relates to business also includes a wide range of chemical technologies and those associated with the understanding of the world and its materials. Specialist staff that work in research, development and design, such as scientists and specialist engineers, are confronted with an even more complex set of technologies with which they must often 'juggle' to benefit the products and processes of the organizations for which they work.

There is scope in this text for only a small sample of examples of the areas of technology that are involved in the various aspects of research and design (in addition to IT and engineering technology which we have already encountered):

- Chemical technology refers to the technology used by chemists in developing new compounds, chemical products and chemical intermediates.
- Biochemical, biomolecular and pharmaceutical technology relates to chemistry as it applies to life. Technological developments in this area have affected the lives of literally billions of people for the better.
- Gene and genetic technology is one of those areas of research that is perhaps at the leading edge of science. By understanding the genetic 'code' of animal and plant life, knowledge is gained in other areas, such as the causes of disease, deformity and the ways in which these can be corrected.
- Materials technology includes such things as metallurgy (the study of metals), ceramics and how these can be used in business products. The implications of materials technology extend to many sectors of business, including motors, brushes, shipping, aircraft, rocketry, surgery and clothes.
- Process technology concerns the technology involved in industrial (particularly manufacturing) processes. It borrows heavily from other areas of technology, depending upon the industry and type of process in question.
- Aerodynamic technology is important to organizations engaged in the design and manufacture of such products as motor cars, aircraft, missiles and bikes of various types. It concerns the flow of air through, past and over product shapes, with the objective of reducing fuel consumption and increasing efficiency. (Have you ever wondered why many cars are more or less the same shape?).
- Acoustic and audio technologies are used by any business engaged in sound. Examples include manufacturers of audio equipment and companies involved in the staging of concerts or concert hall design.

The progress of technology in most of the above areas is just as rapid as it has been in

IT. We need look no further than changes in medicine and in pharmaceuticals to see the rate of progress in the wider technological environment.

Assignment

How would you answer a company's managing director who says that he has sacked his research and development staff because, 'They cost too much money. We can get by with the products we've already got?'

Further reading

Bailey, J. (1993) *Managing People and Technological Change*. London: Pitman.

Edwards, J. and Lewis, C. (1994) *Business Computing Primer*. London: Pitman.

Frenzel, C. W. (1992) *Management of Information Technology*. Thomson.

Harry, M. (1994) *Information Systems in Business*. London: Pitman.

Landauer, T. K. (1995) *The Trouble with Computers. Usefulness, Usability and Productivity*. Cambridge, MA: MIT Press.

Langley, G. and Ronayne, J. (1993) *Telecommunications Primer*. 4th edn. London: Pitman.

McLoughlin, I. and Clark, J. (1994) *Technological Change at Work.*, 2nd edn. Milton Keynes: Open University Press.

Peppard, J. (1993) *IT Strategy for Business*. London: Pitman

Roy, R. and Wield, D. (Eds) (1986) *Product Design and Technological Innovation*. Milton Keynes: Open University Press.

Tom, P. L. (1991) *Managing Information as a Corporate Resource*, 2nd edn. London: Harper Collins.

Zorkoczy, P. and Heap, N. (1994) *Information Technology*. London: Pitman.

28

The international business environment

Learning objectives

After studying this chapter, students should be able to describe:

- The factors that have contributed to the internationalization of business.
- The motivations behind increased internationalization.
- The various internationalization entry strategies.
- The major features and operation of multinational companies.
- How governments influence multinational companies and international business.

28.1 The internationalization of business

One of the most striking features of business growth in the latter half of the twentieth century has been an increase in business growth across national borders. At its simplest, the need to buy and sell across borders is motivated by the fact that no country is entirely self-sufficient. Increased business activity and growth has stimulated increased demand for goods, services and factors of production. In the event that such commodities cannot be satisfied from within national borders, foreign suppliers are sought to meet the demand.

Various favourable factors came together in the years following the Second World War which served to intensify greatly the internationalization of business. These are discussed in the following section. Today, the millions of international trading relationships across the world mean that international business affects, in one way or another, almost every individual and organization. This may be either directly through such things as imports or exports, or indirectly through the use of foreign currency or foreign goods and services (e.g. French cars, Japanese computer equipment, Brazilian coffee).

Factors that have stimulated increased internationalization

How then can we explain the growth in business across national borders? Like many phenomena in business, it has several contributory factors. Some of the most important are discussed below.

The communications 'revolution'
The twentieth century has been distinguished by a number of outstanding innovations in communications technology. Since the industrial revolution in the late eighteenth

century, the pace of change has accelerated as new technologies have been developed. Whereas previously the fastest method of reliable communication was the galloping horse, information travelling at the speed of light can now circulate the Earth several times in less than one second. Furthermore, in addition to the enormous speeding up of communications, an unprecedented number of people all over the world now have access to channels of advanced means of communications. Communications can thus reach many more people than ever before at almost instantaneous speed. The changes in communications technology have been so marked that the term the 'communications revolution' has been coined to describe it.

Over recent years, communications technology has grown in line with developments in computer technology. The 'digitization' of all First World telephone systems in the late 1980s and early 1990s has enabled telephony to be combined with computers. The growth in the use of fax and Email are testimony to this.

The mass media, particularly the medium of television, has also enjoyed expansion coupled with reductions in the real price (i.e. after inflation) of technology. This has offered business the opportunity to advertise and communicate with billions of people world-wide in a way that was not possible earlier. The growth of 'global' brands, such as Coca Cola and the Big Mac is due in part to the promotions made possible by mass communications.

Question 28.1

It has been said that the three most seminal innovations of the twentieth century have been antibiotics, flight and the semiconductor. Defend this statement with evidence.

This may take the form of a class debate, with one side arguing that the above contention is too simplistic and the other side showing how each of these developments has led on to many other innovations.

Improved transport and transport infrastructure

In a similar vein to advances in electronic communication, physical transport of goods has become faster and more reliable through innovations in both vehicular transport and in the infrastructure it uses. The growth and improvements in motor car technology has signalled a huge growth in independent transport, whilst the construction of motorway systems has made transport by road faster and safer. The rapid loading and unloading of ships together with electronic inventory management in shipping services has increased the usefulness of shipping as a means of goods passage between countries. Rail and air services have seen similar advances, with air flights alone increasing within the UK from 10.8 million flights in the year 1972 to over 24 million in 1993.

The net effect of all these changes is that the movements of people and goods is now much faster and more reliable than ever before. Whereas at one time a car travelling from Glasgow to London would take a day, having to go along A-grade roads and through many towns, a modern car can make the journey in around five hours entirely via high-speed roads, mainly motorways. The modernization of road and rail links has been a feature of all industrialized countries.

Market homogenization

According to Professor Theodore Levitt, a noted American academic, 'the world's needs and wants have become irrevocably homogenized'.[1] By homogenization, Levitt means that, increasingly, consumers in different countries want the very same products, without any 'tweaking' to account for regional variations in taste or fashion. It is argued that everybody wants the same global brands, such as Levi jeans, Marlboro, Coca Cola and McDonald's. Whilst in some countries the desire for a brand may be due to the fact that it has some status attached to it (such as Western clothes brands in the Third World), in other cases everybody wants a certain product simply because it is the best available. A company producing a product which is demanded in many or even all parts of the world (i.e. for which demand is homogenized) will have an obvious incentive to internationalize in order to take full advantage of the global demand.

Examples of products which lend themselves to a globally homogeneous demand include:

- some food and soft-drink brands (e.g. Coca Cola, Big Mac);
- consumer electronics (e.g. Intel personal computer chips and general television designs);
- computer software (e.g. Microsoft Windows, FoxPro, WordPerfect)
- pharmaceuticals (e.g. best-selling prescription drugs like Zantac and the antidepressant Prozac);
- defence equipment and aircraft (where the incentive is to have the most up-to-date equipment);
- clothing fashions (e.g. Levi jeans and French ladies' fashions);
- perfumes (e.g. Chanel and Yves Saint-Laurent);
- some alcohol and tobacco brands (e.g. Marlboro, Heineken and some brands of Scotch whisky).

However, there is clearly room for national variations in product or brand design, so it is not the case that *every* product has homogeneous demand. The Findus frozen food brand (owned by Nestlé), for example, produces fish fingers for the UK market, but frozen boeuf bourgignon for the French. Some companies are successful at making adjustments to their products to make them more acceptable to regional or national tastes and sensibilities.

Question 28.2

Suggest reasons for the growth in homogeneous markets. Why do you think it is the case that 'everybody' wants American cola, French perfumes and British pharmaceuticals?

Political stability

The latter half of the twentieth century has been characterized by, among other things, an unprecedented level of concordance between the major First World industrialized nations. Whereas Britain and France spent centuries at, or near to war over a number of issues, the two are now considered to be close allies. Similarly, the Germans, Italians and Austrians, erstwhile aggressors, are now prosperous nations which enjoy friendly relations with all other First World countries.

On the domestic front, it has also transpired that industrialized nations have enjoyed fifty years or more (in the UK, many years more) of stable democratic government. In such political structures, we take for granted things that earlier generations could not. It is almost unthinkable, for example, that Britain would go to war against one of its First World partners or that the UK government would be threatened by insurrection.

Political stability favours business prosperity owing to the presence of certainty. Businesses know that if they make a substantial investment in a politically stable country the investment is as 'safe' as it can be. Of course, not all parts of the world enjoy such stability, and less stable countries tend to characterized by lower levels of business prosperity.

One of the major objectives of some supranational political institutions is to maintain and increase political stability, which in turn encourages business activity. The European Union is an obvious example, but organizations such as the United Nations also help towards this end.

28.2 Motivations behind internationalization

The reasons *why* companies pursue international strategies obviously differ from business to business. In attempting to distil the many motivations down to a few simplified ones, we can identify three major factors.

Market 'push' motivations

Market 'push' refers to the motivation to seek business from foreign markets because of constraints in the domestic ones. A company which has successfully traded in the UK for decades may seek to expand overseas due to adverse changes in its traditional UK markets. The business is 'pushed' abroad by unfavourable conditions at home.

Examples of market push motivations include:

- *Maturity or decline* in the domestic market. The product life cycle we encountered in Chapter 12 says that all products are subject to growth, maturity and, eventually, decline. It may be the case that a product entering maturity in one country (thus stopping the growth the company has previously enjoyed), can be offset by growth in hitherto untapped foreign markets. In some cases the domestic market will reach maturity because 'everybody who wants one has got one', whereas other cases there may be a trend away from buying a certain type of product (e.g. tobacco products).
- *Increased regulation* in the domestic market. Governments that impose 'excessive' regulation (which is a matter of perspective) on businesses will tend, overall, to encourage businesses to seek to invest in areas where regulation is less. Regulation of business, for example by imposing employment laws, health and safety rules, etc., invariably entails cost increases, so it is in some businesses' interests to seek to

expand in countries where regulation is less strict. The 'opt out' that the UK negotiated from the Social Chapter of the Maastricht Treaty of 1992 means that UK labour is in some ways less regulated than most other European Union states and this reduced the incentive for some companies to seek to internationalize away from the UK.

- *High labour costs* (and other factor costs) may be linked to regulation of business, but may also be a function of the standard of living enjoyed by workers in a country. If labour costs in a domestic market rise to the point where it is no longer economically attractive to stay, the business may seek to expand to a country where labour can be bought at more favourable rates.
- *Inappropriately skilled labour* may be a factor for businesses which cannot find an adequate level of skilling in the domestic labour force of their home countries. Whilst training is an obvious remedy for inappropriate skills, it is thought to be the case that certain countries are somehow inherently better at some skills than others. Companies may look abroad to invest if they suspect that the skills of the local labour force will not be adequate over the longer term.
- *High fiscal pressure* may encourage a business to seek international expansion if it must pay what it considers to be excessive taxes in a domestic economy. The same may be true in episodes of prolonged monetary pressure.
- *Political or economic instability* will be a powerful push factor. We have seen that businesses, just like individuals, like certainty and security. Rapid or unpredictable changes in the political or economic environment may not create conditions wherein a business would be happy to remain.

Market 'pull' motivations

Whilst market push motivations encourage a business to look elsewhere, market pull factors, predictably, are those features of a country which are attractive to businesses. They 'pull' businesses into the country because they possess attractive features to businesses which are considering expanding internationally. Essentially, pull factors will be the opposites of push factors.

Countries will be attractive to businesses if:

- there is growth potential in the country's market;
- there is increasing spending power and prosperity (e.g. in 'newly industrialized' nations, like some in the Far East);
- fiscal and monetary pressure is low (the growth of Hong Kong as a centre of inward investment is due in large part to these factors);
- the market for the company's products is undersupplied in the foreign country;
- the country possesses highly skilled workers;
- labour costs (and the costs of other factors of production) are comparatively low;
- there is a more stable political system than the business's home country.

Pull factors are all relative to the home country. It is not, for example, whether a foreign country has highly skilled labour and low tax rates, but whether it has *higher* skills and *lower* taxes than the company's home country.

Portfolio as a motivator

The nature of a business portfolio, as we saw when we considered holding companies (Chapter 4) and external unrelated growth (Chapter 8), is linked to the notion of spreading opportunity and risk. For some 'polycentric' (many-centred) companies, international expansion is sought simply as a method of guaranteeing the company has a meaningful presence in a variety of national markets. Whilst market pull factors will guide such a company *vis à vis* its choice of locations, one of the primary strategic motives will be to ensure that its base is sufficiently well spread to enable it to withstand economic shock and to benefit from growth in different national markets.

One of the features of international business is its unpredictability. The fact is that if a company operates in several national environments, it has more variables to watch than if it operates in just the UK. A downturn in the demand for the company's products in Singapore will have less impact on the company as a whole if the Singapore sales account for only a small percentage of its international total.

28.3 Internationalization strategies

Having looked at *why* companies seek to internationalize, we now come to the question of '*how?*' they do so. A business has a choice of several methods by which it can extend its business interests beyond its immediate national borders.

The entry strategy (entry into international markets) adopted by an organization will depend upon several factors:

- The company's *objectives* in becoming internationalized. The entry strategy must match its purposes. A company seeking to dominate the world automotive (car) market would need to adopt a much more aggressive internationalization strategy than would a local paint company which merely wanted to increase its sales volume.
- The *resources available* for the international expansion. It makes sense that a business must 'cut its cloth' to match its budgets. Some entry strategies are necessarily more resource intensive than others.
- To a certain extent, the strategy chosen will depend upon the *types of products and markets* the company is involved in. Businesses which involve massive amounts of capital expenditure (e.g. oil companies) will need to serve several national markets in order to generate sufficient revenue to repay its capital costs. Similarly, the nature of some perishable food products would preclude their being exported in a conventional way and a more direct investment approach may be more suitable.

    The major entry strategies are:

- exporting;
- international franchising;
- international licensing;
- international (strategic) alliances;
- foreign direct investment.

All of the above strategies are discussed below.

Exporting

The most straightforward internationalization strategy is to take the company's products and sell them to foreign customers by means of export. For a UK based company, the products are made in the UK and then sent by carrier to foreign customers who then pay the UK company in sterling on normal payment terms.

In an organization's history, exporting is usually the first foray it makes into international markets. It is usually the cheapest and most convenient of the entry strategies we shall consider.

Because export sales involve the exchange of money from one currency to another, the competitiveness of British exports depends heavily upon the exchange rate of sterling. A low value of sterling will make British exports more price competitive, whereas a high value will make them less so. We saw in Chapter 23 that, as well as being very dependent upon the exchange rate, exports are one of the major determinants of it.

Britain's traditional export markets were the British Commonwealth countries, such as Canada, Australia and India. Over recent decades, however, Britain's exports have increasingly gone to Europe, particularly the other European Union (EU) states such as France and Germany. The EU accounts for around half of the UK's total exports. This change is partly due to the fact that Europe is nearer than most of the far-flung Commonwealth nations, and partly due to the economic advantages of EU membership, particularly the absence of trade barriers to imports and exports across the national borders of EU states.

Export contracts

Imagine the following scenario. A ship leaves dock at Humberside laden with cars from a British manufacturer. Heading for Holland, the ship unfortunately sinks exactly half-way across the North Sea. The question is this: *whose loss is this – the exporter's or the importer's?* The answer is that it depends upon the terms of the export contract. The fact that carriage of goods over long distances involves many potential risks means that it must be made absolutely clear at what point ownership of the goods changes hands. Hence, export contracts vary according to the point at which this change of ownership takes place.

- *Ex-works* contracts specify the gate of the exporting company as the point of change. The importer effectively collects the goods from the exporter and assumes responsibility for them all the way to the overseas site. Payment becomes due at the point of pick-up. The seller's responsibilities are limited to assisting the importer with the necessary documentation for the export of the goods.
- *Free on rail (FOR)* contracts specify that the exporter assumes responsibility for the carriage of the goods to the nearest rail terminal to the seller's premises. From the train station to the importer's premises, the goods belong to the buyer.
- *Free alongside ship (FAS)* contracts specify that the goods shall change hands once the exporter has delivered them to the docks and places them ready for loading onto the ship. The importer (buyer) assumes responsibility for the goods from the transfer of the goods onto the ship to the destination.

> - *Free on board (FOB)* contracts go a few metres further than FAS. The exporter assumes ownership of the goods up to and including the placement of the goods on the outgoing ship.
> - *Ex-ship* contracts specify that ownership changes hands at a foreign port of the importer's choice. The payment of shipping and insurance charges by the exporter has obvious implications for the cost of the shipment to the importer.
> - *Cost, insurance, freight (CIF)* contracts specify that the exporter assumes responsibility for the shipment all the way to the importer's site in the foreign country.
>
> The export contract chosen will be a point of mutual agreement between the importer and exporter. It follows that the nearer to the importer's site ownership changes hands, the more expensive will be the price of the shipment.

There are a number of advantages to using exporting as an entry strategy:

- It enables a business to benefit from international trade with *no significant overseas investment* and at relatively little setting-up or organizing cost. The use of foreign agents or distributors usually frees the exporter of such responsibilities.
- The exporter's *risk is limited to the value of the shipment*. Compared to direct investment, when a great deal of investment may be at risk by changes in the foreign country's environment, exporting can be an attractive option.
- The fact that little or no set-up cost is involved in exporting means that an organization can *attack several foreign markets within a limited budget*. The business can thus benefit from a wide geographical coverage.

There are also some features of exporting that may make it inappropriate for some businesses:

- *Transport and carriage can be problematic* for some types of goods. This problem is exacerbated when the distance is great or when the goods are of a fragile or perishable nature. The costs of transport and insurance can also add costs to exports that can render them price uncompetitive compared to domestic products in the foreign country.
- *Collecting due payment can be a problem* when the customer is in a different country. Legal complications can sometimes result if customers default on payment or if payment is late. Legal instruments are usually put in place using a bank in the importer's country to minimize the risks of non or late payment.
- Exported goods, when entering foreign countries, are sometimes *subject to tariff charges or other restrictions*. Payment of taxes to a host government by the importer has obvious implications for pricing, whilst some goods are subject to limitations on the quantities imported. Such protectionist measures mean that exporters have many more factors to consider in exporting than if they were to restrict their activities to domestic business only.
- The number of foreign interests that an exporter has means that the company must be *aware of the business environments of more countries than just its own*. Changes

in the internal environment of a country with which the organization does business can affect the performance of the company. An exporter has an interest in the political, economic and sociological environments of all the countries it exports to. This significantly complicates the operation of an exporter's business (although this can said to be a drawback of most entry strategies – not just exporting).

International licensing and franchising

Licensing and franchising across international borders, whilst being different in approach, both offer the same benefit: the gaining of international coverage and income with no direct investment.

When we examined the concept of franchise in Chapter 5, we saw that it was a way in which a business with a transferable business idea can expand by renting the right to use the idea to a franchisee. Expansion by franchise is thus an expansion option which offers the franchisor the opportunity to gain income at little or no extra investment or risk to himself. Because moving to foreign markets inevitably contains an element of risk which may not be so marked if expansion were to be restricted to the domestic market, some companies have opted for international franchising as a means of internationalization. Grand Metropolitan plc, the British food and drink company, chose franchising as the main mechanism of international expansion for its Burger King chain of fast-food restaurants. As at 1992, Grand Metropolitan had granted over 6000 franchise outlets in almost 40 different countries. The wide geographical distribution of the Burger King chain may have been something of a headache to the head office if it had operated each one from the centre. As it is, each Burger King restaurant is a privately operated 'small' business requiring minimal input from Grand Metropolitan's London head office.

Question 28.3

There is a Burger King outlet on the Champs Elysees, Paris. Suppose that, hypothetically, an accident occurs and a lorry crashes into the shop causing the outlet to burn down. Describe the implications of this accident for Grand Metropolitan if:

- The Champs Elysees outlet is a franchise.
- The Champs Elysees outlet is owned directly by the Grand Metropolitan head office.

Licensing is similar in some ways to franchising in that it involves a licensee paying a licensor a fee for the use of a business idea – usually a piece of intellectual property. A licence is a permit granted to a licensee to manufacture or market (or both) a product belonging to a licensor. In international business, a licence will usually afford the licensor the sole rights to use the intellectual property within a certain national market. Whereas franchising involves the use of a business identity, licensing typically involves the use of a brand name, a formulation or a recipe by an existing business.

The benefits to the two parties involved in a licensing agreement are similar to those enjoyed by those in a franchising agreement. The licensor receives low-risk income and increased international exposure of the product. The licensee gains the use of a product which enjoys current success, offering an increased chance of successful business performance.

Licensing is used in a number of sectors of business. Perhaps the best known example is that of brewing. British consumers seem to attach some value to foreign beer brands, and brewers take advantage of this by buying licences to brew certain brands in the UK under licence. Coors lager (licensee: Scottish Courage) is an example of a licensed brand where the licensor is a North American company. It is also used in some scientific industries where a local manufacturer in a foreign country may produce a specialist paint or plastic for the foreign country's market.

International alliances and joint ventures

An alliance of two parties, as the name suggests, is a relationship entered into voluntarily and in which both parties retain their full independence. Of course strategic alliances can be used as a basis for business co-operation on a national as well as an international level, and we must not imagine that such relationships are exclusive to international business. Thompson and Strickland have defined a strategic alliance as two businesses working together by

> ... *joint research efforts, technology sharing, joint use of production facilities, marketing one another's products, or joining forces to manufacture components or assemble finished products.*[2]

Alliances and joint ventures are both quite different concepts to that of a merger (see Chapter 8), where two companies become 'one'. Alliances tend to be ongoing and even semi-permanent, whereas joint ventures tend to be entered into for a particular 'venture' only, such as several construction companies working together on a large civil engineering project. These types of business relationship borrow a term from biology – it is said that they are *symbiotic*, i.e. beneficial to both parties.

International alliances are often entered into as a means of gaining access to foreign markets via the contacts of the partner business in the foreign country. Such relationships often involve *reciprocation*, allowing the foreign partner similarly to use the home country contacts. They can also be used for joint projects where expertise or equipment is shared as a vehicle for meeting both partners' business objectives.

In practice, alliances tend to be relatively short term in nature. This is partly due to the fact that many are entered into for specific projects only, and partly because there is sometimes a certain amount of distrust between alliance partners.

Honda Rover – a successful alliance?

There has been an increasing amount of alliance activity in the world automotive industry. One such alliance was that which existed for fifteen years between the

British Rover Group (then owned by British Aerospace plc) and the Japanese Honda.

The partnership began in 1979. The prevailing market conditions at that time meant that it would be advantageous for large automotive companies to gain access to foreign markets and to benefit from as much expertise as possible in the design and development of new models of vehicle. According to Rover, *'Honda emerged as the ideal partner ... an outstanding reputation for automobile engineering, particularly in the field of engine design'*. Honda, although a successful manufacturer in the Far East, had hitherto failed to make any serious inroads into the substantial European market for cars. The partnership was sealed on 27 December 1979.

The first tangible output from the alliance was the Triumph Acclaim, a car which included parts and technology from both companies. Having sold a respectable 130 000 units across Europe, the Acclaim was replaced in 1984 by 'twins' – the Rover 200 series and the Honda Ballade. Essentially similar 'under the skin' these two models proved successful for both companies, with the Ballade being made for Honda at the Rover plant in Longbridge, UK. In 1981, both companies launched 'executive cars', again sharing many common parts and the same body 'platform', the Rover 800 and the Honda Legend. A later model, the Honda Accord was built at Honda's new £200 million plant in Swindon using body panels made by Rover.

In addition to the significant collaboration in design and manufacture, the two companies also began to collaborate in vehicle distribution. Rover's Land Rover Discovery was sold through Honda's dealer network in Japan, 'badged' as a Honda to gain a wider acceptance in the Far Eastern market.

The alliance was strengthened in April 1990 by the reciprocal exchange of 20% shareholding. This exchange of a financial stake in each other's company was designed to be the basis of a longer term relationship that would continue to work to the advantage of both partners.

The advantages from the partnership can be summarized as:

- Honda's increased access to European markets;
- Rover's increased access to Far Eastern markets;
- improved designs through the sharing of expertise;
- economies of scale through the sharing of many common body parts.

Whilst the alliance was unarguably a success, it came to an abrupt demise on 31 January 1994 when British Aerospace sold its controlling shareholding in Rover to the German BMW company for £800 million. Honda's management were vocal in their anger at the decision, and a few weeks later, on 21 February, announced that Honda had sold its 20% shareholding in Rover.

(Source: *'History of Rover Joint Ventures with Honda,* Rover Group Motors, and press reports on 1 February and 22 February 1994)

Foreign 'direct' investment

A foreign direct investment (FDI), as the name suggests, involves a business actually making a financial investment in another country. This sets it apart from all other entry strategies which all involve conducting cross-border business from a home country base. Due to the fact that a financial investment is made abroad, it is usually the case that FDI occurs only when the organization is very sure that its investment is right, and that it will be 'safe'. There are two broad types of FDI: an existing foreign company can be acquired or a new plant can be built in the foreign country.

Foreign acquisitions

Holding companies often scout around for companies which are appropriate for addition to the group. This often involves purchasing all or part of a foreign business. Shares are bought in the usual ways – via a stock exchange for public companies or in discussion with the owners for private companies. Some British companies are well known for their international acquisition strategies, notable among them being is Hanson plc, which has acquired many businesses all over the world, with a distinct focus on North America.

'Greenfield' development

For companies that wish to invest in a certain country but cannot find an appropriate acquisition, it is not uncommon for a new site to be developed and built on. It is usually the case that 'greenfield developments' of this kind are more expensive and carry a greater risk of failure than acquisition owing to the fact that an acquisition would have an established customer base. Notable greenfield developments in the UK include those in specialised industries where a new site offers the investor an opportunity to gain premises that precisely match the company's requirements. Such investments have been made in the automotive industry (e.g. Honda, Nissan and Toyota) and in electronics (e.g. Fujitsu, Samsung and Siemens).

Whilst it is obvious that FDI exposes a company to higher levels of risk than the other entry strategies, the advantages are potentially significant. It is often entered into when export volumes have built up to such an extent that it becomes more economic to manufacture in the foreign country rather than to export the product. By manufacturing and selling within the foreign country, the company also circumvents ('gets round') the restrictions that exporters sometimes face, such as taxes placed upon imported items and limits set by host governments on the numbers of certain imported goods.

Foreign direct investment – a greenfield development in the UK

Toyota is Japan's largest motor manufacture and occupies the third position (by volume) in the world. In 1991, Toyota's world-wide output amounted to 4.75 million vehicles with a financial turnover of over £30 billion. Operating in 150 countries, the company has 29 manufacturing plants in 22 countries, sells its vehicles through over 7000 dealerships and employs more than 100 000 people.

In the early 1960s, Toyota made its first incursions into the European market by exporting cars to Denmark. Its growth in the EU since then has been substantial.

By 1992, Toyota was selling vehicles in 22 European countries through 3500 dealerships.

The market potential for sales in the EU, as one of the legs of the 'triad' (the Far East, North America and Europe), proved too tempting to miss for Toyota, and in 1989 it announced plans to make a direct investment in a manufacturing plant in the EU. After much discussion, the company chose two sites in the UK and one in Belgium. Toyota's initial investments in the UK – at Burnaston in Derbyshire and at Deesside in North Wales – amounted to £840 million. Its investment at Diest, Belgium, was in a European parts centre and came to £26 million. Construction of the two UK plants commenced in 1990, and the first British Toyotas left the production line in December 1992.

Unlike other Japanese motor companies that have invested in the UK, Toyota did not develop a single 'super-site'. The plant in North Wales is dedicated to the production of engines whilst the company's plant in Derbyshire produces passenger cars for the European market using engines produced at Deesside.

In common with other manufacturers who have made sizeable inward investments into the EU, Toyota's objective in its direct investment manoeuvre was to overcome the import restrictions which the EU places upon imports from outside its borders. By producing from within the EU, the cars produced are British, not Japanese, as far as sales to other EU states are concerned. Of course, direct investment also means that transport costs to other EU states from the UK are significantly less than they would be coming from Japan.

(Source: Toyota)

Philip Morris – foreign acquisitions in the former communist states of central and eastern Europe

Philip Morris Inc. is the largest cigarette manufacturer in the world and the world's third largest brewer. Its tobacco brands occupy 47% of the USA's 500 billion cigarettes per year market and 30% of the EU's total cigarette consumption. The company's 3000 brands also include a wide range of food products. It is the largest world-wide producer of consumer packaged goods, with sales in the year to 1995 of over $65 billion. Its best-known brands include Marlboro, L&M and Chesterfield cigarettes, Miller beers, and a wide range of food products including Post cereals, Kraft foods (e.g. Philadelphia, Maxwell House) and the confectionery brands Toblerone, Suchard and Terry's of York.

The company is based in New York and sells its products in over 170 countries, employing around 155 000 people in its world-wide operations. European, Middle Eastern and African operations are controlled from the Philip Morris offices in Lausanne, Switzerland.

Over recent years, Philip Morris has pursued a strategy of direct investment in the tobacco industries of the former communist countries of central and eastern Europe. Central Europe's cigarette consumption is around 600 billion cigarettes per year, which, unlike demand in some parts of the world, is relatively stable (i.e. it is not in decline). The decentralization of the economies in these states has provided investment opportunities for western companies which, for such reasons as above, wish to gain a market presence in these parts of the world. Philip Morris has had links, through licensing agreements, with companies in central and eastern Europe for over twenty years, so the demise of communism in these countries offered a unique opportunity for expansion (by means of FDI) into these national markets.

Some of its major acquisitions in former communist states of Central and Eastern Europe include the following:

Foreign interest	Year	Country	Value	Shareholding
Tabak A.S.	1992	Czech Republic	$400 million	Majority (>77%)
New build factory – St Petersburg	1992	Russia	Undisclosed	Majority
Klaipeda State Tobacco Company	1993	Lithuania (a Baltic state	$50 million	62.5% (including a new-build factory)
Krasnodar Tobacco Factory	1993	Russia	$60 million	Majority
Almaty Tobacco Kombinat	1993	Kazakhstan	$200 million	Majority
Kharkov Tobacco Factory	1994	Ukraine	Undisclosed	Majority

Source: Philip Morris Inc. Lausanne

Question 28.4

Suggest the strategic reasoning which lies behind Philip Morris's tobacco investments in the former communist states of central and eastern Europe. It may be helpful to look at 'market push', 'market pull' and portfolio factors in arriving at your conclusions.

28.4 Multinational companies

What is a multinational company?

Many of the companies we have discussed in this chapter so far are what we may call *multinationals*. A working definition of a multinational company (MNC) is as follows: *a company which has direct investments in more than one (usually many) different countries.*

For the reasons we have seen in Section 28.1 of this chapter, the growth in multinationalization has been very marked over the past fifty years. The competitive pressures which have built up in international markets coupled with a general relaxation in exchange controls, has meant that MNCs have become an important feature of the international business environment. It is thought that MNCs account for over a quarter of the world's economic output.

It follows from the above definition that most MNCs are very large organizations. The head office of a MNC may operate hundreds of divisions or subsidiary companies in as many countries around the world. The turnover of the MNC may well exceed the GDP of many of the countries in which it operates. Many of the best-known corporate household names are MNCs (Table 28.1).

Table 28.1 Some well-known MNCs

UK multinationals investing abroad	Foreign multinationals investing in the UK
Hanson	Nissan (Japan)
ICI	BASF (Germany)
BP	Michelin (France)
Glaxo Wellcome	Philips (Holland)
RTZ Corporation	Nestlé (Switzerland)
BAT Industries	General Motors (USA)

The operation of MNCs

The geographical distribution of a MNC offers several potential benefits:

- When a company operates in many countries, it has the opportunity to *locate activities in the country to which they are best suited*. The MNC can take advantage of variations in the business environments of the different countries. It may choose, for example, to locate design and development in a country where skilled technical people are plentiful, such as the UK, but to manufacture products where labour is cheaper, such as the Far East. Marketing communications will usually be based in a country with an advanced communications network, such as the UK or the USA.
- *Opportunity and risk can be spread* over many businesses in many countries. The breadth of portfolio renders the MNC more robust in the event of shocks in regional markets.
- MNCs can *take advantage of legal and fiscal differences in the different countries* in which they operate. By employing a creative use of internal transfer pricing, the MNC can significantly reduce its overall tax burden and thus increase net profits. Accountants can, up to a point, make high profits show in countries which enjoy a low level of corporation tax and lower profits in higher tax countries.

The head office of a MNC often operates as a holding company (see Chapter 4). Accordingly, the head office administration of the company usually comprises a small part of the total company operation. The size and importance of a large multinational places a increased significance to the role of the board of directors. The strategies pursued by a large MNC can bring about effects in many parts of the world and can even influence government policies. The senior directors of MNCs tend to be particularly adroit people, many of whom hold several other non-executive directorships, owing to the demand for directors of such a high calibre.

MNCs and governments

When we consider government and business, we usually think of the ways that businesses are influenced by governments. However, the size and economic importance of very large companies means that they can bring their influence to bear upon the governments of the countries in which they operate. Table 28.2 shows how the sizes of the world's biggest companies compare with some countries.

Table 28.2 Comparison of the size of the world's biggest industrial companies with some comparable national economies. (Source: Datastream)

Country or industrial company	GDP or sales turnover (1994–1995) (US$ billions)
UK	1013.6
Canada	541.5
Mitsubishi Corp. (Japan)	174.7
Mitsui & Company (Japan)	170.4
Itochu Corporation (Japan)	166.7
Sumitomo Corporation (Japan)	161.4
Marubeni Corporation (Japan)	149.2
Denmark	147.4
General Motors (USA)	141.6
Turkey	134.5
Toyota Motors (Japan)	108.3
Norway	108.2
Ford Motors (USA)	107.1
Royal Dutch/Shell Corp. (Netherlands/UK)	103.3
Nissho Iwai Corporation (Japan)	100.2
Exxon Corporation (USA)	99.6
Finland	95.9
Portugal	87.5
Greece	77.6
Hitachi Corporation (Japan)	74.0
Matsushita Electric (Japan)	69.5
Ireland	51.8
British Petroleum (UK)	46.2

Traditionally, national governments have had something of a 'love-hate' relationship with some of the world's major multinational companies. Clearly, they can be of enormous benefit to the countries in which they operate in their provision of jobs, their payment of tax revenues and their contribution to GDP, exports, etc. Similarly, their size and their importance to a country can mean they also have significant influence upon governments. Critics argue that not only is excessive business influence upon government anti-democratic (because it is the government and not large businesses which are elected to govern), but also that such influence is usually representative of certain economic opinions only.

Multinationalization and globalization

Some people have confused the terms multinational business and globalized business. Whilst with very large organizations it is often difficult to tell which category they are in, it is generally held that there is a difference. A company is said to be a global business when its multinational expansion has reached the point where it carries out activities in all major parts of the world rather than a selected few centres abroad. Accompanying this expansion is a change in its corporate culture when the business loses its national bias. In other words, it no longer 'feels like' a Japanese company or a British company – its breadth means that it feels like and is seen as a global business. A global company's head office (e.g. in London) does not see the business as divided into 'home' and 'overseas', but as one company of many parts encompassing the world.

28.5 Governments and international business

We saw in Chapter 23 that cross-border business transactions can directly determine some of the economic 'indicators' in a country, such as the exchange rate. Indirectly, international business can affect domestic unemployment, inflation and the rate of economic growth. It is therefore not surprising that governments take an active interest in the activities of internationalized businesses.

Governments have the ability to influence international business across its borders by implementing a range of measures that are primarily designed to act in the interests of domestic (home) businesses. They can also be used to further the political ends of a governing party or to act against the business interests of a foreign state.

The most important objective of governments with regard to international business is to stimulate business activities that will result in a positive entry in the balance of payments statement (see Chapter 23). This includes:

- exports;
- inward investment;
- inward bank deposits;
- a net surplus on cash transactions.

Similarly, it would, in most cases, wish to minimize imports and other transactions which would exert a downward pressure on the value of the currency, although there are offsetting factors that make it favourable for British businesses to invest abroad.

Common political measures used to influence international business are explained below.

Import tariffs

An import tariff or *import duty* is a form of indirect taxation (see Chapter 23). It is a percentage of the price of an imported good added on and collected (in the UK) by HM

Customs and Excise. The percentage added varies according to the category of goods. Such a tax on imported goods serves two purposes:

- it is a source of revenue for the Treasury;
- it provides a price disincentive for importers.

Increasing the price of imported goods is partly designed to protect domestic businesses, which may be disadvantaged if too many foreign goods were imported. It also helps to support the value of sterling.

An example of the imposition of import tariffs concerns motor cars. The UK imposes an import duty of 10% of the purchase price on imported motor vehicles when the source of the import is outside the EU. Hence, if a car is bought from Japan for £5000, the import duty on it would be £500, making the actual import cost £5500. Some goods attract lower rates of duty and others are exempt altogether.

Import quotas

A quota is a maximum limit set by a government for the import of certain goods. It will usually be an annual total and can be expressed either as a number (e.g. an import quota of 15 million tonne per year of chemical X), or as a percentage of total products sold. Percentage quotas might be expressed as 'no more than 15% of all widgets sold in the UK shall be imported from outside the EU'. It follows that for percentage quotas, the actual number will vary from year to year as the total varies.

An example of an import quota set by the UK government refers to car imports. The UK has traditionally imposed an import quota of around 10% on cars imported from Japan. This means that no more than 10% of all new cars sold in the UK may be imported from Japan (the actual quota on Japanese cars may vary from year to year). Note that this quota is a percentage and not a fixed number. Accordingly, the actual number of cars imported will vary from year to year. Other types of product are limited by number.

Exchange controls

Governments can restrict the volumes of trade across their borders by imposing limits on the amount of foreign currency that can be exchanged within a given time period. This sanction is invariably used to restrict the amount of foreign currency that can be bought. Because currency must be bought to purchase foreign goods, exchange controls are an effective restriction on imports.

In addition to the effect of lower imports, exchange controls will also have a positive effect on the capital account of the balance of payments statement. However, as a mechanism of protectionism it is rarely used, as it is viewed as being against the principles of international free trade and perhaps a little unfair. It would be inconsistent, for example, for state A to complain of unfair discrimination with regard to business in state B if state A were to impose exchange controls against state B. In consequence, exchange controls have become increasingly rare between developed industrial countries.

Encouraging exports

Because of the benefits to a domestic economy of exports, governments often set in place measures to actively encourage export activity. Whilst the most important determinants of export value are factors in the domestic economy as a whole, such as manufacturing investment, specific measures can encourage increased exporting.

Exports, like most other business transactions, are sold on credit. This means that goods are sent out and then the supplier must wait for payment to come through. Most domestic transactions are sold on credit periods of 30–90 days whereas export business can often involve credit periods of up to 180 days. Capital projects such as the exporting of civil engineering consultancy can involve much longer credit periods – in some cases, up to five years.

The major governmental body which assists exporters with their export risks is the *Export Credits Guarantee Department* (ECGD). The ECGD was set up in 1919, and since 1930 has helped exporters of invisibles in addition to visibles exporters (see the section of the balance of payments in Chapter 23 for a discussion of these terms). Its purpose is to provide a special type of insurance against two main areas of risk:

- the creditworthiness of overseas buyers (i.e. covering the risks of non or late payment of debts);
- the economic and political risks arising from events in overseas countries.

Prior to 1991, the ECGD insured both short-term (credit terms of less than two years) and long-term (more than two years credit) export business. In 1991, the short-term debt insurance role of the ECGD was sold by the Government to the NCM Group, a Dutch insurance company. The ECGD retains the responsibility for insuring debt involving over two years' credit.

In addition to its 'hard' financial support for exporters provided by the ECGD, the government also encourages and recognizes export performance in non-financial ways. The *Queen's Award for Export Achievement* is an award given to companies whose exports have shown growth or consistency. It applies to all sizes of business and winners receive permission to use the Award's logo on their letterheads and livery.

Inward investment policy

In addition to exports, inward investment is also entered as a positive figure on the balance of payments statement and hence exerts an upward pressure on the value of the currency. Most countries wish to encourage inward investment, as it provides jobs, tax revenues and increases GDP. In some cases, inward investments can also contribute to the UK's exports, which, as we have seen, helps to support the value of sterling. In order to encourage inward investment, it is in the government's interest to maintain relatively low fiscal and monetary pressure and not to allow the value of the domestic currency to rise to an uncompetitive level. In addition, governments sometimes provide grant support in the same way that it might for any company setting up in certain parts of the country. For large inward investments, negotiations between company and government can occur at a very senior level, with assistance packages individually designed to best meet the investor's aspirations.

International sanctions and embargoes

From time to time, governments see fit to impose severe restrictions on trading with certain countries. These can either be on a unilateral basis (i.e. one country prevents its domestic businesses from dealing with parties from the affected country), or on a multilateral basis. Multilateral sanctions are agreed by many countries together, where a ban is imposed from buying or selling to businesses in the sanctioned country.

Sanctions can be partial or total. In 1979, when the former USSR invaded Afghanistan, the US President Jimmy Carter imposed a block on the export of some US grain to the Soviet Union. This was a unilateral partial embargo. At the other end of the continuum, Iraq's 1990 invasion of Kuwait attracted a multilateral total embargo, wherein all countries of the United Nations agreed to isolate Iraq from selling its exports (mainly oil) and from benefiting from imported goods and services.

Such actions are designed to achieve political rather than business objectives. In some cases, they are imposed as a means of punishment, whilst in others it is hoped that the sanctions will precipitate a change in certain political practices (such as an end to human rights abuses or the cessation of violent hostilities). It goes without saying that businesses affected by governmental sanctions do not like such measures, much as they may agree with the political objectives.

28.6 Single markets and trading blocks

An international single market is one wherein business transactions can be carried out across borders as though they weren't there. The UK as a country has a single market because no limitations apply to companies in one part of the country trading with another. A company in England selling to a customer in Scotland need not worry about tariffs, quotas or other protectionist measures because both countries are part of the UK. In an international single market, the member state agrees to allow free movement of goods, services and, sometimes, personnel between them. In this respect, a single market acts as if it was one country. These agreements are sometimes referred to as *customs unions* – agreements between countries to reduce or eliminate customs restrictions pertaining to the import and export of goods and services.

The 'singularity' of a trading block varies. Some allow completely free movements, whereas others retain some restrictions in order to offer some protection to domestic businesses. In any event, such arrangements act as a stimulant to international business.

The European Union

We have already examined (Chapter 21) the European Union (EU), which consists of a community of fifteen nation states. The Single European Act 1986, which was signed by all member states, set the conditions whereby a single market – a common market – could be achieved. Described as 'an area without internal frontiers in which the free movement of goods, persons, services and capital is ensured in accordance with the provisions of this Treaty [The Treaty of Rome 1957]', the European single market came into being at the beginning of 1993. In addition to the single market, the EU also imposes a common external tariff (CET) upon all imports into any EU state. The CET means that all countries in the trading bloc impose the same rate of duty on all goods imported from outside the EU. Plans to bring the various EU national economies into closer concurrence, such as stabilizing exchange rates, harmonizing tax levels and safety standards are expected to render the single market more effective.

NAFTA and other trading bloc

Western Europe's attempt to generate a single market (the EU) has been emulated by countries in other parts of the world. The potential of a trading bloc in Western Europe is matched both by the *North American Free Trade Area* (NAFTA) and by a proposed trading area in the Asia Pacific region. This would include Japan, Australia and the 'Tigers' (such as South Korea, Taiwan and Thailand). The NAFTA area comprises 370 million people and about 30% of the world's economic output, whilst the Asia Pacific area would contain more people (2.3 billion) but with a lower percentage of world trade at about 20% (although this is expected to grow significantly in the future). It is said that the EU, NAFTA and Asia Pacific together comprise the 'triad' of the world's economy – three powerful economic centres containing the vast majority of the world's production and consumption.

GATT and the WTO

Trading agreements exist on the global as well as the regional level. The most prominent agreements in this category are the *General Agreement on Tariffs and Trade* (GATT) and its successor, the *World Trade Organization* (WTO). The GATT agreement began life as the Havana Charter 1948, when 23 countries acted as signatories to what they hoped would become an international trading organization (ITO). As negotiations progressed, it became clear that such a world-wide trading block was too ambitious, and so a general agreement was arrived at. The main points of the agreement were as follows:

- *Tariffs* should not be increased above current levels.
- *Quotas* should be reduced and eventually abolished.
- Each signatory was a *'most favoured nation'*. This meant that trading privileges extended by one member nation to another must be widened to include all of the others.
- The General Agreement recognized that other trading bloc may exist, such as the EU and NAFTA, but these were encouraged to be outward-looking rather than insular as far as trading restrictions were concerned.

GATT has evolved over the years through the staging of several 'rounds' of lengthy and complicated negotiation. The number of countries subscribing to GATT has grown as the various rounds have progressed. With over 100 members, GATT members now account for about 80% of international trade. Overall, GATT has succeeded in generally reducing import tariffs and significantly cutting down on quotas. Recent rounds have focused on attempting to reduce the stark variations in prosperity between wealthy and poorer countries (the 'north–south dialogue').

Assignment

A major far-eastern motor manufacturer is seeking to gain a 'foot-hold' in the substantial European car market.

Questions

- Outline the options open to the manufacturer in seeking to achieve its objectives.
- Discuss the pros and cons of the two main options; those of exporting to the European Union or of directly investing in a car manufacturing plant somewhere in the EU.
- Presuming that the company adopts an FDI strategy, discuss the criteria that the company should consider when deciding which European country to build the plant in.

References

1. Levitt, T. (1983) The globalisation of markets. *Harvard Business Review*. May/June.
2. Thompson, A. A. and Strickland, A. J. (1995) *Strategic Management*. Irwin

Further reading

Chryssochoidis, G, Millar, C. and Clegg, J. (1996) *Internationalisation Strategies*. London: Macmillan.

Daniels, J. D. and Radebaugh, L. H. (1995) *International Business. Environments and Operations*, 7th edn. New York: Addison Wesley.

Doz, Y. (1986) *Strategic Management in Multinational Companies*. Oxford: Butterworth-Heinemann.

El Kahal, S. (1994) *An Introduction to International Business*. New York: McGraw Hill.

Ellis, J. and Williams D. (1995) *International Business Strategy*. London: Pitman.

Ketelhohn, W. (1993) *International Business Strategy*. Oxford: Butterworth-Heinemann.

Ohmae, K. (1992) *The Borderless World*. London: Penguin.

Preston, J. (1993) *International Business. Text and Cases*. London: Pitman.

Taggart, J. H. and McDermott, M.C. (1993) *The Essence of International Business*. Englewood Cliffs, NJ: Prentice Hall.

Taoka, G. M. and Beeman, D. R. (1991) *International Business. Environments, Institutions and Operations*. London: Harper Collins.

INDEX